Product Planning and Management

Product
Planning
and
Management

William S. Sachs
St. Johns University

George Benson
St. Johns University

PennWell Books
PennWell Publishing Company
Tulsa, Oklahoma

Copyright © 1981 by
PennWell Publishing Company
1421 South Sheridan Road / P. O. Box 1260
Tulsa, Oklahoma 74101

Library of Congress Cataloging in Publication Data

Sachs, William S., 1919–
    Product planning and management.

    Includes index.
    1. Product management.   2. New products.
I. Benson, George, 1920–   joint author.
II. Title.
HF5415.15.S22   658.5   80-25648
ISBN 0-87814-149-9

Printed in the United States of America

1 2 3 4 5   85 84 83 82 81

HF
5415. 15
. S22

Copy 1

To Inge and Lillian,
wives, companions, lovers

Contents

List of Figures

List of Tables

Foreword

Products are the *raison d'etre* for the organizations of the 1980's. Society grants businesses the right to operate in return for the provision of products and services. In a very real sense, the sole economic justification for the continued existence of any firm is the development, production, and marketing of want-satisfying goods and services.

The notion of a marketing mix comprised of decisions concerning the elements of product, promotion, price, and marketing channels appropriately blended to satisfy a chosen market target has left a strong imprint upon the curricula of many business programs. Courses in consumer behavior may be found in most undergaduate and graduate marketing programs. Marketing mix elements are represented in different degrees by specific courses. Promotion tends to be well represented by such courses as advertising, sales management, or promotional strategy. The study of the design and management of marketing channels is accomplished in such courses as channel management, physical distribution/logistics, and/or by courses focusing on specific channel intermediaries as retailers and wholesalers. The final mix elements—product strategy and pricing—are relatively less covered in terms of numbers of specific courses offered. As a result (or perhaps at least partially a cause), fewer text alternatives are available in these subjects.

Most books dealing with product strategy tend to be collections of readings or deal with such specific elements as new product development. As a consequence, the instructor who teaches the product planning course often has to resort to utilizing several required texts and handouts in order to provide the coverage needed. These instructors are likely to be highly pleased with this book.

Product Planning and Management is an important book. Professors Benson and Sachs have developed a text that provides thorough coverage of the critical process of new-product development *and* given balanced treatment of the other—equally crucial-subjects such as strategic planning as related to product, portfolio analysis, product life cycle analysis, product elimination and revitalization, organization, new product diffusion and the adoption process, product safety, branding and packaging decisions, and government regulations. A separate chapter focuses on such environmental issues as resource scarcity, energy, ecological questions, and consumerism. Cases facilitate use of the text and an appendix summarizing the major legislation affecting product decisions is included.

In several instances, specific courses have been developed as a result of the publication of a seminal work in a subject area. Such an occurrence took place in 1968 with the publication of Engel, Kollat, and Blackwell's *Consumer Behavior*. If a well-written text providing complete coverage of product planning and management is required in order for additional courses in this area to be offered, the 1980s may witness marked growth in product management courses. Benson and Sachs have written such a book.

Louis E. Boone

Preface

Product development, an activity that seemingly lies outside the mainstream of American life, has more and more become a national concern. The term "product development" is seldom mentioned at public forums, because issues are not thought of in those terms. Product development has broad, vague connotations, while public issues refer to particulars. But these particulars are all manifestations of a larger whole.

The subject of product development is brought into focus every time a consumer protection agency complains about a product defect or a potential hazard or an unfair selling practice. Product development comes into being every time an environmentalist cries out against pollution of our air or waterways or city streets. Product development rises to the fore every time a labor leader calls for quotas on foreign imports or preferential treatment for American products or subsidies to sick industries. Product development assumes a prominent role every time a political figure raises questions about a slowdown in economic growth or the loss of our nation's technological leadership or the decline of the American innovative spirit.

The problems associated with product development in the 1970's had been exacerbated by energy shortages and rising prices, conditions which are likely to persist in the decade of the 1980's. These in turn have increased pressures on corporate management for better product planning and development. Regardless of political persuasion or social leanings, the vast majority of Americans still regard the private sector as the place where the twin product functions of planning and development can best be carried out.

Accordingly, we have sought to handle product development in comprehensive fashion, so as to encompass the management of all relevant activities. For pragmatic reasons, we have adhered to the managerial approach, with emphasis upon analysis. But we have also attempted to accent underlying principles with illustrations and examples.

In actual practice, product development is probably less formal than might appear in this book. But we have not abandoned the concept of entrepreneurship, which underscores innovative behavior and veers away from the traditional view of decision-making. Only when objectives are defined and alternatives given can managers employ optimizing methods. But the central question is: how do ends and means get to be identified in the first place? This process, born in the search for a differential advantage, is not a strictly logical one that can be described by conventional analysis. Though not explicit, the entrepreneurial theme is present nevertheless, like the indominable force that sustains the good guys on a mythical galaxy far, far away.

The book logically divides itself into five parts. The first, including chapters 1 to 3, might be entitled "the environment for product decisions." But the subject is viewed from the perspective of the firm—the problems it is likely to encounter and options available to solve them.

The second part takes up questions of strategic planning. This is a firm's attempt at long-run adjustment of its internal resources to external forces. Strategic planning material is contained in chapters 4 and 5.

Part three concerns itself with organization for new products. It includes issues of responsibility, organizational structure and functions. Chapters 6 and 7 discuss these aspects.

Part four takes up the subject of new product development. Following the interpretation of the process given by Booz, Allen & Hamilton, product development is broken down into various phases: exploration, screening, business analysis, development, testing, commercialization. This part spans chapters 8 to 13. The commercialization aspect, however, is dealt with in terms of the diffusion process, which refers to adoption of innovation by prospective customers.

The book ends, as it began, with the environment. But chapter 14 diverges from the book's format and deals with the subject from a macro point of view, as a societal issue. How has society as a whole been affected by, and responded to, the issues brought on by product development?

In the course of writing this book we have accumulated debts to many. We extend bouquets to our faculty members, Joseph Chasin and Abram Poczter, who read parts of the manuscript and made useful comments. For Louis E. Boone of the University of Central Florida, who read the entire manuscript and gave us many valuable suggestions, we have woven the garlands of praise into a large wreath. We thank our graduate assistants Linda Saladino, Toby Kuh, Myla Schwartz, Alan Zilbert, who all contributed to the preparation of the manuscript. We are grateful to Marie Westerberg and Rosemarie Realmuto for their excellent typing of our manuscript. And we owe an enormous debt, which will go largely unremunerated, to our wives, Inge and Lillian, who patiently abided our irascible and churlish dispositions while the manuscript was being written.

One/ Strategies for Product Management

1/ The Importance of Product Development

A major factor in economic development of the Western world is the process of innovation. It implies doing things differently. To an individual firm, it becomes an important means of achieving a differential advantage. This quest for a competitive edge via product development may have many objectives. The reasons cited most frequently by business executives are corporate growth, cost reduction, diversification, stimulation of sales of complementary products, and reactions to competitive activity.

There are, however, significant variations in innovative activities among the various industries. Four in particular—chemicals, machinery, electrical equipment and communications, and transportation and missiles—expend more than $2.5 billion each in research and development (R&D). This group accounted for a combined total of about $13.6 billion, more than 70 percent of all U.S. industry spending for R&D.

Product development, however, is a risky enterprise as well as a costly one. Most new products end in failure. More than two-thirds of corporate expenditures for such ventures result in efforts that contribute little or nothing of economic value.

Most failures are market related. Business executives attribute the most common causes of failure to poor product choice, inadequate market assessment, and faulty planning and marketing. Corporate management seems to minimize external factors.

Despite high failure rates, benefits to be derived from new products far outweigh risks. Product development is usually managed conservatively, so as to minimize negative financial results.

Products in an Affluent Society

If there is any single economic idea that has dominated public thought, it is one of progress, onward and upward. Regardless of political persuasion or social philosophy, Americans have evinced a deep faith in economic growth. Politicians extol its virtues. Conservatives and liberals alike proclaim it as a legitimate end of public policy. Economists study its manifestations and, like ancient oracles, make enigmatic pronouncements about its future.

1

Forecasts of Gross National Product (GNP), an all-embracing economic activity, are watched with particular interest and reported in the
financial pages of the most prestigious newspapers. This measure
represents the value of all goods and services produced by our economy. A higher GNP, deflated by a general price index, indicates more
goods and services, more jobs, and more income for the average American. Greater real output signifies a higher standard of living and, notwithstanding sprinkles of dissent, is therefore equated with progress
in the public mind.

Economic growth has become a cornerstone of domestic policy. It
has been an avowed objective of every administration from the end of
World War II to the present. It holds out the promise of general well-
being and provides the taxes to pay for expensive government programs
that legislators deem essential to well-being. Nor have the bursts of
inflation in the seventies, together with periodic shortages of key supplies and materials, dampened tellingly the prevailing mood of optimism. While these unwelcome events are not taken lightly, neither are
they regarded as the "normal" state of things. They are aberrations that
should be set straight, so that normal economic growth can run its
course unimpeded.

It is theoretically possible for the economy to grow by expanding the
output of current products. Basic industries, for example, may simply
produce more of the same: mine more coal or iron ore; grow more
wheat or soybeans; transmit more kilowatts of electricity. Similarly,
manufacturing plants and service industries can expand by producing
more of the same in essentially the same way. Increases in population
enhance demand for the same products society produces, such as food,
clothing, and shelter. More hands are also available to produce the
needed goods and services. Many young countries relied on such
"natural" forces in the past, and many third world nations today find
economic expansion of this nature. Or certain raw material-producing
nations, such as oil exporters, rely on output of a single product to build
foreign purchasing power for items that the country lacks.

But there are practical limits to this sort of growth, particularly in an
advanced market economy. In one such as ours, emphasizing private
enterprise, the sum total of corporate product decisions is the prime
element of real GNP. Increases in the total output of business firms do
not merely come from extensions of current activity but from new
activity. Economic growth goes hand in hand with variety and change;
quantitative variation is related to qualitative variation. The economist
John Kenneth Galbraith highlighted this aspect when he contrasted our
modern world with a past world. "Once," he wrote, "more production
meant more food for the hungry, more clothing for the cold, more
houses for the homeless." In today's society, Galbraith perceived that a

burgeoning output "satisfies the craving for more elegant automobiles, more exotic food, more erotic clothing, more elaborate entertainment—indeed for the modern range of sensuous, edifying and lethal desires."[1]

Innovation and Economic Development

Galbraith's contrast of past with present, in terms of output, is symptomatic of a more fundamental cleavage between the two worlds—their attitudes towards both national output and innovation. The ancient worlds were not unmindful of material wealth in all its forms, in the power and pleasures and possessions it could buy. Powerful nations levied tributes on their dependencies. Egyptian grain, extracted from farmers of the Nile delta, and chained barbarians, trained for the arena, supplied the fickle Roman mobs with bread and circuses. But there was no conscious policy of economic betterment for society as a whole by expanding production or increasing productivity.

Nor were the ancient worlds completely unfamiliar with new things. But they did not willfully seek them. They accepted the innovations as gifts of the gods, even as the fire stolen from Mount Olympus, and propitiated their deities with elegant temples and ritualistic sacrifices. The way of doing things was generally the same, year after year and decade after decade. Centuries rolled by, and the ways of producing goods changed little. Even the medieval craftsman, initiated into the mysteries of his guild, adhered to the prescribed ways of his forefathers and passed them on intact to his apprentices, the would-be master workmen of the next generation.

Joseph Schumpeter was the first economist to highlight innovation as a driving force in the economic development of Western nations.[2] He used the term *innovation* in a broad economic sense, which encompassed a triad of products, markets, and organization. The "products group" included both applications of new technologies and new supplies of raw materials.

As firms vie with each other for business, Schumpeter reasoned, they combine factors of production in new ways. Novel arrangements that portend a differential advantage are quickly copied, and even improved upon, by entrepreneurs acting under the competitive pressures of a capitalistic environment. The creative aspect of product policy, to Schumpeter, was the *sine qua non* of business rivalry. The continuous development of products and markets was what brought firms increas-

---

[1] John Kenneth Galbraith, *The Affluent Society* (New York: Houghton Mifflin Company, 1958), p. 140.

[2] Joseph A. Schumpeter, *The Theory of Economic Development* (Translated by R. Opie. Cambridge, MA: Harvard University Press, 1961), pp. 65-85.

ing monetary rewards and, at the same time, society a higher level of well-being. And firms that fail to keep pace with innovative behavior, in Schumpeter's colorful metaphor, are doomed to linger "in the fatally deepening dusk of respectable decay."[3]

Innovation is the alter ego of economic development, and it was no accident that both evolved together through the expanse of time. In the ancient world, innovative acts came haphazardly, as though they were accidents of history. In the modern world, such events crowd in on each other.

It took the human race some 10,000 years to move from an agricultural economy to an industrial one. In this period, innovations were comparatively few and far apart. As late as the eighteenth century, farming was done in much the same fashion as in biblical days. A clumsy wooden plow, drawn by slow-moving oxen, barely scratched the soil. Many areas were bereft of even this rudimentary tool, and men relied on the hoe to turn over the ground. Men swung scythes to cut hay, sickles to reap grain, and sturdy flails to thresh wheat. Life was adjusted to scarcity and threatened by contingency—a drought, a freak storm, an unforeseen frost, an unforgiving pestilence.

Society's emergence from the somnolence of rural life to the quickening pace of city life came to be known as the "industrial revolution," in reality an evolutionary process that stretched out for over a century. During this period, featured by the rise of the factory system and mass production techniques, successful applications of inventions were plentiful—the steam engine, the Bessemer process, the cotton gin, the telegraph, the automobile, and the electric light being a few of the prominent technical breakthroughs. They profoundly transformed the nation's way of life. But they represented individual effort, for the most part, casual and desultory.

The modern period is often referred to as the "technological revolution." It is characterized by organized, systematic efforts for carrying out innovation. New ways of doing things come about through purposeful resolve, through prearranged planning. Corporations have established R&D departments to systematically search for ways to develop new products and processes, harnessing science to these ends. The first corporate R&D laboratory was established in 1876 by Thomas Edison. By the turn of the century, Eastman Kodak, B. F. Goodrich, and General Electric had followed suit. But no more than a hundred were in existence before World War I. By 1960, research laboratories reached well over 5,000 in number, the big bulge coming during and after the second great war.

---

[3] *Ibid.*, p. 70.

The proliferation of industrial R&D laboratories marked an important break with the past. Science and technology now came together in the employ of the production function. Invention shifted from an individual pursuit to an institutional one, carried out by organizations. This institutionalization of R&D literally joined invention with entrepreneurship. Marketing departments, created at staff levels, were charged with seeking out new markets, new ways of stimulating demand, new opportunities for corporate capabilities. And management became wedded to the notion of ever experimenting with new organizational forms to exploit its technology and marketing potentials.

A U.S. Commerce Department study in 1977 reported that technological innovation was responsible for 45 percent of the nation's growth from 1929 to 1969.[4] But this attempt to quantify the implicit relationship between technology and GNP, as others before it, only results in an extremely crude estimate. The usual method is to relate real GNP to nontechnological factors, such as population growth and investment level, and then ascribe any residual to technology.[5] Weaknesses in this method of measuring the effects of technology give rise to highly fluctuating estimates. While most authorities believe that technology spurs economic growth, the exact amount remains elusive.

Product Policy and the Quest for a Differential Advantage

A corporation by law is endowed with perpetual life. But it can only cling to its immortal essence by competing successfully in the business arena. To an individual firm, the choice of products signifies the contests it has chosen to enter and the directions in which its energies will be devoted.

In this sense, the product is fundamental. It determines, among other things, the facilities and technology that are required. It is the company's vital link to the outside world—the customers whom it must win, the competition against whom it must pit itself, the suppliers with whom it must deal, the middlemen through whom it must distribute its vendibles. To paraphrase Marshall McLuhan, the product is the message.

But messages do not exist alone; they require a sender and a destination. Information directed to no one is a futile act, signifying nothing. So products never stand alone without markets, and a firm's product policy is inseparable from its marketing policy.

---

[4] Cited in "Vanishing Innovation," *Business Week* (July 3, 1978), p. 49.

[5] See Edward F. Denison, *Accounting for United States Economic Growth, 1929-1969* (Washington, D.C.: The Brookings Institute, 1974); John W. Kendrick, *Postwar Productivity Trends in the United States, 1948-1969* (New York: National Bureau of Economic Research, 1973).

"Product-market" strategies and tactics have become potent competitive weapons in modern business. In these commercial engagements, the role of product development is highlighted by an industrial structure which long ago ceased to resemble the competitive model postulated by classical economics. In U.S. manufacturing, the top four companies in an industry, on the average, account for about 40 percent of the market. The average eight-firm concentration ratio for American industry runs close to 60 percent.[6]

Industrial concentration does not *per se* betoken a lack of rivalry among corporations. Nor does it rule out price as a competitive form. Many small businesses, when run efficiently, can ring up profits by underpricing the giants. But many large companies may find price competition a poor, ineffective device. A price cut by one colossus can be matched almost immediately by others, and the advantage of an aggressive price policy flitters quickly away. Rather, the more typical method for creating product preferences among customers is to differentiate the offerings.

A product can be differentiated by changes in either its properties or its physical form. Such changes can affect the functions a product performs, the satisfactions it generates in use, the esthetic qualities and symbolic meanings it conveys. Regardless of its effects, the product is endowed with features that differentiate it from its competitors. Economists sometimes refer to this type of strategy as "quality competition."[7] The term quality is defined in the broadest possible context, including color, shape, materials, design, grade, services, etc.

On the other extreme, a product may remain the same but still be differentiated by advertising and promotion. In this instance, a difference exists not in the goods or services but in the eye of the beholder. The advertising profession refers to such attempts at psychological differentiation as "product positioning." Yet the industry is almost unanimous in the opinion that advertising cannot work alone and that a product can best be "positioned" in the consumer's mind when it is indeed differentiated in quality. Procter and Gamble, the leading national advertiser, has always insisted on the primacy of product quality. This widespread attitude is reflected in the fact that changes in positioning strategy are often accompanied by changes in the physical product. Though these differences are frequently superficial, they nevertheless induce a penchant for change and for new products.

Most firms use variations of quality, promotion, and price simultaneously. Regardless of the exact marketing mix, product development

---

[6] U.S. Bureau of the Census, Census of Manufacturers, 1972, "Concentration Ratios in Manufacturing," (MC72(SR)-2.

[7] Lawrence Abbott, *Quality and Competition, an Essay in Economic Theory* (New York: Columbia University Press, 1956).

has become an important element in a company's unending search for a differential advantage.

The specific advantages a firm may derive from new products, most often variations of old ones, are numerous. They accrue to every level of management, from corporate headquarters down to divisions and individual brand groups. They are both strategic and tactical, long-term and short-run. The most common reasons for investing in product development cited by business executives, though not necessarily in order of importance, are as follows:

Corporate growth

Stimulating corporate growth is probably the most important reason for a policy of product development. As in national affairs, growth is paid homage in the highest councils of corporate officialdom. It is regarded as the elixir of corporate life. It is avidly sought after by financial analysts and funds managers and is therefore a powerful factor in capital markets. IBM for many years has been an investment favorite with the financial community because of its growth record. Many companies view steady, regular growth as an imperative and sometimes display excessive zeal in its attainment. Bernard Trueblood, marketing director for Bic, told a Connecticut audience in 1977 that growth-stimulative practices are frequently harmful, when they are "not natural to the company's business."[8] But what is "natural"? Peter Drucker, one of the leading management authorities, defines the "natural" or "right size" as that which results in "the optimal yield from production resources."[9] PepsiCo. Inc., the giant beverage manufacturer, is said to gear its operations for meeting a specified annual growth rate in earnings. In 1972 the board of directors went so far as to replace the traditional stock option plan with a bonus scheme pegged to a 10 percent rise in earnings. Deviations below the 10 percent called for steeply lower bonus payments, so that a rise of only 9 percent in earnings would cut the bonus value by 25 percent.[10]

Growth is a popular theme of public relations men and trade book editors who meticulously catalog new products and ideas coming out of research and development. Although publicity pieces are meant to influence and persuade, they are generally correct in associating growth with product development.

The reason for linking corporate growth with innovation is not hard to discern. There are limits to market demand. No matter how success-

---

[8] "Trueblood Hits 'Bureaucratic' Companies Which Push Stocks Rather Than Sell Wares," *Marketing News* (April 8, 1977), p. 1.

[9] Peter F. Drucker, "Good Growth and Bad Growth," *Wall Street Journal* (April 10, 1979), p. 26.

[10] *Fortune* (September 15, 1975), p. 69.

ful initially, a product cannot be kept intact and also be expected to grow continually, indefinitely, at a constant rate. Sooner or later, sales gains will slow down. Increases in expenditures and corporate effort will result in diminishing returns. To preserve an upward momentum, the company must turn to new approaches, new directions.

Static product lines imply static companies. It is precisely those industries spending most on R&D that have experienced the greatest growth.[11] At times, whole new industries have sprung up from the seeds of new technologies: electronics, color television, synthetic fibers, plastics, automation, alternate energy sources. Companies able to gain footholds in these new industries—and they need not have been first with the innovation—are often able to record impressive gains in sales and profits. These growth fields also witness the formation of independent firms, some of which grow into corporate giants. Xerox Corporation is an outstanding example of a firm built on the success of a new product. Polaroid is another, skyrocketing to preeminence in relatively short time because of the Land camera.

But growth to what ends? Not all growth is economically useful or socially desirable.[12] As a generalization, however, growth yields positive consequences, especially when adroitly directed. With respect to individual firms, available evidence points unmistakably in the direction of greater profit margins. Michael Porter's study of forty-two consumer goods industries found a positive correlation between growth rates and reported profits. The relationship was particularly high for convenience goods, wherein the two variables, growth and profits, showed up with an associated variance of 70 percent ($R^2 = .79$).[13] In other words, 79 percent of the variation in corporate profits were explained by fluctuations in company growth rates.

Another generalization relates profits to firm size. Innumerable studies of industrial structure consistently support the conclusion that profit fluctuations for large companies are less than those for small companies. Because growth tends to increase company size, it also serves to encourage elements that stabilize corporate earnings.[14] To that extent, greater stabilization is introduced into the economy.

[11] Lewis N. Goslin, *The Product-Planning System* (Homewood: Richard D. Irwin, Inc., 1967), pp. 15–16; "The Silent Crisis in R&D," *Business Week* (March 8, 1976), pp. 90–92.

[12] See Carter Henderson, "The Economics of Less," *Business Horizons* (April, 1979), pp. 25–28.

[13] Michael E. Porter, *Interbrand Choice, Strategy, and Bilateral Market Power* (Cambridge, MA: Harvard University Press, 1976), pp. 163–165.

[14] S. Hymer and P. Pashigan, "Firm Size and Growth Rates," *Journal of Political Economy* (December, 1962), pp. 556–569; Herbert Simon, "Comment: Firm Size and Rate of Growth," *Ibid.* (February, 1964), pp. 81–82; M. Hall and L. Weiss, "Firm Size and Profitability," *Review of Economics and Statistics* (August, 1967), pp. 323–327.

Cost reduction

The advantages of cost reduction accrue from "process"-type innovations. They seek to enhance corporate profits not by increasing the quantity or variety of goods sold, but by producing the same products at lower costs.

A great deal of energy-saving research today is directed toward this end. These technological developments, in the main, do not represent radically new processes. But they are gradually changing the face of industry. Manufacturing plants are being built or modified in order to support alternative fuel usage. Water-based paints are being substituted for the petroleum solvent-base paints in industrial processes in order to conserve a potential source of fuel. The use of aluminum and plastics in automobiles is expected to grow significantly over the next several years because they can reduce vehicle weight, and hence improve fuel economy. In 1968 about 86 percent of chlorine was produced by electrolysis, in which the cell anode is made of graphite. Today the graphite anode has been largely replaced by metal to reduce electrical consumption. Because about 50 percent of chlorine production costs represent the cost of energy, the new anode drastically reduces costs. In the long run, process-type innovations tend to raise productivity, and to encourage greater outputs at lower prices.

A low cost producer might choose to lower prices in order to increase sales, if demand is elastic. But the immediate objective of innovation in processing is cost reduction, not market expansion. There is a change in the physical product, however, when the process involves a change in material, such as the substitution of plastics for metal or glass. The physical product can also be altered by cost-saving redesign, such as reducing the number of parts that go into its assembly or simplifying it in other ways. Thus, the long-run effect may well turn out to be a cost reduction coupled with a larger volume of sales.

New businesses

This is a common practice of corporate planning, often referred to as "portfolio management." Essentially, the aim is to effect a change in the firm's product mix, so as to place greater emphasis upon products with brighter profit prospects. Another motive is to achieve greater stability in performance.

Most of the product reshuffling takes place in related business fields. Examples of this sort are legion, for they are today inherent in normal operating procedure. For instance, Stauffer Chemical in 1968 moved to discontinue its low-profit line of general purpose resins and to enter the more specialized area of PVC dispersion resins. Today the company is a major producer for the vinyl industry, with a complete product line and one of the world's largest single dispersion resin plants in Delaware City, Delaware. A soft drink company, anticipating an aging population and a decline in sales of "sweet" beverages, has been expanding facilities that cater to older people, with products like wine, orange juice, coffee and tea.

The other type of change in the product mix, and one that normally makes news in a newspaper's financial section, involves entry into a new field of endeavor. Examples of this sort are also numerous, for they are part of corporate planning. As early as 1961, Martin-Marietta Corporation, a major supplier of missiles, was already planning to abandon the business in favor of manned space flight, which required a radically different technology from that of weapon production. Cigarette companies have for more than a decade been moving gradually into unrelated businesses. W. R. Grace & Company long ago left its traditional shipping business and is today a leading manufacturer of chemicals, with about 82 percent of its earnings derived from chemical products and processes. Recently, the company has been moving into specialized retail fields. AMF, once primarily a producer of industrial goods and services, now is a leading proponent of "active leisure," with almost two-thirds of its revenue coming from leisure-time products. Grumman Corporation has set an ambitious goal of deriving 50 percent of its profits from sales not related to aerospace or defense technologies.

Sales of complementary products

Sometimes, product development is undertaken to stimulate sales of other items in the line. Razors are produced and sold at little or no profit to create a demand for the more profitable blades. The Trac II concept involves a razor which fits the blade. Pool supplies are often stocked by installers in order to sell swimming pools. Spare parts are handled by automobile manufacturers for no other purpose than as a service to dealers. For a good number of years, foreign auto manufacturers were at a decided disadvantage in selling new models, and many still are, because of the difficulty in getting parts. In many industrial fields, firms take on new products to round out their lines, finding the new offerings a help in selling other goods.

Reaction to competition

Probably the majority of all new items coming out of product development represents reactions to competition. There can be only one innovator; the rest are followers. But no firm can afford the luxury of not following and of allowing its competitor to capture the market uncontested. When firms react to innovations of their competitors, their new entries are "imitative" of existing ones and prompted by a strategy that is defensive in nature.

However, imitative products can also be offensive, as in the case of line extensions. These can be conceived as efforts to broaden a mature product line, like a tree setting out new branches and extending its shade. These outpourings hold out potential gains at relatively low risk and have therefore become a major form of new product introduction.[15] They can be developed with little cost in R&D and can normally be produced on the machinery currently in use. They are invariably sold in the same distribution channels as other products and handled by the same sales force. Since such products share the same overhead as the existing line, the firm benefits from lower fixed cost per unit of output. Little wonder that the line extension has gained such popularity in product development!

New Product Intensity

Approximately 50 percent of current sales of major corporations are derived from products that have been introduced within the past ten years, but there are significant variations from industry to industry. Consequently, the type of business in which a company operates, or elects to operate, in large measure dictates product-market opportunities. Table 1-1 estimates, for broad industry categories in select years, the proportion of sales coming from new products four years hence.

Table 1-1
New Products as a Percent of Sales Four Years Ahead

Industry	Spring 1967 for 1970 (Percent)	Spring 1972 for 1975 (Percent)	Spring 1977 for 1980 (Percent)
Iron and steel....................	8	10	5
Nonferrous metals	16	10	6
Machinery	25	24	25
Elect. machinery	26	17	16
Autos, trucks, parts..............	24	40	18
Aerospace	49	41	17
Other transp. equip.	12	4	17
Fabricated metals, instruments.....	18	24	21
Chemicals	20	16	19
Paper & pulp	10	14	8
Rubber	7	12	8
Petroleum......................	7	6	3
Stone, clay, glass	20	11	11
Food & beverages	12	10	11
Textiles	21	15	15
Misc. mfrs.	8	19	4
All manufacturing	17	18	13

Source: Dept. of Economics, McGraw-Hill Publications Company.

---

[15] "The Line Extension That Cost $452 Million," *Marketing Review* (December–January, 1977), p. 6.

As indicated in table 1-1, industries differ enormously in the extent to which they carry on new product activity. Industries such as machinery, instruments, and chemicals can expect from about a fifth to a fourth of 1980 sales to come from products that had entered the market four years earlier. An obvious inference is that companies operating in these fields must pursue with vigor a new product program during the seventies, in order to compete successfully in the eighties. At the other extreme, petroleum, iron and steel, metals, paper, and rubber have rather low net product intensities.

New products also seem to come in spurts in some industries, such as aerospace. In 1970, products introduced four years earlier made up 49 percent of total sales. A decade later, this percentage is estimated at 17 percent, a substantial decline in relative sales volume. But R&D expenditures continue at a high rate. In 1975, they were some eightfold greater than capital spending, most of the R&D funds coming from the federal government.[16]

In most instances, however, government does not shower industry with gifts for innovation. Companies which see new products as a way of achieving a differential advantage must commit funds for their development. The road to innovation is not toll free. Corporate allocations for research and development were estimated at about $25 billion for 1979.[17] This massive expenditure is only part of the cost of bringing new products into the marketplace.

Again, there are marked differences from industry to industry when comparing funds earmarked for research and development. Table 1-2 portrays for sixteen broad, industrial groupings estimated 1978 R&D expenditures as a percentage of the previous year's corporate profit.

As can be seen in table 1-2, four industries have R&D expenditures of more than $2.5 billion each: chemicals, machinery, electrical equipment and communications, and transportation and missiles. These four categories, collectively, spend more than 70 percent of all U.S. industry allocation for R&D. Individually, they also invest a substantial portion of their profits in such activities, ranging from some 29 percent for machinery manufacturers to 83 percent for companies in transportation and defense.

In many subindustries within these four broad groupings, technical superiority has become a major competitive factor. Among the large companies in aerospace, it is common to find internally funded R&D programs running into the $100 million range. Technical features as

---

[16] McGraw-Hill Publications Co., "Historical Research and Development Expenditures and Related Data" (Mimeographed, 7/78), p. 6.

[17] Battelle Memorial Institute, *Probable Levels of R&D Expenditures in 1979* (Columbus: Battelle, 1978).

Table 1-2
1978 Estimates of R&D Expenditures

Industry	Corporate Funded R&D	
	Total (Mils $)	Percent of Profits (%)
Food and kindred products........................	416	9.8
Textiles & apparel...............................	101	3.4
Lumber, wood, furniture..........................	64	1.4
Paper & allied products..........................	293	5.3
Chemicals & allied products	3,149	31.2
Petroleum	973	6.6
Rubber	429	29.6
Stone, clay, glass	240	13.0
Primary metals	561	13.1
Fabricated metals...............................	458	8.5
Machinery	2,863	28.7
Elec. equip. & communic.........................	3,835	32.9
Transportation & missiles	3,710	82.6
Prof. & scient. instru.	1,111	48.9
Other manufacturers	242	3.8
Nonmanufacturers...............................	607	1.2
Total*	19,052	13.4

*Excludes agriculture, forestry & fishing. Totals may not add up to 100% because of rounding.

Source: Battelle Memorial Institute, *Probable Levels of R&D Expenditures in 1978* (Columbus: Battelle, 1977).

speed, maneuverability, and fire power largely determine governments' choices of aircraft. Even General Motors, almost wholly occupied with the automobile, a mature product that has changed in only minor ways in recent times, expects to spend some $6.5 billion on R&D between 1977 and 1981—more than the entire oil industry.[18] Producers of drugs are reputed to have spent about $1.5 billion on R&D in 1978. To bring out a new drug product, on the average, requires about five to seven years of R&D and some $50 million.[19]

Technology is an activity that feeds upon itself. As it shortens the life spans of existing products, it compels firms to vie with each other in turning out a continuous stream of new products. More effort is needed just to keep up. Technological innovation thus becomes a vital factor in sustaining corporate revenue and income. In turn, this speeds further

[18] "How GM Manages Its Billion-Dollar R&D Program," *Business Week* (June 28, 1976), pp. 54–58.

[19] Arlene Hershman and Marjorie Siegel, "Prescription for Profits," *Duns Review* (January, 1979), p. 39.

the rate of obsolescence, the need for developing newer and more effective processes, and the cycle of technological change.

The Effects of Environmental Factors on Innovation

New product development, like all other economic activity of a corporation, takes place in an environmental context, the influences of
which are many. Some are weak, some are strong. Some are positive
and others are negative. But they all exert pressures as to both types
and amounts of new products that come forth.

The economic expansion of the fifties and sixties created a situation
that was highly conducive to innovation. Gross national product in the
decade after 1945 more than trebled, rising from $212 billion to $398
billion. By 1965 this figure had jumped to $676 billion. Personal
consumption expenditures grew apace. Rising national income, like a
sponge in water, absorbed prodigious quantities of goods and services.

The country in the two-and-a-half decades after World War II witnessed not only a bulging population but also a mobile one. A major
characteristic of this mobility was the migration out of large cities into
smaller communities beyond. This new suburbia, intersticed with bands
of superhighways and congested traffic, formed vast, rich markets such
as had never been seen before. Almost overnight millions had learned to
expect two cars in their garages and to stock their homes with the latest
contraptions for comfort and show. Demand swelled for photographic
equipment, sporting goods, fertilizer, lawnmowers, workshop tools,
and do-it-yourself kits. There arose new industries catering to the so-
called leisure-time market, which really imposes more tasks on the liberated, twentieth-century man than was ever thought possible in the
era when a six-day, sixty-hour workweek was universal.

Shopping centers in suburbia sprang up everywhere, flourishing as
vigorously as the hardy crab grass and golden dandelions. Consumers
were offered more alternative products and wider choices within
product categories. In part, this reflected marketers' reactions to rising
discretionary income, which broadens consumers' consideration frames.
Markets that were once broad, almost homogeneous, now became conducive to segmentation. Edibles no longer came in commodity-type lines
but in a variety of forms: health foods, gourmet foods, ethnic foods,
precooked, premeasured, presweetened, low calorie, high protein, and
so forth. Even pet owners were offered numerous choices: wet foods,
dry foods, biscuits, crackers, puppy chow, mature animal meals, beef
chunks, liver snaps, and whatever.

The years of plenty, of rising consumption and ebullient expectations, finally gave way to a more subdued economy. The inflation and
sporadic shortages in the seventies bode ill for innovation. R&D activi-

ties seem to have shifted from long-term to more short-term projects, with an increasing emphasis upon product modification rather than a search for completely new products and processes. Rising costs, coupled with greater uncertainties, have driven industrial research managers to seek the safety of near-term results and a more predictable demand.

The seriousness of the situation was underscored when the White House in 1977 ordered a twenty-eight–agency "domestic policy review" of how governmental policy affects industrial innovation. This was the only review in the previous twenty years transcending the interests of more than one agency.[20]

The effects of adversity, however, are not uniform and, in many instances, may be turned to advantage. Soaring prices of oil, for example, have spurred petroleum and chemical companies to more vigorous efforts in energy research. Texaco in 1976 announced successful development of a process for the conversion of coal into clean fuel gas and synthesis for the manufacture of chemicals.[21] Awarded a large government contract, Exxon pursued research on a catalytic coal gasification process for converting coal to pipeline-quality natural gas.[22] The company also announced the development of the EXOL method, which supposedly achieves a 30 percent savings in lubricating oil, an energy-intensive operation.[23] Union Carbide has been attempting to derive energy products from municipal wastes.[24] The Electrolytic Systems groups of Diamond Shamrock, engaged in extensive research on energy reduction in the chemical industry, recently licensed its chlor-alkali technology to the Peoples Republic of China. This multimillion dollar transaction was probably the first such agreement between a U.S. corporation and China.[25] In all these examples, companies realized that change, even if unwanted, created opportunities for profitable ventures.

New Product Risks

Not only is product development a costly process, but risks run extremely high. This is evidenced by the large incidence of new product failures.

Studies regarding success or failure of new products have disclosed inconsistent results. A study of supermarkets in 1968 estimated that out of 9,450 products introduced, only about 20 percent met their sales

[20] Cited in "Vanishing Innovation,"*Business Week* (July 3, 1978), p. 46.

[21] Texaco, Inc., *Annual Report, 1976*, pp. 25–26.

[22] Exxon Corporation, *Annual Report, 1976*, p. 19.

[23] *Ibid., 1978*, p. 17.

[24] Union Carbide Corp., *Annual Report, 1976*, p. 8.

[25] Diamond Shamrock, *Annual Report, 1978*, p. 18.

goals.[26] An A. C. Nielsen report of food and drug items in 1971 calculated the new product failure rate at approximately 53 percent.[27] Other studies have put failure rates for consumer goods at a low of some 40 percent to a high of 80 percent. The failure incidence for new products in the industrial field seems to run somewhat lower, though there is no agreement on a precise figure.[28] But by all measures, there is a consensus among marketers that the proportion of successful new products is less than adequate.

A somewhat different approach to the success or failure problem is that of Booz, Allen & Hamilton, a consulting firm. Its study of 200 companies, all large and prominent, breaks down the new product process into distinct planning stages, ranging from generation of ideas to commercialization of developed products. Figure 1-1 shows the mortality rate of new product ideas as they make their way through the planning process within a corporation.

Figure 1-1. Mortality of New Product Ideas

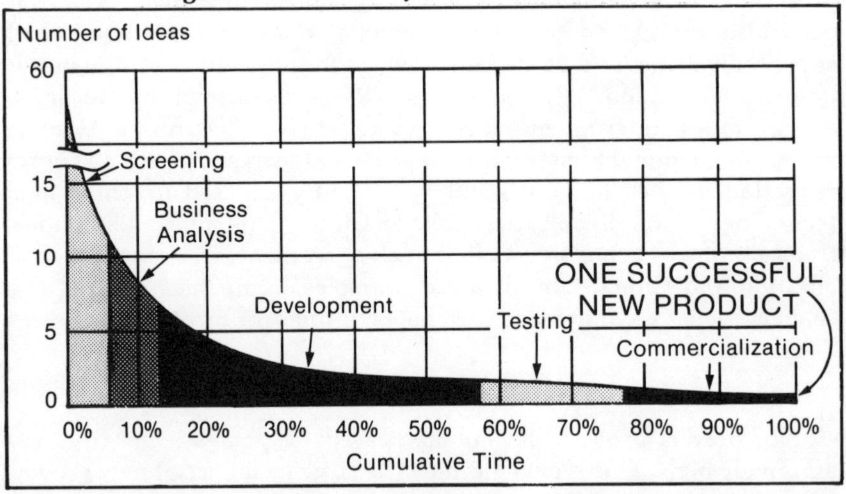

Source: Allen & Hamilton, *Management of New Products* (Chicago: Booz, Allen & Hamilton, 1968), p. 9.

---

[26] Theodore L. Angelus, "Why Do Most New Products Fail," *Advertising Age* (March 24, 1969), p. 85.

[27] "New Product Success Ratio," *The Nielsen Researcher* (1971), pp. 2–10.

[28] David S. Hopkins and E. L. Bailey, *New Product Pressures* (New York: The Conference Board, June, 1971), p. 20; Robert D. Buzzell and R. E. M. Nourse, *Product Innovation in Food Processing, 1954–1964* (Boston: Harvard Business School, 1967), pp. 9–10, 99–105, 122–124, 169–170; C. Merle Crawford, "Marketing Research and the New Product Failure Rate," *Journal of Marketing* (April, 1977), p. 51. However, a 1979 study by The Conference Board found that 67 percent of new products introduced were successful. "Survey Finds 67 Percent of New Products Succeed," *Marketing News* (February 8, 1980), p. 1.

The Booz, Allen & Hamilton study attributes only one commercial success in the marketplace out of every fifty-eight ideas. Since the calculation excludes ideas considered but not screened, the number of ideas needed for one success actually exceeds this estimate.

Figure 1-1 shows idea attrition as it takes place over the planning time span. Most of new product planning, slightly better than 40 percent, is taken up with development. Another 20 percent or so is devoted to testing. This comparatively lengthy period of preparation—development and testing—separates the initial acceptance of an idea from its implementation and, depending on the product, may substantially increase the business risks.

The development and testing periods also consumed, on the average, about two-thirds of all expenses in the evolution of new products. This can be seen in table 1-3, which depicts the portion of expenses associated with each stage of the new product process, according to the Booz, Allen & Hamilton study.

Table 1-3

Proportion of New Product Expenses at Stage of New Product Evolution

Stages of New Product Evolution	Proportion of New Product Expenses, %	Percent Distribution		
		Successful Products, %	Unsuccessful Products, %	Total Products, %
Screening and business analysis ...	15	13	87	100
Development	57	21	79	100
Testing..........	10	40	60	100
Commercialization.	18	67	33	100
All stages	100	30	70	100

Source: Derived from Booz, Allen & Hamilton, *op. cit.*, pp. 10–11.

As table 1-3 shows, 70 percent of all expenses were frittered away on projects that were unsuccessful. Screening and business analysis had the lowest relative effectiveness, with almost 90 percent of the efforts resulting in negative accomplishments. But this phase only accounted for 15 percent of all expenses and, by eliminating supposed failures, reduced waste in the later, more expensive stages. But the high proportion of development expenses spent on unsuccessful products, some 79 percent, must be a matter of concern. The statistics imply that about eight out of every ten technicians and engineers spent their time on projects that never justified themselves commercially.

Reasons for New Product Failure

A reduction of the new product failure rate by only a few percentage points would result in substantial savings to American industry. For example, it is estimated that as many as 100,000 products introduced into supermarkets during the seventies were disappointments. The advertising costs alone for these failures probably ran well over $13 billion.[29] Thus, numerous studies, carried out over the years, have attempted to probe into reasons for such failures.[30]

The reasons for failure, like rate estimates, vary from study to study. The disparities owe partly to definition, partly to sampling and questionnaire design. But broad areas of agreement exist as well. Table 1-4 summarizes the most frequently quoted reasons for failure and groups them under factors that are internal and external to the company.

Table 1-4
Most Frequently Quoted Reasons for New Product Failure

Internal Factors	External Factors
1. Imitative, "me-too" product	1. Lack of effective demand
2. Inadequate market assessment	2. Competitive action
3. Poor market planning and execution	
4. Poor management control	
5. Corporate limitations	
6. Technical deficiency	

Internal factors

Internal deficiencies can be remedied because they are supposedly under management control. Therefore, any improvement in their performance can lead to significant savings by reducing the failure rate.

The evidence stongly indicates the major reasons for failure as being market related, not product related. By all counts, failures that can be traced to technical deficiencies are relatively few. The most serious ones refer to food products that were ostensibly dropped because they lacked appealing taste. Prominent failures of this type were Campbell's Red Kettle and Best Foods' Knorrs, which were said not to be as tasty as Lipton's Cup-O-Soup. But these brands might have foundered because of a market-related problem rather than a technical one. That is, R&D did not create the "proper" taste owing to the difficulty of assessing consumers' taste preferences.

---

[29] "New Products: The Push is on Marketing," *Business Week* (March 4, 1972), p. 159.

[30] E.g., see George J. Abrams, "Why New Products Fail," *Advertising Age* (April 22, 1974), pp. 51–52; Angelus, *op.cit.*; William J. Constandse, "Why New Product Management Fails," *Business Management* (June, 1971), pp. 163–165; Erwin A. Frand, "Why New Products Fail," *Industry Week* (August 11, 1975), pp. 58–60; Hopkins and Bailey, *op.cit.*; William T. Moran, "Why New Products Fail," *Journal of Advertising Research* (April, 1973), pp.5–13.

A more frequently cited reason for failure is the introduction of imitative, "me-too" products. Such entries presumably violate the marketing concept and therefore do not fulfill a genuine consumer need. Industrial goods of this type are seen as offering no comparative advantage. In either event, the "copies" have no reason for being, it is held, and languish in the absence of strong demand.

These assertions may well contain elements of truth. But the evidence to substantiate this position is far from convincing. Studies of the subject have merely documented the fact that more imitative products fail than any other type. By itself, this proves nothing. It is like saying that more whites die than blacks—a highly expected result, for there are more of them. What is lacking is the incidence or probability of failure attached to each type of product and its related costs. In short, the studies have not shown that the failure rate among imitative products is higher than among other kinds of new products and that costs of these failures are proportionately greater.

Other often cited reasons for product failure are poor predictions of market demand and faulty market planning and execution. Improper timing is also a common complaint, but it is usually associated with forecasting, planning, or execution of a program. A deficiency in any one would show up as bad timing.

External factors

Since external elements remain outside the corporation, they are not decision variables. For example, a company can anticipate or react to competitive activity. But it cannot control product planning of competitors or dictate their product offerings. Similarly, a company can influence but cannot control the marketplace. It cannot decree that sales shall be so much, and no less. And markets may turn perverse, despite the best plans.

Yet external factors are seldom mentioned by business executives as reasons for failure. Management seems unwilling to concede anything to forces it cannot control. It seems highly reluctant to admit that failure can come about in spite of carefully planned, competent executive action. If a new product did not make it, someone must have been at fault. To think otherwise would be a tacit admission that valuable resources and stockholders' equity are as much at the mercy of chance as in the firm, safe hands of accomplished professionals. Since most investigations of new product failures rest on surveys with business executives, they reflect a managerial point of view that is turned inward upon itself.

This same view is stated forcefully by Marcus and Tauber, who argue that internal and external reasons for failure are in reality different sides of the same coin. "If consumers reject a product because the

price is too high," they assert, "management erred in its pricing decision. If consumers show little need for a product, management failed to
test the market adequately and forecast sales."[31]

No one would deny that corporate action affects the marketplace.
But the ability to anticipate all contingencies or to bring about all desired results is beyond the realm of reality. How can one forecast sudden predilections for mini-skirts or maxi-skirts or in-betweens? How
was it possible to predict that within a half-dozen years OPEC would
quadruple the price of oil and turn "have" nations into "have-nots"? To
think that management can always set prices or forecast sales unerr-
ingly is to endow it with omniscience.

Perhaps management is correct in deemphasizing external factors
and in building a system of rewards based upon results, not intentions.
In this way an organization strives to improve its decision-making processes and to bring its operations under greater control. And assuredly
there is much room for improvement. Nevertheless, management cannot wish away uncertainty, for willingly or not, it must cope with it.

Time and Uncertainty

One element of uncertainty, and an important one at that, is the
effect of time. The concept of a new product precedes its use by a
relatively long period. When initially conceived, the product might have
been just what the market wanted, but it may have been unwanted by
the time it went into commercial production.

In the grocery field, where products can be pushed to market
quickly, the average time span from concept to introduction is about
three years. For certain metals, chemicals, and paper products, the time
lag averages some five years. Development time for ethical drugs runs
from five-and-a-half to eight years. Relatively long lead times are experienced by manufacturers of aircraft, computers, machinery, and other
technical equipment. Lead times for new energy supplies, measured
from time of access to major commercial production, run from as low as
two to as high as twelve years. This is shown in figure 1-2.

The greater the lead time, the greater the uncertainty with respect
to markets. All sales projections in one way or another undergo time
warps, as it were, and plans must be adjusted continuously.

Time also has another effect: it affects costs. In general, the longer
the lead time to commercialization, the more costs accumulate, and the
larger the amount of investment becomes. This time-cost relationship
becomes especially critical in periods of inflation, when extended devel-

---

[31] Burton H. Marcus and Edward M. Tauber, *Marketing Analysis and Decision Making* (Boston:
Little, Brown and Company, 1979), p. 26.

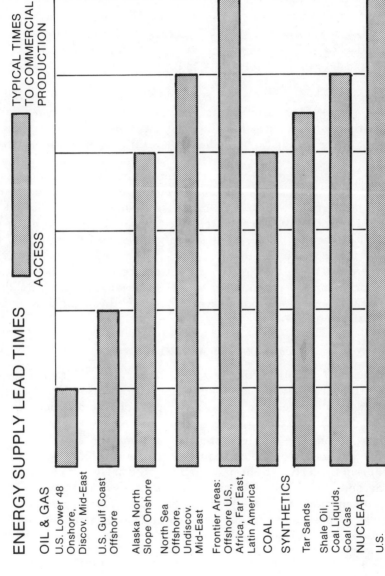

Figure 1-2. Energy, Supply Lead Times

Source: Exxon, *World Energy Outlook* (New York: Exxon Corporation, 1977), p. 33.

opment cycles mean cost overruns. Time is the greatest enemy of the corporate planner.

This was dramatically demonstrated with respect to new ethical drugs. From 1962 to 1972, average development time rose from two to seven years, primarily because of government red tape. Meanwhile, average development costs escalated from $1 million to $11.5 million. The advent of inflation since 1972 brought development cost to an estimated $22 million four years later.[32] These figures reflect the effects of longer development time, more stringent clinical and toxicological studies, and rises in price levels.

From a somewhat different perspective, time magnifies variations between expectations and results. New product plans will seldom coincide with actual outcomes under any circumstances. By its very definition, plans are actions to be undertaken in future time. But variations between expected results and actuality are not randomly distributed. Rather, sales represent forms of patterned behavior, and deviations from plans tend to occur in the same direction. They become cumulative with time. Products with high purchase frequencies are particularly affected by such habit-forming tendencies. If things start off badly and are left unchanged, they are likely to get worse. Consequently, the greater the separation of the thought from the deed—of planning from commercialization—the greater the difference between management expectations and market outcomes. With respect to new products, there is no truth in the homespun proverb about time healing old wounds; it aggravates them.

Are Rewards Worth the Risks?

While costs of putting out new products run high, the rate of success is at a comparatively low level. Yet there is little reason for pessimism. All things considered, the potential benefits of new products seem to outweigh their potential losses.

First, a complete failure, costly though it may be, seldom results in complete disaster for the company. Quite the contrary: that unhappy event is more likely to be brought about by the neglect of new products.

Second, the amount of corporate resources devoted to new products is relatively modest. On an average, American industry spends about 13 percent of pretax profits on research and development.[33] Since the largest part of R&D expenditures goes into salaries and fringe benefits,

[32] Edwin A. Gee and Chaplin Tyler, *Managing Innovation* (New York: John Wiley & Sons, 1976), p. 6.

[33] See table 1-2.

[34] Thomas A. Staudt, "Higher Management Risks in Product Strategy," *Journal of Marketing* (January, 1973), pp. 4-9; Battelle, *Probable Levels of R&D Expenditures in 1978*, p. 11.

they are charged to the period in which they occur and deducted from revenue as an expense. It is conducted on a pay-as-you-go basis.

Research and development expenditures are also conservatively managed in other ways. The bulk of such expenditures is funneled into projects designed to extend or modify existing product lines, improve existing processes, and reduce costs.[34] Hence, spending is directed mainly to support ongoing businesses, not to create new ones.

The same principles apply to costs other than R&D. New products that are related to existing business lines can capitalize on the favorable volume-cost effects of synergism. Commercialization processes also commonly involve a series of careful market probes to assess the probabilities of various outcomes. Such policies of deferring output and distribution are designed to move capital spending on new projects to periods of greater certainty.

Large companies normally have several new ventures going on at the same time. Although some may be considered more important than others, reliance is seldom placed on any particular one. This process of "portfolio management" is not unlike exploration for oil. Many sunken wells turn up dry or with low yields, but a few gushers will more than make up for past disappointments.

In any event, opportunity and risk, like good and evil, can always be found together. New products remain an important means of generating desirable corporate growth, though the incidence of failure runs high. But that is a cost of doing business in a market economy. Hardly ever does a company question whether it can afford a program of product development—it cannot afford *not* to have one.

REVIEW QUESTIONS

1. Does the study of new products deserve the emphasis it receives? Explain your answer.

2. A conscious, organized policy of product innovation can spur economic growth. Growth can also be achieved by expanding the production and consumption of current products. Compare and evaluate the two approaches.

3. Compare a price reduction with a product change as a means of creating product preferences among customers.

4. The importance of new products, in part, is based on the achievement of company growth, cost reduction, and new business. Explain how these strategic results are achieved via new products.

5. Perhaps the basic business reasons for seeking new products relate to growth, cost reduction, profits, new business, and stability. What are more specific reasons?

6. Explain the following statement: "There can be only one innovator; the rest are followers."

7. What are the current environmental forces that will shape the trend of much future innovation?

8. Long lead time for new product development increases risk. Why?

9. What are some of the reasons for new product failures?

10. Why does time generate uncertainty? How does this affect product development risk?

2/ Product Market Dimensions

A product may be defined in one of two ways, generically or psychologically. A physical definition of a product seems preferable to a psychological one because classification is more objective. From the perspective of microeconomics, a "new" product is defined as one new to the firm but not necessarily new to the market. In this sense, a new product can be a revision, modification, or even an imitation of products already existing in the marketplace. The majority of new products are of this sort.

New product development includes both technological and marketing alternatives. The former encompasses three options—the application of conventional technology, its extension, or the development of a new technology. Maintaining the "state of the art" carries the lowest risks, but nontechnical considerations take precedure over technological ones. The development of a new technology may offer the greatest rewards. But breakthroughs of this type are rare and entail the highest risks.

Marketing options are also of three broad types. A firm can attempt to maintain its markets, expand them, or enter new ones. When combined with three product options, a firm has nine wide-ranging product-market alternatives. Strategy consists in a choice of the proper mix.

Segmentation is but an extension of these strategies, their applications to an entire market or to a segment thereof. Criteria for segmenting markets can be objective, such as geography, demographics, socioeconomic data, or usage patterns. Subjective criteria are primarily psychological, such as personality traits, life style, attitudes, perceptions, and preferences. It seems that objective factors can be used successfully to define market parameters. Although psychological variables may discriminate among brands, they present problems both in concept and measurement.

Product Definition

What is a product? The question seems simple and straightforward, but the answer is neither matter-of-fact nor forthright. Oskar Morgenstern, a prominent economist, noted in 1963 that some of the greatest diffculties were encountered in defining a "product" and an "industry."[1] This statement is equally true today. An energetic technology, which creates new products, new materials, and new processes, renders classification a never-ending task. Subtle changes in quality and use patterns occurring over time may also alter the character of a product.

Yet a classification system must be structured. This issue of product definition is not an idle one, imposed upon a reading audience to satisfy an academic convention. Taxonomy is the core of any science. Without a well-defined classification system, widely accepted by a profession, there can be no measurement of basic data or meaningful communication. If the same things are called by different names, there exists a babble of tongues, which can only result in great confusion.

Of course, marketing is an art, not a science. But even art must adhere to a certain discipline in order to perpetuate its techniques and to flourish. A musical composition is not a random arrangement of notes. And a painting is not a random splashing of color on canvas, though some contemporary art may appear that way. Classification is an absolute requirement for even the bare beginnings of organized information and of a marketing discipline.

All products, which include goods and services, can be grouped generically—arranged in accordance with some characteristic. Thus, goods can be classified by categories such as furniture, automobiles, houses, food, etc. These classifications can be set in some hierarchical order, ranging from extremely broad to specifically narrow definitions. Using this form, a good becomes a combination of physical and chemical properties. Services can be described similarly in terms of functions to be performed by the agency that renders them. Almost all industries measure sales of their products by such basic definitions, although the exact breakdowns may vary among companies in the same industry.

Some authorities have advocated a psychological definition of a product. This view holds that a product is not a physical entity but a perception of a physical entity. Therefore, the argument goes, it should be defined not in generic terms but in those which "focus on consumers' needs and wants."[2]

From a consumer's point of view, the perceptual definition of a product may be eminently correct. Indeed, an unchanged product might

[1] Oskar Morgenstern, *On the Accuracy of Economic Observations* (2nd Ed., Princeton: Princeton University Press, 1963), p. 35.

[2] Eberhard E. Scheuing, *New Product Management* (Hinsdale, Ill.: The Dryden Press, 1974), pp. 6-7; Milton I. Brand, "What is a New Product?" Brand, Guber & Co., ed. *Professionals Look at New Products* (Ann Arbor: University of Michigan, 1969), pp.10-13. Also see, Chester R. Wasson, *Product Management* (St. Charles, Ill.: Challenge Books, 1971), pp.3, 13; D. J. Luck and O. C. Ferrell, *Marketing Strategy and Plans* (Englewood Cliffs: Prentice-Hall, Inc., 1979), pp. 163-165.

suddenly be perceived as something novel and, according to this definition, should now be classified as a new product.[3] But it becomes patently obvious—without discursions into taxonomy and related epistemological cal issues—that such a classification system encounters formidable barriers. Perceptions are subjective characteristics and, though real enough, are difficult to measure. These intangibles also seem to be undergoing constant shifts and, if measurable, present data that lack stability. Moreover, no one has yet devised an operational method for classifying products according to psychological variables. Therefore, this book will adhere to tradition and define products generically.

However, there are more fundamental reasons for the generic approach. Physical objects and their perceptions by would-be customers are not identical. Perceptions are demand-related features. But products are supply-related. They derive from decisions of suppliers, not buyers. A firm accepting the "wants and needs" philosophy might try matching its products to the desires and aspirations of potential customers. A firm inclined otherwise might try changing buyers' perceptions, so as to alter their priorities of "wants and needs" and their brand preferences. Many firms engage in both endeavors simultaneously. Regardless of approach, the act of product innovation—the what, how, when, and where of product development—is determined by the producer.

Innovation Relative to Markets

It has been claimed, again and again, that most products promoted as new are not and may be quite jaded in the sense that similar items already exist in the marketplace. Nevertheless, they are different from other forms of output. The amount of product newness is thus a matter of difference between the new entry and those of its competitors. This difference can range from small, trivial dissimilarities to large, yawning separations. It can range from new products that are virtually indistinguishable from old ones to entries so novel as to have no counterpart in the commercial world.

One way of conceptualizing these shades of difference is that of Thomas Robertson, who has proposed a scale running through three categories of newness: continuous, dynamically continuous, and discontinuous innovations.[4] This "newness continuum" regards innovation from the standpoint of its effects on usage patterns. According to this grading scheme, the less the degree of newness, the more continuous the usage patterns. The greater the amount of newness, the more the discontinuity in established patterns of product usage.

---

[3] Robert R. Rothberg, "Product Innovation in Perspective," Rothberg, ed., *Corporate Strategy and Product Planning* (New York: The Free Press, 1976), p. 4.

[4] Thomas Robertson, "The Process of Innovation and the Diffusion of Innovation," *Journal of Marketing* (January, 1967), pp. 14-19.

Continuous innovations

Continuous innovations are thought of as changes in existing products that are relatively minor in scope, such as annual model changeovers in the automobile industry. Innovations of this nature are numerous, going on all the time. A cigarette is made "slim" and heralded as the flavor-giving smoke of the liberated woman. A new package, with a zipper on top and bottom, is proclaimed as the great labor-saving device to free every one-zipper package user from endless drudgery. Often, product alterations may not be apparent, as when minor changes are incorporated in components, manufacturing techniques, or processes. The addition of a common emollient can be enough for a firm to announce a new, miracle body lotion, drenched with exclusive formulae to make every part of the torso feel smooth and soft, like the full breasts of the model doing the commercial.

Many firms find themselves competing on such differences, often superficial. When product features are so weakly differentiated from those of competitive products, firms tend to rely upon marketing as the stalwart of sales—out-advertise the competition, out-position them, out-price them, out-promote them, out-sell them, etc. Indeed, they must, for under such circumstances that is the only avenue open for attaining a differential advantage. The buyer must be made to think that one brand is superior or offers more benefits for the money expended.

Dynamically continuous innovations

Dynamically continuous innovations are mainly revisions of existing products, but they entail major modifications in design. These revisions perform essentially the same functions as the older products but in a uniquely different way.

These innovations are more disruptive of current usage, since they involve the creation of radically new products or processes that compete with older forms. An example of this type of innovation is the electric toothbrush, which is directly substitutable for those manipulated entirely by human power. Another illustration is the IBM typewriter with the memory unit, which competes with older manual and electric models. The introduction of color television, which is directly substitutable for a black and white set, tends to fall into this portion of the newness continuum.

Discontinuous innovations

Discontinuous innovations are new products that have no counterparts on the market. They disturb usage patterns, for they set in motion completely new forms of behavior. Old processes and skills become obsolete, while new ones are called into being. The advent of television or the development of the computer exemplifies this sort of innovation.

Hand calculators and photocopy processes can be grouped at this end of the scale with respect to product newness.

Innovation Relative to Company

Since the decision-making unit for product development is the firm, product newness can be viewed from a microeconomic perspective. From this standpoint, the amount of newness in the marketplace may be unrelated to those of particular organizations. For example, a new product may be markedly similar to others on the market. But that same item can be regarded as brand new by a company that produced nothing like it before. Regardless of its effects on usage patterns, that banal, unoriginal item represents a new venture to that particular firm. Thus, a new product to a company is something that is different from its other output, though it will possess varying degrees of market newness.

When the subject of new products is approached from this microeconomic point of view, every firm has three, broadly based product options. At any given time it can offer any of the following:

1. *The same product.* The company merely keeps the product unchanged, as is, without any alterations whatsoever.

2. *A revised product.* This modification can be major or minor. The latter is by far the more common.

3. *A completely new product.* This is simply one that the company had not offered previously. The range of possibilities is remarkably wide. The product may be similar to those already on the market. Or it may be a major improvement of available alternatives. Or, it may be quite unique, without facsimiles on the market.

These alternatives are not mutually exclusive. Corporations usually turn out many products, and all three strategies can be carried out at the same time, with varying emphasis upon each. Strategy may also shift in relation to a specific product, for what is appropriate one day may be inappropriate at a later time. A company must remain flexible, keeping open all its options, so as to let the strategy fit the circumstances.

Product Options–Technical Options

A firm's choice of product strategy—to stand pat, revise, or introduce a new entry—calls forth the use or nonuse of a given technology. Each product strategy will further elicit technical alternatives varing greatly in terms of both costs and risks. A useful arrangement of such technological input is the simple, three-tier categorization of Lowell

W. Steele, technical consultant to R&D at General Electric. Focusing on the subject from the vantage point of performance, technology is divided into three categories: applications of conventional technology, extensions of that technology, and development of new technology.[5]

Applications of conventional technology

Most R&D programs are of this uncreative nature, seeking solutions through what is already known and readily available. They traverse the familiar knowledge, concepts, and techniques of a professional discipline but do not venture beyond. Their effect, as such, is to maintain the technological state of the art.

In this type of R&D work, technical risks remain low. This does not eliminate risk; it is shifted to other areas. Or product development may evoke considerations other than technological ones. Issues such as costs, sales volume, marketing, and finance usually take precedence over technical ones. When risk swings towards the nontechnological side, the focus of corporate effort tends to move in the same direction.

Extensions of conventional technology

R&D work of this nature aims to refine or improve upon conventional technology, so that the state of the art is expanded, incrementally as it were, beyond its present boundaries. Advances may take place in design, engineering techniques, materials, and processes. An example of this type is the current developmental work for deriving a new generation of catalysts to be used in coal liquefaction and production of synthetic fuels. Another might be exemplified by present work to develop a new type of battery, capable of powering electric vehicles of the future. Extensions of conventional technology contain greater uncertainties as to the required time and effort for project completion.

Development of new technology

Development of new technology is the exception rather than the rule. Work of this nature, usually basic research, is carried on by a number of large companies. But it usually falls outside the scope of operational planning and management. Its results cannot be anticipated. The creation of a new technology also requires a different kind of thinking from that of the typical R&D researcher, who seeks to apply or extend the state of the art. In fact, new ways of thinking or doing are often resisted by technicians immersed in the old technology.[6]

Theoretically, the three product options can be combined with the three technical options to indicate broad types of strategies available to a corporation. This combination, in the form of a matrix, is illustrated in table 2-1.

---

[5] Lowell W. Steele, *Innovation in Big Business* (New York: Elsevier, 1975), pp. 67-75.
[6] *Ibid.*, p. 74.

Table 2-1

Product—Technical Options

Technical Option	Product Option		
	Same Product	Revised Product	New Product
Application		X	X
Extension		X	X
New technology			X

Given a product policy, designated by the column, the matrix indicates technical alternatives, designated by the row. A decision to keep the product unchanged will require no technological input. A revised product, which attests to the prior existence of a similar one, would count primarily on applications, though extensions are possible. An applications strategy also implies that the technical route would unfold few differential advantages, which would have to be found in other directions.

Virtually all revised products can benefit from an extension of conventional technology, such as cost reduction or improvement of product performance. But these benefits must be weighed against costs and risks and compared with other alternatives, for there is often more than one way to attain a goal. Young industries are more likely than mature ones to reward technical efforts with larger incremental improvements. But such potential advantages may also be accompanied by greater risks.

New products, from the standpoint of the individual firm, can be of various types: similar to competitive offerings, differentiated from other entries in the same product class, or all by themselves, with no counterparts on the market. Although products new to a company can employ any one of the three technical options, the most common is application of the old technology. This imitative technological approach has the capacity for producing innovative products. The electric knife involved no new scientific principles or techniques, though the concept of this cutting instrument was highly creative.

Firms that can best exploit this imitative strategy must have capabilities in other areas, particularly marketing and finance. Japanese firms, for example, have demonstrated a remarkable deftness for acquiring foreign technologies and carrying them to successful conclusions.

Companies poised to adopt technical imitation can derive many advantages from this strategy. First, the investment in technology can be based on risk that is calculable, not vague or "iffy." Second, the desired technology is at hand, literally available on demand. Third, the imitator therefore enjoys the privilege of choosing from among competing alternatives. Risks and uncertainties of R&D are cut to a relatively low level. Fourth, supply is more easily adaptable to demand factors.

However, deep pitfalls await the imitator as well. Lacking a technical capability of its own, such a firm must always be reacting to decisions made by others. In industries where new technology is not a major factor, this disadvantage can be exasperating, but it is seldom detrimental. Few opportunities are lost, especially when reaction time is fast. But as the state of the art reaches maturity, no matter what the field, the tendency is towards specialization and a division of labor. A firm that imitates might have trouble in recruiting and training specialists in critical areas. A research program that explicitly mimics developments of others runs counter to the professional values of technical and engineering personnel. Finally, the firm doing little or no exploratory work on its own is in a poor position to anticipate changes in the future. If time is important in the introduction of a new product, the follower is at a decided disadvantage. In general, firms that are most successful as followers possess an R&D capability that can support and improve upon the acquired technology.[7]

Developing a new technology invariably results in products new to the market. These may be of two types. In one instance, the functions are the same, but the product or process is different. Such innovations are substitutes for the existing products, as is margarine for butter and jet engines for engines with propellers. In the other instance, new functions are made possible, such as that by the heart pacer.

In either case, the innovator can insinuate himself into a proprietary position from which he would be difficult to dislodge. On the other hand, costs and risks are great. Even if developed, the new technology must prove itself. A new function must have an effective demand. A competing function must demonstrate a better performance, and usually at lower cost.

The classic failure of an apparently superior technology was the case of Corfam, developed in 1963 by DuPont after some twenty-five years of research. Designed to replace leather for shoe uppers, Corfam weighed two-thirds less. It was water-repellent, resistant to abrasion, and unlike leather, did not have to be polished to keep its shine. Being of uniform thickness, it was responsive to quality control in manufacturing. How could it fail to become another glowing episode in DuPont's continuing saga of better living through chemistry?

Yet fail it did. DuPont's new plant at Old Hickory, Tennessee, encountered a series of perplexing and unforeseen production problems. Rocketing costs far overshot original estimates. From 1964 to 1967 Corfam shoe sales actually rose from 1 million to 20 million pairs, but no significant production economies were effected. Meanwhile, vinyl-coated fabrics, a plastic material, flooded the market in a variety of

---

[7] William A. Fisher, "Follow-Up Strategies for Technical Growth," *California Management Review* (Fall, 1978), pp. 10-19.

colors and embossments, and shoes made from these synthetics sold at about half the retail price of Corfam. Marketing expenses doubled, as compared with the initial budget, but market slippage could not be halted. After seven years of heavy losses, and unable to bring costs down to competitive levels, the Old Hickory plant closed its doors, and the ghost of Corfam, like those of other prominent ventures in which hopes outran performance, haunts the sallow pages of marketing books as a lesson in economics for would-be entrepreneurs.[8]

Product-Market Relationships

By now it should be plainly obvious that a firm's product policy and technological options are incomplete without reference to markets. Products and markets are as inseparable as government and taxes. A new products policy must therefore consider not only its technological but also its marketing dimensions.

No matter how superior, products usually cannot sell themselves. In a past age, the world literally came to the inventor who could make a superior product. Our modern economy, which emphasizes a "free market," finds no virtue in the old adage, "If a man can build a better mouse trap than his neighbor, through he builds his house in the woods, the world will make a beaten path to his door." For better or for worse, the inventor of the rodent-catching contraption must beat a path to the world. New product policy must go hand in hand with marketing policy, for the path can seldom be traversed by one alone.

Theoretically, three broad aims characterize any product policy with respect to markets, defined as classes of potential customers or users. The company can:

1. *Keep its old customers intact.* This is an avowed policy of maintaining the *status quo*.

2. *Expand the market by adding new customers from among potential users.* In mature industries, new customers represent switching from competitive brands. In growth industries, new customers may be won, not only from competitive brands, but from the unrealized potential.

3. *Extend the market by selling to a new class of customers.* This strategy usually calls for entering a new market.

If the three possibilities above are combined with the three product options, the result is nine possible outcomes. This model can be represented by the matrix in table 2-2.

---

[8] See Robert F. Hartley, *Marketing Mistakes* (Columbus, Ohio: Grid Publishing, Inc.), pp. 71-80.

Table 2-2

Product—Market Matrix

Product Market	Degree of Market Newness		
	(1) Same Market	(2) Expanded Market	(3) Extended Market
(1) Same product	1	4	7
(2) Revised product	2	5	8
(3) New product	3	6	9

If emphasis is placed on the column (vertically), the question becomes: "What are the possible product strategies, given a marketing goal?" If emphasis is reversed and placed on the rows, the question is inverted: "What are the various marketing alternatives, given a product policy?"

From a decision-making standpoint, the first alternative is more in keeping with the experiences of most companies. Actually, it is possible to develop a product first and then seek markets for it. This is not unusual in industries with vested interests in specific materials, such as glass, oil, and steel. Such businesses will emphasize efficiency and technological research. But the more common experience is to develop products in response to market demand. Here, the approach to product innovation begins by probing the customer—his wants, his problems, his desires, his frustrations with products currently in use—in order to recognize new product opportunities. Even more important, business strategies are usually formulated in terms of market—to maintain them, expand them, extend them—with specific goals set for investments, sales, expenses, profits.

Same market policy (cells 1-3)

A policy to maintain present customers is applicable in a wide range of circumstances. But it has particular relevance in two situations: when the product, having reached its potential, is the market leader, or when it is declining.

In the former instance, the company may opt to stand pat on both customers and products. If additional increments in product development or promotional expenditures would yield less than incremental returns, logic might dictate a strategy of maintaining the *status quo*. Or the market leader might even settle for small decrements if an aggressive policy in either promotion or product development would create instability in sales and profits. The large American auto manufacturers for many years tolerated the inroads of foreign cars without developing a small car of their own because they stood to lose more by cannibalizing their more expensive, and more profitable, models than they could gain by contesting for a larger share of the small car market. A leading firm in an oligopolistic environment might take a similar "live and let live" attitude, particularly in a raw material or basic industry where processes cannot readily be altered. In general, product development plays a minor role in a busines strategy that contemplates limited growth and seeks to optimize returns.

A firm may increase its revenue and profits even in this static situation—same market, same product—by a beneficial increase in usage per customer. In the industrial field, normal growth will tend to produce such an effect, and many suppliers count on growing with their customers. A similar result, however, can occur in the consumer field. In either situation, product development is of little or no consequence, and marketing is relied upon for achieving these salutary results. For example, Kraft ads on how to make a cheese souffle, hopefully with Cracker Barrel cheese, exemplify an attempt of a market leader to increase customers' per capita usage. Hershey's special recipes, such as those for "Hand-Me-Down" cake, likewise aim at encouraging customers to use more of its cocoa in cooking.

Another stand-pat situation is one in which market dominance has been attained by virtue of patents. Here, technology might be used extensively yet result in no product, new or revised. Pharmaceutical companies, after developing a new drug, commonly patent innumerable minor variations of its molecular structure to safeguard the legal monoply accorded an inventor. Firms in other high-technology industries, such as photography, chemistry, and instrumentation, engage in similar practices to support proprietary advantages. These activities have come under attack from many quarters but have stubbornly persisted. For example, in the fall of 1978 Genentech scientists succeeded in producing bacteria-induced insulin, which was later given to Eli Lilly for testing. At that time, Robert Swanson, president of Genentech, was quoted as saying, "I think we will be throwing up patent roadblocks."[9]

A firm may also attempt to keep its present customers through revised or new products. The former strategy may entail changes in style, which is sometimes referred to as "planned obsolescence." Yearly model changes by auto makers presumably stimulate buying, but in a replacement market by the same class of customers. Stylistic changes in clothing accomplish the same thing. Or products may be added to existing lines in order to exploit marketing capabilities.

Although markets remain constant, product revision can also be undertaken to reduce manufacturing and operating costs. With the price of fuel soaring, many companies in recent years have embarked upon programs to save energy. But there are numerous ways besides technology to achieve lower costs. An unspectacular change in package design can lead to substantial savings in transportation costs. Narrow-

---

[9] Marilyn Chase, "Search for 'Superbugs'," *Wall Street Journal* (May 10, 1979), p. 48.

ing a product line or relocating plants and warehouses or improving physical distribution can also lower expenses. Technological options must therefore be combined, and evaluated, with other approaches in cost-reduction programs.

A no-growth market strategy for finished goods by no means rules out products new to the company. Integrating backwards to supply its own plants with raw materials and components would give a company new products but cause no change in present customers or markets. Such investments are similar to cost-reducing processes; they represent attempts to maintain the earnings flow of an established business and to tighten the grasp on those hard-won gains achieved in the marketplace.

Market expansion strategy (cells 4-6)

This is probably the most common position of companies, each one trying to expand its business. Line functions usually emphasize this goal, with or without new products. A sales manager must do with what he has, and given a product line, he will usually seek to increase sales. In some instances, marketing alone will be relied upon as a strategy for enlarging the number of customers. For example, lowering prices in industries with high fixed costs can have a significant effect on volume. Fare cuts by airlines in 1977 have increased the number of passengers. This larger volume also lowered operating costs per passenger. Market expansion was thus accomplished with virtually no change in the product, and the ensuing efficiency resulted from changes in volume cost variances rather than technology.

But growth in a market cannot be sustained long without resort to product development, usually in the form of revision. The importance of this option to business expansion depends upon the nature of the product and its markets and therefore differs considerably from industry to industry.

Low-priced convenience goods sold in self-service outlets, for example, look primarily to advertising and sales promotion for revenue gains. Technology plays a decidedly minor role in swaying consumer choice of one brand over another. At most, its function is a supportive one. Consumers do practically no comparison shopping, for savings cannot possibly exceed search costs. In such circumstances, objective, dispassionate appraisals regarding the value of "quality" differences among brands can hardly be classified as public information. In the absence of individual search activities or strong noncommercial publicity about a product, the preferences and prejudices of the buying public become shaped by advertising and promotion.

Yet revised products, for the most part of minor or insignificant variety, gush forth in an almost steady stream. The additions of new ingredients in detergents, deodorants, beauty care products, floor wax, and polishes occur with a tireless frequency. Form changes are trumpeted endlessly, such as roll-on, cream, and sprays for deodorants. Commercials shout about changes in package design, size of packages, and color of items, as in bath soaps. Alterations in the flavor of foods, as in Jell-O or soft drinks, parallel changes in color of nonedible products.

But if product quality is of little consequence in the formation of consumer preferences, why the parade of modified products? Why the rush to obliterate old brands and despoil assets, when the "improvements" are assumed to have only a marginal effect on demand?

The fact is that few brands differentiated by advertising enjoy highly inelastic demand curves. Regardless of the promotional budget size, current brand loyalty offers little security in market position with respect to convenience goods. A shopper will have no hesitation to substitute for a brand out of stock. A smoker, finding his regular brand unavailable, would rather switch than fight, notwithstanding claims to the contrary. What is described as "impulse" buying—purchase decisions made with little consideration—has the potential to upset established patterns of behavior, given certain sets of circumstances.

Advertising campaigns must be renewed because, in the jargon of the trade, they are said to "wear out." After a while, commercial messages impart no new meanings or images but act only as a "reminder" that Brand X still exists. In like manner, unaltered brands have a tendency to experience sales erosion. What can a consumer possibly lose by trying something new, especially when the item is low priced and bought frequently? If dissatisfied, the buyer can always go back to the old brand on the next purchase. A new or improved product reverses this inclination to try another brand, giving sales a needed boost.

Product development in convenience goods not only follows from marketing strategy but can also be viewed as an integral part of promotion. It is in fact one alternative among various themes of a copy platform. It offers advertising a means of presenting the brand in a different *motif*, as new and up to date. It is a device, when combined with advertising, to make the promotional mix more effective. Advertising can enjoy a change of pace and perhaps inject a modicum of excitement in its messages. Since costs of such product revision are modest, they may be a small price to pay for the rejuvenation of an advertising campaign. As such, the incremental cost of product revision should be compared with the incremental revenue of this revised product. The increment is the difference between what occurred because of the product revision and what would have happened if no revision had taken place. The latter can only be estimated, based on past trends. The life of the product runs from its introduction until it is replaced by another revision.

In mature industries with entrenched brands, a side effect of this revision-promotion strategy is a higher barrier to entry. Especially when advertising budgets are large, the additional requirements of frequent product changes raises the stakes, or operating costs, in that particular industry.[10]

For high-priced durables in consumer fields, as well as for many industrial goods, product design and technical features are important ingredients in generating demand. Here, product revision may be more vital to market expansion, with the degree of importance varying widely among industries.

When products are differentiated on their characteristics, product modification offers an invaluable time advantage. If the revision is patentable, the time advantage is even more valuable. For example, Texas Instruments, Inc. in May 1977 unveiled three hand calculators, all more powerful than anything previously on the market but at only two-thirds the price of their predecessors. These new machines, designed for the higher-priced end of the market, were all of the programmable type that had grown popular with scientists, engineers, and business analysts. The obvious strategy of Texas Instruments was to expand its share of the market. At the time of this announcement, it was estimated that the new machines gave their manufacturer a year's head start over its nearest competitor, Hewlett-Packard Company.

Market extension strategy (cells 7-9)

Gaining new markets with the same product is most applicable to a geographic strategy, such as Coca-Cola entering China or Pepsi moving into the Soviet Union. Other than this spatial approach, market extension with the same product is rare and makes up the success stories of marketing. Inducing women to take up the nicotine habit in the twenties was one of the first demonstrations of advertising's persuasive powers. Right Guard deodorant, originally advertised for men, added a new class of customers when it changed its theme to a "family deodorant." Marlboro cigarette, originally thought of as a mild, women's smoke, gained a different group of users by building a masculine, he-man image.

But opening new markets with an unchanged product is difficult for a company. Usually, it must exercise a new product option in order to win new classes of customers. Quite often only a minor modification of a product is enough to trigger entrance into other markets. For example, a manufacturer of adult shoes may alter the product for the children's market. Adult dresses may be redesigned for adolescents. Men's electric razors, with slight changes in features, are promoted to the female market. General Electric's ongoing research in silicone sealants

---

[10] Porter, *op. cit.*, pp. 126-128.

has resulted in a variety of related products used in more than thirty different industries, as diverse as construction, electronics, and transportation. Play dough, originally an industrial caulking material, was produced in different colors and marketed as a modeling clay for children. Many industrial tools are adapted for consumer use by making them smaller and cheaper.

A product completely new to the firm normally brings a company into a new market. This development, involving both new products and new markets, is referred to as diversification. The new product aspect of diversification can be accomplished in several ways: by integral development of new lines, by licensing, by acquisitions and mergers, or by any combination of the three.

Market Segmentation Concept

A logical extension of the product-market discussion is the segmentation philosophy. As the word implies, segmentation means dividing a market into smaller parts or units and offering the product to one or more of these segments. Product-market options are thereby expanded, running the gamut from an undifferentiated, whole market approach to one of selective, fragmented marketing.

Since Wendell Smith's thought-provoking article on the subject more than two decades ago, the segmentation ideology has permeated marketing with an insuppressible presence.[11] Every leading textbook on marketing sets aside a chapter for segmentation. Professional journals and trade publications keep grinding out article after article on the topic: bases for segmenting markets, research methods for discovering segments, statistical methods for delineating submarkets.

The more a word is used, the more meanings it tends to take on, both blurring and expanding the original sense. The semantics of marketing is no exception. Almost any marketing tactic that does not embrace the total market might be called "segmentation." Sometimes, regional marketing is lumped under this heading.[12] Any advertising that features a product benefit or attribute can be said to appeal to some "psychological segment" of a total body of consumers. A promotion for drinking beer with lunch can be termed "occasion segmentation," because the midday meal is one occasion among many for having a glass of beer.[13] In a sense, all these interpretations may be correct. At the same

---

[11] Wendell Smith, "Product Differentiation and Market Segmentation as Alternative Marketing Strategies," *Journal of Marketing* (July, 1956) pp. 3–8.

[12] Robert D. Hisrich and Michael P. Peters, *Marketing a New Product: Its Planning, Development and Control* (Menlo Park: The Benjamin/Cummings Publishing Co., Inc., 1978), p. 162.

[13] "Occasion Segmentation Can Help in Profiling Market, Goldman Says," *Marketing News* (April 6, 1979), pp. 1, 5.

time, the segmentation concept becomes grandly vague, like the campaign promises of a politician. If a concept can be perceived as encompassing almost all marketing activity, it becomes too general for any kind of meaningful application. It loses its differentiation and might just as well be called "marketing." Because of the prevailing ambiguity, it would be fitting to go over some of the old ground—even at the risk of distraction—in order to describe the segmentation concept in a more rigid form.

The segmentation philosophy derives from the fact that a market may be composed of diverse parts or segments, each with its own unique behavioral patterns and its own teleological processes. The uniqueness of these segments may reside in use patterns, or tastes, or preferences, or other characteristics. From the standpoint of product policy, firms may strive to gain a differential advantage by creating products specially designed for these individual segments. As Smith defined market segmentation, it is a strategy formulated for a "heterogeneous market by emphasizing the precision with which a firm's products can satisfy the requirements of one or more distinguishable market segments."[14]

A firm adopting a market-oriented approach would develop products to fit the attitudes and expectations of particular segments. Conversely, a product-oriented approach seeks segments that desire the utilities promised by individual products. Either way, products are matched with segments, according to their respective demands. Sometimes, the two approaches are combined to complement each other. But no matter which line is taken—markets, products, combination—certain basic requisites prevail for successful segmentation:

1. *Differential response.* There must be clearly defined differences among segments in terms of market response. It is not enough to delineate differences among people or products. These divergencies must be associated with variations in the consumption of the newly introduced brand.

2. *Sufficient size.* Markets can be segmented in an infinite number of ways, subject only to the imagination of the planner. But the segment must be of a size that matches the objectives of the firm. Each company will of necessity have a different definition of how big is "big enough." To Seymour Cray, head of the firm that bears his name, the relevant segment of the computer market is that portion, perhaps 5 percent in all, that can utilize a super machine for scientific work. On revenues of $17.2 million, Cray Research in 1978 showed a profit of $3.6 million. The company planned to deliver seven computers in 1979 and no more

---

[14] Smith, *op. cit.*, p. 4.

than one a month within the next three years.[15] This volume is palpably sufficient for the company to prosper. But a customer base of this size would be trifling--hardly worth the bother—to IBM, which prefers to service the other 95 percent of the market.

3. *Quantifiability.* Segments must be capable of being identified and quantified. They must have common measurable features that permit them to be distinguished from each other. If they cannot be identified and measured, there is no way to take advantage of their existence.

4. *Stability.* Characteristics by which segments are identified must be reasonably stable over time. Product development and commercialization involve lengthy operations. In addition, any product must have a useful life that comports with return-on-investment objectives. If a segmentation strategy is employed, it would be disastrous for relevant segments to vanish suddenly or to undergo significant alterations.

5. *Accessibility.* The segments must be accessible to the promotional efforts of the marketer. Commercial messages, sales personnel, or some combination of both must be capable of reaching the market segment efficiently. Customers cannot be gained if they cannot be reached.

However, in consumer goods industries, which rely heavily upon advertising, the problem is often one of superfluity rather than accessibility. Unless a segment has unique media habits differing from those of the population at large, communication efficiency tends to be positively correlated with size of the market. Advertising exposure cost per prospect runs high when a target market is small with no distinctive media characteristics.

Indeed, there is some question as to whether advertising to a narrow market via mass media is segmentation at all. Mass media reach out to everyone, prospects and nonprospects, with the latter getting proportionately larger as the former diminishes in numbers. That various sectors of the population do not react uniformly to the same commercial messages is not germane to the issue. Advertisers attempting to cultivate a national market, and having no thought of segmentation, will also find differential reactions. Though Coca-Cola endorses undifferentiated marketing, young people will drink more of the "real thing" than senior citizens. The fact is that generalized, to-whom-it-may-concern messages run counter to the segmentation philosophy, which implies a selective product-market strategy. How much media "waste" is needed before selectivity becomes generalization, however, is a judgmental decision.

The criteria used for segmentation can be classified in either one of two basic ways: (1) behavioristic or objective; or (2) psychological or

---

[15.] Harlan S. Byrne, "Seymour Cray Shows Computer World How to Build Big Machines," *Wall Street Journal* (April 12, 1979), pp. 1, 32.

subjective. Table 2-3 indicates the most frequently used methods for segmenting markets.

Table 2-3
Most Popular Criteria Used for Segmenting Markets

Behavioristic	Psychological
Geographic	Attitudes
Consumption patterns	Preferences
—Usage volume/frequency	Perceptions, images
—Purchase volume/frequency	Personality
—Brand loyalty	Life style
Demographics	Interests, benefits sought
Socioeconomic	Opinions

Behavioristic Criteria for Segmentation

Behavioristic data were used in market analysis long before the advent of segmentation concepts. They are absolutely necessary as a first step in estimating the market's dimensions for a product.

Geographic

Geographic segmentation was one of the earliest forms of dividing markets, for it permitted sales analysis on a basis that conformed to sales territories. A key element in geographic analysis is selection of the information control unit (ICU).[16] This is the smallest geographic unit for which information is kept. The smaller the unit, the more flexibility in aggregating data into larger and more varied configurations. However, smaller ICU's expand the amount of information that must be stored and updated, and they consequently increase costs.

Climate accounts for variations in the geographic distribution of many products, such as skiing equipment, snow tires, building materials, plants, or snowmobiles. In other instances, the response to a product may be associated with differences in habits and residential patterns of localities, such as those between urban and rural, suburbs and central cities, etc.

Consumption patterns

A popular method of partitioning markets on the basis of consumption patterns is that of "volume segmentation." This approach is based on the "heavy half theory," popularized by Dik Twedt of Oscar

---

[16] For considerations in selecting an information control unit, see Bertram Schoner and Kenneth P. Uhl, *Marketing Research* (2nd Ed., New York: John Wiley & Sons, Inc., 1975), pp. 150–154.

Mayer Company. The theory holds that for a wide array of products, half the users may consume as much as 80 percent to 85 percent of the total. Many market studies have indicated that for a substantial number of product categories, a single group of people buy in disproportionately large quantities. For example, 85 percent of cold remedy sales are made to a mere 16 percent of product users. Less than a fifth of all beer drinkers guzzle almost two-thirds of all beer produced.[17] Then shouldn't product development, the reasoning goes, be directed to the market source of the business? Sales and profits will be vastly better where the propensity to consume is greater.

But the "heavy half," or the segment with the highest probabilities of purchase, must be identified. Who are these heavy users? Unless they are known, products cannot be matched with the inclinations and desires of the most productive part of the market. The traditional way of identifying heavy user segments has been by attempting to correlate usage with demographic and socioeconomic factors.

Demographic/socioeconomic variables

Demographic and socioeconomic data are used almost universally in market analysis and product planning of consumer goods. Segments based on such population characteristics are easy to identify, and information is plentiful and updated, thanks to the Bureau of the Census. Goods and services can be created for such diverse segments as the "youth market," the "Black market" (demographically speaking), upper income groups, those below poverty levels, professionals in certain occupations. And, so it can go, with a wide variety of products made specially for particular demographic or socioeconomic clusters of the populace.

The issue of socioeconomic variables as causative factors, however, is still unresolved for a large number of consumer product categories. Convenience goods, especially grocery products, have generally shown low relationships between purchases and social or economic variables.[18] The effects of these factors have also tended to be played down by academicians in recent years, even for products that might be considered discretionary purchases. Blue collar and white collar live in the same suburbs and the same cities, it has been argued. Except for the lower rung of the economic ladder, those below the poverty level, income does not sufficiently differentiate people with respect to acquisitions of material goods. TV sets, autos, stereos, and what-have-you are bought, it is said, by all social and economic classes. In short, an

---

[17] Edmund B. Maher, "Focus Promotion on Heavy Users," *Advertising Age* (January 8, 1979), p. 58.

[18] R. E. Frank, *et. al.*, "Correlates of Grocery Product Consumption Rates," *Journal of Marketing Research* (May, 1976), p. 189.

affluent society has blurred socioeconomic differences as a factor in consumption.[19]

On the other hand, a series of studies in "zip code marketing," a name popularized by *TIME* magazine, has drawn sharply contrary conclusions. These studies entail an extremely crude segmentation of zip code areas, which postal authorities have defined as functional economic units. These zip codes are ranked in accordance with the percentage of households earning $15,000 or more, as reported by the 1970 Census of Population and Housing. These small areas are then divided into quintiles, with each fifth having roughly an equal number of households. Purchases of various products are then matched with each quintile.

For example, 400 names and addresses of recent dishwasher buyers in 1977 were supplied by each of four manufacturers: Frigidaire, General Electric, Kitchen Aid, and Sears. These records were then matched with the appropriate zip codes in the top 100 markets. This study found that homes located in the top quintile accounted for 47 percent of all dishwasher sales.[20] *Golf* magazine, following the same procedure, did a study with 1974 purchasers of radial tires in the San Francisco metropolitan area. Results showed 58 percent of the sales going to 20 percent of people living in the upper income quintile.[21] More than 100 studies covering a great variety of products have indicated similar patterns of demand, not only for high-priced durables, but for such items as frozen foods, wines, and liquor.[22] The results are all the more convincing because quintiles based on a percentage of homes with $15,000 or more income, in 1969 dollars, are poor differentiators. The median income of a neighborhood would be a much better discriminator.

Correlates of New Car Purchases

The zip code approach, which combines geography, consumption patterns, and socioeconomic variables, permits firms to pinpoint business opportunities among population segments. To illustrate how the method might work, this section will report part of a locational study

[19] See R. E. Frank and W. F. Massey, "Market Segmentation and the Effectiveness of a Brand's Price and Dealing Policies," *Journal of Business* (April, 1965), pp. 186–200; Chester R. Wasson, "Is It Time to Quit Thinking About Income Classes?" *Journal of Marketing* (April, 1969), p. 54; Richard J. Reiser, "Why New Products Fail, Why Old Products Falter..." AMA, *Annual Workshop on Advertising Planning and Evaluation* (December 13, 1966), p. 6; William H. Reynolds, *Products and Markets* (New York: Meredith Corporation, 1969), pp. 164–165.

[20] TIME magazine, *People Who Buy Dishwashers, Microwave Ovens, Side-by-Side Refrigerators* (New York: TIME, Inc., 1977).

[21] Golf, *Zip Marketing Report* (Unpublished).

[22] *Ibid.*; TIME magazine, *Marketing Case Histories* (New York: TIME, Inc., 1976) and *A New Approach to Brand Analysis Through Zip Marketing* (New York: TIME, Inc., 1976).

done by the authors. Its objective was not market segmentation. Rather, it sought to develop estimates of new car sales for neighborhoods, which could be combined in various ways to form larger trading areas. The ultimate goal was to locate dealerships near the center of gravity in a trading zone with highest potential sales. Nevertheless, selective results can illuminate key features of a segmentation strategy based on behavioristic criteria.

The first step was to run summary tapes of the U.S. Census of Population and Housing. These records contain socioeconomic data for all zip codes in tracted metropolitan regions. Eight Standard Metropolitan Statistical Areas (SMSA's) were analyzed: Chicago, Detroit, Los Angeles, San Francisco, Bridgeport, Danbury, Norwalk, and Stanford. The last four, all located in Fairfield County, Connecticut, were combined and treated as one SMSA. All zip codes were defined by the following socioeconomic variables:

1. Median family income.

2. Percent of families with income of $25,000 or more.

3. Percent of households owning their home.

4. Median value of home owned.

5. Percent of households owning one or more cars.

6. Percent of households owning two or more cars.

7. Household head, percent white.

8. Percent of adults twenty-five years or older who attended college.

9. Percent of working adults sixteen years or older who were professional or managerial by occupation.

Table 2-4
Average Area Correlations Among Demographic Variables

Variable	#2	#8	#4	#9	#1	#6	#5	#3	#7
#2: Income $25,000+	—								
#8: Attended college	.9	—							
#4: Median home value	.8	.9	—		Cluster I				
#9: Prof/mgr occupation	.8	.9	.8	—					
#1: Median family income	.8	.9	.9	.8	—				
#6: Own 2+ cars	.5	.6	.8	.5	.8	—			
#5: Own 1+ cars	.3	.3	.5	.3	.8	.9	—		Cluster II
#3: Own home	.2	.3	.5	.3	.7	.9	.9	—	
#7: White households	.3	.3	.4	.3	.6	.5	.6	.5	—

Table 2-4 is matrix arranged in a different sequence from the listing above. It shows how all variables correlate with each other.

Traditional marketing statistics cover large areas, such as counties and even entire SMSA's. Taken as a whole, Chicago is not unlike Los Angeles or San Francisco or Detroit. But these broad-based aggregates tend to obscure vast social and economic differences among neighborhoods. Such small localities, often located a few miles or less of each other, may seem like worlds apart in terms of rich and poor, managers and employees, educated and ignorant, who live within their boundaries.

The analysis in table 2-4 indicates two well-defined clusters, marked off by triangles. The first implies a socioeconomic dimension. Neighborhoods with high income also enjoy high home values, and their residents are better educated and more inclined towards professional and managerial occupations than the general population. Low income sections tend to have opposite characteristics—lower property values, comparatively less educated, and more production and service workers. The second cluster reflects possession or ownership of capital goods, at least of houses and automobiles, and is only moderately related to the first. But median income falls within both clusters and supplies the common bond. Income is at once a determinant of residential economic patterns and a limiting factor to man's acquisition of worldly goods.

But simply dividing neighborhoods does not segment markets for products. Is this socioeconomic structure related to new car sales? If not, the analysis remains solely in the realm of sociology.

To answer this question, a random sample of 13,800 new car registrations recorded in the first six months of the 1977 model year was drawn from R. L. Polk lists. The counts were weighted by the reciprocal of the sampling ratio and projected to each zip code area. This permitted calculations of the new car purchase rate per 100 households, actually the probability of a household in a given neighborhood buying a new car. These probabilities were then correlated with the respective socioeconomic data of the zip codes. The results are shown in table 2-5.

With a single exception, all correlation coefficients were significant and positive. The best variable was the percent of homes in an area owning two or more cars. Since new cars, by and large, represent a replacement market, the more automobiles a family owns, the higher the probability that a car will "wear out" and have to be replaced. But income also showed a close relationship with new car sales, and the high degree of interrelationship between multiple car ownership and income suggests that essentially similar sales estimates could be obtained regardless of which variable is used.

The high coefficients also indicate that socioeconomic factors can predict new car buying with a fair degree of accuracy. Consequently,

Table 2-5
Correlations of Demographic Variables
with New Car Registration Rates

Variable	Conn. (n = 37)	Detroit (n = 40)	Chicago (n = 39)	Los Angeles (n = 63)	San Francisco (n = 32)
#2: Income $25,000+ (%)	.54	.50	.30	.63	.57
#8: Attended college (%).....	.64	.65	.48	.64	.55
#4: Median home value ($) ...	.51	.73	.61	.38	.68
#9: Prof/mgr occup. (%)	.67	.69	.45	.64	.45
#1: Median family income ($).	.61	.75	.67	.75	.78
#6: Own 2+ cars (%)	.72	.78	.87	.65	.84
#5: Own 1+ cars (%)	.69	.67	.80	.38	.62
#3: Own home (%)	.71	.49	.80	.49	.70
#7: White households (%)	.55	.56	.46	.17	.47

regression equations were developed for each area and used to make predictions. Table 2-6 compares actual predictions made on the basis of these estimating equations with actual six-month sales, derived from independent data.

Table 2-6
Comparisons of Predicted and Actual New Car Registration Rates

SMSA	Registration Rate Estimates, Percent of Households		Correlation
	Actual, %	Predicted, %	Actual and Predicted
Chicago	7.4	7.8	.81
Detroit	6.9	7.3	.75
Los Angeles	3.3	3.4	.69
San Francisco..........	3.6	3.6	.88

Table 2-6 indicates that sales predictions for metropolitan areas, derived from zip codes, were reasonably good. But more important, a close association was apparent between predicted neighborhood sales and actual buying for these same areas, estimated from new car registrations. There is thus a strong presumption that socioeconomic factors are capable of defining the parameters of the market.

These same factors, however, revealed no observable differences with respect to characteristics of cars bought. No social or economic variable appears to differentiate purchases of various models, such as Chevrolets, Fords, or Plymouths; or of types, such as large, intermediate, or small cars; or of automobiles defined in any other way. One obvious inference is that behavioristic criteria can describe the new car market but cannot explain why demand fluctuates among individual "brands." Given different levels of demand, station wagons and sports cars, domestic and imports, will appeal to the same general areas, for a car is a car is a car. Perhaps these are the limits to segmentation. But the marketing research fraternity, by almost common agreement, has refused to accept this verdict, though offering little demonstrable evidence to the contrary up to now.

Psychological Criteria

If behavioristic criteria have fallen somewhat short as a basis for segmentation, what can fill the gap? Marketing research in consumer goods industries have for many years been involved in psychological measurements and there seek answers to variations in demand. Causal elements that induce general buying behavior, the psychological school holds, are to be found in consumers' minds, and not in their economic or social status. This is quite evident in clothing. The trend towards an increasing number of female managers and professionals is clearly perceived. But this does not help a firm predict what women will buy, dresses or pants or skirts, and especially which styles.

Like behavioristic criteria, psychological ones can be either people related or product related. Attempts to segment markets by personality or life style illustrate people-based factors. Sometimes, life style is described in terms of social and economic data.[23] But more commonly, it is defined psychologically, such as swingers, squares, straights, sociables, unsociables, etc.

Although these psychological variables are intuitively attractive, they have stumbled badly on the pragmatic test of measurement. In addition, customary population descriptors are not available in the same terms. If a desired psychological segment is then to be reached, it must somehow be interrelated with the more traditional descriptions of population, such as demographic, social, and economic data. This "identification" problem has compounded the difficulty and, together with negative research findings as to the discriminating power of personality or life style factors, has dampened enthusiam for this approach to segmentation.[24]

---

[23] E.g., see "How Lifestyle Segmentation Selects Prospects from Zips," *Direct Marketing* (March, 1975), pp. 40–46; W. S. Sachs and C. J. Jain, "Market Segmentation: A Key to Success in Land Selling," *American Salesman* (June, 1976), pp. 30–33 and (July, 1976), pp. 32–36.

[24] E.g., see B. Evans and H. V. Roberts, "Fords, Chevrolets and the Problem of Discrimination," *Journal of Business* (April, 1963), pp. 242–249; Ralph Westfall, "Psychological Factors in Predicting Brand Choice," *Journal of Marketing* (April, 1962), pp. 34–40; W. T. Tucker and J. J. Painter, "Personality and Product Use," *Journal of Applied Psychology* (October, 1961), pp. 325–329.

Product-related endeavors to segment markets psychologically rest on the assumption that opinions, perceptions, and attitudes towards products are the precursors of behavior. Given this assumption, the idea is to seek groups that share similar attitudes and then to adjust the characteristics of products to accommodate these preferences.[25]

One popular form of the product-related approach is that of "benefits segmentation." Its underlying rationale implies that consumers buy products because of the benefits derived therefrom, and that variations in benefits sought leads to market segments.[26]

There are actually numerous ways in which a benefits segmentation philosophy might be implemented. One such method would point product development along the following lines. A consumer survey would try to determine what characteristics buyers ascribe to the ideal product and to those now in use. The result would yield some sort of configuration of product benefits for various brands, as well as for the ideal. The analysis would then attempt to discover "gaps" between what consumers want and what they are now getting.[27] As one author put it, "A new product introduction becomes a search for a position of a product which is preferred over other products."[28]

Held up as an illustration of product segmentation strategy is the case of Ronzoni. Spaghetti sauce has many brands competing for the consumer's purse. But most sauces attempt to imitate the leader, Ragu, and blind tests indicate that consumers cannot differentiate one brand from another in relation to taste. But when questioned by consumer surveys, people say they buy what they do because it tastes better.

Del Monte, Heinz, Hunt, and Chef-Boy-Ar-Dee have all attempted to enter the rich New York market with products similar to Ragu, and all ended in failure. In contrast, Ronzoni came into the market with a somewhat different product, spicier, thicker, and with 6 percent meat, as compared with Ragu's 3 percent. Because this new product ostensibly satisfied a need not currently fulfilled, Ronzoni made inroads in the market whereas the others did not.[29]

---

[25] See Russel I. Haley, "The Implications of Market Segmentation," *The Conference Board Record* (March, 1969), p. 44; Walter Burgi, "What is Segmentation Anyway," *Marketing Review* (January–February, 1976), pp. 11–12. For variant, see William Knobler, "Anticipating What the Consumer Wants: Benefits Research vs. Problem Detection," *Marketing Review* (January–February, 1976), pp. 19–21.

[26] See Russel I. Haley, "Benefit Segmentation: A Decision-Oriented Research Tool," *Journal of Marketing* (July, 1968), pp. 30–35; Daniel Yankelovich, "New Criteria for Market Segmentation," *Harvard Business Review* (March–April, 1964), pp. 83–90.

[27] For a more detailed discussion of multidimensional scaling, see chapter 8.

[28] Norman L. Barnett, "Beyond Market Segmentation," *Harvard Business Review* (January–February, 1969), pp. 152–166.

[29] David A. Schwartz, "Sometimes It Doesn't Pay to Follow the Leader," *Sales Management* (October 16, 1972), pp. 42–44.

Segmentation or Differentiation

Despite some evident successes, there is neither general accord nor unreserved acceptance of product segmentation methods by industry. Measurement techniques have been widely questioned, while benefit listings from consumer surveys are said to be presumptive. Critics point out that so far there has been no hard evidence to show that survey results correlate with future behavior.[30] Without such proof, no one can say with any degree of assurance that information about attitudes and benefits gathered by researchers and transformed into neat statistical charts which seem undeniably final is predictive of actual purchases.

Another group of psychologists have challenged the very basis of such psychological segmentation by arguing that consumers do not form deep-seated attitudes about products, especially packaged goods. Issues such as softness of toilet paper, cleaning power of detergents, and amount of flavor from uncola nuts are essentially trivia and stir no great outpourings of emotion in the breasts of homemakers. Even heavy sales promotion and advertising, it is held, produce levels of consumer involvement that are so low as to make measurement of attitude change to a product or marketing stimulus an extremely dubious undertaking.[31]

The Ronzoni case admirably focuses on the fundamental questions about product segmentation. Was there really a consumer segment looking for a spicier, thicker, 6 percent sauce? And did this group of consumers embrace the new brand because it matched a demand that was already there? Or did the brand appeal to basically the same people who buy Ragu but are willing to try something else just for the sake of variety? Such questions have been left unanswered, despite the millions poured into marketing research annually. It has therefore been argued, and with some justification, that much of what is rationalized as segmentation is really a consumer desire for variety.[32]

Segmentation strategies are undoubtedly suitable for small companies, or small brands, so that they can exploit fringe markets neglected by industry leaders. But the latter follow strategies of product differentiation, giving the market variety, rather than segmentation. A multiple brand manufacturer of detergents, presenting one brand as "making clothes white" and another as cleaning "whiter than white," unmistaka-

---

[30] R. C. Blattberg and S. K. Sen, "Market Segmentation Using Models of Multidimensional Purchasing Behavior," *Journal of Marketing* (October, 1974), p. 18.

[31] Herbert Krugman, "Answering Some Unanswered Questions in Measuring Advertising Effectiveness," ARF 12th Annual Conference, *Proceedings*, pp. 18–23; "New Studies of Brain Functioning...," *Marketing News* (March 25, 1977), pp. 1, 7.

[32] Reynolds, *op. cit.*, pp. 145–147.

bly tries to differentiate each offering. But the advertising is to the same market, and not to distinct segments. This policy rests on the reasoning that a buyer who would forgo one brand may choose the other, and despite interbrand competition, two brands would produce a net gain over one brand only. General Motors has put out 140 different models of 1979 cars and promoted each with a unique appeal. Are there then 140 different consumer segments, each desiring some special combination of auto features? On the contrary, the giant auto manufacturer advertises its numerous models in the same mass media, which ostensibly go to the same readers and viewers.

Market segmentation implies different strokes for different folks. But is marketing witnessing a case of different strokes for the same folks?

Industrial Market Segmentation

Segmentation of industrial markets rests on the same underlying rationale as that of consumer market segmentation. Potential customers are thought of as being fragmented, forming groups with differing demands for goods and services. As a consequence, these groups are postulated to possess their own unique response to product offerings and marketing efforts. The criteria for choosing industrial segments are also the same as those for selecting consumer segments: differential response, sufficient size, quantifiability, stability, and accessibility.

But there are substantial differences between buying units of industrial goods and those of consumer products. The former are organizations, not individuals, and therefore must be classified accordingly. The traditional ways of characterizing organizations are by such objective features as geography, company size, S.I.C. category, product application, or end use. These characteristics might be regarded as "organizational demographics" and have long been used by sellers of industrial products to define their markets. This form of market classification is also referred to as "macrosegmentation" and is most popular with companies practicing differentiated marketing. Such firms may offer different products to different classes of customers. Steel earmarked for can makers is different from that destined to manufacturers of auto parts. The Xerox Corporation has available a line of copiers for various uses, in accordance with type and volume. Firms that engage in differentiated marketing may also employ diverse distribution channels and distinct sales groups within their organizations.

As with consumer segmentation, the demographic approach has been criticized for not sufficiently discriminating among differences in buyer response. As a result, a number of other criteria for industrial segmentation have been proposed. These have generally been of two types, behaviorial and psychological, though the two are not mutually exclusive. Both of these types focus their attention on the decision-making unit within the customer organization, sometimes referred to as the "buying center." But they concentrate on different aspects of the problem.

One approach attempts to define segments by relating them directly to the decision mechanism of the buying center. The criteria for segmentation thus become such factors as distribution of purchase responsibility, types of buying situations, purchasing strategies used, key variables in the decision process.[33] The other method focuses on the individuals who make up the buying center and seeks to classify these participants according to psychological characteristics. These variables include such influences as those stemming from psychographics, degrees of self-confidence, perceived risk, and personality traits.[34] Since both methods center their attention on purchase decision units within companies, either relationships or individuals, they have been referred to as "microsegmentation," in contrast to the traditional method of macrosegmentation.

The early writings urging a micro approach viewed it as an alternative to macrosegmentation. Today, the tendency is to regard microsegmentation as complementary to, or a further refinement of, "organizational demographics."[35] The macrosegments are simply broken down into smaller but more discriminating groups.

This two-step method of segmentation, however, has remained primarily in the realm of theory, not practicality. Endeavors at microsegmentation have almost completely disregarded product development. Rather, they have been used in promotional activities, such as formulating sales strategies, allocating calls among sales personnel, designing sales presentations, selecting advertising media.

Empirical evidence indicates that large concerns do, indeed, practice differentiated marketing. But these practices are a far cry from those

[33] See Patrick J. Robinson, et. al., Industrial Buying and Creative Marketing (Boston: Allyn and Bacon, 1967); J. B. Kernan and M. S. Sommers, "The Behaviorial Matrix—A Closer Look at the Industrial Buyer," Business Horizons (Summer, 1966), pp. 59–72; W. Feldman and R. N. Cardozo, "Industrial Buying as Consumer Behavior," Moyer and Vosburgh, eds., Marketing for Tomorrow... (Chicago: American Marketing Association, 1967), pp. 102–107; J. Choffray and G. L. Lilien, "A New Approach to Industrial Market Segmentation," Sloan Management Review (Spring, 1978), pp. 17–29.

[34] See Daniel Yankelovich, op. cit., pp. 83–90; David T. Wilson, et. al., "Industrial Buyer Segmentation: A Psychographic Approach," American Marketing Association, Conference Proceedings, 1971, pp. 327–331.

[35] See Choffray and Lilien, op. cit.: Yoram Wind and Richard Cardozo, "Industrial Market Segmentation," Industrial Marketing Management (April, 1974), pp. 153–166.

of planned segmentation strategies.[36] One study found that the most common way of dividing industrial markets was via macrosegmentation. But most frequently, it seems, products were modified in accordance with the requirements of individual customers.[37] This finding is hardly unexpected, given the nature of industrial markets. Companies dealing with General Motors are, in fact, doing business with the major part of the automotive manufacturing industry. Firms selling components to IBM are covering most of the computer industry. Individual firms, not groups of firms, make up the most important entities in markets with high degrees of industrial concentration. In these circumstances, suppliers will fit their products to meet the needs of particular customers. At the same time, true market segments become either nonexistent or extremely constricted, offering poor returns on product development. A narrow group of customers may have little appeal if the value of purchase orders is low. Thus, much of industrial product development will seek generality, not specificity, with the potential of being modified for individual users. Such strategies run counter to market segmentation plans, which visualize different products made for particular segments.

REVIEW QUESTIONS

1. How would you define a new product?

2. From a pragmatic point of view, it is the consumer's perceptions that define a new product or determine the degree of newness. However, this approach to a definition creates problems and does not provide useful guidance to the new product developer. Explain.

3. What is meant by planned obsolescence?

4. Develop a list of methods or approaches for changing an old product into a new product. Indicate the degree of newness involved and the degree of profit potential that may result.

5. Describe two or more systems for classifying new products, each system to be all inclusive. Provide new product examples of each.

6. New products can be tremendous sales successes and also highly innovative though based entirely on current technology. Provide four or five examples of such products currently on the market.

[36.] Frederick E. Webster, Jr., *Industrial Marketing Strategy* (New York: John Wiley & Sons, 1979), pp. 87–88.

[37] Wind and Cardozo, *op. cit.*, pp. 160–164.

7. Suggest—for each of the three classifications—two products introduced during the past ten years which at the time of introduction would have been cited as examples of:
    a. continuous innovation.
    b. dynamically continuous innovation.
    c. discontinuous innovation.
    Discuss the degree of risk and profit potential inherent in each.

8. Discuss the degree of risk and profit potential presented by each of the nine categories indicated by table 2-2. The answer can be in the form of two separate rankings, high to low, one for profit and one for risk. Be prepared to defend your ranking.

9. Distinguish between positive and negative product attributes. Cite examples of both.

10. Products and markets can vary not only in terms of newness but also in psychological, behaviorial terms. Develop classification systems for both products and consumers that may provide a possible path to segmentation.

11. Cite examples of market segmentation derived from personal observations. Indicate the nature of the segmentation and if universal applications are possible.

12. Market segments vary in size, in number of competitors, and in degree of dominance of these competitors. Two companies in the same industry, one large, the other small, are planning to introduce new products to one or more segments within their industry. What principles can be outlined that could guide the two companies?

13. Market segmentation can be approached via markets or products. Both methods provide direction for new product developers. Examine and compare the two methods.

3/ The Product Life Cycle

The product life cycle concept, actually a time series, divides chronologically ordered dates into periods such as introduction, growth, maturity, and decline. Each stage presents a company introducing a new brand with different sets of problems, each requiring different solutions. This chapter explores product strategies appropriate to the changing conditions of the product life cycle.

The basic problem in the introductory stage is attaining a level of acceptance that indicates the product has commercial viability. Though a short introductory period has obvious advantages, many firms willfully delay speeding up things in order to decrease risks.

Entrants into high-growth fields have better likelihoods of success if their resources are compatible with the requirements of the new product category. The size of investments is also important, for growth industries call for large resource commitments. Firms capable of acquiring a dominant market position during the growth phase will usually have relative cost advantages because of the experience curve.

Mature products are a major source of revenue and earnings for most companies. Many new products of these firms are product modifications and line extensions, the purpose of which is to maintain earnings flow. But newcomers also enter mature industries with new products. When the new brand is not much different from existing ones, the new entrant is usually one that had been operating on the periphery of the market. Major innovations capable of replacing an entire product category, however, often come from industries removed from the immediate market.

Alternative strategies for dying brands are "harvesting" and elimination. Implementation of the latter strategy depends upon assumptions made as to mobility of resources and disposal of fixed assets.

Because the product life cycle is not predictive, its uses are controversial. Within certain limits, however, it can serve as a guide to product planning and assessments of profit quality.

Product Life Cycle Concept

Products, like all living things, are conceived of as having life cycles, going from birth to youth to maturity to old age. Carried over from biology, the concept contains a certain degree of anthropomorphism, attributing human qualities to inanimate objects. Nevertheless, the idea of a pattern in a product's finite life has proved a useful one.

As with different species of animal life, products vary enormously in age. Some have lived on for generations, and even centuries, such as basic raw materials and staples. Others have tarried their hour or two in the endless progression of time and hardly left a trace that they ever existed at all. But these outward similarities between animal physiology and products are only analogous, useful for proposes of exposition.

A product's life cycle is usually described in terms of sales over time. From a statistical standpoint, it is a time series. The plots differ radically for different products both in duration and shape. At the risk of neglecting these differences, the life cycle concept can be generalized in the form of a parabola or second-degree polynomial. This model visualizes four stages to the cycle: introduction, growth, maturity, and decline. The general pattern, encompassing the four stages, is illustrated in the following diagram (figure 3-1).

Figure 3-1. Product Life Cycle Concept

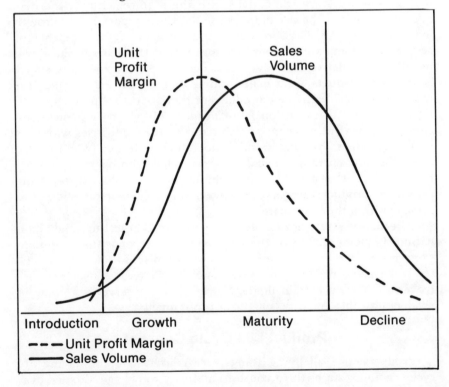

Life cycles for products of individual companies or brands deviate from those of an entire industry or product category. One obvious reason is that introductions of individual brands do not correspond with the birth of a product class. For example, when S. C. Johnson in 1977 launched Agree creme rinse, capturing about a 20 percent share of market within a year, the new entry enjoyed rapid growth, whereas the entire hair care category did not. The growth phase of Tylenol took place when sales of all analgesics indicated a mature industry. The various brands that make up a product category differ not only in timing of their introductions but in product quality and marketing effort. Consequently, variations in their sales patterns are also to be expected. A brand's life cycle must therefore be differentiated from the product life cycle, defined as the sales configuration of a group of items competing with each other and made of similar materials by the same processes. The product life cycle thus measures sales of a generic group of items.

Nevertheless, there are some problems in measuring the product life cycle because of ambiguity in definition of a product category. For example, a 1972 study of the tire industry found the product, called "tires," in the middle of a growth period. But the study also noted subcycles for different product types, such as radials, bias, and bias/belted. Tires using different materials also seemed to be going through their own unique cycles. Thus, no single type of tire followed closely the pattern for the industry as a whole.[1]

An alternative way of looking at the same information is to regard the subcategories as different product classes. This would in effect mean several product life cycles but only because of a change in the definition of a product. Yet this is exactly what innovation does, regardless of semantics. Innovation is dynamic, not static. It assigns products to an abiding state of flux by altering their characteristics, some more so than others. A radial tire may not belong to the same group as a bias/belted tire, though both are known by the name *tire*. There is an inevitable lag between changes and perceptions of those changes.

Parallel developments have taken place with such common, everyday items as cigarettes and beer. The plethora of low-tar brands has created a cigarette group with a sales momentum that is in marked contrast to the lethargic pattern of older types. The new brands began innocently enough as sort of line extensions, differing only in their tar contents. But they were also substitutes for cigarettes with higher tar levels and in time formed a new product category in their own right.

---

[1] F. J. Kovac and M. F. Dague, "Forecasting by Product Life Cycle Analysis," *Research Management* (July, 1972), pp. 66-72.

The light beers, all with fewer than 100 calories, similarly grew at the expense of regular varieties. It can be argued, assuredly and logically, that the two types of beers should be treated as separate products, for their diffusion in the marketplace required completely different sets of strategies and tactics. Then Anheuser-Busch in late 1977 introduced Michelob Light, averaging 150 calories per twelve-ounce can, somewhere midway between light and regular.[2] If more 150-calorie beers appear on the market, perhaps a new "medium" product category will be created. The point, however, is that changes in quality, many small, subtle, and of low degree, can inject variation and diversity into an industry and change the nature of its products.

Introduction Period Strategies

A product's formative stage begins with its introduction into the marketplace and ends with the growth stage, a point at which sales increase at an accelerated rate. The introductory period is characterized by low sales and negative or nonexistent earnings for companies in the field. In some instances, the introduction may be carried out by one company, especially when the new product is protected by patent. In other situations, several companies may be promoting the innovation, as in the early days of color television or in the opening phases of videotapes and cassettes. For the product to survive, it must attain some mimimum sales level or threshold. It must show signs of being commercially viable, of eventually reaching a point whereby satisfactory earnings can be sustained. Each industry—as well as individual firms within an industry—has its own expected threshold values regarding sales and profits.

A short introductory period is highly desirable so as to reduce the negative impact of earnings and cash flow. The sooner the brand gets off the ground, the sooner the financial drain shows signs of abatement. On the positive side, a short introduction dispels some of the uncertainty surrounding a new product and permits investment decisions based on better risk probabilities. To some degree, earnings depend on the accounting practices of individual companies. A conservative financial policy that favors shorter write-offs for new machinery and expensing rather than capitalizing charges where possible will tend to exaggerate losses and understate profits during the pioneering stages. More liberal financial rules will have an opposite effect. These accounting conventions will also affect the shape of the product life cycle, insofar as the accentuation of losses or the dampening of profits tends to restrain aggressive new product introductions. There is less purpose for going all out to build a market position when

---

[2] "A-B Aims to Win by Segmenting Light Beer," *Marketing News* (December 29, 1978), pp. 1, 5-6.

the outcome is in doubt. In general, however, the duration of the introductory stage is largely determined by product characteristics and the nature of resource commitment. The former imposes certain limitations as to what actions are feasible. But it also presents a firm with opportunities, for a product life cycle is not something that is given, something inherent in the product. Its shape and duration are not preordained, running a predetermined course from the day of creation to the day of its inevitable demise. Firms can, in part, influence a product's life span from birth to death notably by the amount and nature of resources they allocate.

Product characteristics

Many new products bring into being new functions or new ways of performing old functions. The greater the degree of such newness, it is held, the slower potential customers are likely to adapt to the newer ways.[3] This generalization has particular relevance to consumer goods, for which old habits must be broken, old learning must be unlearned, and new information must be absorbed and utilized to form new routines. To some extent, a firm may minimize novelty in consumer experience by product design. A beep can assure a person unaccustomed to machinery running with unbroken silence that the hand calculator is working when the push buttons are pressed. An odorless insecticide may have difficulty in convincing consumers that it is efficient in killing bugs. Manufacturers of microwave ovens had to add a feature to brown meat, though the browning process was completely unrelated to actual cooking. This addition was to make the food fit consumers' perceptions of what roast meat should look like.

In the absence of design that radiates familiarity with the way a thing works, it may be necessary to spend heavier than usual to disseminate new information and promote new ways of doing things. Manufacturers of the first low-suds detergents had to teach consumers that cleaning power was not related to suds level. Nevertheless, radical innovations can gain quick acceptance. Television producers had little trouble in getting the public to see the entertainment aspects of the home screen wired for sight and sound.

From the standpoint of usage patterns, the degree of newness is often associated with product complexity. The more complex the new product, the slower its pace of diffusion, or the rate of consumer adoption. For example, some forty companies in 1979 were making personal computers, mainly for offices, professions, and classrooms. The personal computer emerged as a reality with developments in microprocessors, silicone chips no more than a quarter-inch square

---

[3] Theodore Levitt, "Exploit the Product Life Cycle," *Harvard Business Review* (November-December, 1965), p. 84; William D. Zarecor, "High Technology Product Planning," *Ibid.*, (January-February, 1975), pp. 113-114.

used in computations needing limited power or employed as building blocks of large computers. Tandy, a leader in the field, had advertised heavily its $599 model the previous Christmas as an ideal, inexpensive gift for doing a multitude of tasks—preparing tax returns, switching lawn sprinklers on and off, regulating room temperatures, controlling family budgets, teaching children, addressing Christmas cards, and keeping track of important birthdays and anniversaries. Yet few of these tasks were being done, even by the relatively few venturesome buyers who graced their homes with such electronic wonders. Most consumers have neither the technical training nor the inclination to make a home computer serve them with robot-like precision. As time goes on, software will probably be developed further and technological advances will make the machines easier to operate. Meanwhile, sales for home computers grow by painfully small increments as operational complexity is being overcome gradually.[4]

Sometimes, environmental factors conspire with a natural resistance to innovation. This was the case of the automobile, which required some twenty years to grow out of its baby status. Until the nation could build a network of paved highways—and technical performance could be taken for granted—early drivers would be taunted with derisive shouts of "Get a horse!" Today, the most important environmental factor is probably government regulation, notably in areas which affect the public's health or safety, such as foods, drugs, toys, and energy.

At other times, the duration of the introductory phase is contingent upon the development of another, complementary product. Widespread acceptance of color TV sets awaited the advent of telecasts in color. The first color TV sets made their appearance in the early fifties. But less than 150,000 were sold in any year until 1962, when broadcasters offered a sufficient number of hours of color programming. The videodisc is similarly dependent for rising sales on software, a large library of cheap, popular films. A company introducing a product of this type has more control over its operation if it also has the capacity to develop the contingent product or service. Never was this demonstrated more forcefully than by IBM, which captured the lion's share of the market by bundling its hardware with service and software.

Products that are divisible and that can be consumed in small quantites lend themselves better than others to short introductions. This characteristic reduces user risk and encourages trial of the new product. It creates opportunities for companies to make up small but low-cost samples for free distribution among prospective customers. Many low-priced, packaged goods, when introduced with heavy advertising and

---

[4] Mitchell C. Lynch, "A Computer Error: Trying to Use One in Your Own Home," *Wall Street Journal* (May 14, 1979), pp. 1, 33; Richard A. Shaffer, "Texas Instruments Pounces on Market in Home Computers," *Ibid.* (June 1, 1979), p. 8.

sales promotion, can build sales volume rapidly because of divisibility features. A study of 300 commercially successful ethical drugs found the median length of time for an introduction was one month.[5] Detail men, who convey the new product information and dispense free samples, can cover a market expeditiously. Under such circumstances, response is fairly rapid and, if encouraging, is followed up with non-personal promotion. Producers of various types of industrial supplies can avail themselves of similar means to establish a market position for a new product within a brief period of time. Firms producing goods which cannot be broken down into small quantities and which are usually high-priced and complex can use warranties, services, and leasing programs to help overcome the higher risks on the part of users.

When a new product has an almost immediate response, the shape of the product life cycle will not trace out the classical S-curve, as portrayed in figure 3-1. There is no period of gradually rising sales preceding a strong upturn. Instead, the product life cycle assumes an exponential shape, with the largest part of sales gains coming in the early period and subsequent increases occurring at a declining rate. A wide variety of simple, low-priced, divisible products acquire an exponential form under certain circumstances. A curve of this sort is depicted in figure 3-2.

Figure 3-2. Exponential Product Life Cycle

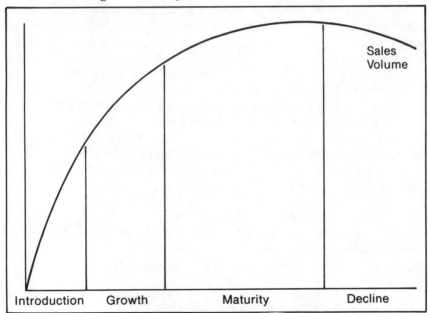

| Introduction | Growth | Maturity | Decline |

[5] William E. Cox, Jr., "Product Life Cycles as Marketing Models," *The Journal of Business* (October, 1967), p. 378.

Another characteristic that can speed up or slacken the length of the introductory period is a new product's differential advantage over older products with which it competes. The most frequent advantages are superior quality or performance, lower prices, greater convenience, better appearance, or greater aesthetic value. The first two are especially important for industrial products, which are purchased on a rationalistic, comparative basis.

The greater the differential advantage, the faster the new product will gain acceptance. But more expensive items are usually compelled to prove larger relative advantages. Capital goods normally have slower diffusion rates than materials and supplies because old machinery and equipment are not easily discarded. Only when savings from a new machine exceed the costs of its acquisition and installation does it pay to trade in the old. Materials and supplies involve similar considerations but without accounting for the effects of capitalization. Their adoption is hastened if they can perform better or cheaper than the older products. Sometimes, however, their acceptance may be dependent upon the machinery and processes in current use. Gas, for example, cannot be used for heating plants with oil-burning systems.

Resource input

The marketing effort expended by the innovating company has a direct effect on how quickly a new product achieves market penetration. Advertising at high saturation levels is not uncommon with new products in the consumer field. A number of low-tar cigarette brands had budgeted more than $40 million for advertising and promotion in their introductory campaigns to push sales up rapidly.[6] The food, beverage, cosmetic, and proprietary drug industries have also witnessed new products starting out with heavy marketing expenditures to get maximum sales in the shortest possible time. For most new products, however, firms move slowly and cautiously.

New products are highly risky and unpredictable. Their record is virtually littered with costly failures that were introduced with great fanfare and high hopes. The value of a short introductory period must therefore be traded off against potential costs of failure.

A new product in the introductory stage of its life cycle usually demands a large allocation of resources, far greater than just marketing expenditures. Most of the time existing facilities are inadequate or incapable of handling the new product. But new plants, equipment, and a logistical support system are long-term commitments that seldom warrant an all-out "make or break" approach.

---

[6] John J. O'Connor, "B&W to Spend a Kool $45 Million," *Advertising Age* (November 28, 1977), p. 8: and "Merit Led 1976 Cigaret Spenders," *Advertising Age* (December 26, 1977), pp. 3, 38-39.

To this heavy fixed investment in facilities must be added the costs associated with production in anticipation of future demand. Speculative inventories must be accumulated before a single sale can be made. While accounting defers inventory as a current asset, in reality operating capital is being committed to long-term usage. Inventory is never liquidated during the commercial life of the product, and it becomes as fixed as plant and equipment but without tax benefits for depreciation. Only goods made to order, such as airplanes, large computers, sewerage treatment plants and the like, can escape inventory investment for finished goods. The necessity for heavy capital outlays argues for a cautious, go-slow approach, for risk reduction may take precedence over a short introduction.

A firm usually has available to it a number of production and marketing alternatives that can affect both the perceived risk and speed of product introduction. For example, components and subassemblies, or the entire product itself for that matter, can be contracted for on the outside. A buy decision would delay investment in plant and equipment until the probability of success rises to an acceptable level, while the pace of introduction might be slowed very little, if at all. But something is invariably given up when buy decisions seek to reduce the risks of make decisions. Costs may be higher than otherwise and, if not reflected in price, would show up in lower profit margins. Or valuable designs might be jeopardized by exposing them to outsiders. Or control over product quality might be lessened, and production schedules might fail to meet desired levels of reliability.

Other alternatives might include employing middlemen instead of establishing a company sales force, utilizing public warehouses instead of constructing private facilities, and shipping by common carrier instead of delivering by company-owned trucks. Any of these steps is capable of postponing investment until such time as demand becomes more certain and of sufficient size to warrant long-term outlays. But reduction of investment risk by such means involves a cost or a trade-off, either explicit or implicit. Middlemen's margins may be higher than one's own sales expenses, and operations may not be as effective. Public warehouses and common carriers may not provide the same degree of control that could be obtained by owned and operated facilities. Nevertheless, substitutions of external for internal capabilities offer certain benefits, the costs of which should be considered in relation to risks.

Many durable goods make their initial appearance on the market with a high price tag. For example, the first hand calculators sold for some $200, but after the market expanded, the same items went for as low as $10. This policy of "skimming" is said to restrict the market, for unit prices are related inversely to sales volume. By discouraging demand through high prices, skimming is also accused of prolonging a product's formative period.

In actuality, a skimming policy is more often a consequence of production and financial decisions rather than a casual factor of demand. When demand is uncertain, as it must be for a new product, companies are in no hurry to build plants housing expensive equipment for supplying hypothetical markets in some hypothetical tomorrow. The new product is normally market tested, if possible, and produced on pilot equipment during its early period. Test markets are often "rolled out," gradually expanded geographically, so as to accumulate evidence that the new product has a good chance of being successful before making heavy commitments for fixed assets. Meanwhile, the makeshift equipment in the initial phase can supply only a contracted demand. So why not try to recoup some portion of development costs at the low volume? Lowering prices hardly makes sense when production facilities are wholly inadequate to satisfy a broader market. When production cannot fulfill market requirements, skimming acts as a convenient device for adjusting demand to the limited supply.

Growth Period Strategies

The growth period commences when potential customers adopt the new product at an accelerated pace. Sales grow rapidly as the market expands. The growth period comes to an end as the market approaches saturation, and sales increases begin to level off.

Without legal restrictions such as patents and government regulations, success breeds emulators. Once there is evidence that a new product has a bright future, the pioneers will find other prospectors ready to share the good news. The most formidable barrier to entry is qualifying to compete successfully in the new arena.

The new competitors are usually companies with resources and capabilities that are conducive to entering the new field, such as in R&D, manufacturing, and marketing. For example, the most successful entrants into new markets for leisure-time products were companies already in leisure-time fields. Those best able to contest for sales of new electronic goods were companies that had been operating in the electronics industry and were familiar with the business. While entry barriers are comparatively low in growth industries, risks climb with higher degrees of incompatibility between a firm's resources and the markets it seeks.

Opportunities to enter growth fields are partly contingent upon the alacrity with which the new product is adopted. The longer the response to the new product, the greater the probability that the eventual market leaders will not be the same firms that pioneered or initiated the innovation. Texas Instruments, with a major share of the market, was not the first to produce a hand calculator. Vinyl tile for floors was initiated by a small, unknown company, Delaware Floor Products, and not by dominant Armstrong Cork. Convenience foods were pioneered by new companies like Swanson, and not by market leaders like General Foods and Campbell Soup. But in most instances, market leaders entered the market early, expanded it, and in the process, grew with it.

When diffusion of the innovation is slow, there is no particular virtue in being first in the market. The giant RCA Corporation was reported as being content to let North American Philips get into the market first with a videodisc while sitting on its own version. William C. Hittinger, RCA's vice-president, was quoted as saying, "If Philips beats us, it may be encouraging. We'll be able to get some information on the kinds of software that sell."[7]

The remark sums up much more than appears on the surface. Sometimes it pays to wait. Time is important, but not at all times. When time is not of the essence, a firm with strong resources actually has an advantage in waiting. If strong in manufacturing and delivery functions, the laggard can modify the original product in a way that brings better performance or significant cost reductions. When coupled with aggressive marketing, this sort of company makes a tough competitor.[8]

Upsmanship associated with a patient, follower strategy in entering growth markets, however, may sometimes backfire. Texas Instruments is a case in point. In late 1973 Itel introduced its 8080 eight-bit microprocessor, which became the industry standard. Texas Instruments tried to do Itel one better by coming out with a sixteen-bit memory in 1975. But the company completely miscalculated the market. Independent estimates for eight-bit microprocessors put sales in excess of $350 million by 1980 but only about a third as much for sixteen-bit models. Texas Instruments figured the latter would be outselling the former by that date. At about the same time, Texas Instruments tried to capitalize on growth by introducing two general-purpose minicomputers. But the other minicomputers were made for what is called the original equipment market, wherein the small machines are subsidiary to the larger system. In contrast, the Texas Instruments entries were complete, independent systems, offering "complete solutions." This attempt to "leap frog" resulted in more problem-handling machines but in few minicomputer sales.[9]

But Texas Instruments persevered, pouring enormous resources into its microprocessor and minicomputer operations. The latter strat-

[7] "RCA's New Vista: The Bottom Line," *Business Week* (July 4, 1977), p. 41.

[8] See H. Igor Ansoff and John M. Stewart, "Strategies for a Technology-Based Business," *Harvard Business Review* (November-December, 1967), p. 83.

[9] Peter J. Schuyten, "Winning and Losing at Texas Instruments," *New York Times* (May 13, 1979), pp. F1, F13.

egy was finally turned around, and Texas Instruments in 1979 ranked fourth as a minicomputer producer. The same year Itel and Motorola introduced sixteen-bit microprocessors, equipment in which Texas Instruments supposedly had an advantage. In the long run, through dogged determination and generous funding, the basic strategy may still pay off handsomely.

Large investments are not something affordable; they may be vital during the growth stage, depending upon the rate of sales increase and size of the market. As demand expands, permanent manufacturing installations and distribution facilities are called into being. Losses of the introductory stage become profits in the growth stage because facilities are utilized more efficiently. Operating economies are achieved largely because of two factors: economies of scale and those of the learning curve.

The learning curve was observed in aircraft production during World War II. Unit production costs tended to decrease by some constant percentage rate over the life of the product, yielding a smaller absolute improvement for each successive period. The Boston Consulting Group expanded the study of cost relationships to functions other than labor and production inputs. The major work was done in 1965–66 in electronics and chemical industries but was later generalized to other fields. The Boston consultants found that costs on value added decline from 20 percent to 30 percent, as measured in constant dollars, every time physical output doubles. The group called this the "experience curve."[10] A curve of this sort is pictured in figure 3–3.

The illustration in figure 3–3 shows an 80 percent experience curve for a hypothetical company, starting with 100 units in accumulated output at a unit cost of $1. The accumulated volume might be 1,000 units, 10,000 units, 100,000 units. That does not matter. What does is that each time the accumulated volume doubles, the unit costs of value added fall by 20 percent. Thus, at 200 units, costs per unit drop to $.80 ($1×.8). At 1,600 units, where accumulated experience has doubled four times from the initial starting point, costs would decline to $.41 per unit ($1×.8⁴). Obviously, the faster the growth rate, the steeper the cost decline.

The implications of the experience curve are far-reaching, as the Boston Consulting Group was quick to point out. Among other things, its analysis placed heavy emphasis on market share strategy for companies introducing new products in growth periods.[11]

Companies gaining market share are also accumulating volume faster than the industry and, hence, the logic goes, are building a more favorable cost structure. This competitive advantage can best be at-

[10] *Perspectives on Experience* (Boston: The Boston Consulting Group, Inc., 1970).

[11] *Ibid.*, pp. 25, 29, 31, 35.

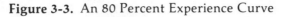

Figure 3-3. An 80 Percent Experience Curve

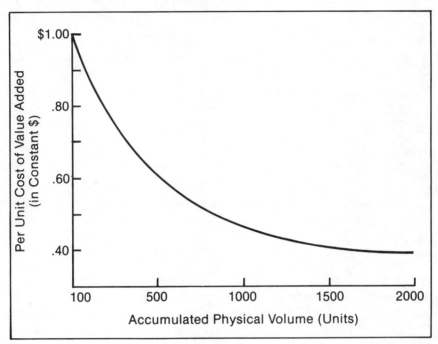

tained in the early phases of product growth, when customers are acquired from the unrealized market potential rather than being won from competitors, which implies overcoming routine transactional habits, established trade relationships, and ingrained brand loyalties. And such early increases yield compounded future returns, for each later share point translates into larger volume and cost differentials.

Given an equally good product, market share becomes a matter of time, effort, and money. It is regarded, in large part, as an outcome of the amount and efficiency of marketing expenditures. A company is thus seen as "buying into the market," with the cost varying in accordance with the efficiency of the marketing program.

But there are qualifications to this strategy. Market share spending has its limits, which for many companies may come earlier than those imposed by decreasing returns to scale. One constraining element is the investment required to support a share expansion plan (see table 3-1).

Table 3-1 shows annual color TV sales during the early years of the product life cycle. If a company began production at about 1959, attained a 10 percent share of market, and thereafter just kept pace with the industry, it would have increased its annual output almost fifteen fold by 1964. In the next two years, there would have been another 257 percent increase, but from a larger base. In addition to expanding pro-

Table 3-1

Color Television Market

Year	Industry Sales (in 000's Units)	Accumulated Company Experience (Assuming a Constant 10% Share) (in 000's Units)
1959	90	9
1960	120	21
1961	147	36
1962	438	80
1963	747	154
1964	1404	295
1965	2694	564
1966	5012	1065

Source: Figures compiled from Electronics Industries Association, *Consumer Electronics 1978 Annual Review* (D.C.: EIA, 1979), p. 13.

ductive capacity, money would also have been laid out for inventory, warehousing, and other physical distribution functions. When a strategy to increase market share is combined with rapid growth, results are highly escalating investments. These often create dislocations and financial strain. The decision of Texas Instruments in the seventies to achieve a dominant position in home electronics probably impeded development in other parts of the company that might have been more profitable.

The amount of investment also depends upon the ratio of long-term assets to sales. The degree of capital intensity exacerbates the investment market share connection. The more capital-intensive an industry, the greater the investment required for a given sales volume. When markets are large, a market share strategy in a capital-intensive industry can strain the resources of even the largest corporations. Giants like RCA and GE found captial generation beyond their means to support modest share targets of 10 percent and 15 percent, respectively, in the computer industry at about 1970.[12]

The crowning touch is that investments, no matter how judicious, never really extricate themselves from jeopardy in the growth period of the product life cycle. The main reason is unstable competitive relationships. Since all companies do not increase their volumes at a uniform rate, significant changes in relative costs can occur quickly. Indeed, it is almost inevitable, as a company's volume each year still looms large as a percentage of its total previous experience. For example, consider our hypothetical TV manufacturer who began making color sets in 1959. If the company just kept pace with the industry, it would still be experi-

---

[12] William Fruhan, Jr., "Pryrrhic Victories in Fights for Market Share," *Harvard Business Review* (September–October, 1972), pp. 101–102.

encing sharply rising sales seven years later. In 1966 it would increase its accumulated volume from 564,000 to 1,065,000 units, an 89 percent gain! Assuming a 70 percent to 80 percent experience curve, this company would lower its value-added unit costs by 18 percent to 27 percent (table 3-1). With such large cost variations from year to year, the entire industry can be thrown into a frenzy should a dominant producer find it advantageous to lower prices below the cost decreases of other firms.

Pressures of this sort on high-cost producers seem to happen toward the end of the growth phase. As growth slackens, competition takes on a more ominous appearance. Rising profit margins begin to falter, and the industry suddenly finds itself overcrowded.

Violent shakeouts ensue, wreaking havoc among firms that rushed in willy-nilly to exploit a growth situation. The electronic hand calculator industry, after a meteoric rise, saw numerous weak firms drop out of competition. The scene was repeated with manufacturers of four-channel gear. When it was introduced into the market in 1971, its boosters saw it as replacing stereophonic equipment. By 1976, even such prominent companies as Radio Shack, a division of Tandy, and Harman-Kardon, a subsidiary of Harman International Industries, dropped their quadraphonic lines.[13] The digital watch industry underwent the same vacillating times in 1977.

These scenarios, together with the evidence gathered by the Boston Consulting Group, suggest a systems-like approach to new products. Marketing, sales, and R&D cannot go off on their own. The greatest marketing plan is useless unless the company has, or can obtain, the necessary capital to support the market share targeted. And if plans should go awry, as they so often do in new product development, care must be taken not to impair other parts of the corporation. Strategy must consider the organization as a whole, especially when a company decides to commit substantial resources to relatively new fields. From this broader perspective, resource compatibility and utilization take on telling importance in the choice of new product endeavors.

Maturity Period Strategies

The maturity stage is reached when sales begin to level off. New users cannot be added indefinitely, and sooner or later the market approaches saturation. This limit prescribes the extent of the market in terms of consuming units. For soap it is almost universal. For eyeglasses, it is confined to those with sight deficiencies, at least until such time as people can be convinced to wear glasses for other reasons.

A mature product can, and often does, experience growth, but at a decreasing rate. As markets become saturated, there are less and less

---

13 Bernard Wysocki, Jr., "Disastrous Debuts," *Wall Street Journal* (March 23, 1976).

new consuming units to be gained. Demand for consumer durables, for example, is largely a replacement one. New car sales are closely tied to used car sales. Capital goods in mature industries similarly find most sales resulting from a desire to replace older equipment and facilities. Nondurables, whether consumer or industrial, can best achieve growth not from frantic explorations for new customers but from greater volume per consuming unit.

The maturity stage lasts as long as no competitive substitutes make their appearance or no strong shifts occur in consumer values or preferences. Soft drinks have persisted in a mature status for generations, just like people who never age beyond forty. According to J. Lucian Smith, president and chief operating officer of Coca-Cola Company, Coke has defied successfully the theory of limited product life.[14] On the other hand, some products hardly achieve maturity at all before they die, such as women's fashions and other types of fads.

As market volume nears its limits, individual companies find that sustaining sales growth has become more difficult. Meanwhile, economies of scale and greater proficiency because of learning no longer push unit costs downward. Productivity gains now come mainly from capital investments. Nevertheless, corporate energies are concentrated on mature, established products, for these are the mainstay of revenue and earnings.

These mature products also represent substantial investments of manpower and capital, and their current market positions are too hard-won to be neglected. As such, they themselves become the objects for product development in attempts to maintain and improve their market positions. It is precisely at the maturity stage that product policy offers the greatest opportunities for extending and changing the shape of the product life cycle. The two most common ways of accomplishing this are by product modification and extension of existing product lines.

Product modification

Modified products, along with line extensions, frequently begin in the latter half of the growth stage. But these are best associated with maturity. Advantages of remodeling a mature product are many. With production and distribution machinery in place, costs of product modification are relatively small. These apply to consumer as well as industrial goods. A study among 121 companies operating in, or supplying, the railroad and computer industries found that of 565 innovations, mainly of the "nuts and bolts" type, two-thirds cost less than $100,000, a relatively modest sum for research development of a commercially viable product.[15]

---

[14] *Marketing News* (July, 1, 1977), p. 1.

[15] Donald C. Marquis, "The Anatomy of Successful Innovation," Rothberg, *op.cit.*, p. 22.

Product changes in the maturity stage are often preferable to other competitive alternatives. For example, it is highly problematical that a mature brand can gain lasting benefits from incremental outlays for promotion.[16] To be most effective, a promotion must have something worthwhile to promote. To develop a new brand and neglect the old may be even more foolish.[17] A regenerated product minimizes risk because it starts from a more solid foundation. It already enjoys a reputation and a group of regular customers.

Edward G. Harness, Procter and Gamble's chief executive officer, told a conference board marketing session in 1977 that product improvement was one of the most effective ways to prolong a brand's life. He noted that Tide, a leading heavy duty detergent, had made fifty-five significant modifications during its nineteen-year lifetime. If a new company product is defined as something different from previous output, no matter how minute the difference, this process might be regarded as having produced fifty-five new products—remodeled ones—under the Tide brand name. But the essential point is that such product changes add distinctive value to items. This form of strategy, however, has a greater effect on individual brand sales than on those of the entire product category.

But some modification goes beyond the brand. The classic example of how a product's life was extended by remodeling is that of nylon. Developed primarily for the military, nylon's first uses were for parachutes. Gradually, it was applied to women's hosiery products and came to dominate that business. Later, DuPont developed more varied uses of hosiery, such as tinted hose and textured garments. Nylon was then extended to other fields: rugs, tires, bearings, and so forth. It has been estimated that had there been no further product innovations after military and circular knit uses, nylon consumption by 1962 would have reached a saturation level of 50 million pounds annually. Instead, actual consumption that year exceeded 500 million pounds.[18] Each innovation boosted sales, producing a new period of product growth and extending the product's life by many years.

Product policy cannot always rejuvenate an old product. Basic changes in purchase patterns or habits may force a decline, such as the trend toward casual, wash-and-wear apparel which brought about less drycleaning. Or a radically superior product may force obsolescence of the old. But that is the hallmark of good management—to determine when to alter a product and when not to spend money in futile efforts.

---

[16] However, see Louis J. Haugh, "Nabisco Finding New Ad Muscle Via 'All' System," *Advertising Age* (June 13, 1977), p. 3.

[17] Nariman K. Dhalla and Sonia Yuspeh, "Forget the Product Life Cycle Concept!" *Harvard Business Review* (January–February, 1976), p. 102.

[18] Levitt, "Exploit the Product Life Cycle," pp. 88–89.

Product proliferation or line extension

This approach calls for the introduction of new varieties in order to extend the market and increase volume of sales. Shavers for women were designed for that purpose. Many of the commonplace, mature products have persisted and prospered by an almost endless series of extensions. Right Guard deodorant, having attained a plateau with its family size, has since extended its line to a Right Guard for antistain and yet another for "double protection," clothes and body. Its competitor, Arrid, has produced deodorants in different forms—sprays, roll-ons, and creams. Kleenex, a brand name that has become generic, has introduced a line of Boutique tissues, casuals and facials. Dial soap sought to revitalize the brand by a series of products of different sizes for different uses—bath soap, family size, and regular—and in different colors—gold, pink, white, etc. Hawaiian Punch, another mature product, has expanded its flavors prodigiously—apple, red, fruit juicy red, cherry royal, very berry, sunshine orange—with a parallel line of low-calorie punches.

By broadening the line and increasing variety, product proliferation appeals to larger, or different, segments of the market. Johnson's baby shampoo was formulated for adults.[19] If the proliferated products are sold in the same channels, such as supermarkets, the company uses retail shelf space more effectively as a billboard for its family of products.

These line extensions can also offer a company relative cost advantages as well as marketing ones. These arise from what is sometimes referred to as "economies of scope."[20] Basically, they involve joint production made possible by technical characteristics of input factors. Such economies are effected whenever the incremental cost of producing a product on existing facilities is lower than producing it separately. This principle is also applicable to multiple brand manufacturers. A firm with a broader production scope, all other things being equal, will enjoy lower relative costs, not only for the particular extension, but for the entire line.

New entrants

In a mature market, established brands are extremely difficult to dislodge. Newcomers are always at a disadvantage because dominant companies, by virtue of greater accumulated experience, have lower operating costs. This cost disparity gives the market leader a commanding position, one so great as to lead the Boston Consulting Group to

---

[19] See B. M. Enis, *et. al.*, "Extending the Product Life Cycle," *Business Horizons* (June, 1979), p. 50.

[20] Robert D. Willing, "Multiproduct Technology and Market Structure," *American Economic Review* (May, 1979), pp. 346–351.

conclude that if resources and insights are equal, "new competitors and small producers can never overtake leaders."[21] The statement is correct, for it is a logical tautology. As a generalization it is useful, for it points to certain relative advantages of brands with entrenched positions. But the statement does contain an "if" clause, and the "if" does not always hold. Neither resources nor insights are always equal, and new competitors do make inroads into mature markets.

Companies in related industries form a major source of new competition. These potential competitors are already operating on the periphery of the market and require but a few short steps to enter. For example, the movement of oil companies into petrochemicals, or even into older energy fields such as coal, was not a radical step. Such would-be entrants are familiar with the new markets and have resources that are compatible. The type of products they choose to introduce depends upon the magnitude of resources they are willing to commit to the venture.

Sometimes, the newcomer challenges the market leader head-on. The entrance of Procter and Gamble into the dentifrice area, first with Gleem and then with Crest, was a frontal attack on Colgate, which enjoyed about 60 percent of the market before the upstart brands made their appearance. Johnson and Johnson's Tylenol was aimed at the heart of the analgesic market, long dominated by Bristol Myers and American Home Products. S. C. Johnson & Sons, Inc., with a $30 million budget for advertising and promotion, launched Agree shampoo in 1978, going against the two leaders, Procter and Gamble and Revlon.

A more common approach, and one with limited liability, is to invest some flank of the market with the new offering. When strong counteraction jeopardizes profits, the leader will normally forgo deterring action. The host of private labels in the packaged goods field, appealing to price-conscious shoppers, is basically an encroachment of this sort. The incursions into the domain of national brands are lamented, admonished, and denounced at almost every convention of the advertising industry. But the private brands are endured, for an effective cure of the malady may be far worse than the disease. In other instances, brands of new competitors may seek to cultivate distinct market segments that dominant companies neglect.

A more serious threat to mature brands is one that would destroy the entire product category. The attack often comes from outside a product's immediate business environment, its industrial or category boundaries. This invasion by outsiders brings new technologies and competitive substitutes that trigger the decline of the old. Synthetic fibers were not innovations of old line companies making cloth but

---

[21] Boston Consulting Group, Inc., *op. cit.,* p. 62.

were carried into textiles by the chemical industry. Jet engines come from GE and Westinghouse, and not from the traditional aircraft engine manufacturers. Innovations in machine tools, such as carbides, were products of the defense industries. Digital watches came not from conventional watchmakers but from firms in electronics.

When the differential advantage of the new product is small, it can be resisted by technology. Steel manufacturers, for example, have designed more efficient and better performing products to redress the balance with aluminum. Canning plants today are being built to use alternative materials, depending upon the price and performance of the metals available. When the crosswinds of change blow hard and differentials are large, survival may rest on the ability, like that of palm trees, to bend with the wind. Gilette, for example, was quick to adopt the stainless steel blade. NCR has remained a major supplier of banking equipment by redesigning its machines to function within a computerized system. Though Timex was unprepared for the new technology that invaded the watch industry, it went out and acquired a small electronics firm capable of producing the necessary components. Thus, an innovation signaling the death of a mature product need not be fatal to its producer.

Decline Period Strategies

The declining stage of the product life cycle is characterized by falling sales and profits, which may be swift or very gradual. Products subject to stylistic elements may come to an abrupt end. Other products, such as steel and beer, have seen sales drifting downward by small degrees. Sales of individual brands will also trend down, following the general direction of the declining product category. But no matter. Whether products age gracefully, like the elegant mansions of the Old South, or break down all at once, like the fanciful deacon's one-horse shay, the eventual outcome is the same—oblivion.

But how oblivion is met becomes the focal point of strategy. Only if decline is inevitable or if the falling trend cannot be stopped do options call for divestment or elimination of the product. Declining brands can be allowed to go on to slow deaths but with severely restricted budgets. Or they can be eliminated quickly and unceremoniously. This decision applies not merely to brands in a disappearing product category but to any brand that management deems beyond the redemptive powers of rejuvenation.

For products allowed to drift downward, there must come a time when they, too, will meet an unequivocal end. The decision here is one of timing: when shall the end come? Though every corporation is likely to have many weak products, most have no formal procedures for dropping their timeworn items.[22] Nevertheless, product elimination decisions must be made, if not formally, implicitly and *ad hoc*.

Budget pruning

Some brands never die, especially if they have developed a substantial share of market. Like old soldiers, they just fade away—and very, very slowly. There is always a hard core who will keep on using an old brand. The decline of nonfilter cigarettes has been exponential. Although soap was displaced by detergents for washing clothes many years ago, Ivory Flakes and Ivory Snow have gallantly held on despite their reliance on new users. The irrepressible idea that detergents are hard on clothing and will irritate a baby's soft skin has apparently been passed from generation to generation of new mothers. The counterpart to this type of slow death in the industrial field is supplies, parts, or components for a discontinued product that will continue in use for some time. Parts for the IBM 360 computer, which has been superseded by newer models, will be in demand for many years to come. Supplying spare parts for older model cars is a thriving business of auto repair shops.

One possible strategy for such degenerated products is budget pruning, often referred to as "milking" or "harvesting." The emphasis here is on budget control techniques, not product elimination techniques.

This strategy rests on the proposition that with proper budget control, slow-dying brands may be profitable for a long time, particularly if they enjoyed high ratios of marketing expenses to sales in their prime. The investments that have been made are sunken costs and have only salvage value and tax write-off benefits. The idea then is to cut all expenses to the bone and let the brands linger on until all possible economic value is gone. These brands may be marginal, and their profit contributions may be small. But as long as some contribution keeps coming in with only minimal effort, the reasoning goes, they can't be all bad. Then why not squeeze out every last bit of financial value?

An outstanding example of the staying power of an old favorite is Camels cigarets. Introduced in 1913, it became the first national brand and assumed the top spot for decades. Today, it is no longer advertised. Yet it competes with some 170 other brands, most low-tar, highly filtered, containing less tar in a pack than in one cigarette of Camels. But in 1979 Camels was still the seventh best-selling brand in the U.S., with domestic sales running better than $250 million.

A trip through any supermarket will readily reveal brands that, left alone, have been fading slowly for many years. HO Farina was a popular cereal for kids when the grandparents of today's offspring were kids. Ex Lax goes back to the same era, when it boasted to grandma about its powers of regularity. Chewing tobacco dates back to the age of speakeasies and trolley cars. Today's middle-aged household heads might still recall pestering their mothers for Ovaltine so they could send in silvery seals from the jar tops and receive Little Orphan Annie decoders, signet rings, and dog whistles in the mail. Vaseline hair tonic still commands loyalty from that hardy group who never accepted the dry look. Olive oil is still used for cooking by older Italian housewives. A surprising number of old products have a great deal of financial value to squeeze out.

Elimination

Two main reasons have been advanced for killing off weak products: better profits and better use of executive time.[23] Actually, only the first reason can be documented and has consequently emerged as the overwhelming concern in product elimination decisions. The benefits of elimination are often discussed in terms of increased sales, longer production runs, less inventory adjustment, more productive use of resources. These factors, which pinpoint the source of profit erosion when examined separately, are all reflected in the bottom line.

The profit criterion, however, does not provide a simple solution to the elimination problem. The main reason is because cost and revenue of sickly products are in numerous ways related to healthy ones. These interproduct relationships might be examined by, at the outset, considering profits subject to two simple assumptions:

1. Profits are calculated as sales minus costs and expense but do not include fixed overhead costs. The latter might be regarded as sunken costs and therefore unaffected by the deletion decision.

2. Resources are completely mobile. That is, production factors can be utilized in alternative ways to produce any pattern in a product line.

Within the past decade, several product elimination models with the above assumptions have been developed by research and consulting companies. One such computer model is PRESS, short for Product Review and Evaluation Subsystem Model.[24] Using standard cost accounting data, it is supposed to identify which products to cut off.

---

[23] See Philip Kotler, "Phasing Out Weak Products," *Harvard Business Review* (March–April 1965), pp. 109–110; David J. Luck, *Product Policy and Strategy* (Englewood Cliffs: Prentice Hall, Inc., 1972), pp. 77–78; S. H. Kratchman, R. T. Hise, and T. A. Ulrich, "Management's Decision to Discontinue a Product," *Journal of Accountancy* (June, 1975), pp. 50–54.

[24] Paul M. Hamelman and Edward M. Mazze, "Improving Product Abandonment Decisions," *Journal of Marketing* (April, 1972), pp. 20–26.

Its prime criterion is a product's marginal contribution to profits, calulated as sales minus variable costs and expenses. This figure, expressed as a percentage of the marginal contribution of all products, is then compared with the relative facilities cost. The result manifests itself as an index number called SIN (Selective Index Number). All products are then evaluated on the basis of SIN values. For example, if a product's relative contribution to profit is 3 percent but it utilizes 9 percent of the plant facilities to do this, its effective SIN value is small and it becomes a candidate for elimination. The actual formula for the SIN index is as follows:

$$\frac{CM_i/\Sigma CM_i}{FC_i/\Sigma FC_i,} \times \frac{CM_i}{\Sigma CM_i}$$

where:

CM_i = Marginal contribution for product i.

FC_i = Facilities costs for product i.

ΣCM_i = Marginal contribution of all products.

ΣFC_i = Facilities costs for all products

Given a relative marginal contribution of 3 percent and a relative facilities cost of 9 percent, SIN = .03/.09 × .03 = .1 .

Such models are useful when resources can be shifted easily from one type of operation to another. This would permit companies to discard low-margin products in favor of more profitable ones. While these models may also have application to cost control, the broader uses are not germane to the problem of product elimination.

Given the assumption of complete mobility of resources, the PRESS model may logically condemn profitable brands to the chopping block. Brands with low SIN indexes may generate profits though not commensurate with the facilities they utilize. But if the resource mobility assumption is dropped and fixed overhead is bought into the picture, then quite different conclusions and decisions might follow.

If resources are considered less than perfectly mobile and fixed costs are included in the financial analysis, it becomes quickly apparent that even a product that sustains a loss does not necessarily go off the market on purely economic grounds. Nor should it! The main reason is because only cash inflows end with the death of a product, but not cash outflows. All variable costs do. But fixed costs are different. Some do and some don't.

Accounting usually classifies two types of fixed costs, those that are constant and those that can be altered. The cost of machinery represents a constant sum that, for accounting purposes, is spread out over many years, depending upon the depreciation schedule. In contrast, an advertising budget is treated as a fixed cost, insofar as it is not variable. But this can be altered or eliminated completely. Accountants refer to such expenditures as "programmed costs." Anything programmed can be unprogrammed or changed.

The constant portion of the fixed costs, however, is not constant in terms of continuance after a brand is dropped. Interest payments on money borrowed to finance equipment purchases will go on whether the brand is manufactured or not. Leasing payments similarly may have to continue until the end of the lease. Taxes on property will accrue whether a plant is open or shut. But other kinds of fixed costs can be eliminated, such as supervisory salaries, utilities, or rent if the space can be subleased.

Table 3-2, a financial statement for a hypothetical Brand X, illustrates this situation.

Table 3-2

Financial Statement for a Hypothetical Brand X

Sales	$1,000,000
Cost of Sales:	
Materials	200,000
Direct labor	250,000
Variable overhead	50,000
Fixed overhead (applied)	300,000
Total	800,000
Gross profit	200,000
Less: Selling and Administrative expenses	
Variable	200,000
Fixed (applied)	100,000
Total	300,000
Net profit	(100,000)

In this example, Brand X shows a loss from operations of $100,000 per annum. Assume there is little hope of improvement. Should it be discontinued?

Before jumping to a yes conclusion, analyze the figures carefully. Costs break into $700,000 variable and $400,000 fixed. The variable costs will disappear with the demise of the brand. Good riddance! But not all fixed costs will vanish. For purposes of this example, say that $150,000 will continue and $250,000 will be eliminated.

Now what? If the brand goes on, it cuts into profits of the company by $100,000. But if it stops selling, it decreases profits by $150,000. Costs saddling a company after the brand is gone cannot be ignored, especially if they can be reduced by the brand's continuance.

At what point should the brand cease to be? If a brand's profit contribution to fixed costs is sales minus variable cost, then the percentage of each sales dollar going toward that end can be expressed as 1—(variable costs/sales). The point of elimination can then be described by the following formula:

$$\text{Point of elimination} = \frac{\text{Eliminable fixed costs}}{1 - (\text{variable costs/sales})}$$

In our example, the point at which Brand X should be eliminated is

$$\frac{\$250,000}{1 - (700,000/1,000,000)} = \$833,333$$

Only when sales drop down to $833,333 does it pay to take Brand X off the market. At any point above this figure, it would cost the company more to discontinue the brand than to keep it going and take annual losses.

In reality, the problem may be somewhat more complicated by the occurrence of joint costs. Or a somewhat similar situation might arise when a declining brand is manufactured on the same machinery that produces other brands. In fact, machinery is purposely designed to have that capability. First, it lowers the risk of output obsolescence. Second, the ability to produce multiple products on the same machine will effect greater operating economies. In either event—joint costs or joint use— the eliminable fixed overhead must be separated from that which cannot be eliminated in a decision to discontinue a brand.

Under absorption costing, each product must carry its share of the overhead, or of joint production costs if that be the case. These costs are allocated to various products in accordance with criteria set up by the cost accountants. That these allocations may not be made objectively is irrelevant. If resources cannot be transformed when a brand is dropped or if unused capacity results, allocated overhead or at least the uneliminable part, is shifted to the remaining brands. The same holds true for distribution when a brand is warehoused with other brands. Its removal from the market transfers a portion of fixed costs to the remainder of the warehoused items. If the company does its own shipping and its trucks travel the same route at less than full capacity, line haul costs are virtually the same as they had been before the brand's deletion. Unless offsetting adjustments can be made in transit schedules, unit transport costs will rise.

The removal of a brand from a product line may also affect sales of other brands in the line. This depends upon the extent to which products are complementary to one another. For example, a company may have trouble selling single-edged razor blades unless it manufactures single-edged razors. Certain typewriters need certain ribbons, and if the latter were discontinued, sales of the former would undoubtedly suffer. Consequently, the degree to which products complement each other becomes an important variable.

To sum up, the decision to eliminate a product is often not a matter of the brand alone. It does not stand in splendid isolation from other products. Both cost and sales effects on other products must be considered. The same factors that organizations have built into their operations to achieve economies for product increments work in reverse for product decrements.

Value of the Life Cycle Concept

Many authorities have suggested that perhaps the greatest significance of the life cycle concept is its potential value in product planning. This implies establishing directions for new product development. It also implies an ability to forecast the shape and timing of cycles.

However, numerous studies have pointed to a wide variety of shapes, and some have even questioned whether accurate forecasts are possible. One study found nine common variants of the product life cycle, which are shown in figure 3–4. Another study of the ethical drugs found six different types of curves, few of which resembled the nine represented in figure 3–4.[25] But more important, there seemed to be no way of relating a product in advance to a specific type of curve.

Probably the most thorough study of the product life cycle was conducted by the Marketing Science Institute. Its investigators analyzed more than 100 product categories in food, health, and personal care. They concluded that only 17 percent of the product classes studied and 20 percent of the individual brands followed a sales pattern that was consistent with the generalized model.[26] This has led some authors to maintain that management would be best advised to forget the life cycle and arrive at policy decision in a pragmatic way.[27]

While the concept has undoubtedly been abused, it can still be valuable in product planning if used thoughtfully—as a framework or as a broad theoretical structure for programs. After all, introducing a brand when the product category is relatively new will mean encountering situations and problems different from those in mature, established industries. In this sort of context, predictive accuracy of the product life cycle is neither necessary nor desirable, for results depend partly on the product programs and their implementation. The product program, not the life cycle *per se*, becomes the relevant variable in assessing sales outcomes.

[25] Cox, *op. cit.*

[26] Rolando Pilli and Victor J. Cook, "A Test of the Product Life Cycle as a Model of Sales Behavior," *Marketing Science Institute Working Paper* (November, 1967) and "Validity of the Product Life Cycle," *The Journal of Business* (October, 1969), pp. 385–400.

[27] Dhalla and Yuspeh, *op. cit.*

Figure 3-4. Nine Variants of the Product Life Cycle

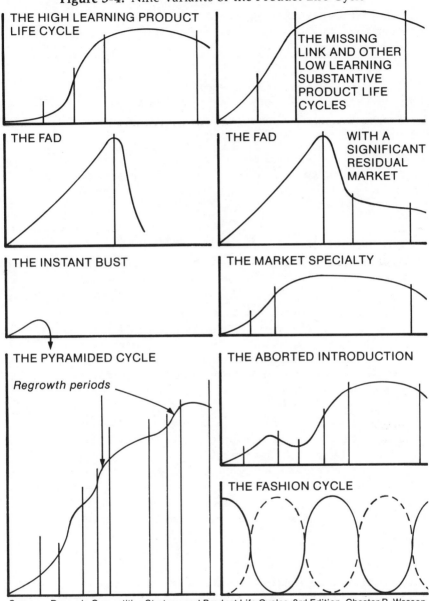

THE HIGH LEARNING PRODUCT LIFE CYCLE

THE MISSING LINK AND OTHER LOW LEARNING SUBSTANTIVE PRODUCT LIFE CYCLES

THE FAD

THE FAD WITH A SIGNIFICANT RESIDUAL MARKET

THE INSTANT BUST

THE MARKET SPECIALTY

THE PYRAMIDED CYCLE

Regrowth periods

THE ABORTED INTRODUCTION

THE FASHION CYCLE

Source: Dynamic Competitive Strategy and Product Life Cycles, 3rd Edition. Chester R. Wasson, Austin Press, Division of Lone Star Publishers, Austin, Texas 78766, 1978.

The product life cycle can also serve as a guide with respect to quality of profits.[28] Just as important as total profits are a company's sources of

[28] Sam R. Goodman, *Techniques of Profitability Analysis* (New York: John Wiley & Sons, 1970), p. 70.

profits. Do they come from mature, growing, or declining products? And in what proportions? As expressed by William S. Woodside, president and chief operating officer of the American Can Company:

> ". . . *management of a three-billion-dollar corporation has a responsibility to both the present and the future. It means utilizing mature businesses to provide dependable cash flow and increasing return on investment. It means supporting embryonic businesses that can become the growth businesses of the future. And it means having lots of businesses in between, at early, at intermediate and late growth stages, to provide increasing earnings per share."[29]*

If expected earnings are the harbingers of future well-being, a product mix planned for future life cycles is the dispatcher.

---

[29] American Can Company, *Report on 76th Annual Meeting.*

REVIEW QUESTIONS

1. What can occur within the uncontrolled external environment that creates a need and opportunity for new products or endangers the continued profitable existence of old products? Include both consumer and industrial products in your answer.
2. Discuss some of the basic changes—developments— that are currently creating opportunities for profitable new products.
3. As a marketing manager for an extensive line of breakfast cereals, of what planning value is the concept of the product life cycle?
4. Describe in general, universal terms the evolution of product X as it travels the path from introduction to phase out.
5. Name two products that you believe are in (a) the birth stage, (b) the growth stage, (c) the maturity stage, and (d) the decline stage of the product life cycle. Cite reasons for your selections.
6. Discuss the progression of changes in promotional strategy for a consumer product during the different stages of the product life cycle.
7. What factors may operate to lengthen the duration of the introductory stage of the product life cycle? Does the manufacturer desire a lengthy introductory period? What can be done to alter the duration of this period?
8. Examine the possible approaches to profit revitalization from the doldrums of the maturity stage.
9. The treatment of product costs affects prices and profits and that in turn affects the decision to discontinue a seemingly unprofitable product. Discuss the ramifications of decision making in this area.
10. What are the implications of the experience curve for a company that is: (a) first to introduce an innovative product, (b) second to introduce a comparable innovative product.

Two/ Strategic Planning

4/ Strategic Planning

Most of the large corporations today engage in strategic planning. This type of planning is long-range and conducted at various levels of management within the corporation. It serves to guide the company as to the direction in which it is going.

Strategy normally begins with objectives, which are translated into goals. These in turn serve as the basis for evaluating product development output. Corporate policy, which establishes acceptable alternatives for meeting goals, defines the criteria that both new and old ventures must meet in order to have management approval.

Strategic planning attempts to match corporate resources with environmental factors. Two external elements in particular are of major importance—population and technology. The first dominates strategy of producers of consumer goods, for people and markets are inseparable. The shifting characteristics of the U.S. population present both problems and opportunities to marketers of consumer goods. Technological change is especially crucial to firms in rapidly growing, technologically intensive industries. To keep abreast of such changes and prepare for them, many firms resort to technological forecasting, the most common methods of which are trend fitting, trend correlation, expert opinion, and scenario writing.

Strategic planning involves budgeting, which allocates the firm's resources among different product lines and businesses. To deal with problems of allocation, diversified firms have turned to portfolio selection theory. There are three basic methods for evaluating the product portfolio: market share–growth rate matrix, market attractiveness-business position matrix, and empirical methods.

Each method has both advantages and disadvantages. But in actuality, they view the product portfolio from different perspectives and therefore can be used in combination with each other.

Strategic Planning Concept

Within the past two decades, corporations have placed increasing emphasis upon formality and strategy in their planning. Neither attribute takes on a compelling urgency in the executive atmosphere of smaller companies or even in large firms with narrow product lines. The president can meet frequently with his small group of managers to assess current operations and make decisions that affect the company's future.

But it is otherwise with large diversified corporations, whose operations reach into far-flung lines of business. This multiformity has led to decentralized management and specialization. It has also created an insistent need for a system whereby decisions of various entities are cohesive, aim in the same directions and, when made by one manager, are conducive to the goals of the entire organization.[1]

The term *strategic planning* was carried over into business from the military establishment. The word *strategy* derives from the Greek term meaning "generalship." Corporate planners, like military strategists, are concerned primarily with the broad strokes of winning a war, and not with any particular battle. From this point of view, strategic planning provides general directions to specific ends.

It addresses itself to potential opportunities that require resource deployment. Strategic plans therefore oversee sources and applications of corporate funds, both for old and new products. No group in a company can engage in a line of business until it is given a budget to do so. While budgets for numerous activities are worked out through negotiation, they are visibly guided by choices of strategy.

Thinking about strategy goes on at all levels of a company. But the goals are not the same at the different levels.

Strategic planning at corporate headquarters contemplates far-reaching options, often with a panoramic sweep. Its interests embrace many businesses, depending upon the size and diversity of the organization. But it is also future oriented. It points to the directions in which a firm should be moving, the businesses it should be in. These company strategies are formulated within a set of rules known as corporate policy. Consequently, strategy takes on a dual meaning. First, it refers to a set of rules for investigating, evaluating, and selecting products and markets. Second, strategic planning narrows the search for market opportunities by adjusting internal capabilities to environmental factors. This is done by assessing a firm's strengths and weaknesses and focusing on areas in which advantages are manifest. By matching capabilities and opportunities, strategic planning postures the firm in the economic sphere of society. The end result of corporate strategy is a definition of a firm's products and markets for the future and a roadmap for getting there.

Strategies for functional units, such as product lines, concern themselves mainly with operational goals and, hence, involve tactical decisions. These are related to such questions as advertising copy, media

[1] R. F. Vancil and P. Lorange, "Strategic Planning in Diversified Companies," *Harvard Business Review* (January–February, 1975), p. 81.

selection, product mix, and sales programs. Since these action programs must conform to corporate plans, they can be thought of as supporting strategies. If the corporate plan is the sum of its parts, then tactics are action programs for carrying out higher level strategies. The relationship between strategic and operational plans is depicted in figure 4-1.

A further distinction between strategy and tactics is the time span to which plans refer. Strategic planning at the corporate level is invariably long-term, running anywhere from five to ten years.[2] Beyond that point plans cease to be operationally useful as perspectives become blurred. On the other hand, operational or tactical plans are for shorter durations, with budgets for functional units reviewed on a continuous basis and usually allocated for no more than a year.

New Product Planning

New product decisions are both strategic and tactical. Cost reduction programs are examples of operational planning resulting in new products and processes. A similar situation prevails with product design changes, the primary goal of which is better use of allocated resources. A decision to include new items in a product line is often linked to functional issues. On the other hand, a resolve to enter a completely new business represents strategic planning.

In small companies, new product strategy is action oriented and closely related to functional goals. Top management, which may include the president only, selects the alternative courses of action. Since the choice of programs determines goals, strategic planning proceeds from the top down.[3]

Strategy in large corporations runs from the bottom up. Senior officers are too far removed from products and markets, especially if they are highly varied, to acquire anything more than a superficial understanding of business conditions. Division managers thus become the main source for identifying relevant issues and supplying data with which to set corporate goals.

The bottom-up process, so common in large organizations, has often been criticized as being inimical to innovative product planning.[4] Division managers are not apt to take kindly to an innovation that conflicts with their own interests. Would they be quick to recognize, much less to recommend, a strategy that calls for the phasing out of their opera-

[2] Parmanand Kumar, "Long-Range Planning Practices by U.S. Companies," *Managerial Planning* (January–February, 1978), pp. 31–32.

[3] P. Lorange and R. F. Vancil, "How to Design a Strategic Planning System," *Harvard Business Review* (September–October, 1976), pp. 75–81.

[4] See Carter F. Bales, "Strategic Control: The President's Paradox," *Business Horizons* (August, 1977), pp. 20–21; Derek F. Abell, "Strategic Windows," *Journal of Marketing* (July, 1978), pp. 25–26.

Figure 4-1. Generic Structure of Plans

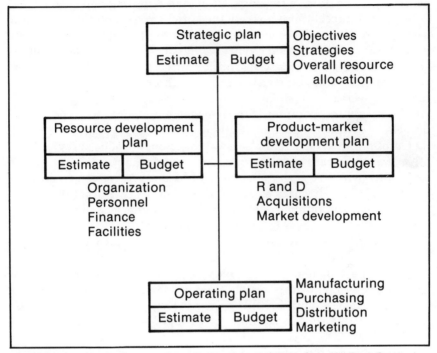

From *Corporate Strategy* by H. Igor Ansoff. Copyright © 1963, McGraw-Hill Book Co. Used with permission of McGraw-Hill Book Company.

tions? The early adoption of innovation is also hindered because many radical ideas originate outside their respective industries. Strategic planning at the division level, critics of decentralization point out, saddles innovation with operational considerations and new products with routine thinking. Priorities tend to support current lines of business and to make use of familiar materials and processes.

But planning at the corporate level exerts influence on the direction of new products despite bottom-up procedures. Though divisional plans may comprise the principal part of the total corporate plan, the two are not synonymous. In practice, there is an interplay, a give and take, between divisional heads and corporate leadership. Though the top cannot extract more than what can be done at lower levels of the organization, expectations are not necessarily the same. Goals set by various divisions, when taken together, usually diverge from results envisioned by top management. The latter may be higher than what divisions collectively think they can deliver. Assuming plans for current products are optimal, the gap can only be closed by new products. Corporate management may thus spur divisions to embark on more aggressive

new product programs. Or it can circumvent divisional programs altogether by going outside the corporation and acquiring new businesses.
If divisional expectations exceed those befitting available resources,
corporate management again has a number of strategic options. It can
borrow funds for promising ventures. It can scale down plans, killing
some projects, so that financial specifications are met. Or it can carry on
both strategies simultaneously, funneling more funds into some ventures and decreasing commitments for others. By controlling the purse
strings of the corporation, top management maintains a pervasive
influence over the product mix outlook.

Corporate headquarters also sway divisional product programs in
other ways. Certain planning functions overlap, since they are done
simultaneously. The corporate choice of business areas can frequently
dictate strategic alternatives at the divisional level. Corporate guidelines, in the form of objectives and policies, further channel divisional
choices into certain areas in preference to others.

Probably the most elaborate system of strategic planning is that of
GE. With more than 200 operating units and some 50 divisions, GE is
one of the most diversified companies in the world, developed mainly by
internal growth. For purposes of strategic planning, a structure called
"strategic business units" (S.B.U.'s) is superimposed over product divisions. All related functional units are grouped into S.B.U.'s. These, in
turn, are sorted into five sectors. The general managers of S.B.U.'s
supervise the planning of individual product lines under their authority.
But the sector executives prepare their own plans, to which S.B.U. plans
must conform. Resource allocation follows top management review
of sector plans and S.B.U. summaries.[5] Whether adding more layers of
management overcomes the criticism of bottom-up planning still remains for the future to determine.

New product planning may look toward corporate strategy for direction, but it is not actually part of that process. It is one of many devices
for implementing a given strategy and, as such, belongs in the domain
of management control.[6] The relationship between strategic planning
and management control is depicted in figure 4-2. This diagram also
shows the results of new product planning being fed back, with the
information used to shape future strategies.

Objectives, Goals, Policies

Regardless of how planning proceeds—top-down or bottom-up—
strategy begins with objectives. On the corporate level, they represent

---

[5] Anthony J. Parisi, "Management: G.E's Search for Synergy," N.Y. Times (April 16, 1978),
pp. F 1, 4.

[6] Raymond M. Kinnunen and Robert H. Caplan III, "The Domain of Management Control," University of Michigan Business Review (May, 1978), pp. 1-9.

Figure 4-2. Strategic Planning–Management Control Relationships

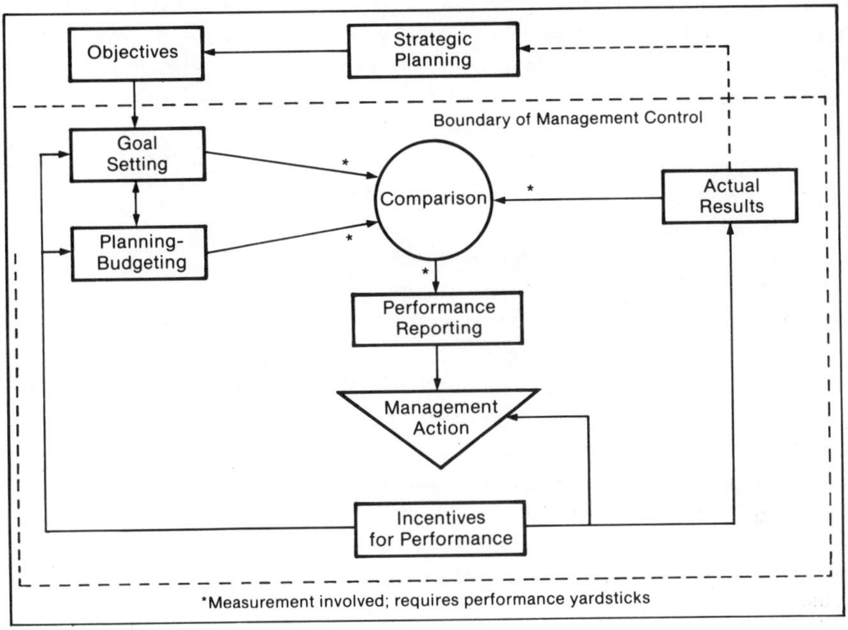

*Measurement involved; requires performance yardsticks

Source: Kinnunen and Caplan III, *op. cit.*, p. 5.

what the firm proposes to accomplish over a given period of time. Since a corporate plan is long-term and covers a wide range of activities, it is of necessity more general than those of subunits. Yet it should, authorities maintain, be specific enough to guide product planning.[7]

Goals are objectives made more detailed both as to performance level and time period. For example, an objective of Consolidated Foods Corporation is to "achieve a maximum return on our stockholders' investment consistent with sound business practices and prudent debt policies." When this objective is refined to specify a 13 percent return on equity as acceptable for 1976 through 1978, it becomes a goal.[8] Since company goals filter down into divisions and product lines, they form a basis for judging new ventures. Though the actual criterion established for accepting a proposed project may be higher than the corporate goal, it is doubtful that any new venture expected to yield less than a 13 percent return on investment would receive management approval to go ahead.

Similarly, AMF stated its major long-range objective was "to grow profitably while strengthening the balance sheet." These objectives

---

[7] See Donald H. Slocum, *New Venture Methodology* (New York: American Management Association, Inc., 1972), p. 8; Douglas W. Foster, *Planning for Products & Markets* (London: Longman Group Ltd., 1972), p. 29.

[8] Consolidated Foods Corporation, *Annual Report*, 1978, p. 6.

were transformed into goals when the company in 1978 targeted a compounded annual growth rate of 10 percent in earnings per share and a 15 percent return on equity.[9] Any new project whose financial performance is forecasted as falling short of these goals will face dim prospects of getting an approving nod from management. Old products would also find it difficult to get money for investment unless the incremental returns would yield at least 15 percent and contribute to per share earnings in accordance with corporate goals.

Corporate policies are broad definitions of alternative means that may be used to achieve desirable goals. In terms of product development, policies outline the scope and nature of new product effort. For example, Consolidated Foods' policy on acquisitions is to seek those "which contribute directly and immediately to our major product lines through strong similarities of product design, manufacturing technology or distribution channels."[10] This policy firmly outlines the types of new ventures the company can initiate through acquisition. Other policy criteria may include growth markets, products with high value added, ventures with synergistic advantages, etc. From this standpoint, policy defines what criteria any new product must match before it is accepted and thus sets forth guidelines for evaluating new product ideas.

Policy formulations may also deal with issues such as business ethics and social responsibility, affirming the company's obligations to its employees, shareholders, customers, and the general public. One view regards these "credo-type" statements as irrelevant platitudes, wholly unnecessary to a corporate plan.[11] Most corporate officers, however, would take strong exception to this opinion.

While management has considerable latitude in carrying out these policies, they are not altogether idle enunciations. A decision to accelerate environmental projects may decelerate work on other ventures. A policy to maintain good customer relations may evoke high service levels or only products that can meet upgraded quality standards. Social concerns might turn product development into channels of action for attaining societal goals. Food companies, for example, continually face the problem—if not internally, then raised by social critics—of producing low-priced, high-nutrition foods in third-world markets, where hunger is a constant companion to large segments of the population. But on the whole, societal policy positions have had but a minor effect on product development.

---

[9] AMF, *Annual Report*, 1978, p. 5.

[10] Consolidated Foods, *op. cit.*, p. 6.

[11] Foster, *op. cit.*, p. 301.

Capability–Opportunity Matching

Strategic planning sets up rules for making product decisions and attempts to match a firm's capabilities with potential opportunities. This process entails analyses of internal resources and environmental factors and fitting one to the other.

A firm's basic resources are physical, financial, and human. A resource audit represents an evaluation of the strengths and weaknesses of an organization. One way of proceeding with the assessment is to draw up a capability profile or a "grid of competence," wherein key resources are rated in accordance with some acceptable level of performance.[12] The analysis can cover such factors as R&D skills, control of raw materials and production quality, nature of marketing and distribution facilities, management depth and financial ability. Strategy may then contemplate where best to employ the firm's strengths. It may also contrive to remedy a deficiency as well as to exploit a proficiency.

For example, a firm with a weak R&D capability may forgo opportunities that depend heavily upon technological leadership. But it may also seek to acquire the necessary technology for the future. Firms with limited financial resources are ill-equipped to pursue a market share strategy in a highly competitive, rapidly growing industry. But a proprietary technology can alter the situation and present attractive options to such firms.

The most advantageous use of capabilities requires a knowledge of the environment in which a firm operates, for that is where opportunities arise. These external factors may include population trends, technological developments, ecological concerns, financial and economic currents, government regulatory climate, and the like. How these uncontrolled variables are joined with those that can be controlled makes up the central theme of strategic planning.

Two environmental factors are of monumental importance—population and technology. The size and quality of the first largely determine the nature of markets for consumer products. Technology governs the range of product alternatives offered to these markets and is of vital concern to firms producing goods and services for the industrial market.

Population

Population changes dominate the interests of most consumer goods manufacturers, for markets are people. Because the impact of these changes do not affect all companies alike, generalizations are presump-

---

[12] Ansoff, *op. cit.*, pp. 76, 92.

tuous and vulnerable. Nevertheless, even a cursory examination of population trends can illustrate some related strategic alternatives.

Projections of population to the year 2000, made by the U.S. Bureau of the Census, indicate a long-term decline in the growth rate. The forecasts contain judgmental factors over which experts themselves may differ greatly. For this reason, the Census Bureau made a number of different projections, ranging from highly optimistic to highly pessimistic. The "best estimates," which postulate a continuation of trends in the main components of population change, are shown in table 4-1.

Table 4-1
Population Estimates 1950–2000

Year	Population (000)*	Average Annual Percentage Change (%)
1950..............................	152,250	1.7
1960..............................	180,650	1.5
1970..............................	204,900	0.8
1980..............................	222,150	0.9
1885..............................	232,900	0.9
1990..............................	243,500	0.7
1995..............................	252,750	0.6
2000..............................	260,400	0.5

*Figures rounded to the nearest 50,000
Source: Projections are those of Series II, *Current Population Reports, Series P-25, No. 704.*

A declining rate of population increase foreshadows a slower growth rate to a people-dependent company. Though a low-growth strategy may be forced by circumstances, few firms are ready to adopt a "small is beautiful" philosophy. To offset the unwanted effects of "national maturity," a firm may cast abroad for markets that are undergoing a more rapid expansion. Or it may seek to operate in faster growing segments at home, for population growth is not uniform.

The most dynamic component of population change is fertility, which, except for a brief period following World War II, has been trending downward. The crude birth rate, defined as births per 1,000 population, peaked at 25.2 in 1957 and has been falling continuously since. The "total fertility rate," a more satisfactory measure, has declined from a high of 3,705 in 1959 to 1,760 in 1976—below the 2,100 replacement level. (The total fertility rate indicates the number of births 1,000 women would have in a lifetime, given an annual rate.)

One evident consequence of declining fertility rates is fewer children. Annual births are actually expected to increase throughout the eighties but at a snail's pace. Females born at the height of the baby boom after World War II will still be of childbearing age in the eighties. But after 1990, the number of babies is projected to decline absolutely. Table 4-2 shows trends of the child population, under fourteen years of age, and projections to the year 2,000.

Table 4-2
Children Under 14 Years of Age (000)*

Year	Under 5 Years	5–13 Years	Total Children
1950	16,400	22,450	38,850
1960	20,350	32,950	53,300
1970	17,150	36,650	53,800
1980	16,000	30,200	46,200
1985	18,800	29,100	47,900
1990	19,450	32,550	52,000
1995	18,750	35,400	54,150
2000	17,850	35,100	52,950

*Figures rounded to the nearest 50,000
Source: *Current Population Reports, Series P-25, No. 704.*

The baby industry—with product lines in baby foods, diapers, oil, powder, etc.—is currently a mature industry. Businesses catering to the children's market, such as those producing toys, candy, and children's clothing, are likewise witnessing the number of product users approaching the upper limits of growth. But the decline in fertility has meant opportunities for other companies, notably those offering birth control devices. Concomitant with a lower birth rate has been a greater desire to avoid the natural consequences of simple pleasures.

Decreasing rates of fertility, in conjunction with longer life spans, will also change the age composition of the population. It will age for the remainder of the twentieth century, and this trend will carry over well into the next. The median age, about thirty years in 1980, will push up to almost thirty-six years by 2000. From 1950 to 1980, the major market growth, in terms of people, took place among children, teenagers, young adults, and the elderly. These were the least affluent segments of U.S. population. In the latter part of the century, the highest growth rate will take place among the most affluent, aged thirty-five to fifty-four. Within these age intervals, earning power is at its peak.[13] Trends and projections for the adult population, aged twenty-five and up, are shown below (table 4-3).

Except for those twenty-five to thirty-four years old, all age groups will show increases from 1980 to 2000. Those thirty-five to forty-four

---

[13] *Current Population Reports, Series P-60, No. 117.*

Table 4-3
Population 25 Years and Older (000)*

Year	25–34 Years	35–44 Years	45–54 Years	55–64 Years	65 Years & Up
1950 24,050	21,650	17,450	13,400	12,400
1960 22,900	24,200	20,600	15,600	16,700
1970 25,300	23,150	23,300	18,650	20,100
1980 36,150	25,700	22,700	21,200	24,950
1990 41,100	36,600	25,300	20,800	29,800
2000 34,450	41,350	35,900	23,250	31,800
	Percent Distribution				
1950	15.8	14.2	11.5	8.8	8.1
1960	12.7	13.4	11.4	8.6	9.2
1970	12.3	11.3	11.4	9.1	9.8
1980	16.3	11.6	10.2	9.5	11.2
1990	16.9	15.0	10.4	8.5	12.2
2000	13.2	15.9	13.8	8.9	12.2

*Figures rounded to the nearest 50,000
Source: *Current Population Reports, Series P-25, No. 704.*

years of age, estimated at about 25.7 million in 1980, are projected to reach 41.4 million by the turn of the century—an increase of 14.3 million, or sixty-one percent. The forty-five to fifty-four age group is expected to grow by 13.2 million within this same time period, a gain of some forty-two percent. Together, this middle-aged group, from thirty-five to fifty-four, will make up about thirty percent of the total population by the year 2000. People over fifty-five will maintain about the same proportion in the total, while young adults, twenty-five to thirty-four years of age, will undergo a relative and absolute decline.

If the sixties and seventies turned attention on the young, the latter part of the century should focus on middle age. And the growing markets should be centered in the more mature life styles and tastes.

In the coming years, few consumer industries will be unaffected by the impact of demographic shifts in the population. These changes will signify exposure to some companies and benefits to others but adjustments in product lines to most.

The giant Coca-Cola Company, for example, provides ample evidence of a firm constructing a strategy for an aging nation. The core market for soft drinks, teenagers and young people under twenty-five, is bound to get smaller. With ninety-five percent of its revenue and earnings coming from soft drinks, Coca-Cola is not about to relinquish its primary business. But it is planning to compensate for the expected contraction of young people. Among these strategies is a strong effort to boost sales in foreign markets, where population is growing rapidly and per capita consumption can be enlarged. Another thrust is diversification into areas catering to middle-aged customers. This included the purchase of the Taylor Wine Company in 1976 for $90 million worth of stock. Another measure was a major expansion of the foods division, budgeting for a two-thirds increase in revenue within five years. The foods division markets orange juice, coffee, and tea, all favorite drinks of mature persons. And finally, Coca-Cola has sought to win sales among older people with its line of diet soft drinks.[14]

By no means does Coca-Cola constitute an isolated example of a company rearranging its priorities to accommodate a changing environment. Cosmetic manufacturers, with more new products to counteract wrinkles, age spots, and greying hair, have evinced an acute interest in middle-aged problems. Gerber has added insurance to its line of baby foods. "Levi's for men" has designed a line of jeans aimed primarily at males aged twenty-five to forty-nine. The biggest spenders for recreational vehicles in the past several years have been middle-aged couples. This same consumer group is responsible for the largest expenditures for travel and recreation-related products and services. According to the Census of Travel, individuals in the thirty-five to fifty-four age bracket do the most traveling, averaging some 3.5 trips per person in a year. A trip is defined as a journey of 100 miles or more away from home. This middle-aged segment of the population forms the backbone of the airline market. Homes with heads thirty-five to fifty-four years of age account for almost half of all household trips taken by airplane. The relevant statistics are shown in table 4-4.

Table 4-4
Household Trips

Age of Household Head	Number of Households (000)	Household Trips		Trips per Household	
		Total (000)	Airplane (000)	Total #	Airplane #
Under 18 yrs.	11	28	3	0.3	0.3
18–24 years	6,992	31,056	3,097	4.4	0.4
25–34 years	16,063	75,518	14,283	4.7	0.9
35–44 years	12,264	69,073	12,881	5.6	1.1
45–54 years	12,700	67,852	11,044	5.3	0.9
55–64 years	11,535	42,164	6,758	3.7	0.6
65 & up	14,917	26,840	4,111	1.8	0.3

Source: Derived from tape of Bureau of Census, Census of Travel, 1977.

---

[14] "The Graying of the Soft-Drink Industry," *Business Week* (May 23, 1977), pp. 68–72.

Companies making products consumed by households, as opposed to individuals, should find brighter prospects in the years ahead. New household formation is projected to move at a 1.5 percent annual rate and add approximately 25 million units between 1980 and the end of the century. The higher growth rate of households than population stems from several sources: postponement of marriage, an increasing divorce rate, and nontraditional living arrangements.[15] The lower population growth should have little effect on such markets as construction, appliances, household supplies, and furnishings.

But there will be substantial shifts in types of products demanded because of changes in the types of households. These spending units will be smaller, with the largest growth in one- and two-person households. Homes and apartments built for large families will have a shrinking demand. With more women expected to enter the labor force, eating habits of the American family will alter markedly. Even now it is estimated that three out of every four homes do not have all their members eating breakfast together. More than 40 percent of adult males shop for groceries, and some 24 percent do their own cooking. The changing role of a homemaker has been a boon to fast food and away-from-home eating establishments. Household equipment and supplies that promise less work for the vanishing homemaker—specialty cleansers, no-wax floors, self-cleaning ovens, microwave ovens—have enjoyed spiraling sales.[16]

Technology

The technological environment, like social and economic factors, contains both positive and negative aspects. To take advantage of opportunities by product design necessitates the anticipation of technological development. Though the future is unkown, strategic planning must consider the possibilities of technical advances in much the same way as it currently evaluates economic and social changes. This is particularly critical in industries of rapid growth and technological intensity, such as instruments, electrical equipment, chemicals.[17] These industries make the greatest use of technological forecasting, for they operate in a climate of fast change. Since there is a lag between a decision to develop a new product and its actual commercialization, a firm must do more than just keep up with technological innovation. It

[15] *Current Population Reports, Series P-20, No. 323.*

[16] See L. J. Shapiro and D. Bohmback, "Eating Habits Force Changes in Marketing," *Advertising Age* (October 30, 1978), pp. 27, 65–66; Larry Edwards, "Soft Sales Challenge Food Marketers," *Ibid.*, 27–103; Joann S. Lublin, "Marketers Discover Free-Spending Group: Affluent Middle-Aged," Wall Street Journal (April 16, 1979), pp. 1, 30.

[17] Arthur Gerstenfeld, *Effective Management of Research and Development* (Reading, MA: Addison-Wesley Publishing Company, 1970), pp. 130–132.

must try to foresee the future, however dimly, for in so doing a firm can actively shape what will be. To wait until it is caught up in events may well be too late.

Technological forecasting is not an exact prediction of future events. Rather, it is an attempt to estimate technical conditions likely to develop and assess the significance of future developments. In this way, a firm can order its technological priorities and systematically plan its R&D schedule over a long horizon.

There are several techniques for technological forecasting, and most firms use more than one. The most popular method, however, is trend fitting. Technological progress in a given field usually assumes the pattern of an S-curve. When the period of rapid growth comes to an end and that of stasis takes over, the prevailing technology is challenged by a competing one. By applying this pattern to several parameters and connecting the tangents of each individual curve, a new S-curve can be constructed.[18] The task of the forecaster is to determine the position of the current state of the art and to postulate which nascent technology would probably replace it.

Related to trend fitting is trend correlation. Instead of assuming that the past will continue into the future, as trend extrapolation must, the trend can be expressed in relation to another trend. That is, the two trends are correlated with each other and an estimating equation is derived from the relationship. But in order for this regression equation to be meaningful, one trend must occur before the other, or "lead" it. A frequently cited example is the relationship between the speeds of commercial and military aircraft, with the latter leading the former. Thus, current flying speeds of military planes indicate probable developments in designs of commercial fleets.[19]

When trends of technical parameters cannot be quantified or cannot serve as reliable guides to the future, forecasters may resort to expert opinion. The most popular such approach is the Delphi method, developed by the RAND Corporation. A panel of experts is asked to respond to a structured questionnaire. Panel members are not supposed to be in touch with each other, so as to avoid persuasion by a few strong individuals and "bandwagon" effects. The specialists, recruited from various fields, are supposed to work anonymously. This assures relatively little influence on an individual by his peers.

After the group is polled, results are summarized and sent back to all members. If there is a disagreement among them, they are asked to reevaluate their responses in the hope of reaching a consensus. After

---

[18] Erich Jantsch, *Technological Forecasting in Perspective* (Paris: Organization for Economic Cooperation and Development, 1967), p. 161.

[19] *Ibid.*, p. 160.

one or more cycles of polling, feedback, and evaluation, results tend to converge towards general agreement. A consensus does not necessarily result, but the range of disagreement is usually narrowed and salient issues are made explicit. The validity of the end results rests in the quality of expertise and the perceptiveness of the specialists' insights.

Another method is scenario writing, in which possible futures are created. A separate scenario is drawn up for each range of problems, with informational content representing value judgments when data are unavailable. Then, often with the aid of a computer, an assessment is made as to how these future goals can best be achieved and the probabilities of doing so. There are several approaches to the analysis, such as developing a set of equations to represent the technological progression. The computer models may be of two kinds, normative or descriptive. The current trend seems to be away from decision models, which yield a "best" solution, and towards information models, which provide information for decision makers to select from alternative futures.[20]

The Product Portfolio Concept

In matching a firm's capabilities to environmental factors, organizational plans are infused with life through budgets. For most of today's large and medium-sized corporations, this involves allocating funds among product lines that span a wide range of businesses. Corporate management must serve as a capital-allocating mechanism among different industries, a function once reserved for the stock market and investment bankers. But capital investment theory, which prescribes the evaluation of investment alternatives by calculating net return and comparing it with the cost of capital, cannot readily be applied to strategic planning. No answer is forthcoming as to whether one division should be given preference over another in capital budgeting or in what proportions the allocations should be made. When extended to many businesses or divisions, traditional investment theory becomes even more cumbersome as an operating device and offers little guidance. To deal with such problems of allocation, multiproduct companies have turned to portfolio selection theory.[21]

The portfolio approach regards a firm's different product lines as separate businesses and attempts to manage these asset-type holdings like an investment house overseeing securities. Each business can be expanded by capital investment, held for net earnings and cash yields, or dropped from the portfolio, either gradually or all at once. These three

---

[20] See P. Kelly and M. Kranzberg, *The Ecology of Innovation* (Springfield, Va.: National Technical Information Service, 1975), pp. 269–273.

[21] Ansoff, *op. cit.*, pp. 13–24.

strategies can, and usually are, employed simultaneously, for a corporation's various businesses are seldom in similar positions at comparable stages of development. The ability to combine different types of assets gives management greater flexibility and a wider range of alternative actions. A risky business, for example, can be balanced against a conservative one in which returns are more certain.[22] A new product with unstable markets can be traded off against new products with more predictable returns. But the central fact is the performance of the entire group of assets, the whole portfolio. The idea then is to manage the portfolio of businesses—shifting, adding, or dropping components—in order to achieve corporate objectives.

Three basic methods are available to evaluate the product portfolio: market share–growth rate matrix, multidimensional factors that evaluate market attractiveness and company strengths, and empirical methods. Each of these techniques stresses somewhat different aspects of the business portfolio, and they can be used separately or in combination with each other.

Market share–growth rate matrix

This is the earliest and probably the most popular method. Developed by the Boston Consulting Group, the model describes all elements of the product portfolio in terms of two factors, relative market share and market growth.[23] All other factors being equal, higher market shares than those of competitors will produce comparatively lower unit costs and higher profit margins because of the experience curve. The Boston Consulting Group thus regards share of market as a proxy for profits. Texas Instruments and Black & Decker are notable examples of companies achieving success by following the implications of the experience curve. Both have used aggressive marketing, disruptive pricing, and standardization in products to attain market share leadership and the consequent status of lowest cost producer. Black & Decker, for instance, is said to sell its power tools from 20 percent to 30 percent less than its major Japanese competitors in their home markets.

In like manner, the market growth factor, which can be described mathematically, derives from the product life cycle concept. Rapid growth corresponds to the early phases of a product's life, slow growth to maturity, and sliding sales to decline.

Both dimensions—relative market share and growth rate—are divided into two parts, high and low. The result is a four-item classification into which all businesses of the product portfolio are assigned:

---

[22] H. I. Ansoff and J. C. Leontiades, "Strategic Portfolio Management," *Journal of General Management* (Autumn, 1976), p. 13.

[23] Bruce D. Henderson, *The Experience Curve Reviewed: The Growth-Share Matrix or the Product Portfolio* (Boston: The Boston Consulting Group, 1973).

1. Low growth–high share.

2. High growth–high share.

3. Low growth–low share.

4. High growth–low share.

To each of these four groupings the Boston Consulting Group has attached colorful but memorable names—cash cow, star, dog, question mark. This version of the product portfolio, with its mixture of animals and things, is depicted graphically as a four-cell matrix in figure 4-3.

Figure 4-3. Market Share–Market Growth Matrix

Relative Market Share

	High	Low
High	Star	Question Mark
Low	Cash Cow	Dog

Market Growth

The market share–growth rate matrix reduces business classification to an extremely simplistic basis. But this accords with the widely held view among corporate executives that relatively few considerations account for the major portion of all business decisions. This point of view, seeking maximum information with minimal data, is given credence by the experience at the Wharton School, which found that large information systems designed for formulating strategy caused worse strategies than doing without the elaborate computer trappings.[24]

Cash cows, with high market shares in stable industries, comprise the mainstay of corporate funds. Since major investments in fixed assets are already in place, long-term capital requirements are modest. Because vendibles are produced for a mature market, the prospects for expanding sales are not bright. The obvious strategy for product lines

---

[24] J. R. Emshoff and I. I. Mitroff, "Improving the Effectiveness of Corporate Planning," *Business Horizons* (October, 1978), pp. 49–55. Also see Gee and Taylor, *op. cit.*, p. 110; James B. Whittaker, *Strategic Planning in a Rapidly Changing Environment* (Lexington, MA: D. C. Heath and Co., 1978), pp. 27–33.

classified as cash cows is management for earnings, which actually represent returns from past investments. The excess cash generated by these products go toward financing new business with more promising potential.

From the standpoint of product development, the strategy is one of investment in R&D and in product modifications and extensions sufficient to maintain market dominance—no more, no less. If overdone, such investments would probably run head-on into the afflictions of diminishing returns. If insufficient support is provided, highly successful products may be jeopardized. This view presumes that managers know exactly how much money it takes to sustain a product's current position. If mistakes are to be made, it would probably be best to err on the profligate side. Here, only the increment over and above that which is necessary is wasted. An error owing to parsimony, however, can depreciate the results of accumulated effort.

The stars, which refer to outstanding performers rather than celestial bodies, boast prominent brand shares in high-growth industries. Yet their cash inflow may be negative and their cash needs may be great. An expanding market lends encouragement to an aggressive sales policy, which must be accompanied by new investments in plants, equipment, and support systems. According to the Boston Consulting Group and most marketing authorities, there is virtue in seeking a bigger market share when growth is rapid. For one thing, the cost may be less than when growth stops, for the effort is directed towards making customers out of new users, and not out of someone else's customers. There is less resistance from buyers and less opposition from competitors.

The quadrant of a firm's portfolio which contains market leaders in young industries, though by no means the only source of growth, is probably the most important one. New product policies that have corporate growth as an objective—and most do—invariably focus on developing stars. New products designed to support brands in mature industries are not of an inconsequential nature, but they offer little growth. It is possible, and the practice goes on all the time, either to slither or muscle into a mature market. But it is the fast-growing markets where opportunities are greatest and where expansion-minded companies concentrate their efforts. True, new product failure rates run high. Yet innovators, on the whole, approach the opportunities with optimism, aspiring to create stars out of their new offerings. When performance does not meet expectations, the newly introduced products can thus be called "falling stars."

The rate at which corporate growth can be accomplished by cultivating high-growth fields depends upon the other quadrants of the product portfolio because cash availability is a balancing factor. The 3M

Company, for example, can manage about 100 new product introductions per year within the financial constraints imposed by top echelon executives.[25] Other companies will have different goals and rules for allocating resources. Above all, growth pursued in this manner must be sustainable. A too rapid rate usually results in cash deficiencies and may show up in low liquidity ratios, shortages in funds required for long-term investment, and higher proportions of debt to equity. Growth that is too slow in relation to cash flow indicates the company is foregoing opportunities. According to the Boston Consulting Group, maximum sustainable growth, assuming no equity financing, can be calculated by

the formula $G = \dfrac{D}{E}(R - i)\, p + Rp$, where:[26]

    G = Maximum sustainable growth of long-term assets.

    D/E = Debt-equity ratio.

    R = After-tax return on assets, in constant dollars.

    p = Rate of retained earnings.

    i = Current costs of debt, after taxes.

The dogs, with low shares in declining markets, have few interesting prospects. One option is to narrow the market to a specialized segment, where the product may compete favorably. If the brand cannot be resuscitated, the best strategy is to eliminate it. The only questions are how and when. The ailing business can be divested, usually through a sale as an operating entity. Another approach is to "milk" or "harvest" the business, cutting back all possible costs so as to capture its cash flow. When the cash stops flowing, the ultimate alternative is deletion of the business from the product portfolio. No matter what alternative is adopted to deal with dogs, the canines are usually given little or no funds for new products.

The question marks are like problem children who give signs of promise but consistently perform below par. These brands, operating in growth fields, are cash drains. And, if the problems remain uncorrected, they are bound to get worse. The conventional wisdom in these instances offers an alternative similar to the advice tough boatswain mates give raw naval recruits having difficulty in adjusting to their new quarters: "Shape up or ship out." But to convert a problem child into a sterling performer may require major financial commitments, with high risks accompanying the effort.

---

[25] Bernard Shaking, "Bet on People," *Barron's* (August 14, 1978), p. 4.

[26] Alan Zakon, *Growth and Financial Strategies* (Boston: The Boston Consulting Group, 1971).

The market share–growth rate matrix provides a convenient framework for outlining broad alternatives. It also affords a ready means of pinpointing strengths and problem areas among a large group of different product lines. In this respect, it is similar to exception reporting, long used in cost accounting to control operations. But the evaluation of specific business units requires caution. For example, there are numerous companies, as well as product lines, with small market shares performing better than market leaders.[27] One inference is that a loss of advantage from having a high market share can be compensated by strengths elsewhere in the corporation.

There may be other situations when profit margins are not related to market share or when the experience curve does not yield a comparative cost advantage to a market leader. A smaller producer may attain lower unit costs than a dominant firm by vertical integration or installation of newer, more efficient machinery. Savings because of better organization or more up-to-date plants and equipment may overcome the advantage of accumulated volume.[28] American steel manufacturers found their greater accumulated experience no match for the modernized, recently built plants of the Japanese. The oriental blast furnaces, of larger size than contemporary American models, can produce 9,000+ tons of molten metal daily, as compared with an average U.S. capability of 2,000 to 3,000 tons a day. They also produce the larger volume more efficiently as they were designed to withstand extremely high temperatures and pressures. In February, 1980, U.S. Steel Corporation, the leading American steel producer, announced that it had signed a three-year contract with Nippon Steel Corporation of Japan for technical aid to increase productivity of its blast furnaces.[29] Procter and Gamble was a latecomer to the toilet tissue market. Yet its greater resources and integrated organization—operating forest lands, manufacturing and distribution facilities—made the firm a low-cost producer and also put it head and shoulders above the rest of the field as a market leader.

Generalizations about cats and dogs are dependent upon specific situations related to a firm.[30] For every seller of a dog or problem child, there is a buyer. What may look like a mongrel to one firm may appear

[27] R. G. Hamermesh, *et. al.*, "Strategies for Low Market Share Businesses," *Harvard Business Review* (May–June, 1978), pp. 95–102; "Market Share-ROI Corporate Strategy Approach Can Be an 'Oversimplistic Snare'," *Marketing News* (Dec. 15, 1978), pp. 6–7.

[28] See Michael E. Porter, "How Competitive Forces Shape Strategy," *Harvard Business Review* (May–April, 1979), pp. 137–145.

[29] Douglas R. Sease, "Nippon Steel Receives U.S. Steel Contract for Advice on Improving Blast Furnaces," *Wall Street Journal* (February 14, 1980), p. 2.

[30] Edward H. Bowman, "Epistemology, Corporate Strategy, and Academe," *Sloan Management Review* (Winter, 1974), pp. 35–50.

like a pedigree to another. A problem child may likewise seem like a
budding genius to the acquiring company. A portfolio analysis will usually find considerations other than those of market share or growth,
and these must be handled as supplemental to the market share–growth
rate matrix.[31] Comparisons of business opportunities or new products
are usually done separately, as they encompass criteria outside the
confines of the two-dimensional matrix.

Figure 4-4. Market Attractiveness–Business Strength Matrix

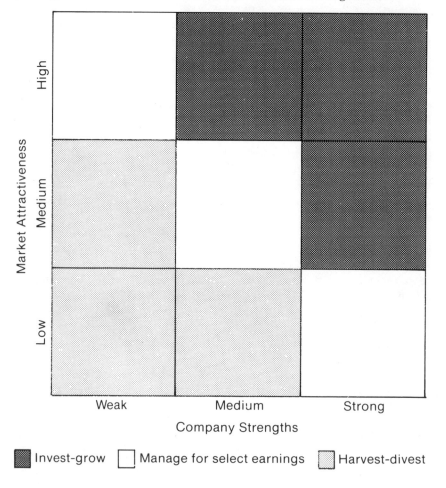

Market attractiveness–business position matrix

This method, too, employs a two-dimensional display to depict business situations of the product portfolio. In some respects, this approach is a modification of the two-factor, Boston Consulting Group matrix. The growth axis, however, is converted into a multifactor index of market attractiveness.[32] In like manner, the market share axis is transformed into an index of business strengths. Share of market and industrial growth are usually included among the factors. But the approach is multidimensional. The format is presented graphically as a nine-box diagram, which is illustrated in figure 4-4.

The diagram in figure 4-4 relates market factors to company resources. The weightings of each factor, which make up the overall score of attractiveness and strengths, are determined by management judgment. High ratings on both internal strengths and industry attractiveness suggest investment opportunities. When the two indexes fall towards the low end of the scale, the analysis indicates that a harvesting or divestiture strategy is in order.

Factors used in this multidimensional approach may include nonfinancial and qualitative elements, such as patent protection, ecological issues, product liability, and the like. The same format can be used to assess different investment proposals for new businesses. Figure 4-5 shows how new business ventures can be compared with each other by matching external and internal factors.

The chart shown in figure 4-5 is the same as in figure 4-4, but it has been transformed into an "identity chart," which compares four proposed projects. According to this particular visual display, the new business proposals were weighted by twelve factors, six for business attractiveness and six for company capability.

This company apparently believes that any project with a total index of less than seventy points has a poor probability of being successful. Hence, Project I would definitely be passed over. Projects II and III are marginal and might be considered if the fitness factors, in management judgment, can be improved. Project IV, with a total score of 100 points, seems to have a high likelihood of commercial success, which translates into business attractiveness plus company strength. Thus, the transformed attractiveness–company fitness matrix can be used as a basis for screening and analyzing new product proposals.

The nine-box matrix is more flexible than the four-cell product portfolio inasmuch as it can include many more variables. It can also be applied to evaluation of new business investments as well as to current

---

[32] William E. Rothschild, *Putting It All Together: A Guide to Thinking* (New York: AMACOM, 1976).

products. As illustrated in figure 4-5, the same format can also be used to create composite scores for the various businesses, current or prospective. The weightings that make up such scores are judgmental, and sometimes called arbitrary. As such, results of these analyses represent management expectations rather than probable outcomes. Some companies, like GE, have thus sought to blend management expectations with empirical data, so that hopes for the future can be judged against likelihoods of their attainment.

Figure 4-5. Business Attractiveness–Company Fit Visual Display

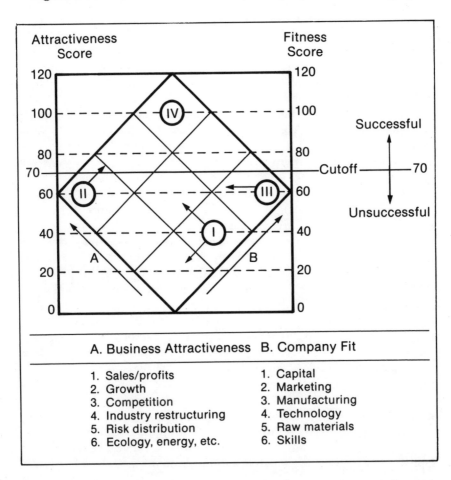

A. Business Attractiveness   B. Company Fit

A. Business Attractiveness	B. Company Fit
1. Sales/profits	1. Capital
2. Growth	2. Marketing
3. Competition	3. Manufacturing
4. Industry restructuring	4. Technology
5. Risk distribution	5. Raw materials
6. Ecology, energy, etc.	6. Skills

Adapted from D. Bruce Merrifield, "Strategic Analysis, Selection and Management of R&D Projects," *AMA Management Briefing* (New York: AMACOM, a division of American Management Association, 1977, p. 20).

Empirical methods

The best known and most influential body of empirical data emerged from Marketing Science Institute's PIMS project, now being carried on by the Strategic Planning Institute. PIMS, an acronym for "profit impact marketing strategies," identified some thirty seven profit influences in analyzing statistics of 602 businesses during a three-year period. A major finding of PIMS is one that marketers have long suspected. The analysis provides ample evidence that share of market is related to return on investment. This relationship is depicted graphically in figure 4-6.

Figure 4-6. Market Share–Pretax ROI Relationship

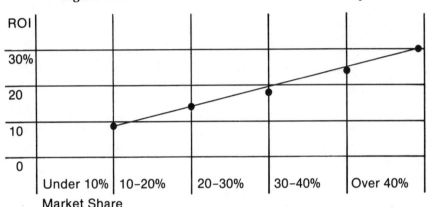

Figure 4-6 shows that, on the average, each ten percentage points in market share was accompanied by five percentage points in pretax return on investment. However, market share by itself is not a strong determinant of profitability, although it is the most important of all individual factors. That is, all factors combined, according to PIMS, account for about 80 percent of the total observable variance in profitability.[33] But less than one-fifth of this 80 percent, or some 15 percent of the total variation, can be attributed to market share. The remainder is associated with other factors.

Among the other important elements associated with profitability is product quality, which seems to go hand in hand with market share. Superior quality is related to high market share, and vice versa. Of all

---

[33] Sidney Schoeffler, "SPI Seeks Science, Not Single, 'Oversimplistic' Strategy Variable: Another Look at Market Share," *Marketing News* (February 9, 1979), p. 1.

products ranked superior in quality, about half enjoyed market shares of
26 percent or better, In contrast, 47 percent of the inferior-rated products held market shares of less than 12 percent on the average. The
distribution of market shares for products of varying quality is shown
in table 4-5.

Table 4-5
Percent Distribution of Product Quality by Share of Market

Percent of businesses with...	Market Share		
	Under 12%	12–26%	More than 26%
Inferior quality	47%	33%	20%
Average quality	30%	36%	30%
Superior quality	23%	31%	50%
No. of businesses	(169)	(176)	(176)

Source: Sidney Schoeffler, *et. al.*, "Impact of Strategic Planning on Profit Performance," *Harvard Business Review*, (March–April, 1974), p. 141.

How does market share, together with product quality, affect profitability? This is shown in table 4-6, wherein average return on investment is calculated for each combination of market share–product
quality grouping.

Table 4-6
Effect of Market Share and Product Quality on
Pretax Return on Investment

Market Share	Product Quality		
	Inferior	Average	Superior
Under 12%	4.5%	10.4%	17.4%
12%–26%	11.0%	18.1%	18.1%
More than 26%	19.5%	21.9%	28.3%

Source: Schoeffler, *et. al., op. cit.*

As shown in table 4-6, the best returns on the average were achieved
by brands with high market share and high quality. But brands with low
shares of market made good showings if they possessed superior quality. Such low share–high quality brands yielded investment returns
averaging 17.4 percent before taxes, an acceptable level. It would thus
seem that good quality is a decided advantage in bringing out new
products to market.

Market share also appears to be of greater importance with respect
to infrequently purchased products.[34] These tend to be industrial

---
[34] Buzzell, *et. al., op. cit.*, p. 97.

goods or high-priced consumer durables. Market share–profitability relationships are less evident in convenience goods, which are less strongly differentiated. This lends support for using a new products policy as a competitive weapon.

PIMS can complement the judgmental methods by blending them with actual experience. In this way, executive desires can be assessed against probable outcomes in the real world. Such analysis can be invaluable in planning because it helps to define goals more realistically. But like all experience, valuable though it be, it is embedded in the past, while strategy must address itself to the future.

REVIEW QUESTIONS

1. Explain the meaning of corporate mission, objectives, policy, strategy and planning, and implementation with respect to new products.

2. Differentiate between general objectives and specific objectives.

3. Explain the meaning of strategic planning.

4. Explain the relationship of goals to tactics.

5. New product decisions are both strategic and tactical. Describe the type of product decisions that are tactically oriented and those that have strategic intentions.

6. Compare the process of strategic planning in the small unidivisional firm with that of the large multidivisional firm.

7. Explain the meaning of new product policy and provide hypothetical examples.

8. New product suggestions are judged by reference to the firm's mission, objectives, goals, and policies. Use hypothetical examples to illustrate the judgment process.

9. When a firm's relative strengths and weaknesses are being determined, what are the principal areas of examination?

10. What is the relationship between a firm's strengths and weaknesses and the existing conditions in the firm's external environment?

11. Contemplate the broad strategic product problems that many consumer goods companies are facing in light of the expected long-term changes in the age distribution of the population.

12. The trend of household formation differs from that of population growth. Why and what are the consumer spending implications for the future?

13. How can a firm's strategic product planning take advantage of technological forecasting?

14. Explain the central thesis of the product portfolio approach to strategic product management.

15. Briefly outline the Boston Consulting Group's philosophy of product portfolio management.

16. What are the pitfalls of the somewhat simplistic approach of the Boston Consulting Group to product management?

17. What are the major profit influences uncovered by the PIMS study? Explain the relationships.

5/ Product Mix Alternatives

New products can support existing businesses or create new ones. A business can be defined in terms of three dimensions: markets, products, and technology.

Most large and medium-sized firms are diversified, operating in different business fields. Diversification can be either offensive or defensive. In the former instance, the strategy offers a firm the means of taking utmost advantage of opportunities. In the latter instance, the firm adopts diversification to avoid future adversities or to rectify present conditions deemed undesirable.

Diversification can be related or unrelated to a firm's existing product lines. Related diversification can move in a vertical or horizontal direction, with synergistic effects derived from either way. The unrelated or conglomerate form derives no advantages from synergy.

Development of new products can be approached internally or externally. Both methods are used simultaneously.

An R&D capability, which concerns itself with a new product's physical characteristics, is necessary to the internal route. Real growth of R&D in the seventies averaged about 2 percent per annum. The slowdown was especially marked in basic research, the real growth of which has been negligible over the last two decades. As a consequence, its percentage of total industrial R&D expenditures has declined steadily from 1960 onwards.

The external approach to diversification and new products can come through several sources: mergers and acquisitions, licenses and patents, or joint ventures. There are, however, important constraints for firms seeking these routes, especially that of mergers and acquisitions. These corporate takeovers must be carried out within the rules governed by national antitrust legislation.

Defining a Business

Strategic planning, carried out at different corporate levels, gives shape to the businesses a firm operates. In like manner, new product activities define a firm's businesses of the future. Yet top managements seldom make such definitions purposefully or explicitly. As Abell and

Hammond astutely observe, decisions concerning new products are made piecemeal on the basis of a project's merits, and not on the basis of overall strategy. The definition of a future business thus becomes dependent upon action instead of action depending upon the definition. Such planning, the authors conclude, are at odds with the rationalistic view, which, as subscribed to by most managements, holds that a future can be determined, fabricated like an item coming off an assembly line, and controlled for volume and quality.[1]

One reason for this dichotomy is that the two forms of planning have different requirements and make use of different theoretical structures. Strategic planning, with its widespread adoption of portfolio selection theory, focuses on cash flows among corporate businesses. New products, with its dedication to capital investment theory, focus on returns over the life of newly created assets. Strategic planning must acknowledge the presence of uncertainty in varying degrees. New product decisions usually assume that all uncertainty is converted into risk and that rewards can be calculated from expected values and probabilities.

Even the "company resources–market attractiveness" approach, which sees return on investment as the central fact in manipulating a product portfolio, differs from that of new products in several important respects. The former, like most strategic planning efforts, paints its canvas of corporate businesses in broad strokes. It allocates resources in accordance with prospective returns but makes few inquiries as to why and how. On the other hand, new product decisions call for minute detail and exhaustive analyses of a business and its environments. But corporate planners cannot apply such information to each part of a company's portfolio without bringing down the entire planning process into an unwholesome morass of elaborate trivialities. The demand for sparsity of information follows a common sense line of reasoning. While few business activities run according to ironclad rules, exceptions will do little harm when they are spread over a portfolio of many products. But individual new product proposals cannot tolerate generalizations, for a deviation from the norm is an unequivocal failure. Rather, they must be regarded as unique, discrete entities to be analyzed in detail and considered on their own merits.

Broad units of analysis are also preferable in strategic planning in order to match cost and revenue. Cash flows and investment returns cannot be compared satisfactorily when they partake of common costs. Ideally, each business unit in a strategic plan should have its own marketing, production, and R&D, so that costs can be traced directly to operations. But joint costs are no hindrance to new product evaluations.

---

[1] Abell and Hammond, *Strategic Market Planning*, pp. 396–397.

Such costs, in fact, are often desirable because they indicate the existence of synergy and possibly a more efficient utilization of resources.

As explained in chapter 2, new product decisions include three major elements that define a business—markets, products, and technology. A business definition then poses three basic questions:

1. Who is served? (markets)

2. What is served? (products)

3. How is the product served? (technology)

These three factors of a business—markets, products, technology—are interrelated, influenced by and influencing each other. Illustrative of this interdependence are the printing trades. Developments in offset printing during the sixties and early seventies created a growing demand for phototypesetting. But the demand was highly diverse. Machines in use ranged from simply operated Selectric typewriters to complex phototypesetters driven by large computers. Even manufacturers of supplies were able to alter standard items to meet the diverse requirements of customers. Small companies, such as Chemco Photo Products, were able to compete in film with the industry giants, Eastman Kodak and DuPont, by serving the low-quality end of the market. Recently, cameras based on a laser technology have entered the marketplace, ostensibly to meet the close deadlines and short work schedules of newspapers. These cameras produce plates directly from page mechanicals and so eliminate film development altogether.

Firms may emphasize one aspect of the market-product-technology triad more than others, depending upon the nature of the business. In general, innovative products come about as a response to the pull of market demand rather than the push of technology.[2] This is sometimes referred to as the "wet noodle" principle. Innovation is likened to a soggy noodle, which can be moved more easily when pulled than when pushed. Regardless of the prime cause, an act of innovation can occur anywhere.

New Products–New Businesses

Although a new business implies a new product, not all new products lead to new businesses. A firm's stream of new products can flow in various directions, with wide-ranging alternatives. At one extreme, a new product may be developed for a business already being pursued, such as a detergent manufacturer adding another washing agent to the line. At the other end of the continuum, the new offering may go into a

[2] Frank H. Healy, "Industry's Needs for Basic Research," *Research Management* (November, 1978), p. 16.

business distinctly different from anything a company presently operates. And there are varying degrees of similarities and differences in
between.

If a business is defined as a combination of markets, products, and
technology, which the early part of this chapter has done, then the
concept of a business becomes an elastic one. The same product may
serve diverse markets, such as one tire maker selling retail and another
plying the industrial route. Both manufacturers are in the tire business.
But are they in the same business? Similarly, the same customers can be
wooed by marketers of different products, as steel and aluminum industries competing for the patronage of can makers. Because the major
elements of a business will seldom meld in identical proportions for
all firms, even competitors may define their businesses somewhat
differently.

Notwithstanding the delicate nuances of definition, a product can be
developed either for an existing business or for one that differs from
those in a firm's current portfolio. When the latter situation prevails, it
is referred to as diversification. The majority of large companies today
embrace diversification as a way of life, operating in many different
lines of business. From 1950 to 1970, single business firms among the
Fortune 500 fell from 30 percent to a meager 8 percent.[3]

The advantages of being diversified are many. To a particular firm,
motives can be offensive, defensive, or both.

In the first instance, diversification can put a company in a convenient position to capitalize on new opportunities by virtue of operating
in more varied situations. These favorable occasions can arise from
entry into new markets and product lines, adoption of new processes, or
appropriation of new technologies. Moreover, diversification can create
conditions for utilizing financial resources more efficiently. Cash can be
routed from areas of surpluses to those of deficiencies, reducing the
need for working capital. Funds can be transferred from high cash flow
businesses to low ones, producing a better overall balance in the firm's
portfolio.

Defensive diversification seeks protection from possible adversity in
the future or redress from unfavorable conditions in the present. Both
motives may be present at the same time.

Spreading investments among diverse businesses serves as a hedge
against adverse effects of competitive and technological shifts. It sets
limits, so to speak, to a firm's contingent liabilities. Consequently,
companies have sought to avoid dependence on a narrow product line or
on markets that are dominated by few buyers. Though doing well,
many companies in aerospace and missiles saw themselves vulnerable to

---

[3] M. S. Salter and W. A. Weinhold, "Diversification Via Acquisition: Creating Value,"
Harvard Business Review (July–August, 1978), p. 166.

the changing winds of politics and moved to lower their reliance on government orders.

Poor prospects in traditional fields have spurred firms toward diversification. Cigarette companies have for many years been decreasing their relative stakes in tobacco and enhancing their positions in foods and beverages. U.S. Steel from 1974 onwards has been investing heavily in chemicals, where growth is higher than in steel. One reason Pillsbury acquired Green Giant in 1979 is that it bought insurance against the threat of surging meat prices, which might injure profits of Burger King, the corporation's leading source of revenue.[4]

Another type of defensive diversification aims at stabilizing revenue and earnings. This can be accomplished by adding businesses with counter-seasonal or cyclical sales patterns, so as to minimize fluctuations in demand. RCA's acquisition of C.I.T. Financial in 1980 was motivated in part by a desire to offset cyclical businesses in electronics, broadcasting, and car rentals with a more steady earnings flow largely unresponsive to alternating waves of prosperity and recession. Greater stability is also achieved by spreading risk, whereby adversity in one field might be offset by successes elsewhere.

Whether diversification efforts are offensive or defensive, they are either related or unrelated to a company's present mode of operations. On the one hand, the new business may share facilities and resources with existing businesses, a form of mutual aid known as synergy. This happens when a resource in one business provides a competitive advantage to another business. On the other hand, the new business may have nothing in common with any other operating unit of the corporation except that of central financial control. Corporations characterized by diversified businesses with little relationship to each other are often called conglomerates. A prime example of a conglomerate is the LTV Corporation, with operations in industries as dissimilar as aerospace, meat and food products, steel, and common carriers in ocean transportation.

New businesses that are related can proceed in one of two directions—horizontal or vertical. The first refers to businesses in the same industry. The second form of diversification entails starting up new businesses at different levels of production in related industries.

To summarize, new ventures can move along many different paths. The main routes are as follows:

1. New products can go into an existing business or a new one.

2. The new business may be related or unrelated to a firm's current operations. Related businesses can yield synergistic benefits.

---

[4] "Pillsbury's Ambitious Plans to Use Green Giant," *Business Week,* (February 5, 1979), p. 87.

3. If related, new businesses can move in horizontal or vertical directions.

The diagram in figure 5-1 charts the possible movements that new products may take.

Figure 5-1. Possible Routes for New Products

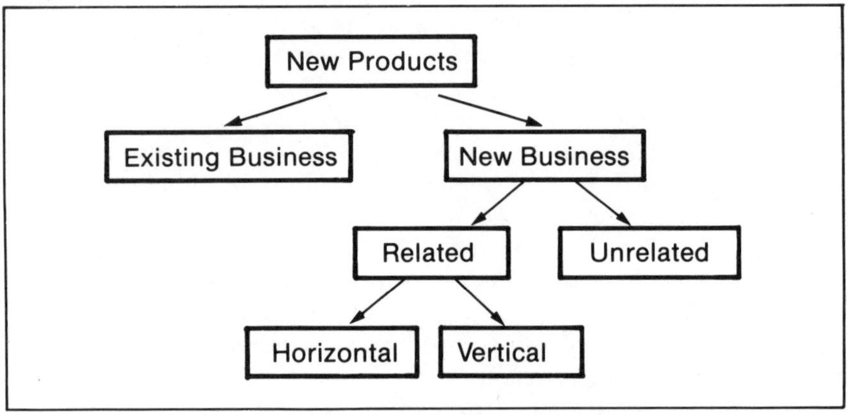

New Ventures and Synergy

The closer a new product is related to ongoing businesses, the lower its relative cost for development and commercialization. This is why modifications and line extensions are so highly popular. Striving to advance present operations, these new offerings are most compatible with a firm's existing resources—people, skills, physical and financial assets.

But synergy can also be realized in diversification. New products moving in horizontal or vertical directions and bearing some relationship to existing assets may yield salutary effects.

A horizontal diversification sends out its different product lines into fields with manifest affinities. A manufacturer of dog food deciding to begin a line of cat food would illustrate a new product that adds horizontal diversification. Other examples are General Foods marketing beverages as diverse as coffee and Kool Aid; CBS expanding in the media field from broadcasting to magazine publishing; a swimsuit manufacturer introducing "wearabouts," items for lounging on the beach.

Investments in product lines that are related promise greater efficiency and lower average costs. Such products can share the same production facilities, the same warehouses and distribution agencies, and often the same sales and marketing personnel. If a company is not operating at a maximum capacity, which is quite common, a new line closely related to others will absorb some proportion of fixed costs. In short, savings can accrue from economies of scale, rationalization of production, and technical innovation.

Chances of success are also enhanced when the new business has available a high level of competence in a relevant area. This key factor may be in marketing, production, or technology.

Synergistic advantages arising from competence in marketing are admirably demonstrated in the grocery field, which offers wide scope for diversification within established business areas. Products carried by typical retail outlets are large in number and highly varied. An average supermarket features some 7,000 items, foods and nonfoods, with no salesmen to steer customers to particular brands. The manufacturer seeking these outlets must assume the role of channel captain, solely responsible for creating demand. But those companies that have become skillful in marketing goods via self-service outlets, it is generally felt, can transfer their know-how and organizational competence to almost any item retailing in this manner.[5]

Perhaps the outstanding example of a company developing new businesses in the grocery trade by virtue of marketing ability is Procter and Gamble. Applying its marketing expertise and distribution network to packaged goods, P&G was able to carve out for itself huge shares of market in a wide variety of areas: household cleaners, soaps, dentifrices, paper towels and toilet tissues, personal care products, coffee, baby diapers, cake mixes. In almost every instance, the formula for success was the same—excellent distribution coverage in retail outlets, accompanied by heavy advertising and promotion.

New products reaching out for diverse fields can also be aided from the technical side, as with GE. One important set of product lines embodies items as different as major appliances, TV sets, and light bulbs. These products have little in common with respect to channels of distribution or markets. Many are sold directly to both consumers and industry through separate agencies. Some businesses are almost as far apart as those of LTV Corp., except for their common roots in an electrical technology. And these binding elements may, in some instances, be as slender as the delicate thread suspending a busy spider. Such hybrid-like diversification spans numerous customer groups and product categories and gives rise to more specialized business units. In turn, this strengthens the impetus for further extension by offering advantages from specialization.

New ventures can also derive synergistic effects by pursuing the route of vertical integration. This form of diversification can be done

---

[5] Louis W. Stern, "Acquisitions: Another Viewpoint," *Journal of Marketing* (July, 1967), p. 43.

either forward or backward. Forward integration, as the term implies, carries activities closer to end users. Backward integration connotes the reverse, a movement toward the raw material.

The benefits of forward integration, in large measure, depend upon the starting point. If diversification proceeds from the raw material or component stage to finished goods, opportunities may be created for a widening market. A prime example of this strategy was afforded by Texas Instruments, originally a semiconductor manufacturer, moving into consumer electronics, first into calculator markets and later into digital watches. Wedded to the concept of volume, Texas Instruments drove down prices to expand sales rapidly and capture a big share of growing markets. With superior R&D skills and manufacturing ability, partly aided by declining unit costs as volume rose, the firm introduced a wide variety of designs at constantly lower prices. In a span of about five years, Texas Instruments became a dominant force in the consumer electronics business. By bringing its products closer to their end use, Texas Instruments also increased the value added of its output.

The movement from raw materials to finished goods, however, is not without its problems. It may lead to markets with which the firm has little experience and limited knowledge. Even the thrust of Texas Instruments into the consumer end of the trade was sometimes in doubt in spite of its advantages in production and technology. Its marketing ineptness and indiscreet pricing actions at times infuriated most of the nation's retailers.[6]

A second potential danger is if the raw material producer, by moving into finished goods production, now begins to compete with its own customers. Monsanto, a supplier of basic chemicals, found itself in that kind of situation when it developed All dishwasher detergent. To avoid customer ill-will and loss of business in its more important product lines, Monsanto sold its competitive finished goods facilities to Lever Brothers, a detergent and soap manufacturer.

Forward integration may also commence at the manufacturing stage and move closer to the end user in varying degrees. A forward step is taken when a manufacturer relying wholly upon middlemen begins taking on channel functions and physical distribution activities. In these instances, new products or widening markets are incidental. Rather, the objectives are improved profit and better control over the flow of goods in distribution channels, though the two do not always go together. Direct sales by manufacturers eliminate middlemen and middlemen's markups as well. Storage in company warehouses and deliveries in company trucks, provided volume is sufficient, do away with profits to

---

6 "Texas Instruments Shows U.S. Business How to Survive in the 1980's" *Business Week* (September 18, 1978), p. 67.

outside agencies. This was the main reason the Ranier Corporation, operating in forest products, started a carrying company. With plants located near sources of raw materials and customers spread throughout the world, Ranier drastically reduced its transportation costs by going into the ocean shipping business. The ultimate step in forward integration is selling directly to the end user, which is often accomplished with industrial products. Consumer goods are more difficult to integrate completely, particularly at the retail level. Sometimes, however, it can be accomplished, as with gasoline stations owned and operated by the large oil companies.

The market aspect of backward integration is seldom important, though product development is required. This is essentially a capital-intensive strategy, for sales will show no increase whatsoever after intercompany eliminations if no raw materials or components are sold to other firms. But profits may rise to the extent that it is usually cheaper producing raw materials internally than ordering from the outside. If the raw material or component end of the business is operated as a profit center, the additional profit to the corporation is reflected in the difference between external sales and incremental costs and expenses in obtaining that revenue. Reported returns for the profit center, however, pose problems because of transfer prices and conventional cost accounting.

Vertical integration may also reduce risks by giving the firm much greater control over supplies. It reduces company exposure to variations in price and disruptions in the flow of materials. But these advantages may be more apparent than real if the raw materials are under the control of a foreign nation with internal instability.

Internal Approach to New Ventures

New product development for either related or unrelated businesses can be approached internally or externally. The do-it-yourself method is a virtual necessity for new products meant to support or expand current businesses. This does not imply that outside agencies will not, or should not, be used in such circumstances. On the contrary, many companies make excellent use of specialists to supplement their own capabilities. But a firm can hardly hope to compete successfully if it must look to the outside to obtain a relative advantage in a business it actively pursues. The issue is one of emphasis. To depend upon outside agencies for success is to run a business on the brink of peril. This supports the proposition that a firm's resources should be compatible with the business in which it is engaged.

The internal route to new products can also be advantageous when development aims at new businesses. Return on investment can be generous, especially when there is synergy between the new venture and the firm's resources. The closer the relationship between the new business and existing product lines, the greater the synergistic effects.

Another advantage of internal development is realized from accounting for R&D expenditures. These costs are generally expensed, which permits more than 50 percent of the cash expended to be recovered quickly through a favorable tax treatment. In most instances, however, R&D makes up a minor part of the total costs of establishing a new business. But the larger the R&D portion in relation to capitalized costs, the less expensive will be each dollar spent in setting up the new venture.

The developmental aspects of the physical product are normally determined in R&D. Industrial R&D includes both basic and applied research in science and engineering, as well as design and development of prototypes and processes. This definition, adhered to by the National Science Foundation (NSF), divides R&D into three parts: basic research, applied research, and development. NSF has defined each segment as follows:[7]

1. *Basic Research.* The purpose of basic research is the extension of scientific knowledge by exploring underlying cause-and-effect relationships. As defined by NSF, basic research projects in industry typify "original investigations for the advancement of scientific knowledge . . . which do not have specific commercial objectives, although they may be in fields of present or potential interest to the reporting company."

2. *Applied Research.* Applied research is directed towards practical applications of knowledge, specific ends concerning products and processes. It is "targeted," using research findings to solve problems in development and design. Consequently, applied research differs from basic research mainly in terms of company objectives.

3. *Development.* According to NSF, development embraces "the systematic use of scientific knowledge directed toward the production of useful materials, devices, systems or methods, including design and development of prototypes and processes."

R&D Trends in U.S. Industry

Both the absolute dollar amount of R&D and its configuration will differ markedly from industry to industry and company to company. Yet firms are part of a broader social and economic system and, for all their differences, are subject to a common set of influences. These underlying trends in U.S. industry consequently affect the amount and types of new products developed internally.

---

[7] National Science Foundation, *National Patterns of R&D Resources, 1953–77*, NSF 77–310, p. 19.

Despite the fact that much of R&D ultimately becomes embodied in products, there is no known method of measuring its performance. Hence, expenditures or input are used to assess R&D activity rather than output. In these terms, industrial funds allocated to R&D have risen each year without interruption from about $4.5 billion in 1960 to an estimated $24.6 billion in 1979. Annual figures for industry R&D funding are shown in table 5-1. Performance figures relate to the value of work actually done, regardless of whether funds came from industry or government.

Table 5-1

Industry R&D Expenditures, by Funding and Performance
(in Millions of Dollars)

Year	Industry Funding		Industry Performance	
	Current Dollars	1972 Dollars	Current Dollars	1972 Dollars
1960	4,516	8,025	10,509	18,556
1961	4,757	8,206	10,908	18,729
1962	5,123	8,432	11,464	18,786
1963	5,456	8,675	12,630	20,014
1964	5,888	9,126	13,512	20,888
1965	6,548	9,809	14,185	21,185
1966	7,328	10,179	15,548	21,580
1967	8,142	10,731	16,385	21,596
1968	9,005	11,211	17,429	21,724
1969	10,010	11,842	18,308	21,659
1970	10,439	11,535	18,062	20,191
1971	10,813	11,386	18,311	19,329
1972	11,698	11,698	19,539	19,539
1973	13,278	12,654	21,233	20,140
1974	14,854	12,789	22,867	19,601
1975	15,787	12,582	24,164	19,178
1976	17,634	13,066	26,677	19,730
1977	19,724	13,807	29,823	20,713
1978	21,780	13,961	33,250	21,299
1979*	24,626	14,431	37,450	21,943

*Estimates of Battelle, Columbus.

Source: Estimates of expenditures in current dollars, National Science Foundation, *National Patterns of R&D Resources, Funds and Personnel in the United States, 1953-1978-79, NSF 68-313*. Estimates for 1972 dollars derived from cost of research index, Battelle, *Probable Levels of R&D Expenditures in 1979*, p. 14.

The increase in dollar expenditures is somewhat misleading because inflation ate into most of the growing corporate budgets. As prices rose, less and less R&D could be purchased with the same dollars. When expenditures in current dollars are adjusted for inflation, the impressive 146 percent increase during the past decade shrivels to a paltry 22 percent, or a little better than 2 percent per annum on the average. This compares with an average annual rate for industry funding of almost two-and-a-half times for the ten years previous, indicating a slower pace in R&D activity.

The adjustments for inflation shown in table 5-1 have not followed the common practice of using a GNP deflator for calculating R&D costs. The reason is because the general price level includes both goods and services, whereas R&D is made up mainly of the latter. Salaries dominate itemized expense sheets. Real R&D costs were thus calculated on the basis of the Milton index, as extended by Battelle, Columbus. Helen Milton in 1966 began gathering information from a representative group of R&D performers and compiled a cost series that ended in 1970. Battelle, Columbus has rebased this index to 1972, disaggregated costs by major R&D sectors, and projected the figures to succeeding years.

Even the small real growth is somewhat misleading because a larger portion of R&D budgets is being earmarked for what might be called "previous externalities." These are benefits that accrue to a firm not by reason of its own actions but because of conditions that prevail in society. For example, industry was once permitted to transport and burn coal with no regard to the dust and sulphur dioxide emitted into the atmosphere. Since the public assumed the burden of environmental pollution, industry was unwittingly given a subsidy in the form of lower energy costs. These conditions have since been reversed, and now "negative subsidies" are being mandated. Industry is being forced to rectify society's past mistakes, laxities, and permissiveness—sometimes with a vengeance. When current costs of such externalities are considered, the real growth in industrial R&D funding might well evaporate into nothingness.

Industry also performs almost half the R&D funded by the federal government. When this is combined with its own expenditures, industry carries out about 70 percent of all R&D performed in the United States (see figure 5-2). In terms of performance, industrial R&D expenditures have indicated virtually no real growth during the past decade. Expenditures peaked in 1968 at $21.7 billion, as expressed in 1972 dollars, and for the next ten years averaged about $20.1 billion. (See table 5-1.)

As industrial R&D funding has experienced a slowdown, basic research has suffered a decline since 1960. In the past quarter century, basic research fell from about 7 percent to 4 percent of total R&D funds provided by industry. The declining proportion and rates of change are delineated in table 5-2.

Figure 5-2. Industrial Performance as a Percentage of Total R&D Expenditures in the U.S. (in Constant 1972 Dollars)

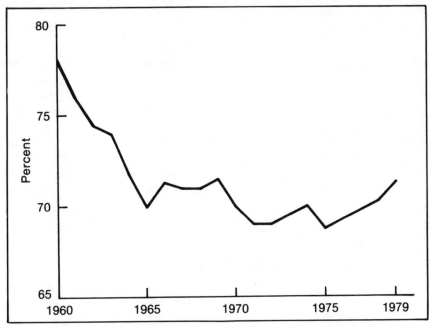

Source: Frank H. Healy, "Industry's Needs for Basic Research," *Research Management* (November, 1978), p. 16.

Table 5-2
Relative Expenditures for Basic Research
(in Constant 1972 Dollars)

Year	Basic Research as a Percentage of Total Industrial R&D Expenditures (%)	Percent Change (%)
1960	7.3	—
1965	6.9	—0.49
1970	4.9	—1.97
1975	4.4	—0.51
1976	4.3	—0.5

Source: Healy, *op. cit.*, p. 14.

Despite real economic growth, basic research budgets in 1975 averaged only 9 percent higher than those of 1960 in terms of 1972 dollars. The reasons for industry neglect of R&D are many. The main ones, however, are those dealing with top management sober control, project selection, economic conditions, and government.[8]

Top management control

While the research community has maintained its ardent faith that basic research ultimately redounds to the benefit of society, top corporate management has succumbed to gnawing doubts. Actually, four industries account for more than three-quarters of all basic research— chemicals, electric equipment and communications, aerospace and missiles, and machinery. High costs and vague promises of returns have relegated such investigations to the corporate giants, such as GE, AT&T, and DuPont. As one author described basic research, "It is a high-stakes gamble, to be undertaken by those who can best afford to lose the bet."[9] But even those who can ante up the high stakes do not like to lose. Unable to demonstrate that its budgets resulted directly in payoffs, basic research fell increasingly under the sway of business control. Some writers have gone so far as to claim that business control systems, especially in large corporations, are inimical to innovation.[10] In any case, the era of undirected research has come to a resolute end. In 1976 more than 40 percent of member firms of the Industrial Research Institute reported having a top-level R&D policy committee, a structure unheard of ten years before. Opinions veered sharply as to whether fundamental scientific investigations were legitimate business activities, with most corporate executives viewing them as belonging to universities. And there most of basic research now resides.

Project selection

R&D funding in most corporations has passed over to operating divisions that, by controlling the budget, also control project selection. Together with management's desire for payoffs, operating divisions have placed increasing emphasis upon development, not research. More and more, R&D has become "targeted," seeking opportunities through the exploitation of available technology and not by attempts to extend it. Returns are wanted now, not in some far away future.

Economic conditions

The buoyancy of the sixties, which created a climate wherein basic research could thrive, gave way to the more sober mood of the seven-

---

[8] See George E. Manners, Jr. and Howard K. Nason, "The Decline of Industrial Research—Causes and Cures." *Research Management* (September, 1978), pp. 8–11.

[9] Dan Cordtz, "Bringing the Laboratory Down to Earth," *Fortune* (January, 1971), p. 107.

[10] James D. Hlavacek and Victor A. Thompson, "Bureaucracy and New Product Innovation," *Academy of Management Journal* (September, 1973), pp. 361–372; and "Goliath or Tom Thumb?" *Business Management* (December, 1969), pp. 35–36; J. G. Hughs, "Breaking Down the Barriers to Innovation," *Marketing Review* (January–February, 1977), pp. 16–18.

ties. Economic weakness and general inflation, fueled by rising energy costs, have put a damper on profits. At the same time, a decline in the real value of accrued depreciation has made the replacement of capital assets more difficult. The result of this balance sheet malady has been an investment lag not only in plant and equipment, but in research that generates new technology. An active R&D program makes little sense when a firm is squeezed for investment funds to implement the R&D results. Since basic research can be regarded as a discretionary expenditure, it is one of the first items to be axed in a period of economic retrenchment.

Government

The federal government affects industrial expenditures for basic research in two ways—through support and regulation. First, cries on all sides for less waste of taxpayers' dollars have moved government to the path of mission-directed projects, with cutbacks in basic research. Moreover, an increasing portion of such research flowed out of business and into universities. Second, the heaping pile of government regulations mandated some diversion of traditional R&D to what business regards as peripheral areas. With R&D departments strapped for funds, basic research inevitably suffered.

Role of Government

Cast in a dual role of supporter and regulator, government plays a leading part in how the R&D drama unfolds. But how can this be in a society that professes faith in the free enterprise system? A strict interpretation would reveal all technical development as belonging in the private sector and government action as being an unwarranted intrusion. Like most political theories, that of free enterprise is adulterated. It mingles freely with welfare economics, which justifies government intervention into R&D when the market mechansim fails to provide benefits required by the public interest. Traditionally, these R&D efforts have been in fields calling for large capital investments that private industry is not prone to make, as in weapons and defense systems.

But the vast size of the expenditures gives government a dominating position. By choice of projects, the federal government marks out areas in which innovation takes place. These choices create a demand for scientists and technical personnel and direct training programs, college curriculae, and graduate students into particular fields.

While the proportion of federal R&D funding has been moving downward, falling from 66 percent in 1964 to 50 percent in 1978, government is still the biggest spender (see figure 5-3). Its $23.8 billion in 1978 affirms Washington as the center of R&D planning.

Figure 5-3. Federal Funding as a Percent of Total R&D

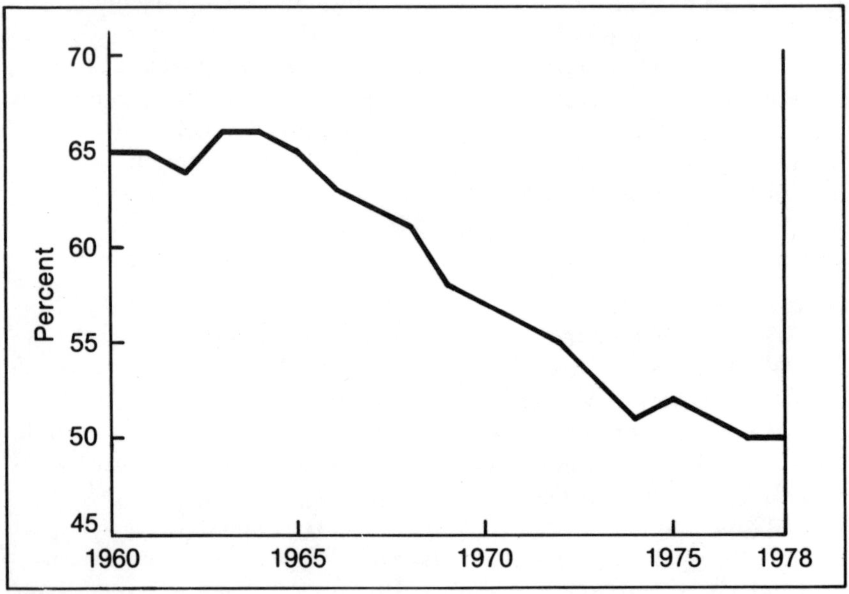

Source: NSF, 78-313.

Total government outlays for R&D have risen some 60 percent within the past decade. But the increased expenditures were not able to buy large amounts of R&D. When adjusted for inflation, government R&D funding reached its peak in 1966 and, like that of the private sector, has been on a downward trend since. Government budgeting for R&D in the past decade, as expressed in constant dollars, showed an average decline of 2.4 percent a year. The downward path of government R&D funding, as adjusted for the shrinking purchasing power of money, is depicted in figure 5-4.

As important as how much is spent on R&D is the question, "On what is the money spent?" Three agencies, the Department of Defense, Department of Energy, and National Aeronautics and Space Administration, claim the lion's share of R&D funding, at least 75 percent of the total. Though the agencies themselves are multifunctional, the major portion of government expenditures is being funneled into projects related to military and space programs. In terms of innovation, this government largess has bestowed comparatively few benefits on the civilian economy. The sharp rise of R&D expenditures for energy is a recent occurrence, spurred on by a series of sporadic crises. Estimated shares of 1979 federally funded R&D, by function, are shown in table 5-3.

Figure 5-4. Federal R&D Funding (in Constant 1972 Dollars)

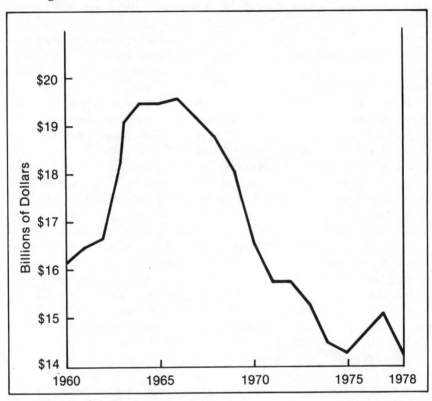

Source: NSF, 68-313.
Note: Current dollars estimated by the National Science Foundation were deflated by the
Milton index, as extended by Battelle, Columbus.

Table 5-3
Percent Distribution of Federal R&D Obligations, by Function (1979)

Function	Percent of Federal R&D Funding
National defense	49.5
Space	12.1
Health	10.8
Energy	10.1
Environment	3.9
Science and technology	3.8
Transportation and communication	3.0
Other	6.8

Source: National Science Foundation, *Science Resources Studies Highlights*,
NSF 78-317.

There is general agreement on the propriety of government planning when public money is at stake. Differences of opinion exist only as
to priorities—on what projects should the public money be spent? But
there is no consensus on the propriety of government regulation, which
gives officialdom a voice in business allocations for R&D. This issue
came to the fore after 1970, when there was a veritable explosion of
rules and regulations affecting R&D.

Government regulations have stimulated new products in many
ways. Auto safety laws have given rise to a variety of safety belts, air
bags, shatter-proof glass, etc. Energy-saving edicts have likewise
brought forth more efficient heating, more energy-efficient appliances, more economical motors and engines, and cost-reducing processes in manufacturing. Legislation has encouraged innovations that
promise a cleaner and healthier environment, while penalizing those
with opposite effects.

But the benefits sought by law makers, however commendable,
were often accompanied by bureaucratic ineptness and waste. Federal
agencies mushroomed by the dozens, with little or no coordination
among them. Companies in the steel industry must comply with more
than 5,000 regulations issued by twenty-seven different federal agencies.[11] The automobile industry estimates that legal mandates siphon
off between 30 percent and 50 percent of its huge multimillion dollar
budgets. In 1974 a vice-president of General Motors asserted that government regulations cost the company more than $1.3 billion, making
work for the equivalent of 25,300 employees.[12] The head of Du Pont in
1977 claimed that were present trends to continue, the firm will spend
$3 billion by 1985 to combat air, water, and noise pollution but that 75
percent of this expenditure "will buy no discernible improvement in the
environment."[13] J. P. Stevens in 1979 estimated that almost one-fifth of
its R&D spending was earmarked for environmental, safety, and health
regulations.[14] And so it goes. The Code of Federal Regulation adds up
to roughly 70,000 pages, and some heads of research and development
report spending more time filling out government requests and reports
than doing the research itself.[15] Innovation is literally being stifled
by mountainous piles of paperwork.

---

[11] Leo-Arthur Kelmenson, "Whatever Happened to U.S. Innovation," *N. Y. Times* (February 4, 1979).

[12] P. F. Chenea, "The Costs and Effects of Regulations," *Research Management* (March, 1977),
pp. 22–26.

[13] Howard K. Nason, "The Environment for Industrial Innovation in the United States,"
Arthur Gerstenfeld, ed., *Technological Innovation: Government/Industry Cooperation* (New York:
John Wiley & Sons, 1979), p. 73.

[14] "R&D Spending at 683 Companies: Another Record Year," *Business Week* (July 2, 1979),
p. 52.

[15] Kelmenson, *op. cit.*

Figure 5-5. Number of Drug Innovations in the U.S.

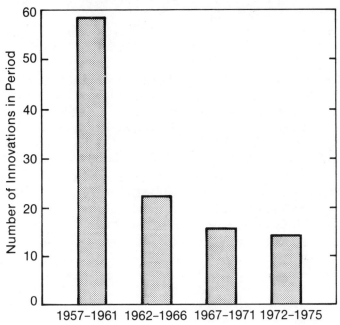

Source: Arthur Gerstenfeld, "Government Regulation and Innovation," Gerstenfeld, ed., *op. cit.*, p. 180.

Critics of government cite the drug industry as a prime example of how the heavy hand of regulation reduced the output of new products and deprived American industry of leadership. In 1960, U.S. firms controlled more than half the world market, and their technological advantage seemed unassailable. But shortly thereafter the FDA began to tighten its regulatory code. Demands multiplied for more data, more documentation, more testing for approval of new products. Research and development costs soared to outrageous heights. Average development costs escalated from $1 million in 1962 to some $22 million in 1975. Average time for FDA approval stretched from six months at the beginning of the period to three-and-a-half to five years a decade later.[10] More of scientists' time was diverted to paperwork, and more of R&D expenditures went into satisfying bureaucratic regulations. As expenses skyrocketed, cash flow dried up and the number of new drug products fell precipitously (see figure 5-5). The world market share of American companies, which once seemed firm and growing, became flabby and shrinking. From 1966 to 1976 the American share of the international market dropped from 53 percent to 40 percent. Though still dominant,

---

[16] Gee and Taylor, *op. cit.*, p. 6.

the American companies never realized the full measure of their capabilities not because of their mistakes, but because of their government's regulations and red tape.[17]

Regulatory barriers to innovation, however, have not been all one-sided, stemming only from legislative enactments. Industry has often acted from narrow economic motives, with little regard for societal consequences. On the other hand, legislators have persisted in an advocacy approach to social issues. While politically expedient, a mixture of opposing views does not necessarily lead to an efficient solution of economic and scientific problems. For example, mandating safety features in automobiles brought an impressive reduction in fatalities. But could a better result have been achieved by reducing speed from 55 miles per hour to, say, 40 miles an hour, and at a lower social cost? Perhaps not. But that is not the point. Unfortunately, alternatives of this sort were never seriously considered because they have no political constituency. In a similar manner, government efforts to overcome energy shortages have been slavishly devoted to maintaining gasoline-fueled transportation, with the least possible inconvenience to motorists. If innovation is to be a factor in economic policy, it cannot be conducted effectively by acceding to the whims of diverse, and frequently opposing interest groups.

External Approach to New Ventures

No matter how large a company or the depth of its resources, the outside business environment offers many opportunities for reaching out into new product lines. The directions are virtually unlimited. There are several ways of getting to new products via the external route, of which the main ones are mergers and acquisitions, licenses and patents, and joint ventures.

Mergers and acquisitions

In 1977 there were forty-one acquisitions valued at $100 million or more each. This number compares with thirty-nine takeovers of comparable value the previous year and a mere eleven in 1975. While these large mergers were relatively few in number, they monopolized the headlines in financial jounals and business sections of newspapers. But the total number of acquisitions in 1977, regardless of size, stood at 2,224, the vast majority of which were small businesses or divisions that were sold or divested.[18]

---

[17] P. Hodgkins, "Unexpected Effects of Government Intervention," *Science and Public Policy* (April, 1977), pp. 142–148.

[18] Ralph E. Winter, "Conservative Firms Bent on Profit Growth Join the Merger Chase," *Wall Street Journal* (April 11, 1978), p. 1.

The same considerations that prod a company to expand from within are present in mergers and acquisitions. The end remains the same; the means are different. The end visualizes an alteration in the product mix to meet a company's objectives, be they growth, stability, survival, or returns on investment. Then why go the acquisition route rather than the do-it-yourself approach? From the standpoint of product policy, there are four main advantages to be attained from acquisition: less time, risk, cost, and financing effort.

Acquisitions reduce time. There is no long process of R&D development: tedious experiments, interminable testing and delays, recurring modification in design. There is no long period of market testing: months of planning brand strategy and counterstrategies, more months of searching for a proper brand name, of testing package designs, of calculating volume reactions to price changes. There is no long wait for production facilities to be built and shakedowns to be completed before the new product can go national. There is no difficult work, often stretching into years, of building a franchise from the ground up. A signing of documents and the ceremonial approval of stockholders are all that are needed to accomplish the diversification objective. And returns on investment begin to come in immediately.

What other internally developed new product can generate instant profits? Paul J. Bumphy, senior vice-president of finance at Anchor Hocking, commenting on the value of acquisitions: "It takes years to build a new business, and we want to get there a little quicker than that."[19] Raymond F. Good, executive vice-president of Pillsbury, sounded the same refrain in commenting on Heinz' acquisition of Weight Watchers. It gave his competitor a "big step forward," he said, in an industry where new product development was "time-consuming and costly."[20]

Inflation has reinforced attempts to save time. By raising the discount rate on the value of money, time becomes more valuable in relation to returns, and pressures mount for quicker paybacks on invested capital.

Acquisitions reduce risk. There is little probability of product failure, of wasted effort, and of capital being dissipated on something that won't make it. Marketing executives are by their nature ebulliently optimistic, for how can they push a new product unless they believe it to be a winner? But the facts are otherwise; most new entries turn out to be losers. If a company pushes into a field with which it is unfamiliar—a new technology, a new market requiring new channels of distribution, a new operation—risk is all the greater. In contrast, the acquired

---

[19] "Heinz Leaps into Low Calories," *Business Week* (March 5, 1979), p. 57.
[20] *Ibid.*

firm is an ongoing business, of known size and profitability. Return on investment can be calculated with far greater certainty from a proven track record.

However, not all acquisitions are successful. A Booz, Allen & Hamilton study of 120 acquisitions, all by large companies, indicated that 61 percent were appraised by management as "satisfactory." Some 25 percent of corporate marriages were rated as of "doubtful" value, while 11 percent ended up in separation or divorce. But divestiture does not imply a loss on the resale. At any rate, even an unsatisfactory acquisition is seldom an all-or-nothing proposition from an investment point of view. There is also evidence that results get better as management gains experience with acquisition activities. For example, companies reporting five or more acquisitions rated good results for 70 percent, as compared with 54 percent for firms that made one or two acquisitions. Management appraisals are shown in figure 5-6.

Acquisitions lower costs. That is, most of the time it is less expensive to buy capabilities rather than duplicate them by an internal development program. Some authorities claim the rewards of external diversification to be lower than those of internal expansion.[21] But in the past several years, replacement costs for plant and equipment have risen sharply. The escalation, however, is not reflected in balance sheets by the historical cost basis of calculating assets. These are actually underdepreciated by accounting convention. Therefore, one company acquiring another makes the purchase on a base that discounts for the overstatement of capital—a much better alternative than paying for the same long-term assets at current market prices. The depressed state of the stock market, brought about in large part by inflation, has provided an added incentive to shop around for assets. As of July, 1979, about half of all issues listed on the New York Stock Exchange were selling below reported book value. Standard & Poor defines book value as total assets, excluding good will, minus all liabilities, minority interests, and liquidating value of any preferred stock outstanding. Insofar as economic imbalances encourage investments to go into acquisitions of existing facilities, they tend to perpetuate the present investment lag in our economy.

Acquisitions may, at times, be easier to finance than internal expansion. Capital markets may not be propitious for raising money for long-term projects at the time it is wanted. Inordinately high interest rates, a

---

[21] "Growing from Within May Pay Off Faster," *Business Week* (September 17, 1966); S. R. Reid, "Reply to Weston/Mansinghka," *Journal of Finance* (September, 1971), pp. 937–946. However, see J. F. Weston and S. K. Mansinghka, "Tests of Efficiency Performance of Conglomerate Firms," *Ibid.,* pp. 919–936; Paul J. Halpern, "Empirical Estimates of the Amount and Distribution of Gains to Companies in Mergers," *Journal of Business* (October, 1973), pp. 554–575.

Figure 5-6. Management Appraisal of Acquisitions
(by Number of Acquisitions per Company)

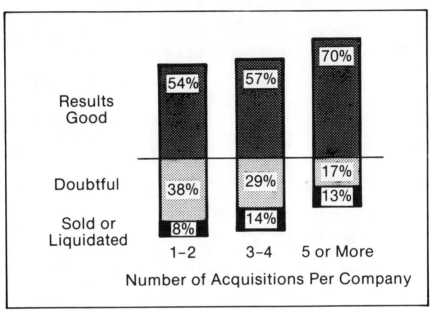

Source: Booz, Allen & Hamilton, *op. cit.*, p. 15.

frequent occurrence in recent years, may further discourage borrowing for new facilities. On the other hand, cash may not be required for an acquisition. In fact, the majority of acquisitions normally involve an exchange of stock rather than cash in order to take advantage of tax benefits. In other instances, a merger can be effected by a simple stock swap, so that cash does not leave the surviving firm and debt is not created. The external route to expansion thus offers flexibility in financing.

Because acquisitions lead to essentially the same results as internal product development—a new bundle of goods and services—Booz, Allen & Hamilton proposes that both kinds of activities be viewed from the same perspective. How will the new products, acquired or created, affect the future of the company? According to the consulting firm, the approach to acquisition should parallel that of internal development, and the mechanics of acquisition should be broken down into a series of defined tasks. The recommended steps are as follows:[22]

1. *Exploration.* A company needs to identify carefully its fields of interests, so that the search is more productive. A strong focus directs exploration to the most fruitful areas.

---

[22] Booz, Allen & Hamilton, *op. cit.*, p. 14.

2. *Screening.* Possible candidates turned up in exploration are evaluated quickly and expeditiously, so that the major effort is spent on those companies that evoke the most interest.

3. *Investigation.* During this analytical phase information is gathered and evaluated but without contacting any company being considered. Preliminary proposals are drawn up and kept in readiness for the next phases.

4. *Proposition.* Direct contact is made with the other firm to determine its interest in the proposition.

5. *Negotiation.* A positive response will lead to a period of negotiation. A negative response might end the quest or trigger an attempt at an unfriendly takeover. Either way, this stage is terminated with a definite yes or no.

6. *Integration.* The acquired firm must be integrated into the parent company. The legal status must be transformed into an economic entity and an effective, commercial operation.

Licenses and patents

A patent, and a license to it, arise from legal efforts to protect property rights of investors or of those who own inventions. These rights are initially conveyed in the form of a patent, issued after filing an application with the U.S. Patent Office. It confers on its owner exclusive rights to the patent for a period of seventeen years. The owner, by virtue of government fiat, can exclude all others from manufacturing, using, or marketing that which has been patented.

This patent is issued when something basically new has been created. Something that existed before but was simply not known is not patentable. A discovery of a scientific law, knowledge of natural phenomenon, or ideas as to cause-and-effect relationships cannot claim exclusivity under patent laws.

There are two main types of patents: those for products and those for processes. In the first instance, the product itself is patented, for the innovation affects the product's physical attributes. In the second, the patent covers only a phase of a production procedure, with no rights to a product or its design.

An owner of a patent has the right to its assignment or license. An assignment is an outright sale, with the transfer of all rights of ownership conveyed to the assignee. A license is a right to use the patent for certain considerations in accordance with specific terms. But legal title to the patent remains with the licensor.[23]

---

[23] Bernard J. McNamee, "A Primer on Patent, Trade Mark, and Know-How Licensing," *MSU Business Topics* (Summer, 1970), pp. 11–20; F. M. Scherer, *Industrial Market Structure and Economic Performance* (Chicago: Rand McNally, 1970), pp. 379–399.

A firm may wish to license a patent for a variety of reasons. If unused, the company might as well obtain revenue from an asset instead of letting it stand idle. A high proportion of all licenses are granted to competitors, ostensibly extended to protect the firm's proprietary rights against infringement, but the licensor may also expect to obtain other licenses in return. When granting a license, the licensor is usually obliged to protect the license from all infringements of the patent and from any suits brought by third parties. The licensing firm will often provide technical assistance as part of the contract.

On the other hand, the licensee has certain obligations, assuming that the patentee will develop manufacturing and marketing capabilities to bring the patent into commercial usage. The licensee is granted only the right to use the innovation, for which a royalty is paid. Payments can be in a lump sum or spread over the term of the license. Usually they are based on the dollar volume of sales and checked by independent auditors paid for by the licensor. A licensee should insist on a contract with a "most-favored-licensee" clause for protection against the licensor giving better terms to competitors.[24]

The obligations and responsibilities of licensee and licensor are normally spelled out in a formal contract. This document also includes the length of time covered by the agreement and conditions whereby either party can terminate the arrangement.

Buying a patent outright, or rights to its use, is actually a halfway measure between acquisition and going it alone. The firm does not obtain a going business. It must expend its managerial talents, capital, and production and marketing facilities to bring the innovation to fruition. It must undertake technical research, if necessary, to satisfy market demand. These considerations are of particular importance in the early stages of commercialization. But the firm avoids costly delays in R&D and saves expense. If technical research proves necessary, resources are devoted to incremental improvements. There is no need to start from scratch.

A patent is more licensable when it involves either an extension of technology or a process innovation. If the patent is more than just a combination of known features, imitation costs are higher. R&D is required to "invent around" the patent, which raises costs and lengthens time. Likewise, a process patent has a higher license demand than a product innovation because of its greater imitation costs. Because physical attributes remain unaltered, the product is no giveaway to the process. The latter cannot be imitated by inspecting the output. On

[24] William Marcy, "Patents and Licenses," *Research Management* (November, 1972), pp. 58–64. Also see Raymond S. Chisholm, "The Role and Functions of Patent Departments," *Ibid.*, pp. 69–71.

the other hand, the innovating firm may desire stability more than potential gains from price warfare and view licensing as the best way to garner incremental profits.[25]

Joint ventures

Joint ventures are created when one or more companies create a third organization to conduct a new business. These organizational forms are widely used when either the risk or capital is too great for any single firm to bear. Joint ventures are common in the oil and gas industry where exploration, development, and distribution can best be accomplished by pooling resources. The Alaskan pipeline, built by a consortium, exemplified this approach. Real estate projects that require extraordinarily large investments may employ a pool of corporate resources to get started. A third major use of the joint venture is in setting up new businesses abroad, wherein the company takes on a partner in the foreign country.

Another type is for two companies to create a third entity with each contributing in accordance with their resources. For example, a technology-based company might supply the technical know-how, while the other partner is counted upon for marketing skill and finances. This provides a joint venture with advantages stemming from strengths of the respective partners. These types of joint ventures appear most frequently in the chemical industry, where new products require diverse abilities, both in technological and marketing fields.[26]

A major reason for joint ventures is capital formation and risk pooling, as in oil and real estate industries. But small firms with technological resources are afforded a ready means of raising capital and acquiring a marketing competence by entering into a joint venture with a larger company. The other partner, in return, acquires an expertise that apparently had been lacking.

Government and Antimerger Policies

Though corporations are always on the lookout for ways to change their product mix by external methods, notably mergers and acquisitions, the activities are hemmed by legal boundaries. Having long espoused a doctrine of competitive benevolence, the government has enacted a series of laws that, though not always consistent, outlaw corporate mergers under certain circumstances. These situations exist when a consolidation threatens to restrain trade or to interfere with the free interplay of the market. This is the only legal basis for government

[25] Robert W. Wilson, "The Effect of Technological Environment and Product Rivalry on R&D and Licensing of Inventions," *Review of Economics and Statistics* (May, 1977), pp. 171–178.
[26] Lee Adler and James D. Hlavacek, *Joint Ventures for Product Innovation* (New York: AMA COM, 1976), pp. 10–11.

opposition to mergers and acquisitions; it must prove adverse consequences to competitive activity.

Federal antimerger legislation dates to the late nineteenth century. The Sherman Act of 1890 forbade "combinations or conspiracies in restraint of trade." This law was evidently passed to head off the wave of consolidations by forming trusts, which circumvented state charters forbidding one corporation to buy stock in another. The "trust" permitted stock of the merging companies to be lodged in a group of trustees, who then issued trust certificates to the owners.

Nevertheless, the horizontal-type mergers that Congress sought to stop were hardly impeded. The Standard Oil case of 1911 weakened antitrust activity further by ruling that only "unreasonable" restraints of trade were illegal.[27] To prove a conspiracy was difficult enough, but to demonstrate the "unreasonableness" of it all was virtually impossible.

As a consequence, Congress in 1914 enacted Section 7 of the Clayton Act, which forbade stock acquisitions that lessened competition. This law, too, became a dead letter because most corporations eschewed stock as a method of control. Instead, they acquired the assets of the company taken over, a practice believed to be outside the jurisdiction of Section 7. In 1950, alarmed by the rising tide of asset acquisition, Congress once more sought to close the floodgates by passing the Celler-Kefauver Act. This law proscribed all consolidations that might substantially lessen competition "in any line of commerce in any section of the country."[28] In effect, this gave the government power to bar effectively any merger if it could be shown that an adverse competitive result came about in one relevant market or submarket.

Since horizontal mergers reduce the number of competitors in a line of commerce, share of market becomes the dominant concern of the antitrust division. Lessened competition is reflected in higher concentration ratios. Other factors, however, are also examined, with the main thrust directed at the likely impact on the entire industry.

The antimonopoly considerations in vertical mergers are more complicated than in the horizontal type. Forward integration through merger or acquisition assures the raw material or semifinished goods producers of a market while constricting outlets to competitors. In backward integration, the acquiring firm achieves an advantage over competitors by securing its source of supply. The economic objection to such mergers as antisocial is that they represent transfers of assets. In contrast, a firm expanding by internal expansion creates new assets, thereby increasing the net capital formation of society.

---

[27] *U.S. v. Standard Oil of N.J.*, 221 U.S. 1 (1911).

[28] See Peter Hilton, *Planning Corporate Growth and Diversification* (New York: McGraw-Hill Book Company, 1970), pp. 124–127.

This economic argument, though eluding hard proof, also applies to conglomerate mergers and is related to the "potential competition doctrine" enunciated by the Supreme Court.[29] It visualizes a firm that is generally regarded as a possible entrant into a market serving as a force that spurs competitive activity. Firms already in the market will act competitively, reducing prices and cutting costs to discourage the entry of newcomers. This is the so-called "edge effect," resulting from a would-be competitor standing poised at the edge of the market. If that potential entrant comes into the market by virtue of an acquisition, the theory holds, the restraining factor to anticompetitive behavior has been removed. Firms need not fear possible crowding and need not strive to keep prices competitive. On the other hand, entrance into the market by internal expansion is seen as enhancing competition by the addition of a strong rival. For example, Procter and Gamble had to divest itself of Clorox because of the critical role played by advertising in new product introductions. As the nation's leading national advertiser, P&G was considered a forceful potential competitor in the liquid bleach industry.[30] Similarly, the government sought to prevent Exxon from acquiring Reliance Electric in 1979 on grounds that the giant oil company had considered moving into electric machinery by developing its internal resources.

So far the potential competition doctrine has been strictly theoretical, unsupported by empirical evidence from actual court cases or economic research. The few studies that have been undertaken have failed to confirm edge effects and limit pricing when firms in an oligopolistic market are confronted by potentially new entrants.[31] Yet it hardly seems to matter that the basic opposition to corporate mergers rests on a flimsy foundation. The imaginary world of corporate behavior is as real to the disputants of a merger as the metaphysical arguments were real to the medieval schoolmen. Then perhaps this modern, materialistic age may yet recapture scholasticism's fine art of deductive reasoning, as exemplified by St. Anslem's dictum, "I know that I may learn."

---

[29] See Peter D. Steiner, *Mergers* (Ann Arbor: University of Michigan Press, 1975), pp. 255–287.

[30] *FTC v. Procter and Gamble Co.*, 386 U.S. 568 (1967).

[31] L. W. Phillips and L. W. Stern, "Limit Pricing Theory as a Basis for Anti-Merger Policy," *Journal of Marketing* (April, 1977), pp. 95–96.

REVIEW QUESTIONS

1. A company's business can be the result of prior broad-stroke strategic planning; or conversely, the business may be the result of many prior piecemeal decisions relating to individual new products. Compare the two approaches.

2. Based on the definition of a business as consisting of a triad— markets, products, technology—provide examples wherein a change in markets only resulted in a new product. Do the same for products and for technology.

3. New products are positioned and old products may be repositioned. Explain.

4. Compare offensive vs. defensive new product ventures.

5. Describe the relationship a new product should bear to the company's existing products if synergism is to develop.

6. New products may be attained via internal self-development efforts or by outside purchase or merger. Compare the advantages and disadvantages of the two approaches.

7. Why purchase a license if you can acquire a company?

8. Product diversification is one means of achieving a measure of stability. Discuss the various approaches to diversification.

9. Given the opportunity to enter upon or widen a policy of diversification, what considerations should rule the decision?

10. What has been the recent trend of expenditures for basic R&D and the causes of this trend?

11. What has been the role of government in controlling R&D expenditures? What has been the effect of this control?

12. Both basic and applied research generate new products. Define the two approaches and differentiate them as to their contributions to new product development.

Three / Organization for Product Development

6/ New Product Organization: Responsibilities

The participation of senior management is an important element in the success of new product programs. The extent of such participation depends upon the expected payout, size of capital outlays, and the degree of change anticipated in the overall product mix.

Another important factor for new product programs pertains to establishing responsibility for carrying out new product programs. Responsibility can be set at the corporate level, the divisional levels, or the operating level.

Corporate new product departments are feasible when the output of various divisions have similar markets and technologies. The corporate thrust is also appropriate when the objective is to develop markets or products that are not in the firm's normal lines of business.

Setting responsibility at the divisional level is advantageous for companies with highly differentiated product lines. Vertical and conglomerate organizations best fit this mold.

When responsibility is lodged below the divisional level, the choice rests between some functional department or a product manager. The most popular department is that of marketing. But responsibility can shift to R&D when marketing requirements are more or less routine and technical ones are important. Responsibility vested in product managers is most appropriate when the new product is an extension or a modification of an existing product line.

Setting Responsibility for New Products

The management of new products, like that of existing ones, is shaped by forces both internal and external to the firm. Setting up an organizational form for new product activity involves three related questions, sequenced in the following order:

1. Who is responsible for new product tasks? Or phrasing the same question somewhat differently, where should responsibility for new products be lodged?

2. What tasks are to be accomplished? Responsibility for these tasks has meaning in relation to getting something done.

3. How are the tasks to be accomplished? This question involves both structure and function.

Writers dealing with new products, in an almost endless refrain, have echoed the theme of top management responsibility for successful programs. The same opinion pervades the councils and deliberations of the business community. When senior management displays a strong interest in new product programs, gets involved with their operations, and appropriates sufficient funds to their development, they are pushed vigorously and enthusiastically. When interest wanes at the top, programs languish for want of nourishment.

Conceptually, all new product planning can be rationalized as the legitimate responsibility of upper echelon executives. Since the chief executive officer and his top lieutenants are in charge of strategic planning, they determine the firm's product mix. They chart the future courses of corporate business and, in doing so, lay out the master plan for new products within the entire business plan.

But top management involvement is another matter. This hinges on the importance that has been assigned to new products in the overall plan. High-placed executives get big salaries, and their time is best spent on weighty matters, those that have a material effect on the performance of the corporation. Consequently, the nature of a company's business and its future businesses conditions top management support. Industries that reward innovative firms with competitive advantages— chemicals, electronics, machinery—will have high-level executives concerned with new products. Industries that are slow to change, with innovation relegated to only a minor role in company performance, will delegate new product activities to lower level executives.

A second factor in executive involvement relates to the kind of new products under consideration. Those that demand substantial capital outlays or that would have a significant effect on the product mix will engage senior executives. A firm's president should—and normally does—play an active role in acquisitions and mergers. He should not— and normally does not—take part in planning a new package or other such minor product modification. Regardless of general top management involvement, high or low, there will be differences on specifics.

A third element in the location of new product responsibility is the existing organizational structure. Small companies, typically with narrow product lines and simple, functional structures, have two options. Most likely, a top official will take charge of innovative efforts. But minor, unimportant improvements might be handed down to a functional department, such as marketing or R&D. Large, complex organizations, broken down into various divisions, have many more alternatives. Responsibility can be lodged at the corporate level, the divisional level, or below the divisional level. The last choice, which parallels the situation in a small company, permits responsibility to rest with a functional department. In complicated organizations, it can end up with some product or market manager group. Responsibilities can be concentrated at a single point or split into various arrangements. The different possibilities are outlined in figure 6-1.

Figure 6-1. Responsibility Options in a Divisional Company

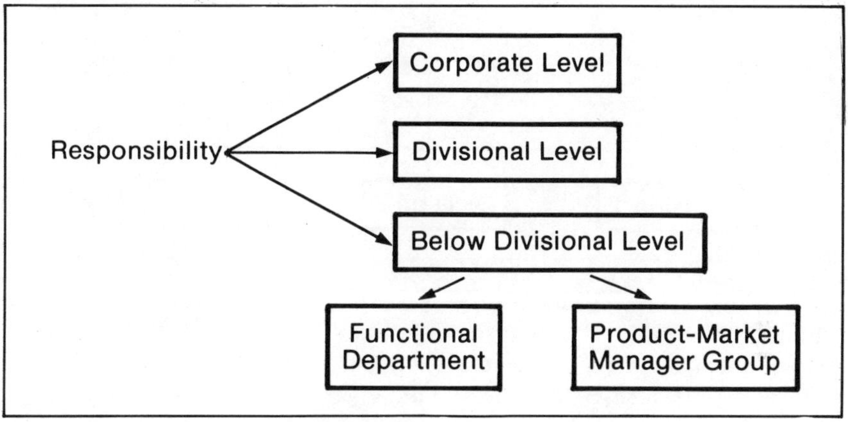

New Products at the Corporate Level

Establishing a unit at the corporate level and vesting it with responsibility for new product development is feasible under a range of circumstances. Such a move is extremely auspicious when the output of various divisions is closely related to both markets and technologies.

A division is normally a profit center organized around a group of related products. As these divisions multiply and proceed in either vertical or conglomerate directions, operations become more dissimilar, incongruous, and varied, especially those of production. Centralizing new product development of such divisions gets to be unwieldy because of the need to assemble and manage highly diverse skills. Corporate functions begin to overlap those of the divisions, and as redundancy increases, costs mount. These trends mitigate against new product units at the corporate level, especially those inclined towards self-sufficiency.

Divisions inclined towards a horizontal direction also take on specialized functions. But their technologies and markets remain related, and centralizing the common elements of their operations can add to efficiency. The General Foods reorganization in 1973, which combined the new products groups of all grocery divisions except coffee, was confidently expected to enhance productivity of innovative efforts.[1] Figure

---

[1] "GF Stresses New Product Area in Major Reorganization Move," *Advertising Age* (February 12, 1973). pp. 1, 57.

6-2 depicts an organization with responsibility for new products residing at the corporate level.

Figure 6-2. New Products at the Corporate Level

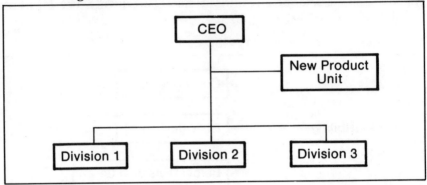

Another set of circumstances favoring a corporate thrust occurs when development strays into unfamiliar fields. Operating divisions would normally neglect these areas, for they fall outside traditional spheres of business. Seldom would a division, evaluated on the basis of financial performance, allocate funds to venture into brave new worlds. Unless that task is assumed at the corporate level, such opportunities would be missed. Centralized laboratories at Bell Telephone, GE, Westinghouse, and RCA, for example, pursue research that divisions would ordinarily prefer not to undertake. These corporate efforts do not replace, but supplement, those of operating divisions. An organizational chart with specialized responsibilities at both corporate and divisional levels is represented by figure 6-3.

Figure 6-3. New Products at Corporate and Divisional Level

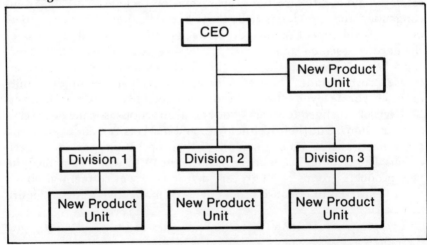

There are both advantages and drawbacks to having new product responsibility set at the corporate level. Among the former is greater effectiveness and control of innovative activities. Centralized research laboratories, for example, are usually larger than the scattered, decentralized units linked to divisional operations. The larger size permits hiring a more specialized, technical staff equipped to handle a wider range of problems. This superior capability is of particular importance to firms caught up in rapidly advancing or new technologies.[2]

Corporate new product units are also insulated from the daily pressures and crisis atmosphere that infect operating personnel. The group's outlook can be more deliberate, impersonal, and catholic, which is in keeping with the long-range views of corporate leadership. New product programs are afforded greater scope for experimentation and wider horizons for exploration. Reporting directly to corporate headquarters, the new product unit has a direct line of communication to top management and numerous fringe benefits that accrue from a relationship impregnated with status. Propinquity to the source of corporate power also facilitates involvement of senior executives and accommodates both control and support of new product programs.[3]

The elements that lend strength to a corporate new product unit are also sources of its greatest weakness. Its isolation from the commotion and turbulence of operations, so necessary for an all-embracing view, makes the unit unresponsive to the urgencies of the marketplace. A request for all possible haste can easily be shrugged off as frantic behavior of nervous salesmen. Unfortunately, such emotional outpourings are all too common in sales organizations. But the people isolated in corporate headquarters, with little intimate knowledge of the cross-currents of demand and competitive activity, have no true way of genuine discrimination. They cannot readily separate the apparent from the real, the contrived from the authentic, the probable from the unconditional.

The comparative isolation of the corporate unit from operational departments makes it necessary to integrate differentiated structures. This is by no means unique to new product organization, but nowhere in the corporate environment is the problem as acute.[4] One reason is because technologies must be transferred from one group to another and from one place to another in the course of development. But a new

---

[2] Steele, *op. cit.*, pp. 120–121.

[3] David S. Hopkins, *Options in New-Product Organization* (New York: The Conference Board, Inc., 1974), pp. 7–9.

[4] Jay W. Lorsch, *Product Innovation and Organization* (New York: The MacMillan Company, 1965), pp. 3–6.

product unit at the corporate level accentuates separation, both organizationally and spatially, and exacerbates the tasks of integration.[5]

New Products at the Divisional Level

Divisional responsibility for new products is most likely when operating units have highly differentiated product lines, as in vertical and conglomerate organizations. Requiring different specialists to manage the intricacies of new products in particular fields dictates a decentralized approach. If these divisions are also large, well-staffed with competent people who are capable of innovation in their respective areas of interest, efficiencies are to be gained by fixing the locus of new product responsibility at the divisional level.

As compared with a centralized approach, the divisional effort would make new product development more attuned to the exigencies of business. Those who work on new products, conversant with the capabilities of their functional departments, would be more able to make necessary adjustments expeditiously. Lastly, shorter lines of communication would tend to make organizational endeavors more cohesive. There would be a more intense commitment on the part of those who have to get the job done, for they are under the same direct authority as the new product unit. An organization with new product responsibility at the divisional level is diagrammed in figure 6-4.

Figure 6-4. New Products at the Divisional Level

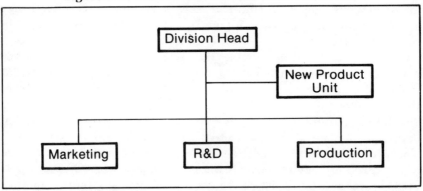

According to figure 6-4, the new product unit is conceived of as a staff function. In this situation, it would normally report to a senior executive within the division. This type of organizational arrangement is deemed most appropriate when projects are likely to demand relatively large budgets, with prolonged periods of development.[6] The higher the stakes, the greater the probability that top management will

---

[5] See Lowell W. Steele, "Speeding the Transition of R&D to Commercial Use," *Research Management* (September, 1975), pp. 30–34.

insist on exercising control, which is its prerogative. The divisional level is also suitable when new product development cuts across product lines.

A new product unit at the divisional level in many ways enjoys the same advantages as its counterpart unit at the corporate level. No matter what form or structure this unit takes, its new product efforts are set apart from the day-to-day activities of operations. Yet its connections with the turns and changes of current business may be strong and intimate. Some of the unit's personnel may work for, or even head, functional departments as with committee forms of organization. The new product unit has fast and easy access to information, which is invaluable in planning programs and determining projects. And its programs can be hammered out in an environment relatively untainted by competing, short-range goals of product lines and operating units.

Setting prime responsibility for new products at the divisional stratum automatically places the job an arm's length away from senior management. This has two major effects: it aids integrative processes and gives direction to the division. Integration is encouraged because functional departments are more prone to cooperate and act energetically on requests from high authorities. There rests the power for rewards and punishments. The unit contributes to divisional planning because its recommendations, making their way to top management, become intertwined with other aspects of mapping the division's goals and directions. Insofar as strategic planing for the entire corporation proceeds bottom-up, this new product group has a hand in the corporate plan.

The problems with establishing divisional responsibility roughly parallel those at the corporate level. Separated from the movers and the doers, the new product units might be looked upon as elitists and "ivory tower" dreamers, whose schemes are as impractical as dreams can make them. Operating personnel may say of these new product planners what George Bernard Shaw once caustically remarked of teachers: "Those who can, do; those who can't, teach." This type of attitude is symptomatic of friction between developmental and functional departments and leads to difficulties in the transition of technologies within the development process.

On a somewhat different plane is the contention of redundancy and misplaced emphasis. This view holds that managing new products is not essentially different from managing old products, that new product development is only one part of a firm's total product development. At any one time, new products account for only a portion—and most of the time a small one at that—of a company's products and markets. Then why elevate new product management to a position of preeminence

---

[6] Hopkins, *op. cit.*, pp. 9–11, 26.

by divorcing it from the ordinary, more important activities of a corporation? To do so, proponents of this view argue, is to place undue emphasis on a function that can be merged into the firm's normal operations. It is not for new products to integrate operations but to be integrated into the main body of operational functions.

New Products Below Divisional Level

A division has many nooks and crannies where new product responsibility can be placed. But responsibility housed anywhere below the divisional level becomes associated with operational activity. For this reason, it is difficult—if not impossible—to consider the locus of responsibility at these lower divisional levels as though it were unrelated to structure and function.

A division contains several operating groups or departments capable of managing the development of new products. The task of assigning prime responsibility boils down to a choice of one. Which unit can best follow through on what must be done to get the item from concept to market? Responsibility placement thus tends to be dependent upon what is—the existing organizational structure.

This decision is quite unlike that of giving responsibility to a unit at the corporate or divisional levels, which traditionally lack basic functions that can accommodate new product development. If responsibility for new products is desired at these upper hierarchical levels, new structures must be created. Over the past two decades, a variety of such structures has come into being, associated with organizational shifts of top management. There have been changes at lower divisional levels as well, but these sprang up, by and large, from fundamental changes in the way operational units function.

The new product approach at lower levels of management is largely dependent upon how a division produces and distributes its existing products. These are the primary tasks of a division, and new products must adjust to them. There are basically two options: a firm can assign prime responsibility for new offerings to one of several functional departments or to product and market managers.

Functional departments

The functional type of organization is the oldest and by far the most common. Divisions operating on the basis of functional departments usually have narrow product lines. In turn, this narrows the choice down to which department should take on responsibility for new products.

In the majority of instances, the designation for new product responsibility is between marketing and research and development, with the former department being favored most of the time. Figure 6-5 illustrates a division in which responsibility for new product development has been assigned to the marketing department. The generic organizational form, however, would be the same if responsibility were shifted to any other functional department.

Figure 6-5. New Products in a Functional Department

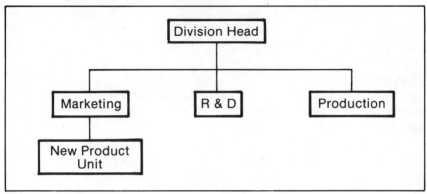

When responsibility for new products is given to a functional department, marketing is the most popular choice. Its greatest advantage is that marketing people, in constant touch with customers, are sensitive to the shifts and turns in usage patterns. They are in the best position to keep a pulse on trends in sales, prices, competitive activity, distribution, and services—all important in bringing a new product to commercialization. Responsibility is usually centered in those efforts that are critical to an outcome. And in most instances, it is the marketplace that determines the success or failure of a new project.

The critical factors in consumer goods ordinarily rest with marketing. But this is also true of many industrial products flowing into distribution channels in which the competitive edge comes about because of long-time relationships between buyer and seller. A satisfactory experience in the past is an irreplaceable advantage when soliciting experiences for the future.

New product development in high technology fields is also greatly influenced by the components of a marketing program. Equipment that is custom-made or highly complex frequently requires extensive servicing—installation, debugging, maintenance, and repair. In other situations, a new product program depends heavily on establishing relationships with distributors and agents, especially when a new product is destined for markets not serviced by the company's regular distribution outlets.

And sometimes, a marketing innovation is more important than a product innovation, even for scientifically based output. Such was the case of a manufacturer of specialized nursery equipment, as related by Louis H. Goldfish, of Technical Marketing Associates, to an AMA conference in Boston.[7] Business prospects for the manufacturer were assessed as dim because of declining birth rates and shrinking numbers of maternity wards. While copying the gloomy report, rumor has it, the analyst was struck by the circumstances of the copy machine company—not altogether dissimilar from those of his own firm. The copier manufacturer did not make a sale of equipment. Yet revenue kept coming in every time a copy was made. Accordingly, the nursery equipment firm changed its marketing tactics. Incubators were placed in hospitals free of charge, but fees were paid for each "baby day" the machine was used. In turn, the hospital would pass through these charges immediately, so it did not tie up its cash. This program apparently reversed the pessimistic outlook.

The greatest danger in putting marketing in charge of new products is its short-range outlook. Its primary concern is present sales, moving goods now, and its efforts bend in the direction of achieving the largest sales volume. Absorbed with the turbulence and incessant drive to make sales, neither time nor inclination augurs well for future planning. The rush of current events tends to crowd out thinking about future products. A trade-off of current for future sales will tend to be perceived as a losing proposition, since any new product usually starts out with low figures. This is particularly true if the new product might act as a substitute for an old one to which there is a strong sales commitment.[8]

The close contact of marketing with customers may be of advantage in modifications and line extensions. But marketing personnel usually run into difficulty when confronted with new products involving scientific concepts and complicated technologies. They may well find themselves unable to cope, unable to direct technological development and integrate advanced scientific thinking. Even their response to customers—and this is their supposed wellspring of strength—may be slow if they are unable to keep up with the latest developments in research and technical design. Many industrial marketers recruit their sales and marketing force from among those with technical and engineering backgrounds. Marketing departments have also created staffs of missionary salesmen and service people who spend time in the field with customers' problems and can feed back product information to research and development. Nevertheless, marketing-led new product efforts in technologically oriented fields may suffer severe handicaps because the generals are inept at mapping out strategy.

---

[7] "High Technology Market Research Can Find Foibles That Affect Sales," *Marketing News* (July 13, 1979), p. 4.

[8] D. E. Vinson and J. H. Jackson, "New-Product Ideas Need Special Management," *Management Review* (December, 1973), p. 28.

When technical innovation is the critical point for the success of a venture, responsibility is focused on research and development. An analogous situation exists when marketing requirements dictate fairly routine procedures but technical performance is all-important in customer acceptance of the new product. This is pointedly exemplified by the pharmaceutical industry, whose markets can be covered by detail men quickly and intensively. The prime necessities for market introduction are brochures, free samples, and footwork. But necessary for market acceptance is the quality of the product itself, its therapeutic effectiveness. A somewhat similar situation presents itself in the government market, where buyers determine specifications and actively select their suppliers.

If the strengths of technical leadership are opposite those of marketing, the reverse is also true. R&D and marketing stand like mirror images with respect to new products.

In fact, many authors have commented—from as far back as the turn of the century—on the differences in the occupational orientation of technicians from that of marketing and sales, and even business in general.[9] Trained in a technical discipline, many researchers are steeped in the values of science. That is not to say their orientation is antibusiness. There is no need to elicit from the musty past the Veblen-like dichotomy which pits the "constructive" values of the engineer against the acquisitive and "predatory" values of the businessman. After all, engineers did hire out to a business corporation, and their desires to put successful new products into the marketplace may be just as intense as those of marketing people. Some companies, such as 3M, even encourage inventors to ride with their products into commercial production and manage them.[10] These actions seemingly are based on the premise that it is easier to train a technician in marketing than to expect a sales person to become proficient in the laboratory.

However, another widely held opinion holds that placing responsibility for new products in R&D deprives the program of a market orientation.[11] On the whole, scientists and engineers lack market wisdom and sensitivity to the needs of customers. Such insensitivity to market trends may be desirable in the laboratory, for it removes a possible constraint on creativity. But it may also be fatal when the same technician assumes the role of managing a new product. It ignores a basic

---

[9] E.g., see Lorsch, *op. cit.*, p. 15.

[10] "How Ideas Are Made into Products at 3M," *Business Week* (September 15, 1973), p. 224.

[11] E.g., see W. V. Muse and R. J. Kegerreis, "Technological Innovation and Marketing Management: Implications for Corporate Policy," *Journal of Marketing* (October, 1969), p. 5; "A Closely Managed Activity," *Industrial Research* (August, 1974), p. 39; John D. Aram, "Innovation Via the R&D Underground," *Research Management* (November, 1973), pp. 24–26.

reason for success since engineering excellence, superior design, and technical elegance can only be justified by market demand. Unless purchasing actions are analyzed and understood, the very basis for new product development is unsuspectingly forgotten.

Regardless of where, or on whom, responsibility is placed, R&D and marketing are looked upon as being dependent upon each other. A harmonious working relationship is essential if products and markets are to be matched. The input of each group is needed. Consequently, management consultants have stressed the need to achieve consensus and organizational integration. A number of integrating mechanisms have been tried: hierarchies of authority to channel activities along desired lines; group dynamics to moderate discord and disharmony; management coordinators to smooth the flow of different tasks. Yet management personnel still seem to be grappling with the problem of how to bring about a spirit of collaboration and teamwork.

One approach has been the creation of what is called a "nominal" setting. It seeks to have group members working individually on specific tasks. Confrontations, criticisms, and challenges are avoided. Yet a consensus can be reached by polling decision-making groups and having them reconsider disagreements until some broad areas of agreement are reached through modification of opinion. The Delphi method of problem solving exemplifies a nominal setting.

The other approach, and by far the more common in business, goes under the label "interaction." The fact that a consensus is reached does not necessarily clear the way for smooth working relationships. If people are to work together, the reasoning goes, they should be able to meet and resolve differences face to face. Hence, the interacting mode brings opposing groups together to air divergent points of view in a give-and-take atmosphere. Yet it is highly debatable whether such dialectics, conducted *vis-à-vis,* either solve problems or endear groups to each other.

In recent years, experimentation has suggested that a combination of nominal and interacting processes is superior to one alone.[12] But the verdict on this form of conflict resolution is not final.

Product-market managers

Responsibility for new products can be turned over to product or market managers, provided the division is organized along these lines.

---

[12] A. Van De Ven and A. L. Delbecq, "Nominal Versus Interacting Group Processes for Committee Decision-Making Effectiveness," *Academy of Management Journal* (June, 1971), pp. 203–212; William E. Souder, "Effectiveness of Nominal and Interacting Group Decision Processes for Integrating R&D and Marketing," *Management Science* (February, 1977), pp. 595–605.

An organization of this type would typically sport product lines with large numbers of items. In this arrangement, a layer of management is actually superimposed on the functional units.

The product management system goes back more than fifty years, having orginated at Procter and Gamble. It made little headway until the sixties, when a rapid proliferation of products created a burden that was too heavy for the chief marketing executive and his small staff. Its greatest gains were made in packaged goods companies. All functional departments of marketing were left intact, with the possible exception of advertising. But managers were added to assist the marketing head with planning and coordinating individual brands and product lines.

New product organization under a product management system can take many forms. One such possibility is depicted for a consumer goods division in figure 6-6.

Figure 6-6. Product Management System in Packaged Goods

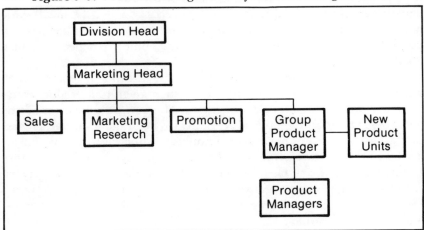

The diagram of a new product unit attached to a product group is more theoretical than actual. It expresses a case of extreme decentralization, which exists in relatively few companies. Most companies assign responsibilities to brand managers directly, particularly for product modifications and often for product extensions. These types of new products are considered part of the marketing tactics to expand an existing line—part of normal operating procedure. Responsibility for their development then naturally flows to those in charge of promoting the product line. In instances where new products are other than modifications or extensions, work may have been initiated elsewhere within the corporation but turned over to a product manager at some point in development.

A study by the Association of National Advertisers in 1974 found the following proportions of its membership using product managers: packaged goods, 85 percent; other consumer goods, 34 percent; industrial goods, 55 percent.[13] These percentages reflect the organizational form of large companies, since big advertisers are more likely to belong to the ANA.

However, it is not quite proper to lump all product managers together. Profound differences arise between those in consumer goods companies and those working in the industrial field.

The product manager in a consumer goods company tends to handle fewer products than his industrial counterpart.[14] Companies that embrace a multiple brand philosophy, found mainly in packaged goods, have each brand run by a separate product manager, called a brand manager. The one brand–one manager system aids new products by giving them a "product champion," an individual who devotes his full time to planning and coordinating the new offering, who strongly believes in and is dedicated to its alluring success. Indeed, he must work hard to obtain a satisfactory outcome, for he is evaluated on the brand's performance, and often his future with the company depends upon a good showing.

When the new product is other than a modification or extension of an existing brand, it will usually suffer when given to a product manager in addition to his regular obligation. The new assignment tends to get crowded out by the normal work load. The brand manager, judged on the basis of current business, cannot permit himself to be diverted by a future promise, no matter how glittering. The new product may interfere with his primary task. In this respect, packaged goods marketers who use a different manager for each new brand are highly effective in the later stages of development, as in product research, test marketing, and commercialization.

On the other hand, the product champion in the packaged goods company may be a weak reed upon which a new product can lean. A large company may leave this white knight two to four levels beneath a position with important decision-making powers and authority to get plans carried out. The multiplication of line extensions and flankers have also forced companies to hire young, inexperienced people as product managers. Unwilling to gamble business outcomes on novices, top managements have deemphasized the product manager's decision-making functions—let alone entrepreneurial ones—and redefined job

---

[13] Quoted in Victor P. Buell, "The Changing Role of the Product Manager in Consumer Goods Companies," *Journal of Marketing* (July, 1975), p. 4.

[14] Philip Kotler, *Marketing Management* (3rd ed., Englewood Cliffs: Prentice-Hall, Inc., 1976), p. 409.

specifications as gathering information, communicating plans for approval, and monitoring performance.[15]

New product leadership by managers under the best of circumstances typically encompasses modifications of existing products and line extensions. But even these endeavors are becoming problematical. Brand managers in the large packaged goods firms were once thought of as managers with responsibility but no authority. Now, the responsibility aspect of their job is also slowly being diluted.

Product management in consumer goods, as shown in figure 6-6, is an outgrowth of the marketing department, an extension of its functions. A manager's greatest concerns are advertising and promotion, for these constitute the most important means of moving goods. The product manager for industrial goods, especially when product attributes assume importance in selling, cannot easily ignore technical and design features. He will consult with technicians and engineers just as frequently as with sales people. He will visit with prospective customers to discuss product and usage problems, for the main emphasis of the marketing mix is not advertising or promotion but personal selling. In new product development, he is more apt to stand in an intermediary position between technical and marketing departments and is thus more effective in integrating diverse functions. The integrative role is much more necessary in industrial than in consumer goods. Cast in an intermediate role, product management in an industrial company can be depicted as shown in figure 6-7:

Figure 6-7. Product Management in Industrial Goods

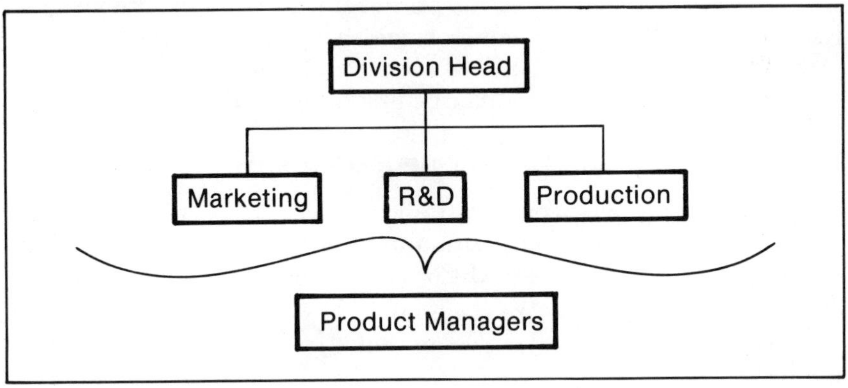

A more complex organizational form exists when market managers are added to the product management system. The result is a matrix form, with managers having overlapping functions. The marketing

---

[15] Buell, *op. cit.*, pp. 6–7, 9–10.

manager concerns himself with all products moving into the market over which his responsibility extends. Markets can be defined in various ways, such as industrial classification, customer type, or geographic area. The product manager looks after a product distributed in all markets. Such a matrix is charted in figure 6-8.

Figure 6-8. Matrix Form of Organization

PRODUCT MANAGER	MARKET MANAGER		
	Market 1	Market 2	Market 3
Product A			
Product B			
Product C			

New products can be developed and introduced by either the market or project manager. The matrix organization is most effective when particular products or groups of products with sufficient volume can be fitted to the different markets. Consequently, each market manager, in effect, divides responsibility with each product manager in a product-market segment. The system lends itself to checks and balances. Under such conditions, the organization presumably runs on the premise that two hands are better than one, for one always watches the other. But the system contains duplication of effort, conflicts of interest, problems in communication, and general difficulties in managing.

The Corporate Personality

Two major studies conducted about a decade apart—one by the American Management Association and the other by the Conference Board—have, like students of the occult, brought into their discussions intangibles that almost defy definition. Both studies have boldly upheld the "corporate personality" as an important determinant of new product organization.[16]

Though indistinct, the personality concept helps explain diversity in common business situations. Companies operating in the same markets with competitive products do not go about their tasks in the same way.

---

[16] Karl H. Tietjen, *Organizing the Product Planning Function* (New York: American Management Association, Inc., 1963), pp. 59–60; Hopkins, *op. cit.*, pp. 94–123.

Similarly, companies organized along parallel lines, with similar spheres of work and comparable job descriptions, will conduct themselves differently.

For example, the lines of communication between people working on new products and those in other parts of the company may be casual and informal. Business relationships may involve personal friendships, compatibility, and common interests. Or the lines of communication may be stiffly formal, flowcharted in an organizational diagram, with chains of command and reporting. The same channels of communication can also produce different degrees of conflict and cooperation. Both the loci and modes of conflict resolution may also differ among companies, though organizational forms remain highly similar.[17]

Corporate personality can be characterized as a company's style and philosophy. Style refers to the manner in which a company conducts its affairs, its *modus operandi*. Philosophy implies the existence of some underlying rationale for its way of doing things, as well as for the things it does. The Conference Board study attempted to isolate the salient elements of style and philosophy, based on executives' judgments. According to the Conference Board, the four main factors were as follows:

1. *Opinions held by the chief executive officer.* Since new products can be regarded as "front-end planning for growth," the company head must take a hand in the choice of structures for planning new products.

2. *Centrality-diffusion trade-offs.* There is an obvious need for retaining centralized control but an equally obvious need for maintaining decentralized decision making. A wide variety of possible options exists for having both at the same time. The exact arrangement results from managerial views and operational pragmatism.

3. *The critical area.* When the critical area is perceived to lie with customers, the new product focus will be market oriented. Sales hinging on product characteristics will shift internal emphasis towards the technical side. Again, there is no single solution, but a wide assortment of alternatives.

4. *Views on innovation.* A widely held opinion views ongoing activities monitored, controlled, and concerned with the immediate as incompatible with innovation. But if the new product process is so different as to require special organization, the question still remains as to what kind. Related issues deal with the extent to which this special device, no matter what form it takes, can direct and control new product planning without stifling creativity at the same time. Many firms have experimented with possibilities and still are.

If a company's way of handling new products expresses its unique personality, the organizational issue becomes an unsettling one. It re-

---

[17] Lorsch, *op. cit.*, pp. 94–123.

fuses to submit to the rational mind seeking synthesis, where every part is in its proper place, bearing a logical relationship to all others and to the whole. It means that almost every generalization will have a large number of exceptions, which makes it no generalization at all. Despite variation among individual companies, new product planning has many characteristics that are common to all firms. Therefore, it may still be meaningful to examine the organization for new products from the standpoint of structures and functions, notwithstanding the existence of great diversity. This is done in the next chapter.

REVIEW QUESTIONS

1. Assume you are a new product management consultant called in by a company to establish an organization for product development. You are given *carte blanche* as to the specifics of how, what, when, where, who, etc. Prepare a list of appropriate guidelines for such an organization unhampered by the limitations of previous politics.

2. A company may have arrived at its current new product organization by way of a sweeping reorganization or by means of a number of minor organizational changes. Discuss the merits of the two approaches.

3. In multidivision firms, the new product organization can report to the top management of either the division or the corporation. A significant number of such firms may deem advisable a multilevel new product organization—one reporting to the division and another to corporate management. Discuss the appropriateness of the three possibilities.

4. Is it feasible to have more than one new product organization within a division operating simultaneously? Explain the circumstances and type of organizations involved.

5. New products are developed and introduced by the firm, operating as a combined force of separate functional departments. However, these functional departments exhibit diverse and possibly opposing interests. Describe the selfish interests of each of the four functional departments. Should the organizational placement of the new product organization be affected by these departmental interests?

6. The responsibility for the commercial development of new products can be assigned to one of the four functional departments, or it can be established as a general management responsibility. Ad-

herents of the marketing concept would probably argue in favor of the marketing department as a home for the new product organization. Discuss the relative merits of the different possibilities.

7. The primary job of a new product organization is to coordinate the firm's efforts to successfully devise, produce, and commercialize products. Coordination requires an acceptable and recognized interface between the various departments of a firm. Discuss the possibilities for such an interface.

8. A basic function of a new product organization is to supervise the daily activities of the R&D department. Is this statement true or false? Explain your answer.

9. Who should manage the new product organization—a technical type or a business-oriented person?

7 / New Product Organization: Structure and Function

Companies that introduce a steady stream of new products in their normal operations usually create special structures to handle such activity. They cannot divert the main attention of their functional departments to jobs that are considered peripheral. The one exception is the product manager. The specially created forms are new product departments, new product committees, ad hoc committees, venture teams, and task forces.

These basic arrangements for handling new products can be differentiated by permanent status, which implies continuity, and responsibility level, which identifies the unit's direct source of authority. These two characteristics also influence the operational effectiveness of the organizational structure. Other attributes that affect operational efficiency are the new product unit's self-sufficiency, exploratory range, degree of product specialization, and personnel time commitment.

The divisional new product department is most common in companies with sales volumes of $50 million or more. These structures also have the highest retention rates, having been discontinued by only 22 percent of the firms using them. On the other hand, venture teams have the lowest incidence of use.

The size of firm has a significant effect upon the structural form used for new products. Large firms rely upon new product departments at the corporate and divisional levels. Small firms make greater use of functional departments, committees, and product managers. But product type also has an effect.

The different structures display a wide variation in functions. New product departments tend to be highly involved in almost all phases of new product activity. New product committees are active during the early stages, while product managers, venture teams, and task forces show greater involvement as a project moves toward commercialization.

160

Structural Forms for New Products

Corporate agencies charged with managing new products go by a great variety of names—new product planning, new product development, new product management, new business, venture management, etc. The plethora of titles gives the mistaken impression that organizational forms are as plentiful as listings in a business directory and heaps confusion on a subject already in disarray. Differently named units do the same things and agencies with the same names do different things. The exposition of new product organization must then start, as many discussions do, with structure and function.

Business firms are organized to carry out the production and distribution of goods and services. These primary tasks are performed without regard for age or newness of products. A new product may occasion plant construction and the setup of different distribution networks. But the organizational form does not basically deviate from what is; it has merely acquired more units of the same kinds, such as sales, production, servicing, etc.

In small companies, a new product is often handled in the same way and by the same units as existing products. There is no change in the day-to-day functions except that the company may have more personnel and turn out more products. Large firms must also depend on their functional departments to produce the new products and to get them into distribution. But introducing new products in greater numbers, they regard their development as an ongoing activity and must organize specially to carry it out.

There is, however, a wide choice of alternatives in the way a new product organization is set up. Like small companies, the larger firms can rely upon what is already available and assign new products to existing functional units. Or they can create entirely new structures. Or they can blend old and new forms in various arrangements. The most popular form of using existing resources is the employment of product managers for new product development. The most common organizational structures established especially for new products are new product departments, new product committees, ad hoc committees, venture teams, and task forces. These six organizational structures—one already existing and five specially created—can conceptually coexist within the same company.

The six basic formations can be differentiated further by characteristics of permanent status and responsibility level. The permanency attribute refers to whether the unit is permanent or temporary. Permanent units have continuity and may be assigned different projects from time to time. Temporary units are usually given one-time assignments upon the completion of which they cease to be. The responsibility factor identifies the corporate level to which the new product unit reports and from which it takes direction.

Identifying units by the three organizational characteristics, regardless of names or titles, yields twelve possible structures. (See fig. 7-1.)

Figure 7-1. Generic New Product Structures

Permanency Status	Specially Created Structure	Responsibility Level	Abbr.
P*	New product dept.	Corporate	Cp. dept.
		Division	Dv. dept.
		Operations	Op. dept.
	New product comm.	Corporate	Cp. com.
		Division	Dv. com.
T**	Ad hoc committee	Corporate	Cp. ad hoc
		Division	Dv. ad hoc
		Operations	Op. ad hoc
	Venture team	Corporate	VT
	Task force	Division	Dv. TF
		Operations	Op. TF
	Existing Structure		
P*	Product manager	Operations	Pr. Mgr.

*Designates permanent status.
**Designates temporary status.

Each of the configurations shown in figure 7-1 is unique and can be identified by its characteristics. If a unit is described as being organized separately or as a department, having permanency, and reporting at the individual level, it is considered a divisional new products department, no matter what name it is given by its management. For purposes of simplification, however, the number of generic structures has been reduced to eight. The rationale is that some structures have almost completely overlapping functions. For example, a task force will have the same characteristics and perform essentially the same functions irrespective of the corporate level to which it reports. The same holds true for the new product and ad hoc committees. By grouping structures that are highly similar, the number of generic forms were reduced to eight and can be described as follows.

Corporate new product department (CP Dept.)

This unit is positioned to serve all other divisions within the company and reports to general management at the corporate level. Or it may concentrate on products unrelated to those of existing divisions. It is self-sufficient to a high degree, requiring little actual support from other parts of the firm. It often tends to be the largest, single unit in the company dealing with new products. It boasts a permanent, full-time staff, consisting of both technical and nontechnical personnel. Firms that emphasize technology in their new product efforts may attach a centralized, technical laboratory to this department.

Divisional new product department (DV Dept.)

This department initiates and coordinates new product development for a division's product lines. A divisionalized company may have a new products department assigned to each division. This department is usually staffed with permanent, full-time managers who may fall back on the services supplied by functional departments with a high degree of self-sufficiency. Such departments would embrace specialists with functional expertise and might even have a complete R&D unit, though this is rare.

Operational new product department (OP Dept.)

This unit operates below the divisional level, reporting to an executive heading a specific product group. It consists of a manager, who often works alone. As such, the structure is really a one-person department, functioning at the operating level. It represents a strict rendition of decentralized management and supposedly provides quick response to the needs of individual product lines. The head of this new product unit, often called a new product manager, depends upon the functional units of the division to carry out all programs.

New product committee (COM)

This is a standing committee at either the corporate or divisional level and therefore constitutes a permanent structure. It is staffed with personnel from different parts of the company, and its members do not work full-time on new product activity. Nevertheless, the committee has continuity and, in many instances, responsibilities similar to those of a new product department. But its power is advisory. Seldom can it act on its own; it must rely upon the performance of nonmembers.

Ad hoc committee (Ad Hoc)

Existing at every operating level, such bodies are set up to pursue specific tasks. They are composed of specialists needed to manage certain aspects of new product activities, such as screening, coordinating test markets, brainstorming, etc. The group operates on a part-time basis, dividing its time between regular duties and newly assigned ones. When the committee completes what is was formed to do, it is disbanded. As such, it lacks continuity; it is temporary. Several ad hoc committees may exist simultaneously, and personnel may serve on more than one committee.

Venture team (VT)

This unit is frequently established at the corporate level with a manager selected directly by top management.[1] Made up of a small interdisciplinary group, the team works full-time on a specific mission. It is frequently provided sufficient resources to carry out its charter and operates independently of functional departments. Not only is the product concept of the project significantly different from that of current product lines, but the investment is relatively large and the time span for development comparatively long.[2] This explains top management's concern with the choice of team leadership. When ventures are completed, they become integrated into the firm's operations, either as new divisions or as parts of existing ones.[3] Project failures lead to discontinuance of the venture team, for it has no reason for being. In either event, the venture team is a temporary arrangement, lasting only as long as it takes to bring the venture to a conclusion.

Task force (TF)

A task force is established to perform both integrative and coordinating functions. This special unit made up of specialists comes into direct contact with functional departments through which it must operate. The mission is usually specified in advance, and the team remains in existence for the life span of the project. At its termination, individual members return to their regular positions. These teams, too, are temporary in nature, and several task forces can be working simultaneously within a company.

---

[1] Wilemon and Gemmill, "The Venture Manager as a Corporate Innovator," *California Management Review* (Fall, 1973), p. 4.

[2] See Hill and Hlavacek, "Learning from Failure," *Ibid.*, (Summer, 1977), p. 12; Hlavacek and Thompson, "Bureaucracy and Venture Failures," *Academy of Management Review* (April, 1978), pp. 242–248.

[3] Karl H. Vesper and Thomas G. Holmdahl, "How Venture Management Fares in Innovative Companies," *Research Management* (May, 1973), pp. 30–32.

Product manager (PR Mgr.)

Firms operating with product managers may assign new products to them, especially those involving line extensions and modifications.[4] Although product managers are permanent, they may or may not work full-time on a new product.

Characteristics of Effectiveness

The responsibility level and permanency status help distinguish agencies that handle new products within a firm. But these characteristics also influence operational effectiveness. For example, permanent units allow the staff to build experience and master skills in developing new products. Reporting to higher levels of management is also viewed as favorable in securing the necessary cooperation from various parts of the organization.

Other attributes that impinge on the operating effectiveness of new product efforts are time commitment, self-sufficiency, exploratory range, product specialization, and leadership specialization. These factors, however, are not completely independent of each other.

Time commitment

This is one of the more important characteristics molding the effectiveness of a new product unit. It refers to whether agency personnel are committed to the new offering on a full-time or part-time basis. Full-time assignments free individuals from all other work, permitting complete concentration on new product activities. There are no diversions, no disruptions, no hindrances from other quarters. Operating on a full-time schedule, personnel become specialists in developing new products. They take part in a division of labor and inherit the benefits of specialization.

Self-sufficiency

The closer any unit comes to being self-sufficient, the less its dependence upon any other unit within the firm. It is a rough measure of resources afforded in order to carry out a designated task. Being able to control its own actions, the new product unit avoids bottlenecks arising from prior commitments elsewhere, uncooperativeness, or plain apathy in others. As such, self-sufficiency buttresses effective action. On the other hand, a self-sufficient unit may find itself isolated from the rest of the company and become unresponsive to business exigencies. It also increases overhead costs, particularly for technology. To have a self-sufficient unit is to imply that R&D will be incorporated into the same

---

[4] For discussion of product management, see chapter 6.

new product entity. In high technology industries, R&D is considered the central fact in a firm creating a self-sufficient new product unit.

Exploratory range

This attribute pertains to how far a new product unit can go in its search for new businesses. It is usually given authority, sometimes formally, sometimes implicitly, to explore certain fields for new product ideas. This exploratory range is related to the unit's responsibility level. The higher the position within the organization, the wider the unit's latitude to seek promising opportunities. In contrast, new product units on the operational level are typically confined to narrow product lines. In turn, the question of effectiveness is related to product and leadership specialization.

Product specialization

This characteristic indicates the extent to which a new unit is confined to its area of expertise. A unit that focuses its search for new

Table 7-1
Structural Profile

Characteristic	CP Dept.	DV Dept.	OP Dept.	COM	PR Mgr.	TF	VT	Ad Hoc
Time commitment								
Full-time	X	X	X			X	X	
Part-time				X	X			X
Permanency status								
Permanent	X	X	X	X	X			
Temporary						X	X	X
Leadership specialization								
Yes	X	X						
No			X	X	X	X	X	X
Self-sufficiency								
Yes	X						X	
No		X	X	X	X	X		X
Exploratory range								
Broad	X	X		X				
Narrow			X		X	X	X	X
Servicing level								
Corporate or division	X	X		X		X	X	X
Product group or line			X		X			
Product specialization								
Yes			X		X			
No	X	X		X		X	X	X

Source: Adopted from George Benson and Joseph Chasin, *The Structure of New Product Organization* (New York: AMACOM, a division of American Management Assn., 1976), p. 13.

concepts on a narrow product line is operating within a definite range of specialization. Narrowness implies a deep understanding and intricate knowledge of that which is examined. It presupposes that decisions will be based on a high degree of expertise and that plans emerging therefrom will consequently be efficient. But whether this type of myopia is effective is an open question. Lacking breadth of vision or authority to pursue breadth, the new product unit may let opportunities go unnoticed under the tapered focus of specialization.

Leadership specialization

The unit may be directed by a specialist or a generalist. A structure is allegedly more effective when led by a specialist. However, it is more important for subordinates to be specialists rather than the leader. It is they who must do the detailed work, where expertise affects results.

Table 7-1 matches characteristics of effectiveness with particular organizational forms. This results in a structural profile.

The structural profiles are derived from "either-or" scoring, which involved some degree of subjectivity. For example, product managers were rated as having a part-time commitment to new products on the grounds that the majority had responsibility for ongoing products. Venture teams were judged as self-sufficient, though there is probably some reliance on functional departments by various groups. But the ensuing profiles are indicative of structural characteristics.

While each structure is unique, some are highly similar to others in terms of characteristics. Specifically, there are four structural pairs which agree on six out of seven characteristics. These closely matching pairs, and the factor that differentiates them, are as follows:

Pair	Differentiating Factor
CP Dept.-DV Dept.	Self-sufficiency
VT-TF	Self-sufficiency
OP Dept.-PR Dept.	Time commitment
TF-Ad Hoc	Time commitment

The existence of similar profiles does not, however, support an inference that comparable structures are necessarily substitutes for each other. The characteristics upon which scoring was based are not the only determinants of new product structures. Moreover, the importance of the different characteristics to individual companies is likely to be dissimilar, with total profile values depending upon the particular configuration of characteristics. Lastly, weightings for the same characteristic probably vary among individual firms. That is, each company attaches a different importance to these characteristics and tends to modify the structural attributes of its new product units in accordance with corporate resources, product lines, and existing organizational arrangement.

Given such information—relevant data about a company and its new product requirements—can the best structure for new products be deduced? To some extent, logical alternatives can be delineated.

For example, a small business introducing new products on occasion might well find the ad hoc committee a satisfactory device to attain its goals. Were the flow of new products to speed up, this same committee might be given a permanent status and be converted into a new product committee. A somewhat larger company in the same circumstances may opt for the services of full-time specialists and set up a new products department at the operational level. Or perhaps it may go one step beyond and establish the more elaborate department at a divisional or corporate level. Table 7-2 matches possible new product structures with company characteristics. Each feasible alternative, given key characteristics of the firm or new product situation, is designated by an X.

Table 7-2
Matching Structure to Firm

General Characteristics of Firm Division	CP Dept.	DV Dept.	OP Dept.	COM	PR Mgr.	TF	VT	Ad Hoc
Size/resources								
Large	X	X	—	—	—	X	X	—
Moderate	—	X	X	—	—	X	X	—
Small	—	X	—	X	X	X	—	X
Product divisions								
Dissimilar	—	X	X	X	X	X	X	X
Similar	X	X	—	—	—	X	X	X
Not divisionalized	—	—	X	X	X	X	X	X
Product lines								
Consumer	X	X	X	X	X	X	—	X
Industrial	X	X	—	X	—	X	X	X
Service	—	X	—	X	X	X	—	X
New product demand								
Continuing	X	X	X	—	—	—	—	—
Sporadic	—	—	—	X	X	X	X	X
New product concern								
Innovative	X	X	—	—	—	X	X	X
Imitative	X	X	X	X	—	X	—	X
Line extensions	X	X	X	X	X	—	—	—

Source: Adapted from Benson and Chasin, *op. cit.*, p. 18.

Each horizontal line of table 7-2 indicates feasible alternative structures considering one factor exclusive of all others. For example, a large firm might best consider a new product department at the corporate or divisional level, a task force, and a venture team. A moderate-sized firm might consider the last three options, in addition to a department on the operational level. When a company is both moderate in size and concerned with innovative products, then a divisional department, task force, or venture team appear to be possible alternatives. The choice might be narrowed further if other characteristics or situations were to be considered.

Examining data in a column indicates which characteristics are appropriate for each new product structure. For instance, the new product department at the corporate level would be suitable for large firms who have divisions in similar or related businesses and a continuous flow of new products, innovative or imitative, going to both consumer and industrial markets. Other structures best match other sets of characteristics and product lines. The obvious logic is to choose that structure which best matches a firm's characteristics, products, and markets unless some overriding consideration intrudes and points in another direction.

Divisional new product departments appear to be most versatile. Reading down the column in table 7-2, possible matches can be observed over a broad spectrum of company characteristics and product-market situations. It is highly flexible as to size of staff and adaptable to new product programs. The company must, however, have a constant flow of new product activity to justify the fixed or programmed overhead.

The task force also appears fairly versatile but only when new product introductions occur sporadically. This limitation confines its general use to small companies. Staffs can be expanded or contracted to fit the required new product effort and are readily disbanded when the project is ended. Task forces used in large companies take place under special circumstances.

The new product department at the corporate level is a relatively inflexible structure. It is best suited to large companies that have a continuous flow of new products. Its capacity for self-sufficiency tends to make this agency effective. But its efficiency depends upon the similarity of the firm's divisions or the relatedness of their products. Highly dissimilar product lines would yield no economics through centralization. In fact, it would probably increase expenses by creating duplication because the different divisions would most likely carry on new product activities on their own.

The new product department on the operational level matches the needs of a moderate-sized consumer goods manufacturer, little concerned with technological innovation. When the broad objective is line extensions and the exploitation of present markets, the manager of the one-man department can plan and coordinate new product development at a modest cost.

New product committees are best used by smaller firms, where new products emerge on occasion. These permit present personnel to be employed on special tasks, with little or no increase in overhead. If technological innovation is not a prime concern, the new product committee can guide and coordinate the project through its development and commercialization. The ad hoc committee is not structurally effective but can be adapted to individual, small-scale projects.

The least flexible structures are those using product managers and venture teams. The first alternative depends upon the prior existence of a product management system. Even then, it is most appropriate for line extensions and product modifications. It is most useful in the small company in which major products are consumer goods. The venture team is applicable mainly to large-scale projects outside the normal business areas in which the firm operates.

Incidence of Generic Structures

To ascertain the extent to which the various new product structures are in use, George Benson and Joseph Chasin undertook a survey among firms, or divisions of firms, with reported sales volume of $50 million or more. The sampling frame for the study was the Standard Directory of Advertisers. Some 1,050 questionnaires were mailed to new product executives or to senior marketing officials of the companies selected. The following results are based upon usable questionnaires received from 267 firms (table 7-3).

Table 7-3
Usage of New Product Structures

Organizational Structure	Currently in Use, %	Past/ Abandoned, %	Never Used, %	All Firms, %
CP Dept.	13	10	77	100
DV Dept.	42	12	46	100
OP Dept.	15	22	63	100
COM	29	21	50	100
PR Mgr.	34	22	44	100
TF	17	25	58	100
VT	8	12	80	100

Source: Benson and Chasin, *op. cit.*, p. 21.

Ad hoc committees were excluded from the questionnaire because they were assumed to exist in most firms at some point in time. Also excluded were external agencies, such as consultants and research services.

As shown in table 7-3, the divisional new product department is most prevalent, being currently used by 42 percent of the companies reporting. It also has the highest retention rate, having been continued by 78 percent of all firms that had ever tried working with this particular structure. The high retention rate suggests a basic satisfaction with this type of new product organization.

The next most popular structures are those of product manager and new product committee, with current usage of 34 percent and 29 percent, respectively. But these structures also display relatively high levels of abandonment. Only 61 percent of all firms that had once used product managers for new products retained them for the job. The comparable figure for new product committees was 58 percent. Presumably, these agencies were dropped in favor of full-time departments in the face of mounting new product demands.

Operational new product departments, task forces, and venture teams disclose a low current incidence but higher past usage. The first structure is probably being surplanted by more effective organization as firms expand. Task forces and venture teams are temporary bodies, here today, gone tomorrow, figuratively speaking. High discontinuance rates would thus be expected.

The venture team also has the lowest incidence of use, presently existing in only 8 percent of the surveyed companies. And 80 percent of the firms had never used this form of organization, despite its popularity in the trade press and academic journals. Its suitability to projects with high risks in nontraditional fields of new business imposes a strict limit on potential users. Likewise, the corporate new product department has a low usage incidence because of its inherent appeal to large companies able to justify an organizational structure demanding a large staff and substantial resources.

The next table (table 7-4) shows the incidence of new product structures among large and small firms. A "large" firm is classified as having a sales volume of $150 million or more.

As expected, the size of the firm has a significant influence on the existing structures in use. Large firms reveal a heavier incidence of departments at the corporate and divisional levels. These companies require permanent units with full-time staffs and sufficient new product volume to support the relatively high fixed costs. Some firms have a lower level of new product activity and tend to find temporary structures or those with part-time commitments adequate for their needs. For example, only 6 percent of small firms have new product departments at the corporate level, as compared with 21 percent of the large firms. But even then there is undoubtedly a qualitative difference. The small companies with departments at the top are mostly nondivisionalized, and therefore, a small department, often headed by a senior officer, handling new products for the entire company. This is in sharp contrast with the heavily staffed unit of the big firm, with access to centralized R&D laboratories. On the other hand, the small firm makes greater use of operational departments, committees, and product managers.

Table 7-4
Usage of New Product Structures by Firm Size

Organizational Structure	Currently in Use	
	Large Firms (%)	Small Firms (%)
CP Dept.	21	6
DV Dept.	47	40
OP Dept.	12	19
COM	22	34
PR Mgr.	25	38
TF	16	18
VT	11	6
Base*	(101)	(137)

*The number of firms does not add up to 267 because some firms failed to supply dollar volume data.

Source: Derived from Benson and Chasin, *op. cit.*, p. 22.

The percentages in table 7-4 add up to more than 100 percent, indicative of multiple structures. Some 59 percent of the firms studied reported the existence of only one type of unit to handle new products. But a substantial number, 41 percent, designated the operations of two or more types, with responsibility divided. This is shown in table 7-5.

Table 7-5
Number of New Product Structures

Number of Different Forms	All Firms %	Firm Size		Principal Products	
		Large %	Small %	Consumer %	Industrial %
One	59	58	60	65	53
Two	28				
Three	10 } 41	42	40	35	47
Four plus	3				
Total	100	100	100	100	100
Base	(267)	(101)	(137)	(107)	(105)

Note: Subgroup totals do not total 267 because some firms did not provide classification information.

Source: Benson and Chasin, *op. cit.*, p. 25.

The nature of a company's products rather than its size is associated with the number of different new product structures in use. Almost two-thirds (65 percent) of all firms in consumer goods placed their reliance exclusively upon one type of unit, as compared with but 53 percent among manufacturers of industrial products. This divergence ostensibly arises from the nature of the new product process. The development of new consumer goods is single-minded, as it were, dominated by one set of considerations. Marketing factors eclipse all others in importance, dictating the feasibility, and even the specifications, of the new product. That is not to say that product quality is of no consequence or that shoddy goods can be sold as easily as those of better grade. But, by and large, marketing assumes primacy and brings all other new product activities under its aegis. In the industrial field, however, product characteristics take on greater significance. New product development must often repose confidence in R&D, while commercialization brings into play completely different skills. When no single activity holds sway over all others, responsibility for coordinating diverse groups and integrating specialized skills must of necessity be more diffused.

To what extent do individual new product structures stand alone? And if they partake in a division of labor, how are they combined? Table 7-6 shows the occurrence of paired combinations of new product structures. The figures shown in brackets denote the relative frequency with which a particular structure exists as the sole unit for managing new products within a firm.

Table 7-6
Paired Combinations of New Product Structures

Forms or Organization	CP Dept. %	DV Dept. %	OP Dept. %	COM %	PR Mgr. %	TF %	VT %
CP Dept.	(46)	3	8	7	6	22	32
DV Dept.	8	(61)	13	18	9	33	36
OP Dept.	8	4	(40)	13	14	16	14
COM..................	14	13	25	(20)	43	44	18
PR Mgr.	14	7	30	50	(39)	38	18
TF	29	14	18	26	19	(7)	23
VT	20	7	8	5	5	11	(9)
Base:	(35)	(111)	(40)	(76)	(89)	(45)	(22)

Note: Column percents may add to more than 100 percent because a number of firms have more than two new product organizational forms, resulting in multiple pairings.

Source: Benson and Chasin, *op. cit.*, p. 25.

Table 7-6 reveals that departments having permanent status and staffed with full-time employees have the greatest likelihood of being accorded sole responsibility for new products. This is particularly true of the divisional departments, of which 64 percent have no partners with whom to share new product efforts. Corporate departments, with greater separation from the functioning businesses, rank behind their divisional counterparts as sole managers. Some 46 percent of these units go it alone. When responsibility is shared, task forces and venture teams are the most likely copartners. These combinations suggest that the department initiates the project and, at some point in its development, turns it over to another group.

In contrast, structures that are temporary in nature or operate with part-time personnel seldom exist alone as new product units. Of all new product committees, only a fifth find themselves working alone on new products. Half the time these bodies are coupled with product managers, whose managerial duties complement committees' advisory functions. Some 26 percent of the committees work hand in hand with task forces, whose full-time employees can carry through on specific tasks. Task forces and venture teams exist alone to a lesser extent than the committees, for their roles apply to specific tasks or projects.

Functions of New Product Structures

The metamorphosis of an idea into a full-blown product competing in the marketplace involves a series of separate, distinctive tasks. Theoretically, permanent new product units should follow development through from start to finish, acting as participant, coordinator, or supervisor. When different types of units share responsibility, each may manage a different function or a separate part in the developmental sequence. In practice, however, logical work flows are not universally observed. The work delegated to a new product unit may be governed as much by company politics and personalities as by structural elements and special requirements.

Table 7-7 shows which functions are performed by the different new product units. The list of jobs numbers sixteen in all, grouped into seven basic functions.

The data indicate a high degree of variation in the jobs done by the different units. They also tend to confirm the conclusion of Booz, Allen & Hamilton that it is difficult indeed to pinpoint responsibility for new product tasks because there is no commonly accepted basis.[5] But certain generalizations can be made.

Corporate and divisional new product departments tend to be involved in practically all phases of new product activity. In terms of listed tasks, involvement averaged more than 70 percent. Their lower in-

---

[5] Booz, Allen & Hamilton, *op. cit.*, p. 18.

volvement in the later phases of new product development, as in test marketing and commercialization, suggests that these activities are removed from the departments and turned over to other units. Their high involvement in screening—practically 100 percent—indicates an active part in idea generation and selection for possible projects to be undertaken. Small departments on an operational level, frequently run by a single individual, usually have no authority to allocate funds for exploration, market evaluation, or product testing. The manager of such a department can only recommend. To get funds, he must go to management with hat in hand. The larger departments on a corporate and divisional level have considerably greater latitude to authorize expendi-

Table 7-7

Functions of New Product Structures

Tasks	CP Dept. %	DV Dept. %	OP Dept. %	COM %	PR Mgr. %	TF %	VT %
1. Initial screening	100	97	90	71	83	27	45
2. Fund authorization							
Exploratory activity	74	66	31	62	41	11	31
Market evaluation	57	65	19	58	47	13	40
3. Authorize R&D effort							
Make feasibility study	77	77	50	67	43	22	40
Develop prototype	71	69	35	74	47	23	45
4. Time schedules/budgets							
Prepare time schedule	80	89	75	45	64	66	72
Monitor time schedule	82	90	77	59	72	60	54
Prepare budget	80	81	64	37	58	48	59
Monitor budget	80	85	60	50	57	44	50
5. Authorize product testing							
Consumer testing	62	63	36	40	65	28	54
Test marketing	57	59	41	53	67	30	59
6. Test marketing							
Preparation of plan	74	80	80	33	88	50	45
Control preparation	62	63	70	23	67	44	50
Responsibility for test marketing	57	56	65	20	70	32	50
7. Launching/commercialization							
Participate in launching	77	74	68	40	89	52	68
Control launching	48	53	53	35	71	32	59
Task involvement average	71	73	57	49	64	36	51
Base:	(35)	(111)	(40)	(76)	(89)	(45)	(22)

Source: Benson and Chasin, *op. cit.*, p. 28.

tures. But roughly one-third must also propose in order to get funding; only higher management can dispose.

New product committees are active in the early phases of new product development. They are often used as agents in initial decisions, authorizing funds for evaluation and R&D effort. As the project moves towards its final stages, committees participate less and less in the decisions.

Product managers participate in screening, but their involvement ebbs during the intermediate phases of new product development. The final phases, which include test marketing and commercialization, find them highly involved in the new product effort.

Venture teams and task forces have relatively low involvement in the listed tasks, particularly in the early stages. Both are more active in preparing time schedules and budgets, as well as in test marketing and commercialization.

The next table summarizes the data by designating the level of involvement—high, medium, low—of particular unit types in the basic phases of development.

Table 7-8
Extent of Involvement

Stage	CP Dept.	DV Dept.	OP Dept.	COM	PR Mgr.	TF	VT
Screening...............	H	H	H	M	H	L	L
Authorize funds	M	M	L	M	L	L	L
Authorize R&D...........	M	M	L	M	L	L	L
Schedules/budgets	H	H	M	L	M	M	M
Authorize testing	M	M	XL	L	M	L	XM
Test marketing...........	M	M	M	L	M	L	L
Commercialization	M	M	M	L	H	L	M

Note: H denotes 80 percent or more involvement; M indicates 50–79 percent involvement; L means less than 50 percent.

Source: Benson and Chasin, *op. cit.*

What a unit does is invariably related to where it gets its directives and sends its reports. Reporting is typically to a principal officer in one of the following areas: general management, marketing management, R&D, or new product management.

A new product unit reporting to general management is assumed to have maximum authority and prestige to obtain cooperation from other parts of the company. A unit placed under marketing management is presumably more sensitive to customers' needs, but reactions to drifts in the marketplace may come at the expense of long-term planning.

While excellent relationships may exist between this new product unit and marketing people, demands to other functional departments may be regarded as trespassing. Except for the new product department at the corporate level, direction from R&D was relatively minor, running at less than 10 percent for all new product structures. The next table indicates the extent to which the various structures for new products report to general and marketing management.

Table 7-9
Proportion of Units Reporting to General
and Marketing Management

	Reports to			
Organizational Form	**Gen'l. Mgt. (%)**	**Mktg. Mgt. (%)**	**Other* (%)**	**Total (%)**
CP dept....................................	60	14	26	100
DV dept....................................	58	28	14	100
OP dept.	25	37	38	100
COM	70	20	10	100
PR Mgr.	25	55	20	100
TF	41	13	46	100
VT	45	4	51	100

*Includes no response.
Source: Derived from Benson and Chasin, *op. cit.*, p. 27.

Corporate and divisional departments, as well as new product committees, report most often to general management. Though far behind, marketing management ranks next. Operational level departments and product managers, positioned on the side of operations, report most frequently to a marketing executive. Task forces and venture teams, both having special assignments, answer mostly to general management. But about one-fifth of these groups failed to respond as to the destination of their reporting. This relatively high level of nonresponse possibly reflects the great variety of circumstances and ambiguity of their existence.

In general, top executives seem to acknowledge not merely that new products are important to corporate welfare but that they require a special type of management. Also accepted is the notion that new products development should be regarded as being on the same level as functional departments in reporting to general management. But as the exact configuration of organization forms are highly diverse, there seems to be no best way to organize for new products.

REVIEW QUESTIONS

1. List and discuss the factors that influence the type of organizational structure selected for the development of new products.

2. New product organizations assume different forms, but all have the same objective. Considered collectively, what are the basic functions of these organizations and who are the participants?

3. List the five most important structural characteristics that determine the effectiveness of a new product organization and explain what each contributes.

4. How much decision-making power and control over the development budget should be given to the new product organization?

5. When does the new product organization's job start? When does it end?

6. There may be considerable differences between a new product department as described in the textbook and a comparable department under the actual operating conditions of a particular firm. Explain.

7. Outline the basic similarities and differences between a:
   a. venture team and task force.
   b. new products department and committee.
   c. corporate new products department and division new products department.

8. Discuss the feasibility of having:
   a. a venture team report to a divisional new product department.
   b. a new product committee report to a group product manager.

9. What is the new product role of the product or brand manager?

Four/ The Product Development and Management Process

Exploration

The idea is the start of new product planning; without a concept there can be no product. The search for ideas, however, is not random. The corporate plan serves as a guide for exploration. It points in the direction of the most desirable areas in which to look for new entries.

A new products department may derive ideas directly or indirectly. Both approaches may be undertaken simultaneously and vary between highly structured and loosely unstructured procedures.

Direct methods rely heavily upon the creativity of company personnel. The techniques utilized include group sessions, such as brainstorming, synectics, and focus group interviews; and individual analysis, such as morphology and consumer surveys.

Indirect methods refer to ideas arising outside the new products department. Therefore, its influence and control over the flow of ideas are indirect. The sources for these ideas may be within the company or external to the corporation. In any event, the new products department must establish a communication network so that ideas can readily flow from those who have them to those who can use them.

The Beginning of a Process

The new products process can be viewed as proceeding in stages, a series of steps that starts with an idea and ends with commercialization. This progression can be described as follows:

1. *Exploration.* The objective here is to search for ideas that will yield valuable additions to the company's existing product line.

2. *Screening.* Screening entails a preliminary evaluation of new product ideas. Its objective is to screen out the weak proposals quickly and inexpensively so that only the most promising ones are given the attention they deserve.

3. *Business analysis.* A detailed evaluation is undertaken only of those proposals that have passed the screening stage and seem to offer the highest probabilities of meeting management objectives.

4. *Development.* New product ideas that have been evaluated favorably are transformed into tangible, concrete products or processes.

5. *Testing.* The product—prototype and final form—is tested with resellers and ultimate users in order to determine buyer reactions.

6. *Commercialization.* Commercialization marks the commencement of full-scale production and marketing for purposes of introducing and establishing the product in the marketplace.

In reality, these several phases do not occur in isolated, self-contained stages, one following the other in rigorous sequence. Rather, they overlap and are carried on concurrently, interacting with and influencing each other. Exploration, for example, is not completely independent of the criteria on which concepts are evaluated. Product testing is often carried out in conjunction with development. A detailed business evaluation must sometimes wait until test market results are in. Some substages may be omitted altogether, while identical analytical techniques may be used at various stages of the new product process. The exact forms are highly varied and must be tailored to particular situations.

The division of the new product process into distinct states is primarily for purposes of exposition. This procedure permits a system to be broken down into its components and examined part by part, all the while realizing that each segment is interwoven with others that make up the whole.

Responsibility for Ideas

The idea is the starting point for any new product. The deed then follows the thought. But thoughts, like deeds, must submit to organization and management. To be used effectively, ideas must be managed effectively. Good management implies assigning responsibility for the job and controlling its implementation. These tasks become especially important because input for new products may come from many different departments within a company, as well as from numerous sources outside. As such, the unit with responsibility for new product ideas is also a coordinating vehicle for the creative efforts of many people, both inside and outside the organization.

Responsibility for new product ideas is usually centralized in a new products group or department. Some companies split the new business function into search and development, using different personnel for each. The job of the former is to generate ideas, the latter to appraise and develop the viable ones. In this way, people do not evaluate their own ideas. Other companies employ the same personnel for both tasks, especially smaller firms, where scale of operations does not encourage narrow specialization. But the idea-generating function maintains a certain degree of constancy from company to company, regardless of organizational structure. The objectives are to gather new product ideas, no matter where they originate.

If the department contains creative individuals, it may generate ideas of its own. But it must also look beyond itself to recognize promising concepts that originate elsewhere. Ideas can come from almost anywhere inside or outside the company, and therefore, their main sources should be accessible to the new products group. For example, the new products group should maintain a close liaison with other departments of the company that are most likely to produce new product ideas, such as marketing and R&D.

Those in charge of search operations serve more or less as a collection medium, a conduit through which all new product ideas must flow. The number of ideas that make their way to this central agency depends upon several factors, such as the ability to identify the major sources of ideas and to encourage transmission from source to destination, or from those who have ideas to those who can use them.

The unit charged with developing ideas should establish a method of reporting, so that people with ideas can better understand what is wanted and submit them in a uniform manner. The search agency should then record all ideas received, by source, and their eventual disposition. Record keeping is not just for the sake of storage or to satisfy a bureaucratic inclination to accumulate trivia. Rather, such records are useful in period reviews, for time often puts things in different perspectives.

Ideas that seem hopelessly impractical one day may become eminently reasonable at a future date. As late as 1974, there was no solar energy industry. The notion of harnessing the sun's power to heat homes and run factories was a fantasy of science fiction writers. Four years later this intriguing reverie had materialized into a $150 million market and is practically doubling from solstice to solstice. The Solar Energy Industries Association, a trade group, contained some 1,000 members by 1978—several industrial Goliaths and a bedraggled army of would-be Davids—all seeking treasures in the glistening rays of the sun.[1]

A similar change in outlook took place with respect to industrial sugar, 15 billion pounds of which is consumed by soft drinks, baked goods, and other food manufacturers. Until the mid-sixties, no American firm indicated any strong interest in the commercial possibilities for fructose corn syrup, or glucose isomerase, as a food sweetener. The basic enzyme and the essential technology to produce it were known for more than a decade. But it was not until a dramatic rise in world sugar

---

[1] Anthony J. Parisi, "Profits From the Sun," *N.Y. Times,* April 30, 1978, pp. F1, 7.

prices that domestic companies suddenly discovered the potential of isomerized corn syrup as a substitute for liquid sugar.[2]

Successful new products, like outstanding athletes, are objects of high interest only because they are out of the ordinary. In fact, the ratio of proposals to eventual successes is a meager one. The vast majority of all new product ideas never survive the initial screening stage. In order to have a sufficient inventory of ideas for development, it is necessary to generate large numbers and great variety at the outset. For this reason, the search group must create an environment that would encourage a strong, steady flow of ideas. There is never, in a literal sense, an excess supply of them. The emphasis in exploration is one of sheer magnitude; refinement in quality comes later at the evaluative stage.

Role of the Corporate Plan

At first glance, the exploration of new products can extend in almost any direction. But in practice, the areas of search are normally prescribed by the corporate plan.[3] New product ideas must be compatible with the firm's long-term strategy. The strategic plan, based upon an assessment of corporate resources—of strengths and weaknesses, of favorable and unfavorable aspects of the environments in which operations take place—will usually delineate areas that are deemed most opportunistic. The logical choices for new products would naturally be those that highlight areas of strength.

For example, a company with a strong organization geared to sell to supermarkets may seek product ideas in the packaged goods field. A firm that excels in engineering and manufacturing but is weak in R&D might decide to concentrate its efforts on imitative products. A firm with a high competence and reputation in a special line of endeavor may be reluctant to wander far afield, wishing only to exploit its unique assets. Because the corporate plan sets the parameters for business ventures, the exploration for new product ideas, to a large extent, becomes a search for synergy. The closer an idea "fits" a corporate plan and therefore a firm's capabilities, the lower its risks.

An organization can expand or contract its options. But even under the most favorable circumstances, choices are limited, for resources are limited. The ill-fated incursion of GE into the computer business is by now a textbook example of how a capital-intensive venture proved too much even for one of the largest diversified companies in the world. On a more modest scale were the failures of the 3M Company, with sales of

---

[2] James P. Casey, "High Fructose Corn Syrup—A Case History," *Research Management* (September, 1976), pp. 27–32.

[3] See chapter 4.

$4 billion, more than 90 percent industrial, in becoming a major force in packaged goods. In 1974 3M actually beat other marketers in the booming plant care category with Precise, a time-release plant food. But problems in sales and distribution and an inability to deal with the trade prevented the company from capitalizing on its opportunity. Similarly, in 1976, the company failed to make headway in another growth area when it introduced Ensure skin care lotion. According to 3M, the product could protect skin by repelling water, cold, etc. But the explosion of other entries by more experienced consumer goods manufacturers led to the market withdrawal of Ensure.[4]

The corporate plan may also link product alternatives with financial considerations. Many companies will eschew new business ventures below a given earnings or sales potential. The Nestle Corporation, for example, expects projected annual sales of at least $10 million after a brand has been on the market five years.[5] H.J. Heinz normally avoids products with less than a $10 million potential.[6] Here a floor is placed on revenue or income expectations. Other companies may put a ceiling on capital spending for new projects. Or they may impose other restrictions, such as having all expenditures funded internally.

To illustrate, a medium-sized dairy company sets forth its new product policy as follows: "...to contribute to the division's volume and profit growth by developing new, improved products to capitalize on the division's major competitive strength—its perishable-product production and distribution system."

The document then outlines the most desirable characteristics these new products should possess. There are three basic criteria:

1. It must meet strategy specification; that is, it must be sufficiently perishable to benefit from distribution through _____'s store-door delivery system...

2. It should be a dairy or dairy-related item. New products that are dairy or dairy related can be expected to benefit from the established consumer franchise, from the company's control over the dairy cabinet in many wholesale accounts, and from the division's technical knowledge of dairy processing...

   This is not a mandatory requirement, as was the first criterion. Nondairy items are being distributed successfully, largely because they can profit from the competive advantages provided by the refrigerated store-door delivery system.

[4] Nancy F. Millman, "Task of 3M Unit: The Neglected 'M'," *Advertising Age* (April 24, 1978), p. 24.

[5] *Nestle's News* (January–February, 1976), p. 5.

[6] Curt Schleier, "Heinz Reverses Poor Image in New Product Development," *Product Mar keting* (May, 1977), p. 23.

3. It should provide an adequate return on invested funds. The division has established a target of _____ percent return before taxes, which is considered satisfactory for new products. The estimated development and testing costs should be included in the total investment account along with capital equipment costs.

In this particular instance, the range of different product categories was severely limited by the perishable requirement. Because the field was restricted, the intensity of exploration had to be increased so as to provide a sufficient amount of viable ideas. In other instances, fields for exploration may be exceedingly broad, such as General Electric's decision in the sixties to enter the nuclear power, computer, and jet engine industries. If the search budget is held constant, expanding the field will decrease the intensity of exploratory effort. If the intensity is given, a broader field will tend to increase budgetary requirements. At any rate, top management establishes the parameters for exploration, so that it does not become an unwieldy, wide-reaching excursion into fruitless areas. The established guidelines mark out the directions, where to look and how intensely.

A Systematic Approach to Ideas

Lodging responsibility for new product ideas in a single department prods the search to go on systematically. Consequently, new ideas are more the result of planned action than of mere accident.

But the way in which such orderly, goal-directed behavior takes place varies greatly from company to company. It may be ceremoniously formal or openly casual. A company suggestion system may have all the trappings of untainted formality. Or lunches with key R&D and marketing people may be inimitably informal, even though business is the immediate occasion for the meal. While new product departments may carry on in both ways at once, emphasis on one approach over another is plainly a matter of style.

Regardless of outward appearances, a new products group may come by ideas directly or indirectly. In the first instance, ideas emanate directly from the personnel in the exploratory group. They may be obliged to other people for suggestions, advice, enlightenment, or inspiration, but the ideas are essentially their own. They thought of them. They created them.

In the second instance, ideas come from outside the search group, as from a contest or an employee suggestion box. The new products department may have initiated the contest or stimulated the suggestions. But it has only a tenuous, virtually nonexistent control over the flow of ideas. These arise not at the pleasure of the department but at the convenience of other people. The output of ideas can be influenced by cajolery, inspiring examples, monetary rewards. But the effects are indirect. People can be encouraged but not made to think about new products. Such encouragement can be enhanced immeasureably by a favorable organizational climate.

As previously defined, a new product is new only to the company, not necessarily to the market. As such, a new product idea represents an arrangement of elements that the company currently lacks. The mental constructs which relate to new products may come in three distinct forms: new product ideas, problems, and generalities.

New product ideas

These are components arranged in a novel or unconventional manner. Such ideas are capable of being conceptualized, perhaps in different ways, and developed into concrete entities that are called products. But they must also contain an additional element, a potential for commercial value. Given these ingredients—novelty and potential value—this is the preferred form in which new product ideas should be molded. They then stand prepared to be screened.

Problems

Many thoughts come in the form of problems rather than complete ideas. That is, they identify some aspect of a product or process that can be improved but do not explain how to do it. They localize areas where some modification or change might yield a differential advantage over what is and so contain the germs of new product ideas. They spotlight, so to speak, what should be done to create a new product. If relevant, the solution transforms the problem into a new product concept. Problem solving may thus be the stepping stone to new product ideas.

Generalities

Many ideas for possible development arrive wholly incomplete, vague, and unformed and might apply to almost any potential product. For example: "We should make a dog food that tastes better." The same thing might be said about any food, whether made for canine or human consumption. Sometimes, product planners can convert such generalities into new product ideas. But insofar as such suggestions are more indefinite than problems, there is less likelihood of producing genuine, new product ideas.

Direct Generation of Ideas

To avoid undue reliance on others, search groups will attempt to generate new product ideas directly by their own efforts. It is, by far, the most reliable way. In doing so they will also use numerous methods. These can be divided into two broad categories: group techniques and individual analysis.

The most common forms of group techniques are brainstorming sessions, synectics, and focus group interviews. Those that emphasize individual endeavors include morphological approaches and consumer surveys. Direct methods for generating new product ideas can thus be represented as follows:

Figure 8-1. Plan for Generating Ideas Directly

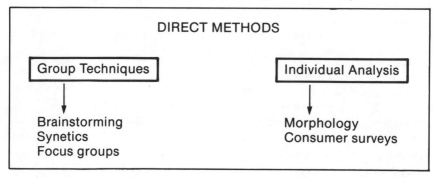

Regardless of methodological primacy—groups or individuals—the methods are means, not ends. They serve as devices to stimulate the imagination, to open broad vistas for the mind to wander. They act as sparks to ignite the fires of creativity. The important thing in creating novel ideas is not the market research method but the people who use it. It is the creative ability of the company personnel, their flair for originality, uniqueness, and freshness. Formal research techniques seldom yield innovative ideas by themselves. Only people do. It is the people concerned with innovation who formulate new product ideas from research material.

Brainstorming

Brainstorming dates back to the late thirties, though it did not come into vogue until the fifties. It was especially popular with advertising agencies, where it was employed to arouse creative ideas regarding promotions, copy treatment, slogans, and names for new products. The technique is still used today, though it may go under different labels, such as "group discussion."

While there are variations in exactly how brainstorming is conducted, all such activities have certain elements in common.[7] They rest on the assumption that people are more productive when working together as a group than alone as individuals. The group atmosphere, proponents of brainstorming maintain, gives rise to a gush of ideas by people interacting with one another. It sets off a chain reaction that is highly contagious, as it were, so that ideas thrust out by one individual draw forth fecond thoughts in others.

---

[7] See Charles H. Clark, *Brainstorming: The Dynamic Way to Create Successful Ideas* (Garden City, N.Y.: Doubleday & Company, 1958).

Working sessions are small, usually ranging from five to ten persons. Participants are chosen from different parts of the company, such as sales, production, or finance, so that diverse points of view are brought to bear on the subject at hand. The prevailing mood at these meetings is one of easygoingness. Practitioners advocate adherence to what is called "deferral of judgment." Negative comments about ideas, however mild, are ruled out. This taboo supposedly keeps down hostility and inhibition, for there is no fear or ridicule or criticism when someone proposes an idea that may seem like bright, blue sky.[8]

The objective of the meeting is to elicit as many ideas as possible, quickly and uncritically, regardless of their merit. Elaboration on those worthwhile can come later by the new products people when the taped session is played back. The moderator plays a key role, some being much more effective than others. He must control the pace of the session, enforce the ground rules, and keep discussion on track without appearing authoritarian or bossy.

One variant of the method is what is referred to as reverse brainstorming. Instead of accentuating the positive, the session focuses on the negatives. The group is asked to think of everything it can about things that are wrong with a product. This approach produces problems, which can often be transformed into creative new product solutions.

While brainstorming produces ideas quickly, the quality of ideas is often berated. The technique actually does not lend itself to problems that embrace complicated elements and call for sequential thinking. Brainstorming can at best cope only with "single node" problems, for it virtually prohibits, as though by design, considerations of complex relationships, evaluation aspects, and even familiarity with the subject under discussion. It attempts to elicit "top-of-the-mind" ideas. This has led some critics to see profundity replaced by superficiality and thoughtfulness by shallowness and to regard the entire group concept as a poor substitute for more competent staffs.[9] Others, who would prefer greater individual initiative, have questioned the creative efficacy of the group, as compared with people working alone.[10]

Of total ideas resulting from these "rap" sessions, a rather low percentage is usable. This proportion may be no less than that derived from other methods. But the amount of effort expended, it is claimed, is comparatively greater. The time of ten executives tied up for several hours is not inconsequential. Available evidence also suggests that

---

[8] See George M. Prince, *The Practice of Creativity* (New York: Harper & Row, 1970), p. 45.

[9] E. Patrick McGuire, *Generating New-Product Ideas* (New York: The Conference Board, 1972), p. 15.

[10] T. J. Bouchard, "Personality, Problem Solving and Performance in Small Groups," *Journal of Applied Psychology* (February, 1969), pp. 1–29; R. F. Maier, *Problem Solving and Creativity in Individuals and Groups* (Belmont, CA: Brooks/Cole, 1970).

novel solutions are highly restricted among ideas that come forth from brainstorming.[11]

Focus Group Interviews

The conduct of focus group interviews bears a striking resemblance to that of brainstorming. It is somewhat unstructured and relies on the spontaneous interaction of the group. But participants are consumers rather than employees and usually have been recruited by a market research house. As such, focus group interviews can be thought of as brainstorming with consumers.

The focus group is widely used by advertising agencies, mainly for guidance in creating advertisements. It is often employed in the testing stage of new product development, both to test product concepts and evolve a campaign strategy. But sometimes group research is undertaken to solicit new product ideas.

As the name implies, this type of group discussion focuses on some definite marketing or product aspect: a brand name, an advertising theme, a product's characteristics. The reason for such centralism is to keep the line of inquiry revolving around the important question, the pivotal theme. While this procedure cuts down on irrelevant and idle chatter, it also restricts the scope and novelty of ideas.

When focus groups are used to elicit new product ideas, they present more basic conceptual difficulties. For one, consumers can hardly be expected to invent products—to enunciate needs that are not obvious or to conceive of entities that do not actually exist. If the typical consumer were queried about his entertainment needs in the early forties, he would not have mentioned the idea of a movie screen, wired with sound, prominently displayed in his living room. If two decades later consumers were surveyed about their needs for handling numbers, who would have suggested a portable electronic contraption that fits in the palm of one's hand? Yet even grade school children today tote these electronic devices into their math classes, and substantial numbers of adults do basic arithmetic by pressing buttons. At best, focus group interviews concern themselves with existing products and usually with their problems.

These group sessions have often been criticized for their lack of representativeness. Samples are composed mainly of women, outgoing and articulate, who have the time and inclination to participate in this sort of activity. Results are thus exploratory in nature and cannot be projected to the population in general.

Another shortcoming of the focus group pertains to the quality of response. Respondents, critics say, try to impress the panel with their

---

[11] Arthur Gerstenfeld, *Effective Management of Research and Development* (Reading, MA: Addison-Wesley Publishing Co., 1970), p. 100.

intelligence and tend to act like experts at these group sessions. Henry Schachte, consultant and former president of J. Walter Thompson Co., put the proposition thusly:[12]

> *In decision presentations, some people . . . still think that the client deciders want information. What they really want is reassurance, some pseudo-guarantee that the recommended decision is safe . . .*
>
> *Which is why focus group "research" is so much used and abused. Reviewing the results of the group session (maybe six or eight people), someone always includes a disclaimer—"of course, this is only for guidance." The warning is ignored as completely as the Surgeon General's wisdom about cigarettes.*
>
> *Fact is, when you're presenting something as abstract . . . and you're trying to get consensus among the traditional room of approvers, you've got to lean on something. Today, the voices of six to eight consumers often speak louder than your judgment. Sad—but so. Because the approvers must lean on something "objective" to soothe their fears of failure.*

A third deficiency of focus group sessions relates to interpretation. Results are like a collective "stream of consciousness" narration. They are subjective and so are inferences drawn from them. When analyzing a tape, there may be nearly as many interpretations as interpreters.

These criticisms are not, however, relevant to new product ideas because the focus group interviews are not utilized in an evaluative manner. If they can be made to produce ideas at a satisfactory cost comparable with that of other techniques then they will have served their purpose well.

Synectics

The synectics technique was popularized by William J. Gordon and George M. Prince in the late fifties while they were employed at Arthur D. Little, a consulting company. In 1960 the two men left the company and set up their own firm, Synectics, Inc.

Gordon and Prince combined group dynamics with problem-solving procedures. Consequently, synectics partakes of certain aspects found in brainstorming, but the differences between the two are highly significant.

The term synectics is a coined word derived from the Greek. Literally, it means a union of dissimilar elements. As applied to idea generation, it implies creative solutions through a combination of diverse components.

Accordingly, the group itself is composed of specialists from different fields, resembling somewhat the operation research teams that be-

---

[12] Henry Schachte, "Today's (Bad) Corporate Advertising Credo Is: Don't Stick Your Neck Out," *Advertising Age* (August 15, 1977), p. 49.

came fashionable in the fifties. In the same vein, the synectics approach calls for a structured orientation, beginning with a problem statement and proceeding in a well-marked sequence of steps to a possible solution. But unlike operations research synectics espouses the theory that creative solutions depend partly, and perhaps mainly, upon intuitive, irrational processes. A better understanding of these thought patterns, the theory holds, enhances the probability of successful problem solving.[13]

Thus, the technique combines rationality with antiintellectualism, cold logic with soaring fantasy. For example, direct analogies, often drawn from nature, are resorted to in order to create a speculative mood. Participants are also asked to imagine themselves as the personification of the simile. "Imagine you are a homing pigeon. What does it feel like?"[14]

An example of the main stages of synectics, referred to as excursions, is given in the following table:

Table 8-1
Example of an Excursion

Stage	
1. Problem as given	Participant stated he would like to solve the problem of how he, an amateur, could build a regular brick wall.
2. Analysis	He explained the practical difficulties he experienced.
3. Problem as understood	How to make a novice a consistent bricklayer.
4. Direct analogy	Homing pigeon. (Reason for choice: a young pigeon has to learn to return to the same place consistently.)
5. Personal analogy	A participant described his fee ngs as a homing pigeon.
6. Compressed conflict	The personal analogy led to the choice of the compressed conflict. Unreliable habit.
7. Second direct analogy	Sleep was chosen as an unreliable habit. Consideration of dreams led to the second compressed conflict.
8. Second compressed conflict	Active sleep.
9. Fantasy force fit	Engage mind on another problem during bricklaying.

---

[13] Prince, *op. cit.*, *passim.*

[14] Brian C. Twiss, *Managing Technological Innovation*, (London: Longman, 1974), p. 114.

10.	Practical force fit	Put patterns on the brick, so that atten tion is directed to creating a regular pattern.
11.	Suggested solutions	Inscribed datum lines on bricks. Patterns or wavy lines on bricks. Color coding.

Source: Twiss, B. C., *Managing Technological Innovation* (Longman Group Ltd.: London, 1974) p. 115.

The team of experts that makes up the panel is held together for a longer time than that of brainstorming sessions, and they focus on a particular problem. The moderator often makes use of flowcharts to plot or sequence progress of the team from problem definition towards solution, and several meetings may be needed. Ideas are carefully evaluated or appraised critically, for the emphasis here is on quality, not quantity. Given a problem, the team strives to attain the best possible solution.

Morphological Methods

Morphological methods postulate creativity as an output made up of two or more precepts arranged in a unique way or related to each other in new combinations. Given this supposition, the search for novel ideas can achieve completeness by identifying all relevant parameters of a product area and deducing all possible combinations.

One form of this approach is attribute listing, often used in product design. The first step is to divide a product into a catalog of factors. The product is described as completely as possible, with all attributes listed in great detail. These attributes are then combined in every conceivable way. This set of all possible combinations, by definition, must also be the set of all possible ideas. The objective then is to search among these alternatives for the most promising ones.

In actuality, alternative combinations can run into the millions. This array by its sheer size makes analysis difficult, if not impossible. In one way or another, by fair means or foul, the number of alternatives to be considered must be reduced, simply from the standpoint of practicality.

But how can this be accomplished without eliminating some very good ideas at the same time? One suggestion has been heuristics—rules of thumb developed from past experience.[15] Some cross-classifications may not seem promising at all based on events of the past. Others may already have been tried and found wanting. In any event, trial-and-error methods can generate a more selective set of alternatives by discarding those that appear to have little potential for success.

[15] Edward M. Tauber, "HIT: Heuristic Ideation Technique—A Systematic Procedure for New Product Search," *Journal of Marketing* (January, 1972), pp. 58–64.

Table 8-2
Two-factor Cross Classification

Food Forms		Packages											
	Aerosol	Bag	Boil in Bag	Bottle	Box	Can	Envelope	Flow-thru Bag	Jar	On a Stick	Pan	Sack	Tube
Biscuit	1	2	3	4	5	6	7	8	9	10	11	12	13
Bread	14	15	16	17	18	19	20	21	22	23	24	25	26
Burger	27	28	29	30	31	32	33	34	35	36	37	38	39
Butter	40	41	42	43	44	45	46	47	48	49	50	51	52
Cereal	53	54	55	56	57	58	59	60	61	62	63	64	65
Cocktail	66	67	68	69	70	71	72	73	74	75	76	77	78
Cookie	79	80	81	82	83	84	85	86	87	88	89	90	91
Crust	92	93	94	95	96	97	98	99	100	101	102	103	104
Custard	105	106	107	108	109	110	111	112	113	114	115	116	117
Dip	118	119	120	121	122	123	124	125	126	127	128	129	130
Dressing	131	132	133	134	135	136	137	138	139	140	141	142	143
Fish	144	145	146	147	148	149	150	151	152	153	154	155	156
Fondue	157	158	159	160	161	162	163	164	165	166	167	168	169
Frosting	170	171	172	173	174	175	176	177	178	179	180	181	182
Fruit	183	184	185	186	187	188	189	190	191	192	193	194	195

Table 8-2 (continued)
Two-factor Cross Classification

Food Forms	Packages												
	Aerosol	Bag	Boil in Bag	Bottle	Box	Can	Envelope	Flow-thru Bag	Jar	On a Stick	Pan	Sack	Tube
Glaze	196	197	198	199	200	201	202	203	204	205	206	207	208
Ice cream	209	210	211	212	213	214	215	216	217	218	219	220	221
Jelly	222	223	224	225	226	227	228	229	230	231	232	233	234
Juice..........	235	236	237	238	239	240	241	242	243	244	245	246	247
Meat	248	249	250	251	252	253	254	255	256	257	258	259	260
Pancake.......	261	262	263	264	265	266	267	268	269	270	271	272	273
Pie...........	274	275	276	277	278	279	280	281	282	283	284	285	286
Pizza..........	287	288	289	290	291	292	293	294	295	296	297	298	299
Salad..........	300	301	302	303	304	305	306	307	308	309	310	311	312
Sandwich......	313	314	315	316	317	318	319	320	321	322	323	324	325
Soup..........	326	327	328	329	330	331	332	333	334	335	336	337	338
Tea	339	340	341	342	343	344	345	346	347	348	349	350	351
Vegetables.....	352	353	354	355	356	357	358	359	360	361	362	363	364
Waffle.........	365	366	367	368	369	370	371	372	373	374	375	376	377

Source: Tauber, "HIT: Heuristic Ideation Technique—A Systematic Procedure for New Product Search," *Journal of Marketing* (January 1972), American Marketing Association, p. 61.

Morphological methods have been carried over from technical situations to development of ideas for consumer goods. One such study dealing with the food industry produced 300 grids from a list of 554 variables.[16] For purposes of illustration, a two-factor matrix from this study is shown in table 8-2.

Advantages that can be derived from morphological methods are telling. They offer a systematic approach for developing many alternatives from which to choose. The sample cross-tabulation of only two factors—packages and food forms—generated 377 combinations, as shown in table 8-2. The twenty-nine rows of food forms multiplied by the thirteen columns of packages yields 377 word pairs.

Two aspects of the procedure assume paramount importance. First, the entire operation rests on the presumption that someone posseses the knowledge to identify, thoroughly and completely, all relevant variables from which to elicit combinations. Second, the output emerges only in word sets. The word sets in table 8-2, for example, show up as Biscuit-Aerosol (1), Bread-Bag (15), Burger-Box (31), etc. By themselves, these word combinations are no more meaningful than those of a Scrabble game. Some of them are downright silly, as number 1, which suggests a biscuit packaged in an aerosol can. But they are only meant to serve as cues to stimulate the imagination, for it still takes a highly creative individual to transfigure two curtly worded attributes into a practical product idea.

Consumer Surveys

Firms producing goods and services destined for the consumer market can often find new directions and opportunities in population surveys. This approach, when employed in a search for new product ideas, veers markedly from the more prevalent procedures. The common procedure is to evolve the idea first and then seek market reaction to it. The survey, in contrast, relies on direct consumer responses as the source of ideas. It views demand as a circumstance which, if understood, can generate new product concepts by revealing consumers' wants and needs, latent and actual. In this instance, exploration works at evaluating consumer behavior and market response and, consequently, overlaps somewhat with the business analysis stage.

Market-based techniques are distinguished by their great variety even when undertaken to develop ideas. These surveys, however, can be divided into two broad classes:

1. Those concerned with behavioristic aspects of marketing, such as product usage, purchase, ownership, and the like.

---

[16] *Ibid.*, p. 60. For application of the same technique to household products, see Charles L. Alford and Joseph B. Mason, "Generating New Product Ideas," *Journal of Advertising Research* (December, 1975), pp. 27–32.

2. Those concerned with psychological characteristics, such as consumer attitudes, preferences, motivation, and the like.

Some surveys will combine behavioristic and psychological features, but even then, they will normally emphasize one over the other. While new product ideas can often be suggested from behavioral measurements, surveys of this nature tend to be evaluative. On the other hand, exploration tends to lean heavily toward the psychological side.

The research field that deals with the human mind appears widely diverse partly because such intangibles as mental constructs are not fully understood. The art of measurement involves many conceptual difficulties and engenders some controversy among practitioners. Many of them see the entire body of knowledge in this field as grossly inadequate and lacking coherence.[17] Yet general theories have developed and are being utilized.

One such generalization is the linear compensatory model, which maintains that an individual's attitude towards an object is determined by its attributes. Some values regarding particular attributes may be positive, some negative. But the positives and negatives simply cannot be added or subtracted to calculate an aggregate value. The prime reason is that separate attribute values are not of equal weight in shaping an overall attitude towards a product. The model thus expresses a person's predisposition as:

$$A_j = \sum_{i=1}^{n} V_i B_{ij},$$

where:

j = Product.

i = Product attributes or characteristics.

A_j = Overall attitude towards the jth product.

V_i = Value or importance attached to the ith attribute.

B_{ij} = Belief as to whether the jth product offers the ith attribute.

This model suggests that attitudes can be measured and expressed mathematically. It also sees a person's overall attitude as a function of values pertaining to product attributes (V_i) and beliefs as to whether the product possesses such characteristics.[18] It further implies that atti-

---

[17] See "Attitude Research Lacks System to Help it Make Sense: Gardner," *Marketing News* (May 5, 1978), pp. 1, 3.

[18] Gilbert A. Churchill, Jr., *Marketing Research* (Hinsdale, IL: The Dryden Press, 1978), pp. 228–229.

tudes are aggregative, that they can be measured separately and then combined somehow to form a "total score."

Multidimensional Scaling

The usual method in attitude research is to have consumers rate products on some type of scale. The exact form varies from survey to survey and from researcher to researcher. But all scales share a common feature in that they visualize the product being rated as placed at some point along a continuum.

Within the past decade, a number of new analytical techniques have emerged to deal with such scales. Perhaps the most promising is multidimensional scaling (MDS). Traditional attitude research normally compares two or more brands on different characteristics but one at a time. The analysis is thus unidimensional; it reveals little as to how product attributes relate to one another. MDS takes an opposite approach, one that is disaggregative. It starts with evaluation of the whole and then attempts to infer attitudinal components that account for differences among products. It is essentially this approach that lies at the heart of the new analytical methods.

Figure 8-2. Perceptions of Pickup Trucks

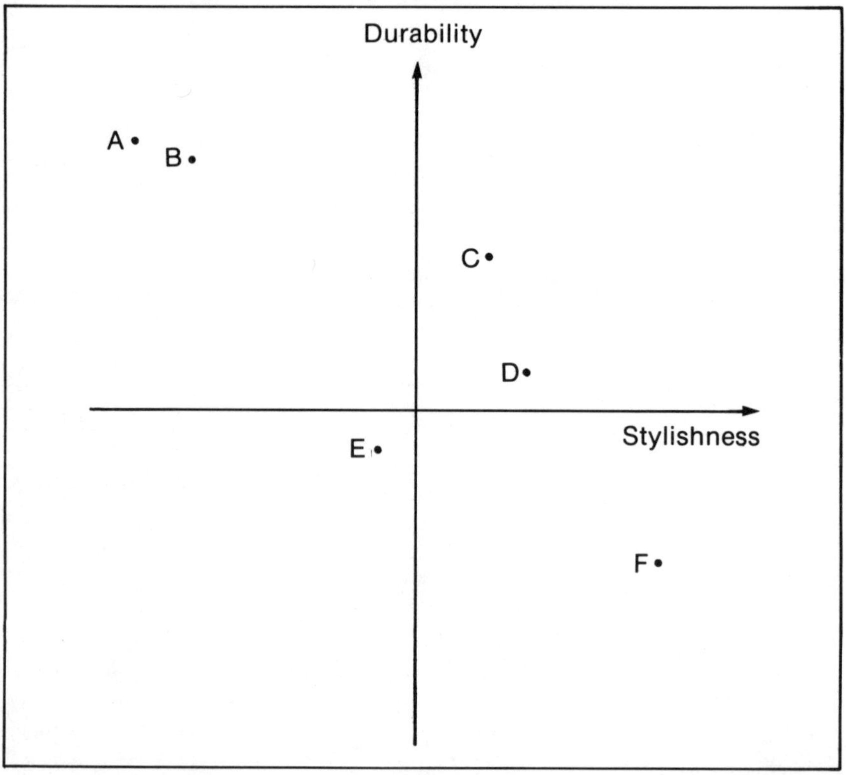

Basically, MDS is a computer-based technique. It takes information obtained from surveys, such as brand perceptions and preferences, and transforms it into a set of points in multidimensional space. For example, a two-dimensional map of how prospects in several western states preceive different makes of pickup trucks is shown in figure 8-2.

MDS can offer many insights into new products. For one, it indicates salient attributes in consumers' perceptions of products and in their comparisons of different brands. In figure 8-2, these main elements are durability and stylishness in various combinations.

Second, it denotes psychological proximity, defined as the distances between brands on the perceptual map. This is supposed to signify the degree of competition among brands. For example, truck makes A and B are close to each other. On the other hand, the more distant make E presumably competes more directly with makes C, D, and F. An examination of psychological distances offers clues as to ways in which to differentiate new products.

Third, the analysis may disclose an ideal combination of attributes that can be incorporated into a new product. This is accomplished by developing a configuration of brand preference rankings from survey

Figure 8-3. Joint Space Map

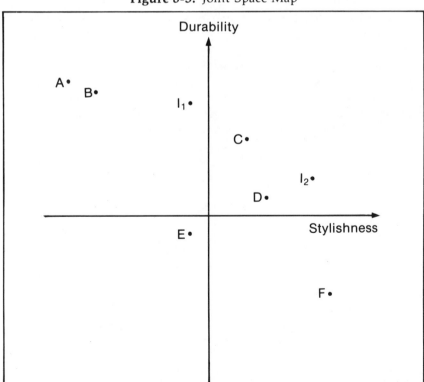

data. The clustered responses would then represent ideal points for population groupings. When ideal and perception points are plotted on the same map, it is referred to as a joint space configuration. Figure 8-3 shows two ideal clusters, I_1 and I_2, on a two-dimensional map.

An implicit assumption of this model is that consumers are prone to buy products that match their ideals. The ideal points can then be viewed as market segments, groups of consumers with similar tastes and preferences.

Consequently, viable market segments for new products might be discovered in joint space configurations. One approach is called gap analysis. It seeks key areas that, positioned near ideal points, contain no existing brands. If a new product can be developed for such empty space, proponents reason, the offering will appeal strongly to the segment located in close psychological proximity.[19]

Yet MDS has not escaped criticism. Most serious is the challenge to its basic assumption that equates product similarity with substitutability. Similary perceived products often are competitive. But they need not be. A person may see yogurt resembling ice cream but have no thought of interchanging the two. To take an extreme example, shaving cream might be perceived as looking like whipped cream—and TV producers at one time showed the former as representing dessert topping. On the other hand, very dissimilar products may compete with each other, as do ice cream and candy in vending machines and sleeping pills and warm milk before going to bed.[20]

Besides certain conceptual problems, MDS also suffers from computational ones. The output requires a computer program, and indeed, many are available. But there is some question as to whether different programs given the same data produce substantially similar results.[21] Nevertheless, the newer techniques are being used increasingly to explore marketing segments in which opportunities for new products exist. As their popularity increases, so will their applications, and more reliable and cheaper algorithms are bound to be developed.

Motivation Research

Other prominent market-oriented means to new products embrace a family of techniques associated with motivation research. These studies try to find out why people act the way they do, withhold or release their discretionary income, and choose one brand over another.

---

[19] Also see Schoner and Uhl, op. cit., pp. 424–425.

[20] Ann Keely, "Product Equivalency as a Measure of Brand Substitutability," Marketing Review (October–November, 1979), pp. 13–16.

[21] See Donald S. Tull & Del I. Hawkins, Marketing Research (New York: MacMillan Publishing Co., Inc., 1976), p. 356; Harper W. Boyd, et al., Marketing Research (4th ed., Homewood, IL: Richard D. Irwin, Inc., 1977), p. 290.

Motivation research leans heavily on clinical psychology for its theoretical structure and actual practice. Its proponents carried over into marketing a number of clinical applications, such as depth interviews and projective techniques. They counseled the application of these techniques to consumers *en masse* in the belief that market needs could be found by probing beneath the surface of consciousness.

Austrian-born Ernest Dichter, widely regarded as the dean of motivation research, describes his approach as follows: "I probe into the underlying reasons that motivate a person to buy a certain product, then advise the company how to improve whatever it is they are trying to sell."[22]

Dr. Dichter gathers small groups of consumers for "therapy" sessions. The same probing in depth can also be carried out in consumer surveys, with interviews taking place in respondents' homes. This technique, says Dichter, lets consumers daydream, so that they "will give you enough insight . . . to translate consumers' wishes into something tangible."[23]

The heyday of motivation research was the fifties, when the voice of Sigmund Freud and his disciples spoke loud and clear to a receptive audience in the business world. Many new products did emerge as the result of daydreams. But the new ideas were more likely to originate not from the reveries of consumers but from the dreams of psychologists who were perceptive and innovative, like the fabulous Dr. Dichter.

Motivation research has waned considerably since the halcyon days of the fifties. In part, it has been replaced by focus group interviews, which are cheaper and quicker. In part, market research and new product departments have realized that creativity springs from the minds of the individual practitioners, and not from the subconscious desires of the consumer body.

Problem Inventory Analysis

While some projective techniques have persisted, they tend to place less emphasis upon psychoanalysis. One such approach is problem inventory analysis.[24] This method calls for a sample of consumers to receive a list of problems and for each problem to name products that come to mind.

The basic interviewing device is sentence completion, a projective technique. But the relationships between problems and products are fairly apparent, and unlike motivation research, there is no attempt to

---

[22] Leonard Russ, "Dean of the Motivation Researchers," *N.Y. Times,* (September 18, 1977), section 22, p. 8.

[23] Ernest Dichter, "Keeping New Products New," *Professionals Look at New Products,* p. 58.

[24] Edward M. Tauber, "Discovering New Product Opportunities with Problem Inventory Analysis," *Journal of Marketing* (January, 1975), pp. 67–70.

get beneath the level of consciousness. Rather, the survey is more in the nature of recall; sentence completion is simply used to get consumers to play back their bad experiences with products. The features of reverse brainstorming are also obvious in problem inventory, insofar as the study focuses on the negative. But this method calls for problem-type quests to be carried out with consumers through sample surveys rather than with groups of employees.

Problem Detection

Problem detection, employing the consumer survey as the data-gathering instrument, also accentuates the negative side. But here, a hypothetical list of problems and solutions is given for each product. Consumers are then queried about all three aspects—problems, solutions, and products.

The William Knobler Company has developed a rating system based on these interviews.[25] The first step is the calculation of a problem score, which is supposed to represent the importance of a problem. Second is a frequency score, connoting how often the problem occurs. Third is a preemptibility score, designating the proportion of respondents unable to name any competitive brand that offers a solution to the problem. Knobler then combines these ratings into an overall opportunity score, which presumably rates the potential value of a solution.

The search for problems came partly as a reaction to what for lack of a better name might be called the needs-and-wants theory. This view argues that by inquiring into consumers' needs, wants, and desires, it is possible to create products that meet these requirements. But as Tom Dillon, board chairman of BBD&O describes people:[26]

> They'll tell you what qualities and attributes they want in products. They will tell you what they think they need. They will tell you what they think they're going to do.
>
> There is only one problem with their replies. If you listen to them, you will likely go broke.
>
> Because when you talk to the consumer about what she wants and needs in the future, all she does is play back what she has been told ... Advertising copywriters tell her what she should want. Parents and teachers have told her what she should want. The government tells her what she should want. And probably some members of her family have been pretty vocal on the same subject.

[25] William Knobler, "Anticipating What the Customer Wants: Benefits Research vs. Problem Detection," *Marketing Review* (January–February, 1976), pp. 19–21.

[26] Tom Dillon, "Forecasting 'Wants and Needs' of the Consumer," speech at American Marketing Association, New Products Conference, April 20, 1978.

One of the arguments for stressing the negative, whether reverse brainstorming, focus groups, problem inventory analysis or problem detection, is that results are practical and actionable. For example, Dillon claims that a problem-gathering search on an ordinary food product can "expect to have from 100 to 200 defined problems associated with it."[27] The development of the GE electric knife is said to have resulted from problems consumers had in cutting frozen foods. Tom S. Carroll, president and chief executive officer of Lever Brothers, attributed the birth of Close-Up to oral hygiene dissatisfaction with existing brands. In more recent days, it was consumer dissatisfaction in shopping for a light bulb that led to Turtle-Lite, Westinghouse's new challenge to GE.[28] And according to S. C. Johnson executives, Agree, the top-selling hair conditioner, can ascribe its success to solving an old problem of creme rinses leaving hair oily and greasy. But the product was also introduced nationally in 1977 with a $7 million ad budget, along with a $7 million sampling program that distributed some 31 million small bottles to potential customers.[29]

Synthetic Methods

In the past several years, methods have emerged that explore both wants and needs and problems, such as quadrant analysis and magnitude estimation. These methods have been used in product testing.[30] But with a little ingenuity, they can be employed just as well in exploration.

They purport to investigate both attributes and dissatisfactions. Either element by itself, supporters argue, fails to tell whether those who place a high value on a product characteristic are currently satisfied with its performance.

The positive-negative combination might be accomplished by conducting a survey and asking respondents to rate attributes in accordance with their importance and the degree of satisfaction with them. Consumers ascribing importance to an attribute form the basis for the analysis. For each attribute, the level of importance is plotted against the level of satisfaction, yielding four quadrants, as in figure 8-4.

The high importance–low satisfaction quadrant is the key to this analytical approach. It presumably reveals vital areas where current

---

[27] *Ibid.*

[28] Iver Peterson, "Bulb Snatching in Supermarkets," *N.Y. Times* (May 14, 1978), pp. D1–11.

[29] See "S. C. Johnson Tries Again on Personal Care," *Business Week* (February 14, 1977), pp. 34, 66.

[30] See David S. Rauch, "Two New Methods for Integrating Consumer Needs and Test Satisfaction," *Marketing Review* (February–March, 1978), pp. 16–19;Howard K. Moskowitz and M. B. Schoenwald, "Ratio Scaling," *Ibid.* (April–May, 1978), pp. 13–16.

Figure 8-4. Quadrant Analysis

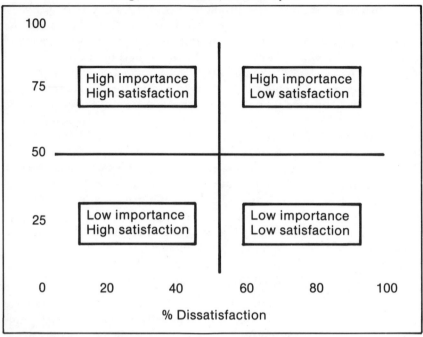

products have failed to perform satisfactorily and thus where opportunities exist for new product entries.

To compare "amounts" of subjective values for product attributes requires a scale with ratio properties. Such a scale was first developed by a group of Harvard psychologists in the fifties to measure intangible qualities such as noise level perceptions. But it was not until 1975 that such "magnitude estimation" scales were adopted to marketing research. A possible derivation of comparative values is shown in the following hypothetical table:

Table 8-3
Example of Magnitude Estimation

Attribute	Importance Rating	×	Percent Dissatisfied (%)	=	"Need" Units Unsatisfied (#)
A	80		20		16
B	60		50		30
C	40		30		12
D	70		35		25
·	·		·		·
·	·		·		·
·	·		·		·

The above table indicates that attribute A is considered more important than B. But most consumers are satisfied with how their current products perform on attribute A. On the other hand, about half are dissatisfied with attribute B, and consequently, a new product that would solve the problems pertaining to B would be a strong competitor.

Whether a survey accentuates the positive or negative or combines the two, the market-oriented search tacitly accepts a rationalistic philosophy of consumer behavior. It has, in effect, adopted the marketing concept as its starting point. It embraces the idea that new product concepts originate in the attitudes of potential customers. Underlying this point of view are certain basic assumptions:

1. The demand for new products is largely independent of supply.

2. Consumers are keenly aware of their wants and needs, as expressed by their attitudes, preferences, dissatisfactions, or any combination of the three.

3. Consumers are capable of conveying these feelings to interviewers, and analysts can translate these responses into quantitative terms.

4. Consumers will act in ways that are highly consistent with their attitudes, preferences, and dissatisfactions, as described in surveys.

5. R&D can develop a physical product that matches a survey's description as to what consumers demand.

Indirect Sources of New Product Ideas

New product ideas can come from almost anywhere, from secretaries to top executives, from production workers to supervisors, from laboratory technicians to outside salesmen. Creative outputs can also orginate outside the immediate confines of the corporate structure in that polymorphous environment where a firm operates. Inasmuch as its contol is indirect, a new products department must maintain liaisons with the major sources from which ideas come forth. How else to harness this creative energy? Even more, the department must establish a communication network, a two-way affair, which would facilitate transmission from those who have ideas to those who want them.

The major sources of new product ideas, inside and outside the firm, can be summarized as follows:

Table 8-4

Major Sources of New Product Ideas

Inside Company Sources	Outside Company Sources
Sales	Customers
Marketing	Competitive products
Research and development	Inventors, agents, brokers
Top management	Consultants, services
Purchasing	Advertising agencies
Production	Distribution channels
Customer service	Patents, research labs
Employee suggestion system	Printed sources (public)

Inside Company Sources

While all employees are potential sources for new product ideas, some are more productive than others. Marketing, sales, and technical research personnel are generally the prime originators of new product ideas. The relative importance of the different components, in large part, is determined by the nature of the industry. Technologically advanced, product-oriented firms will lean heavily on research and development for new ideas. Industries with opposite characteristics will place greater reliance on personnel in marketing and sales operations.

A national survey with new product executives in 267 major corporations revealed major internal sources for new product ideas as follows (table 8-5):

Table 8-5

Major Internal Sources for New Product Ideas

Internal Source	Percent of Mentions (%)
Sales/marketing.................................	62
Top management executives......................	37
Research and development	24
Production department	14
General employee suggestion box	7
All companies...................................	100
Sample base:	(267)

Unpublished data. For details of the survey, see Benson and Chasin, *op. cit.*, p. 7.

Since the percentages add up to more than 100 percent, new product ideas apparently spring from multiple sources. But if we were to eliminate top management, whose new product effort is neither continuous nor full-time, then corporations rely heavily on one internal source.

Market-oriented firms, especially consumer goods producers, find sales and marketing departments as the most productive vehicles for new product ideas. Technologically oriented industries tend to emphasize R&D and production as a prime source of innovation.

Marketing/sales

Almost two-thirds of all new product executives mentioned sales or marketing personnel as important bearers of new product ideas. Sales persons, who received more mentions than any other group, can be particularly useful in this endeavor. The sales force is a company's primary link to its markets, the ultimate judges as to the success or failure of new products. In constant touch with customers, sales personnel are veritable receptacles for market information. They receive advice and information on practically every call they make—satisfactions, complaints, problems, acceptances, and rejections when they do not get the order.

Ways for turning sales intelligence to good account are many. Some companies, especially those marketing industrial products, have their sales people conduct limited surveys with customers. If the respondent feels there is a genuine interest in his views and that the purpose of the inquiry is not to gather testimonials for sales pitches, he is prone to talk freely about his experience with products.

Sales reports can be a literal gold mine of information, especially if they include comments about customers' suggestions, complaints, problems, and the like. Sales meetings can also serve as occasions to probe for new concepts or to find out about problems users may be having.

About one-fourth of all firms surveyed cited product managers as originators of ideas. These personnel, whose main responsibilities include market planning and monitoring, center their attention on products in the marketplace. They must evaluate not only the performance of their own brands but that of competitive ones. Since product policy is a vital aspect of competition, the product manager is cast in the role of advocate of new product proposals, often in self-defense as a reaction to competitive pressures.

Another aspect of the sales and marketing effort is service. Companies whose products must be serviced or require technical support have a direct line to end users. Service call records usually detail breakdowns, malfunctions, limitations, all of which really imply problems with existing products. By the same token, these deficiencies may suggest a means to redesign and improve equipment in current use.

Some companies engage in missionary sales, sending out technical people to assist users and would-be customers with all sorts of equipment problems. These technical representatives, as well as service personnel, sometimes get involved in trying to fit the company's equipment to some unique task or to some job for which it was not originally designed. Such applications or adaptations may have the potential to open new markets and instigate new concepts.

Top management

Next to sales and marketing, top management was mentioned most often as a significant source of new product ideas. In part, this reflects corporate structure. In small and medium-sized companies, top officials are likely to be actively concerned with new products. Such companies may actually lack a full-time new products unit, and corporate brass may head committees to generate new product proposals. But much of top management's involvement probably stems from its contacts with outside sources, both at home and abroad. Despite the existence of functional departments, corporate officers continue to receive inquiries and solicitations regarding new procedures. These should be, and usually are, passed on to the appropriate unit within the organization.

New product executives rated senior management low on degree of importance as a source of new product ideas—far below that of sales, marketing, or R&D. This seems to confirm the disjunctive, secondary role of top executives. Nevertheless, their value as an idea source is frequently neglected.

R&D/production

The development of new product ideas is one function of R&D, but its relative importance in idea generation depends largely on the nature of the product. In some industries, such as pharmaceuticals, industrial chemicals, and electronics, emphasis rests on research, patents, and technological innovation.[31] When these become the most critical aspects of product development, new product ideas are most likely to originate in the laboratory.

The dominance of technological rather than marketing factors implies that the product is uppermost. Products seek markets, so to speak. For that reason, a firm can benefit from a close liaison between technical and marketing personnel. To familiarize technicians with marketing operations, R&D people are often kept abreast of sales developments. Sometimes, they even accompany sales persons on calls to get firsthand information about customers' problems and a more personal sense of market forces.

One idea source on the technological side is a byproduct of value analysis. Value analysis takes place as part of product design. It calls for a systematic review, part by part, with the objective of lowering costs to a minimum. The analysis covers processes, product functions, component size and shape, nature of materials used, and anticipated produc-

---

[31] Pessemier, *Product Management*, pp. 412–415.

tion runs. But often, the most significant cost savings are achieved by changes in design.[32] When conducted with imagination, value analysis might also result in new product ideas.

Purchasing is yet another possible source, though associated with the supply side. This activity necessitates a line of communication with sellers, many of whom from time to time are in the process of introducing new products. These offerings—parts, components, supplies—may also give rise to modifications or reformulations in a company's existing products.

Products purchased are subject to periodic review. These analyses may reveal that a firm can make a component cheaper than the price it pays on the outside. Such circumstances can lead to new products by way of integration and sometimes to substantial marketing opportunities as well. For example, the decision to manufacture its own film opened new profit opportunities for Polaroid.

Employee suggestion systems

Employee suggestion systems are widespread; approximately three-fourths of the largest 500 companies have them.[33] Such programs, however, are concerned with suggestions of all kinds, and not merely with those of new products.

A variety of methods exist for encouraging ideas from employees: internal memos, articles in house organs, presentations, special appeals for suggestions, contests, and cash awards. These are the most common ones to which companies resort. But good public relations are also vital; a high morale is conducive to better employee cooperation. Nothing is more discouraging to a person who submits an idea and begins to feel that it was wantonly disregarded. The receipt of ideas should therefore be acknowledged promptly, and later, each person who offered a suggestion should be informed of its ultimate disposition. If an idea is rejected, the reasons should be given so that the sender will have a better understanding of what is wanted next time.

Public relations people are fond of citing the uninterested employee who unexpectedly comes up with the great idea. One such popular story is the saga of Pampers, the disposable diaper. It all began when a doting grandfather was baby-sitting with his first grandchild and had to change a diaper. He brought his problem—a difficult one for grandfathers—to the attention of his company, Procter and Gamble. Convinced that similar problems applied to other consumers, P&G succeeded in solving it and, in the process, became the leading diaper manufacturer in a multimillion dollar market.

---

[32] Karger and Murdock, *op. cit.*, p. 108.

[33] McGuire, *Generating New-Product Ideas*, p. 22.

The common experience, however, indicates that employee suggestion systems have not been very productive in furnishing companies with new product ideas. In large corporations particularly, people concerned with narrow functions cannot readily envision business opportunities of much broader scope. Prosaic day-to-day tasks also mitigate against creative thinking about activities outside normal routines. Therefore, it is incumbent upon new product departments to solicit ideas selectively. They must make special efforts to enlist the support of those most concerned with new products or those most likely to have ideas and suggestions.

Outside Company Sources

External sources for new product ideas are numerous, and companies differ greatly as to where they concentrate their efforts for outside assistance. There is also considerable variation regarding the extent to which external ideas are sought after and used. The major sources outside the company as reflected in a survey of new product executives are as follows:

Table 8-6
Major External Sources for New Product Ideas

Major Source	Percent of Mentions (%)
Customers	28
Competitive products	27
Foreign products	22
Research facilities, labs	22
Inventors, agents	22
Patents	19
Consultants	18
Advertising agencies	18
Distribution channels	15
Commercial listings	11
Public	7
All companies	100
Sample base:	(267)

Customers

In theory, the customer is king. But only slightly more than a fourth of all companies surveyed went before the sovereign to discern what he wants. Consumer goods manufacturers that solicit royalty for ideas do so through a variety of market research techniques discussed previously. But in many industrial fields, customers frequently develop ideas, even designs, and give the specifications to manufacturers willing

Table 8-7

Source of Innovative Product Designs in Two Selected Industries

Innovative Products First Developed by	Process Equipment (%)	Scientific Instruments (%)
Users	67	77
Manufacturers and "others"	33	23
Sample base:................................	(49)	(111)

Source: Eric von Hippel, "Successful Industrial Products from Customer Ideas," *Journal of Marketing* (January, 1978), p. 41.

Figure 8-5. Returns on Innovative Investment

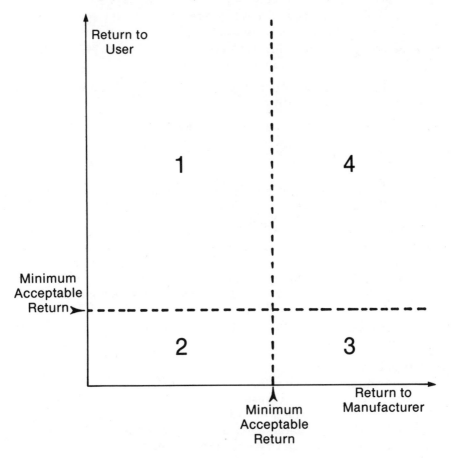

Source: Adapted from Eric von Hippel, "Has a Customer Already Developed Your Next Product," *Sloan Management Review* (Winter, 1977), pp. 65–69.

to invest in product engineering. Such user companies, having a need for innovative equipment or processes, find it worthwhile to conduct active search into areas they may have no intention of getting into. The results of a study in two industries, process equipment and scientific instruments, designated users as the most important source of new product concepts.

This study, conducted at the Sloan School of MIT, defined an innovative product as one having significant functional advantage over competitive entries, according to the opinion of users. This definition probably tipped the scales in favor of users. But it also underscored a noteworthy principle. Many industrial firms are engaged in search activities, especially when the need is great and the likelihood of an outside company fulfilling the need is low. This theory can be represented as follows:

One axis in the above diagram represents the expected return on investment to the user, the second axis to the manufacturer. The dotted lines denote the minimum return acceptable to each type of investor and divide the entire diagram into four parts:

1. The area in which only the user will have enough incentive to invest in the innovation.

2. The area in which neither party will deem it advisable to invest in innovation.

3. The area in which the manufacturer will seek to innovate.

4. The area in which both parties see advantages in expending effort to innovate.

The particular diagram (figure 8-5) indicates an opportunity to innovate as being attractive to the user, but not the manufacturer. Investment to the user can here be justified in terms of potential savings to be gained. On the other hand, the manufacturer here needs a high minimum return and ostensibly would incur high risk. Other configurations suggest other eventualities. In practice, it is difficult to calculate returns on innovations. Nevertheless, the theoretical framework may be useful as a conceptual tool.

Competitive products

Competition was one of the most frequently mentioned sources of new product ideas. No company can act as though it were an island. What a firm does is influenced to a large degree by what others do. The survey results also indicate that many imitative products are defensive in nature as companies try to match or improve new entries from competitors.

This sort of competitive "bandwagon" effect was boldly demonstrated by the low tar trend within the tobacco industry. In 1975, low tar brands made up less than 11 percent of the U.S. cigarette market. By 1977 they had grown to almost 25 percent of the total and are expected to reach 40 percent in two or three years if smokers continue to discard the older brands in favor of low tar varieties. As a consequence, the number of new brands have increased in great profusion. The leading six tobacco companies by 1980 were marketing more than sixty low tar brands, twenty-six percent of which were introduced during 1977.[34]

Secondary sources, such as the trade press, provide listings of new offerings for many industries. Syndicated research services operate in many of them, such as store audits and warehouse retrievals for packaged goods. Each industry will usually have its own unique sources of intelligence. But information about competitive products is necessary in most instances.

Foreign products

As American companies expand their international operations, more ideas from abroad will make their way to our shores. Many ideas borrowed from foreign markets and foreign competitors have proved successful in domestic markets. The most obvious ones are foreign-made automobiles, which had garnered more than 20 percent of the domestic car market by 1980. Domestic auto manufacturers have also adopted these foreign designs through sponsored imports and foreign-developed models. In recent years, even technology, once the almost exclusive asset of America, has been imported from abroad.

To some extent, foreign markets act as a testing ground. But success abroad is no assurance of similar results at home. Tastes and habits are not the same, and good sellers abroad can easily backfire in the American market. Knorrs soup, highly regarded in Europe, failed dismally in the United States. So have Colgate-Palmolive attempts to introduce European brands into this country. Considerable care must be exercised in the transference of an idea across national lines.

Research facilities

Our nation abounds with industrial research labs specializing in new product ideas. Those already developed can be easily obtained either by outright purchase or license. Besides working on their own projects, these research labs also provide services on a contract basis. They are most effective when desired product characteristics can be specified in some detail, but a technological solution has been elusive.

---

[34] See "Cigarette Makers Go All Out for Low Tar Brands," *Business Week* (October 31, 1977), pp. 82–86; D. R. Sease, "Cigaret Companies Vie for Low-Tar Smokers, a Fast Growing Breed," *Wall Street Journal* (March 21, 1978), pp. 1, 18.

The most notable example of a research lab following through on technical development of a highly successful product is that of the Xerox copier. The process of making copies, later named xerography, was first demonstrated by Chester F. Carlson in 1938. At that stage of its development, however, the invention was only in rudimentary form. It was commercially feasible but required considerable technical work before it could be readied for marketing. But substantial progress did not occur until Battelle Memorial Institute of Columbus entered into an agreement with Carlson in 1944 to develop the process in exchange for royalties from commercial sale or licensing. Successful development by Battelle Memorial and an eventual license to Haloid Corporation led to the introduction of the first Xerox copier, a nonautomatic machine, in 1949.

Research labs are of two broad types: profit and nonprofit organizations. Well-known examples of the former are Arthur D. Little, at Cambridge, Massachusetts, and Research Corporation of New York. The latter firm also acts as an agent in marketing patents for other research houses. Notable among the nonprofit segment are such organizations as Battelle Memorial Institute, Mellon Institute Research Foundation, and Rand Corporation. Listings of industrial labs and research centers can be found in various publications of Gale Research Company.

Nonprofit research labs are frequently affiliated with universities, many of which have come to regard royalties from patents as an important contributor to income. Like their counterparts in the noneducational world, they will accept outside projects on a fee or contract basis. But they generally insist, as a condition of employment, that they reserve the right to publish all research findings.

Research laboratories, whether private or quasi-public, offer many advantages to firms seeking new product ideas. The most prevalent is that their newly developed concepts, if suitable, reduce a firm's research expenditure. Other major benefits are:

1. A firm may lack the necessary research facilities or staff, common among small companies. But even larger ones may fall short of specialized equipment or personnel.

2. A company's facilities are operating at full capacity, and expansion is neither urgent nor desirable.

3. Time is of the essence, but a shift in work schedules or resource allocation is not feasible.

4. The company, for one reason or another, desires to assign a problem to a different group working in a completely different environment.

Inventors/patents

Research institutions are one of many sources where patents originate. Other significant agents are companies, individual inventors, and government.

Only a small portion of patented products or processes actually reach the market. The majority lie dormant, held in abeyance by many companies for a variety of reasons. They may not conform with company objectives. Or they may be out of tune with normal operations. At any rate, firms tend to accumulate a surplus technology, which is often negotiable.

Companies possessing dormant patents and with no plans to convert them into marketable items are often willing to license them to others. A number of firms, such as North American Rockwell, Owens-Illinois, and Boeing, to name just a few, have actively engaged in marketing their surplus technology.[35] General Electric, for example, publishes descriptions of patents that can be licensed—both its own and those of other companies—in *New Business Opportunities,* a quarterly sold by subscription to anyone interested in new products. Suppliers of basic materials conduct research into new applications of their wares, and many of them are quite anxious to license patents as a means of increasing sales.

Since the federal government is the largest single sponsor of research and development, it controls a vast number of patents. Most of them fall into the area of public domain and are readily available for license to firms and individuals. Because they are public property, the government will not grant an exclusive license.

Sometimes, government-sponsored research in one area spills over into others. The space program in the sixties, for example, had to explore producing and developing food in places devoid of life. At the same time, state hatcheries were grappling with problems of conservation and ecology. It was felt that the fishing industry was taking too much of the ocean's bounty, reducing animal life and upsetting the natural balance. Union Carbide, then engaged in space research, was given an assignment to develop plate-size fish from eggs. This process is called aqua culture. It involves incubating fish eggs, growing the baby fish in fresh water until they reach a certain size, and then transferring them to a more natural habitat.

When the project came to an end, Carbide remained in aqua culture. It set up an independent company, Domsea Farms, and developed a number of fish products under the Domsea label. These items were test marketed for both consumer and restaurant sectors, first in several minimarkets and later in Atlanta and Minneapolis. National plans for

---

[35] McGuire, *Generating New-Product Ideas,* pp. 43, 44.

commercialization were drawn up, with *pro forma* financial statements and budgets. But fish was not exactly Union Carbide's cup of soup. It was not a business the firm wished to enter. Consequently, Domsea Farms in 1979 was sold to the Campbell Soup Company, whose resources were far more compatible with the development of fishy assets.[36]

The U.S. Patent Office registers more than 50,000 patents annually. These are listed in the *Official Gazette*, a weekly that provides an abbreviated description of patent registrations. Other government agencies issue literature and provide assistance with respect to new products and processes.

Despite the massive organization of research effort, the inventor working on his own has endured as a mover of technological innovation. But his output is frequently communicated by patent brokers or other organizations that specialize in marketing ideas.

Middlemen handling patents work on a fee or commission basis. The commission is set at some agree-upon percentage of royalties that might accrue as a result of a sale. In some instances, however, patent brokerage firms have been accused of charging high fees but affording inventors very little help in selling their patents.

Patent attorneys sometimes act as agents for their clients, handling sales as well as legal details. Such attorneys may also serve as "scouts" for industrial firms, remunerated for their efforts by finder's fees.

Consultants

For the small company virtually devoid of a technical department, a consultant may be a necessity. But a large company may also find him useful. His prime value is experience. Many consultants were at one time employees of big successful companies, working on product development. Consequently, their expertise may often shortcut certain procedures, reduce time, and save money. When hired for specific projects only, there is no increase in overhead. Lastly, a project may require a specialist that the company does not have.

Advertising agencies

Advertising agencies also perform consulting functions, usually in the latter stages of product development, as in drawing up a marketing plan and conducting market tests. But they will also render assistance in coming up with new product ideas at the request of the client. Some full function agencies also maintain new product departments. Young and Rubicam, for example, contains a section that works on all phases of new products, beginning with the idea and ending with commercialization.

---

[36] Interview with Union Carbide executives.

Figure 8-6. Example of a Patent Listing

PATENTS

GRANTED MAY 23, 1978

GENERAL AND MECHANICAL

4,090,264
LEG PROSTHESIS
Johnnie W. Thompson, Rte. 3, Box 263, Pelzer, S.C. 29669
Filed Nov. 26, 1976, Ser. No. 745,092
Int. Cl.² A61F *1/04, 1/08*
U.S. Cl. 3—27   **19 Claims**

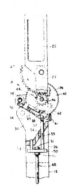

1. In an artificial leg device having an upper support member, a lower support member, a mechanical knee joint connected between said upper and lower support members, locking means carried by said lower support member for locking said upper and lower support members in a locked position to support the weight of the wearer, the improvement comprising:
  (a) said knee joint having a double-joint pivot connection connected between said upper and lower support members comprising:
  (i) a pair of linkage arms pivotally connected at a first pivot to said upper support member and at a second pivot to said lower support member,
  (ii) gear drives means connected between said upper and lower support members permitting said upper support member to turn about said first pivot while said lower support member turns about said second pivot providing smooth synchronous motion therebetween and increased knee bend flexibility, and
  (iii) a pair of tie arms pivotally connected to said upper and lower support members for maintaining said upper and lower supports at substantially the same angle relative to the knee joint connection during bending of the knee.

4,090,265
PARTITION WALL FOR WET CHAMBERS
Heinz Georg Baus, Ulmenweg 46, Thun, Switzerland (3601)
Filed Nov. 24, 1976, Ser. No. 744,875
Claims priority, application Germany, Dec. 2, 1975, 2554097;
Dec. 2, 1975, 2554098
Int. Cl.² A47K *3/4*
U.S. Cl. 4—154   **15 Claims**
1 Partition wall for wet chambers particularly for bathrooms or stall showers having several slidable wall panels with each wall panel suspended in an upper guide rail and with each wall panel having a lower guide ledge guided in a lower closed guide member, said lower closed guide member being shaped with steplike guide rails one above the other and having one continuous upper surface with said lower guide ledge disposed

above the upper surface of the steplike guide rails, said wall panels having permanent magnets installed in said lower guide ledges of the wall panels, said guide rails having keeper means, and each wall panel disposed against a surface of a guide rail

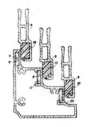

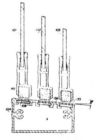

and held by magnetic force resulting from the attraction of said permanent magnets and said keeper means, in a direction perpendicular to the plane of the wall panel, and guided at said surface.

4,090,266
SWIMMING POOL CONSTRUCTION
John W. Price, P.O. Box 783, Moncton, New Brunswick, Canada
Filed Mar. 15, 1976, Ser. No. 667,018
Claims priority, application Canada, May 17, 1976, 242142
Int. Cl.² E04H *3/16*
U.S. Cl. 4—172.19   **11 Claims**

1. A wall assembly for a swimming pool comprising a con-

Source: *Official Gazette* (May 23, 1978), p. 1193.

Advertising people are drawn towards new products in the normal course of agency-client relationships. But a unique approach is taken by Jack Cantwell Associates, which solicits new business by developing new products. This agency first develops a product and then seeks a client to market it, being content to handle the advertising for the account. Naturally, such products are usually consumer goods and do not require complex technology in development.

Distribution channels

Marketing middlemen, such as wholesalers, manufacturers' agents and brokers, and retailers, are often a fertile area for ideas. Like internal salesmen, they are in close touch with customers and are familiar with their operations and sensitive to their problems. Middlemen are also independent businessmen, often dealing with more than one supplier, and consequently come by competitive information.

Some firms make a concerted effort to solicit opinions and advice from resellers. But there is no readily available manner in which to do so. Several companies have set up advisory boards selected from among their distributors. Others have promoted contests among their dealers and offered awards for new product suggestions.[37]

Unsolicited ideas

Practically all companies receive ideas from the public, entirely un-solicited. A few may have some value. But such letters are also the bane of legal departments, for they are possible grounds for litigation and damage claims.

If a company uses an outside idea, the originator is entitled to com-pensation. But the origin of an idea is not always clear-cut. A sugges-tion, by coincidence, may be similar to one already developed by the company. Or it may be common knowledge but not as yet put into effect. Such vagaries give rise to disputed claims as to authorship and hence to legal claims against the corporation. Courts have even ruled in favor of an individual when the idea that was submitted pertained to an expired patent, which would automatically make its use available to everyone.[38]

Companies have therefore sought to reduce lawsuits by setting up strict procedures for handling unsolicited ideas. A commonly practiced method is to insist that all senders sign disclosure statements, which stipulate that the firm has no obligation if the idea is already known or not used.

---

[37] *Ibid.*, p. 30.

[38] Karger and Murdock, *op. cit.*, p. 116.

REVIEW QUESTIONS

1. Exploration or search for new ideas should be restricted to specified fields of interest, though other fields may offer higher profit potentials and return on investment. Is this statement true or false? Explain your answer.

2. The process of exploring for new ideas would appear to be very simple. However, the process can be poorly or incorrectly executed. Some aspects may be overlooked completely. Explain what can go wrong with the exploration phase or how it can be poorly executed.

3. Assuming that you were appointed new product director for a manufacturer of health and beauty aids with $100 million in sales, what sources would you utilize to secure a steady flow of new product ideas related to your industry?

4. Prepare a checklist of sources for new product ideas. These sources would be searched routinely by the new product organization.

5. What would you suggest the company do routinely in order to stimulate and encourage the production of new product ideas from within the firm.

6. Are unsolicited new product suggestions from the public a fruitful source of new product ideas for the firm? Discuss the legal problem associated with such ideas.

7. A manufacturer seeking new product ideas relating to hand cleansers sought advice from a consultant. The consultant suggested an heuristic ideation approach—the cross-classification of product attributes listed under two or more dimensions relating to the product. Construct such a cross-classification for a hand cleanser based on attributes relating to physical form and package form.

8. Compare brainstorming and focus group interviews as techniques for generating new product ideas. What, if any, are the limitations of these techniques?

9. There is more work for the R&D department in a product-oriented company than in a marketing-oriented company. Is this statement true or false? Explain your answer.

10. A product-defined business organization approaches the search for new products differently from that of a marketing-oriented firm. Compare the two approaches.

11. Patent protection and trade secrets serve the same purpose. Compare the two methods.

12. New products derived from internal R&D become profitable faster and are less subject to failure than new products resulting from the acquisition of another company. Is this statement true or false? Explain you answer.

Screening

Screening, though part of the evaluation process, is essentially an elimination technique. By filtering out ideas that are apparently deficient, waste is cut down and time spent on ideas that have survived screening becomes more productive.

The criteria established for screening are derived from the same source as that for search—the corporate plan. These criteria are concentrated in three broad areas: products, markets, and finances.

Actual screening procedures, varying markedly among companies, can range from simple, yes-no checklists to elaborated scaling. In larger companies, where many new product ideas may flow from search to evaluative units, the screening process is usually a multistage procedure, employing different screening devices. Although all screening techniques have deficiencies, they are nevertheless useful in new product selection decisions.

Purpose of Screening

Developing new products is both complicated and time-consuming. Costs run high and risk is ever present. A sound business policy therefore demands that each project be evaluated before funds are committed to its development. Once it reaches the marketplace, what was done cannot easily be undone. It stands or falls on its own merits.

Actually, the evaluative process is stretched out in time, regulated by how long it takes from the inception of an idea to its readiness for market introduction. At numerous points along this span new data became available, previous analyses undergo modification, and management contemplates anew its past decisions in the light of more recent information. Screening refers to the very beginning of this assessment activity. It concerns itself with sorting the raw ideas, qualified and sharpened by the search team, into those that look attractive and those that appear jaded.

In a way, time is an ally of management; commitments for a project can be revoked at any date prior to commercialization. But recision is not without penalties. This pact with time carries a high price tag, for it is generally accompanied by mounting costs. The longer the alliance exists, the greater the cost for the security it ostensibly proffers.

Postponing to the last possible moment a decision to go ahead with a new product may buy a reduction in risk. But by no means can this outcome be regarded as imminent. In fact, delaying tactics might just as easily have the opposite effect. The new product development process—from concept to commercialization—probably suffers more obstructions, adversities, and handicaps from delays in management decision than from anything else.

A study of 200 leading companies indicates how stakes get progressively higher as the new product process approaches commercialization. This is shown in table 9–1.

Table 9-1
Cumulative Costs of New Products

| | Cumulative Expenditures (%) | |
Stage in the New Venture Process	Expenses	Total Expenditures*
Screening and business analysis	15	9
Development	72	39
Testing	82	54
Commercialization	100	100

*Includes capital expenditures.
Source: Booz, Allen & Hamilton, *Management of New Products*, pp. 10–11.

As table 9–1 indicates, almost three-quarters of all expenses have been incurred by the end of the development phase, on the average. Taking capital outlays into account, as shown in column 2, the major portion of all necessary expenditures has already been spent before commercialization is reached.

Such figures attest to the fact that the critical decisions take place at the beginning of the activity chain, before large amounts of money are budgeted and disbursed. This line of reasoning leads to the inevitable conclusion that emphasis should be directed to the start of the process, where it counts. A sound beginning is the nucleus of control over subsequent steps. Numerous companies have indeed taken this approach, concentrating on appraisals very early in the life of a new product idea. This is often referred to as preliminary evaluation or screening.

The Evaluation Process—An Example

While screening connotes evaluation, the exact dividing line that sets it apart from business analysis remains somewhat vague. There is often a gray area that overlaps the two. At Ralston Purina Company, for example, new product ideas are filtered through successive evaluative tests before they are turned over for development. But the point at which screening ends and the more thorough, in-depth analysis begins is difficult to determine. A brief description of the firm's appraisal process is as follows:[1]

1. *Judgmental screening.* The company's new product department makes a rough judgment as to the merits of each idea. Of the several hundred such proposals submitted during a year, from twenty five to thirty are selected for continuation in the appraisal procedure.

2. *Preliminary consumer reaction tests.* The remaining ideas are tested with small samples of consumers. Actually, these surveys involve concept testing. Each idea is described in a short paragraph of between thirty and forty words and submitted to prospective buyers to elicit their degree of interest.

3. *Preliminary marketing criteria evaluation.* Each idea is evaluated with respect to salient considerations outlined by management. These criteria include expected sales volume, product uniqueness, stage of the life cycle, degree of competition, and inherent consumer appeal. To be passed along, an idea must attain a designated rating level.

4. *Preliminary feasibility evaluation.* The new product ideas are then passed along to research and development, where they are assessed as to their feasibility in manufacturing. Existing patents are investigated to determine whether the new product would cause conflicting claims and possible litigation. Broad estimates are also made of required development time and capital equipment that might be needed.

5. *Preliminary concept test.* This is a follow-up to step 2. Alternative presentations of the concept are made to small focus groups in order to develop a promotional or positioning stance for the product.

6. *Final concept test.* This phase attempts to identify the characteristics of consumers to whom the product appeals and the size of the various population segments. Collection of such information usually calls for a large, broad-based sample of consumers.

7. *Final marketing potential and feasibility evaluation.* This entails a thorough business analysis. It requires refined estimates of price structure, profitability, capital outlays, and return on investment. Products that pass this last step are graduated to the research and development department to be prepared for further market tests and commercialization.

If the screening-business analysis distinctions are maintained, then probably steps 1–4 can be labeled screening. Steps 5 and 6 require considerable effort, cost, and detail and therefore can be viewed as business analysis. But the division is arbitrary and highly subjective, and the only useful purpose it serves is one of exposition.

---

[1] E. Patrick McGuire, *Evaluating New Product Proposals* (New York: The Conference Board, 1973), pp. 60–61.

Nature of Screening

As screening is practiced, there are many differences among companies, even among those in the same field. For example, concept testing is far from universal. The degree of elaboration and embellishment in screening procedures varies widely from firm to firm. Nevertheless, screening procedures do have certain features in common no matter how diverse the practice.

One distinguishing mark of screening is its comparatively quick, simple procedure of evaluation, as contrasted with business analysis. Not much effort or money is expended in screening activity. On the other hand, business analysis denotes a more thorough, painstaking appraisal of opportunities inherent in a new product idea.

Second, screening is linked directly to the selection process. Ideas that can withstand the rigors of screening tests are translated into formal documents, earmarked for more detailed investigation and possible development.

But screening stands out, conspicuously so, as an elimination technique. As the name implies, the procedure is analogous to passing masses of gravel and dirt through a filter in a search for nuggets. The gold-bearing rock remains on top of the wire mesh, along with worthless stone and mineral deposits. But the possible places where the shiny metal lies hidden are reduced enormously. There is no need to examine every particle of dirt in the search; selection is made from among what is left after screening.

The rationale for what is basically a rejection technique stems from the fact that very few ideas end up as successful products, perhaps one or two out of every hundred. In that event, the probability of working on a worthwhile proposal is .01 or .02, low indeed. But if screening can weed out those ideas that are manifestly poor, deficient, or limited, the probability of working on a productive concept increases. This probability doubles whenever the list is pared by half, provided that good ideas are not discarded at the same time. The typical screening operation discards about 75 percent of all prospective ideas.[2] In this manner, wasted effort and false starts are reduced, the amount of reduction depending upon the efficiency of the screening process.

Establishing Screening Criteria

Criteria for screening derive from the same guiding instrument as that for search, the firm's product policy as embodied in the corporate plan. Consequently, the responsibility for setting guidelines by which new products are judged rests with top management.

---

[2] Booz, Allen, & Hamilton, *op. cit.*, p. 9.

Screening criteria are apt to be more formal and elaborate in larger firms, where bureaucracy becomes an indispensable adjunct of control. New products involve people from various parts of a corporation, and the bigger the enterprise, the more impersonal the relationships among personnel. In such instances, structured, well-defined guidelines may be necessary for effective, well-planned action. New product proposals in large firms are usually reviewed by several layers of management. Consistent data must thus be available for cogent, well-reasoned decisions.

But even in the same company, the relative size of a project affects the scope of evaluation. Larger projects entail heavier investments and palpably greater risks. Under these conditions, all segments of management would press for a systematic, businesslike appraisal that is probably set forth in the company's manual of operating procedures.

These standards display little uniformity, vacillating greatly from company to company. Some managements endow new product planners with wide latitude in their choice of proposals. Others are highly restrictive, hemming product selection by exacting, circumscribed rules of evaluation.

In either circumstance, senior management reserves for itself the ultimate yes-no decision. When standards are narrowly defined, the ideas that qualify must conform fairly well to corporate goals. When a policy is vague or nonexistent, staff planners will actually design one in accordance with what they think senior management prefers or will accept. But regardless of how diligent middle management acts in such situations, there always remains room for divergent opinions and groups working at cross-purposes. Some observers have even placed development shortcomings and product failure on the doorstep of liberal guidelines.[3]

Regardless of latitude given planners, variations in criteria would still be the rule because of inevitable differences in companies—in their resources, in their competitive positions, and not least, in their philosophies. The first two are obvious. Every set of market and financial statistics proclaims the inequality among competing firms. The third type of difference is more subtle but nonetheless pervasive. For example, new product development is greatly affected by a particular management's risk aversion. According to Ronald Paul, president of Technomatic Consultants, a Chicago industrial consulting firm, "A company's management philosophy includes the *kinds of* decisions that it's comfortable with."[4] It is not risk *per se* that determines management's response

[3] C. Merle Crawford, "Strategies for New Product Development," *Business Horizons* (December, 1972), pp. 50–51, 57.

[4] "Paul: 'People Plus Organization Yield New Industrial Products'," *Marketing News* (December 30, 1977), p. 1.

but its attitude toward the type of risk and the way it is handled, as well as the personality of the business.

The relationship between management attitudes and a set of standards by which to judge new product proposals can be demonstrated by the example of H. J. Heinz. The company had been struggling for many years to break into attractive, profitable markets with a string of new food products. But failure dogged its steps. Such brands as Great American Soups, Happy Soups, Heinz salad dressing, and a fruit drink forebodingly named Help made their brief appearances and then quickly faded into nothingness.

The markets that Heinz had entered with these new products were dynamic and fast growing. But they were also intensely competitive, for they were the primary fields invaded by large, aggressive marketers, with sizable budgets committed to advertising and promotion. With Heinz management apparently unwilling, or unable, to risk large sums that in the event of failure could only be written off as sunken costs, the company changed its standards for approving new product ventures.

Heinz analyzed static, neglected, relatively uncompetitive markets, where management felt more comfortable with the type of risks incurred, and introduced new entries in these categories. Its first new product success in nearly a decade was scored in 1976 with Chili Fixin's, a formulation that contained all the ingredients and seasoning to make chili except ground beef, which consumers were supposed to add.

Introducing new products into mature, non-growth situations is not exactly what most marketing consultants would recommend. It would surely not meet the screening standards of such prominent food marketers as General Foods, General Mills, and Kraft. But they were successful for Heinz, and perhaps, at last, the company has found criteria that match its capability and management temperament.[5]

The most compelling reason for establishing evaluative standards is their useful role in new product development. Among the important functions of screening criteria are the following:

1. They provide a proper perspective for product planners, consistently pointing their efforts in the direction of corporate goals.

2. They cut down on wasted motion by steering planners away from projects that do not conform to policy set by top management and hence have little chance of receiving approval.

3. They provide a unity of purpose, allowing diverse groups to work together with a certain cohesion. New product search, for example, will concentrate in those areas that are most likely to meet screening criteria.

---

[5] "Heinz Reverses Poor Image...," p. 23.

4. They make arbitrary decisions less likely, even when pet ideas come directly from influential quarters.[6] Such proposals must still go through the same evaluative processes and be judged on common factors, hopefully in much the same way.

Types of Screening Criteria

Despite their diversity, screening criteria usually concern themselves with three elements: products, markets, and finances. A Conference Board study of 203 manufacturing and service firms reveals that the considerations mentioned most frequently are as follows:

Table 9-2
Most Frequently Mentioned Considerations Among Major Companies

Product Criteria	Market positioning
• Newness	• Effect on existing product line
• Fit with existing facilities and skills	• Competitive status
• Proprietary position	• Distribution characteristics
• Servicing requirements	**Financial Criteria**
• Technical feasibility (development and production)	• Overall profit contribution
	• Return on investment
• Legal considerations	• Investment requirement
• Organizational support	• Profit-risk ratio
Market Criteria	• Effect on cash flow
• Market size, share	• Accessory income possibilities
• Market growth	

Source: McGuire, *Evaluating New Product Proposals*, pp. 5–25.

Obviously all items in the above list will not affect every company in the same way. A consideration deemed imperative by one firm may be of only passing interest to another. Crucial elements—those that can make or break a new product—are similarly not identical for all corporations in all situations. Even the same factors, such as proprietary position and market growth will be given different definitions by different companies. Despite a certain degree of commonality or affinity, screening criteria of individual firms will differ from those of any general list. Standards for judgment must, of necessity, be tailored to the markets, resources, and organizational biases of the particular entities to which they refer.

Moreover, the criteria designated by any given firm are not of equal import. Some policy standards are vital and must be observed if a new product proposal is to get approval from senior management. When

---

[6] See Donald E. Vinson and John H. Jackson, "New Products Ideas Need Special Management," *Management Review* (December, 1973), pp. 24–25.

corporate policy calls for confining all activity to the food industry, a nonfood item is obviously out of place. The specification for a market of minimum size relegates all ideas that cannot reach that bottom figure to the trash heap, for their potential does not justify investment in the eyes of management. If a firm lacks the technical and managerial skills to produce or market an item, it hardly matters how profitable projections are. The odds are that management will turn thumbs down on that project. Each management, of course, will place different values on factors, depending upon its philosophy and risk-taking attitudes.

Because corporate plans explicitly acknowledge some considerations as being of far greater significance than others, many corporations have more than one set of screening criteria. A grocery products manufacturer, for example, has established two groups of standards—one that is mandatory for practically all products and another that describes expedient or desirable qualities of new product ideas. Planners are instructed to take both sets into account, as outlined in the following checklist:[7]

"Must-have" criteria

1. Be a manufactured food or beverage product, preferably one that entails more than, say, packing vegetables.

2. Be salable in large, expanding territories and capable of yielding $5 million in annual sales volume on a going basis.

3. Fill a perceived need with a sufficiently defined group of heavy users for the product.

4. Have unique product characteristics that offer distinctive benefits to the user.

5. Have a trading profit contribution of 20 percent to 25 percent.

"Would-like" criteria

1. Be a reasonably priced, high-volume packaged good.

2. Be easily proliferatd by line extensions and additions.

3. Provide the basis for a continuing business with a minimum life span of three to five years.

4. Be compatible with and able to carry the company's brand name.

5. Offer rapid payout (twelve months minimum, twenty-four months maximum).

6. Lend itself to mass media advertising.

---

[7] Quoted in McGuire, *Evaluating New Product Proposals*, p.27.

7. Be processable 60 percent in frozen form and 40 percent in other forms.

Multistage Screening

The existence of a double standard—"must-have" and "would-like" criteria—suggests that screening be done in stages. It makes little sense to proceed with an idea that violates a given rule. A preliminary assessment of mandatory requirements would therefore conserve time and effort by confining all subsequent screening activity to ideas that conform to basic corporate policy. Only if an idea passes the first test of compulsories would it progress to the next level of evaluative checks.

This sequence can be extended in several ways, with screening itself taking on various refinements as it progresses. There are several reasons that would justify such progressive modifications. The main one is that a firm usually has more good ideas than it can use. Resources are usually not sufficient to go ahead with all ideas that comply with primary criteria and, for that matter, with secondary ones as well. In short, all ideas that survive a simple checklist screen cannot possibly be developed. If a choice must be made, the logical one is to select those ideas that are perceived to have the greatest potentials.

The implementation of this rationale calls for at least a two-step procedure. Ideas that pass the preliminary stage are then appraised further for the purpose of estimating their relative values, so that the best of the lot can be selected. The assessment in these later stages is more thorough than in the initial ones but not nearly in as much detail as in the next, business analysis portion.

An example of multistage screening is that of Battelle's Columbus Laboratories, a private, nonprofit organization engaged in scientific research and development. These studies, funded by both government and industry, total more than 1,700 in a typical year, encompass highly diverse fields, and cover a wide range of new products and processes. Battelle's screening procedures for corporate development activities identify three different categories of screens: culling, rating, and scoring.[8]

Culling criteria, based on management guidelines for new investments, tend to be absolute. A project either meets them or it does not—yes or no with no in-between responses. Each criterion stands by itself as a critical element, like the "must-have" standards of the grocery products manufacturer cited previously.

Ratings are not mandatory by themselves, like culling criteria, but can be answered by a yes or no. Does any single firm control more than

[8] H. Ronald Hamilton, "Screening Business Development Opportunities," *Business Horizons* (August, 1974), pp. 19-21.

40 percent of the market? Will sales have a seasonal pattern? Will marketing require heavy, nonpersonal promotion? Such criteria are grouped into cost-homogeneous units, and a proposal must meet some minimum score for the group as a whole. For instance, a new product idea must rate favorably on some designated percentage of all criteria in the set.

Scoring refers to a range of values for each criterion. Individual scores then are summed to produce some composite value for the new products idea. Since scoring is much more expensive than culling or rating, it is usually done last.

Typical survival rates at each stage of screening are shown in table 9-3 (according to Battelle's experience).

Table 9-3
Screening Survival Rates: Battelle Columbus

Screening Class	Survival Rate for Ideas Entering Class (%)	Cumulative Survival Rate (%)
Culling	30–60	30–60
Rating	40–70	12–42
Scoring	50–75	6–30

Source: Hamilton, *op. cit.*, p. 21.

Whether a firm adopts a multistage approach depends upon its corporate structure and especially upon the number of ideas flowing from search to evaluation. A few ideas can obviously be screened at a single session; there is no good reason for breaking up the screening process. But when an organizational structure exists to generate a continuous stream of ideas, the more elaborate procedures are conducive to efficiency. Consequently, the multistage method does not apply to many small and medium-sized firms, where resources are limited, new product ideas are not actively pursued, and formal, evaluative units are nonexistent. On the other hand, screening in steps is most prevalent in large companies.

Ideas may also be processed one at a time or in batches. Screening several ideas in one operation may offer certain economies. But more importantly, the batch process seems to provide greater regularity and better control in the flow of proposals from screening to business analysis. Since the probability of failure in screening tests is decidedly greater than that of passage, the one-by-one procedure may run up against a string of bad luck, like a series of losing choices at a roulette wheel. Several consecutive ideas may fail to make it in the later screening stages and thereby create a void in parts of the evaluation process. If this is not a significant consideration, the individualistic approach is a feasible alternative to handling ideas in groups.

Preliminary Screening

A preliminary screen is the first, rather rough attempt to judge the value of a new product idea. It is relatively simple but must contain those imperatives enunciated in a firm's policy decisions. To illustrate the principles of a preliminary screen, a checklist of basic requirements was derived from the policy statement of a consumer goods company. These criteria, which are fairly typical, can be described as in table 9-4.

Table 9-4
Example of Basic Criteria for Preliminary Screening

---

1. The item should be in a field of activity in which the corporation is engaged.
2. If the idea involves a companion product to others already being manufactured, it should be made from materials to which the corporation is accustomed.
3. The item should be capable of being produced on the type and kind of equipment that the corporation normally operates.
4. The item should be easily handled by the corporation's existing sales force through the established distribution pattern.
5. The potential market for the product should be at least $_____.
6. The market over the next five years should be expected to grow at a faster rate than GNP.
7. Return on investment, after taxes, must reach a minimum level of ____ percent.

The above checklist has translated the primary criteria into statements that can be answered yes or no by inspection or quick referral to secondary data. With the exception of the last item, ideas can readily be evaluated as yes-no propositions by almost anyone knowledgeable about the business. Technical questions, such as those relating to equipment and materials, can be referred to the appropriate departments whenever the appraiser is in doubt. But a yes or no answer should be forthcoming without spending much time to research the point at issue. A violation of one necessary condition is enough to shelve a proposal. For secondary criteria, usual practice dictates a minimum percentage of affirmative mentions as a provision for pursuing an idea.

Item 7, the return-on-investment criterion, departs radically from the remaining ones in terms of ease and precision with which it can be judged. An accurate forecast is difficult even for an existing product, and it requires considerable effort. How then does one estimate return on investment for something that is not yet an actuality?

Opinions on the subject are highly diverse. One school of thought has an abiding faith in the subjective beliefs of managers when reinforced by Bayesian decision rules. It therefore advocates that subjective estimates be used as data. At the other extreme is the view, a minority one, that return on investment has no place in screening criteria, for it is not unequivocally available.[9] Because it cannot be validly determined, it should be conveniently forgotten. Some businessmen have even maintained that, notwithstanding the need for financial analysis and control, roughly 90 percent of all business decisions regarding new products can be made on the basis of underlying, nonfinancial information.[10] If so, this would further buttress the logic of the latter point of view.

But most managements insist that an idea be able to satisfy an investment goal before money is spent for detailed analysis. Return on investment is probably one of the first issues top management will inquire about, regardless of informational quality. And subordinates are not prone to tell their superiors that everything they want to know is not always knowable.

In fact, the way in which appropriations are made for new projects has been likened to a "propose-dispose system." Lower echelon executives propose, senior officials dispose.

This call for project justification is the inevitable consequence of a rationalistic view of innovation held by practically all corporations with the same zeal as an article of faith. They see new product risk as something that can be researched, analyzed, and forecast and hence new product development as something that can be directed, controlled, and managed. Good management further implies minimizing risk in relation to potential rewards, and therefore, justification for action must precede the action itself. How else can such activity be funnelled into an orderly, logically considered direction? Consequently, lower level executives who are usually delegated the responsibility of carrying out new product proposals must get approval before they can act. They have sometimes been called "entrepreneurs without authority" because the vital entrepreneurial decisions are handed down from the top. At any rate, a project must be justified in financial terms if it is to receive a budget for development. Some authorities have thus recommended that criteria dealing with profitability and financial data be deferred to the last step of the screening process, as they are the most difficult and expensive to ascertain.[11] In this way, higher cost screening, it is argued, would be applied only to those ideas that have qualified on the other counts. But this position is somewhat ambiguous, for it is readily acknowledged that estimates of revenue, costs, and profits signify only

---

[9] Roderick White, *Consumer Product Development* (London: Longman Group Limited, 1973), pp. 66–67.

[10] C. J. Mathey, "New Approaches to the Management of Product Planning," *Research Management* (November, 1975), p. 13.

[11] Hamilton, *op. cit.*, p. 17.

crude guesses and that good figures cannot be derived in the screening stage. The statistics, such as they are, merely represent very early thought about subsequent, in-depth analyses. While they may have some value in avoiding bewilderment and unsuspecting reversals later, they contribute little to the quality of a decision that concerns itself with screening ideas. Under these conditions, it is just as logical to include return-on-investment criteria—if haphazard guesswork must be made—at the beginning, in the preliminary screen. Why waste much effort on the improbable, on a prediction that will be highly unreliable in any circumstance? In fact, to expend much effort for arriving at more reasonable estimates would countervail the main purpose of screening—a relatively fast, cheap filter. Relegating such investigations to a later stage of product development, when projections become more detailed and realistic, yields its own rewards.

Product Profile Ratings—Ranked Data

Product profile analysis seems to be a widely used method of screening in the later stages. Its main purpose is the comparison of various proposals, so that the most promising survivors of the preliminary tests can be impelled forward to the business analysis phase. Though there are a great many variations, the technique basically calls for ideas to be rated in terms of a number of key characteristics.

One form of such a rating system is the simple ordinal measure, wherein each criterion is scored on a five-point scale. The categories are arbitrary and can be designated by letters A to E. The A might be made to stand for very good, the C for average, etc. If each idea is then rated on eleven different criteria, the basic design can be represented as follows:

Table 9-5
Example of Ordinal Rating Scale

Criteria	Very Good (A)	Good (B)	Average (C)	Poor (D)	Very Poor (E)
1			X		
2		X			
3	X				
4	X				
5			X		
6					X
7		X			
8		X			
9			X		
10	X				
11		X			

The ratings in table 9-5 can also be presented in graphic form. A profile chart derived from rating criteria on the ordinal scale is illustrated in figure 9-1. The numbers at the column heads represent the criteria by which the idea is rated. The rating scale, from A to E, is shown as rows. While this chart suggests continuous data, which they are not, the form facilitates comparisons of product profiles that can be made by the use of overlays.

Figure 9-1. Example of Product Profile in Graphic Form

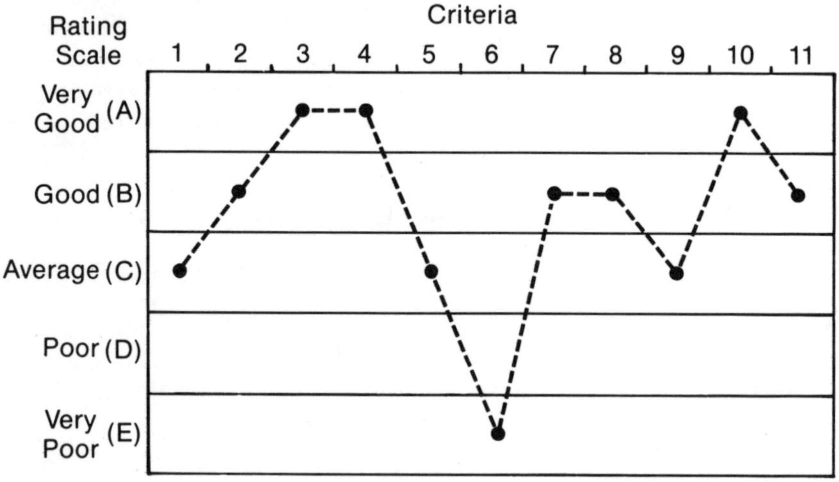

Note: Figure 9-1 was made to conform to data in table 9-5.

Whether in tabular or graphic form, product profiles based on ranked data are extremely difficult to evaluate. In effect, comparisons are done visually because the properties of ordinal scales do not permit meaningful arithmetic operations to be performed. Statistical descriptions and summary information are thus confined to positional measures, such as medians, quartiles, percentiles, and the like.

For example, the criteria in the illustration given (table 9-5 and figure 9-1) were actually listed in order of decreasing importance. That is, criterion 1 is of greater import than criterion 2, which in turn is more vital to a new product than criterion 3, etc. Now suppose idea X went through this screening and obtained an A rating on criterion 1 and a B on criterion 2. Another new product idea, Y, came up with an opposite result—a B score on criterion 1 and an A on criterion 2. One cannot actually say which idea is better, X or Y. The difference between criteria may be inconsequential, whereas that between very good and good may be momentous. Or the reverse may be true.

Even if the importance of the two criteria were equal or known, any interpretation about differences that separate the two ideas can only be subjective. An A score is apparently better than one of B, but that by itself does not say how much better. When there are several criteria, the problem becomes even more formidable, for one cannot tell whether a difference between ranks A and B is equal to one between B and C. In short, there is no way of measuring the difference between scores by which criteria are judged.

Only at the very extremes are answers clear-cut. A product profile with mostly A ratings can be distinguished rather easily from one with scores clustered in B or C. But when patterns are not quite as distinct or when they take on irregular shapes, sorting the best ideas from a large lot becomes a troublesome task, to say the least. For this reason, screening procedures have favored more quantitative methods, those that lend themselves to usual mathematical manipulations. As a consequence, the most popular such technique has become the summated rating.

Product Profiles—Summated Data

The system of summated ratings is very much like that of ranked data but with certain modifications. The most important of these are as follows:

1. As with ranked data, ideas are rated as to their expected performance on various criteria. But the ratings are in terms of numerical values. When scoring is done by several people, results for each criterion are averaged.

2. Each criterion is given a weight in accordance with its presumed importance to the success of a new product.

3. Weights and scores are multiplied and their products added to obtain a single overall rating for an idea. This summated score obviously facilitates comparisons of different ideas. A summated rating can then be described as:

$$R = \sum_{i=1}^{n} W_i S_i$$

where:

R = Overall rating.

W_i = Weight of the ith criterion.

S_i = Score of the idea on the ith criterion.

n = Number of criteria used in screening.

To illustrate this sort of rating system, we will take the sames data shown in table 9-5 and introduce the necessary modifications. Thus, each criterion has been given a weight, an arbitrary one, and numbers 1 to 5 were substituted for letters A to E. The results are shown in table 9-6.

Table 9-6
Example of Summated Ratings

Criteria	Weight	Very Good (5)	Good (4)	Average (3)	Poor (2)	Very Poor (1)	Total
1........................	.15			X			.45
2........................	.12		X				.48
3........................	.11	X					.55
4........................	.10	X					.50
5........................	.10			X			.30
6........................	.09					X	.09
7........................	.08		X				.32
8........................	.07		X				.28
9........................	.07			X			.21
10........................	.06	X					.30
11........................	.05		X				.20
Total	1.00						3.68

In the above example, the sum of the weights is 1.0. Thus, the maximum score of any idea is 5.0. If an idea scored "very good" on all criteria, its summated rating would add to 5.0. The idea rated in the illustration (table 9–6) received an overall score of 3.68, which is close to two-thirds of the maximum. This would probably place the idea somewhere on the borderline between acceptance and rejection, though the exact cutoff point in most instances is a judgmental decision arrived at by trial and error.

Summated ratings apparently permit ideas to be compared with each other on a common basis, so that the highest rated can be given priority. They also provide a ready means of judging each new idea in the light of past experience and estimating the risk involved. Nevertheless, these rating systems are not without flaws, and their usefulness, some critics maintain, may be significantly impaired on several counts.[12]

One type of objection deals with the uses and abuses of scaled data. Simply assigning numbers to categories like "very good" and "good" undoubtedly allows integers to be added, subtracted, divided, and multiplied. Such calculations, representing values attached to various ideas, can then be gauged on a common yardstick. But do these arithmetic exercises, it is asked, make interpretations more meaningful when applied to real market situations? Embellishing ordinal scales with equal-

[12] See Marshall Freimer and L. S. Simon, "The Evaluation of New Product Alternatives," *Management Science* (February, 1967). pp. B279–B292.

looking intervals between categories rests on an assumption, surely a flimsy one, that increments of importance between successive ranks are equal. In short, the conversion of ranks to numerical values is somewhat arbitrary. However, this might be better accomplished through paired comparisons and the "Law of Comparative Judgment."[13]

Other difficulties with summated ratings concern themselves with the ability of managers to rate ideas as finely and precisely as scaling implies. Do managers really have a deep enough understanding to know exactly how ideas, when formed into products, will perform in the marketplace? Critics say no. They maintain that managers are given far more credit than they deserve. To think that any person can tell how a hypothetical product will behave in a hypothetical market of some hypothetical tomorrow, with little more than a bare description of the idea, skeptical observers hold, is to endow executives with powers that border on omniscience. If such were the case, new product failures would be a rare occurrence, a situation highly contrary to fact.

Another possible source of bias is that scores may be related to weights assigned to individual criteria. That is, an evaluator may judge an idea one way if the basis for judgment is unimportant. But he may turn around and score the idea quite differently when the same criterion takes on increasing weight. Higher stakes may introduce greater cautiousness.

Evaluators may also not be steadfastly consistent in their scoring of ideas, a familiar human failing. But this deficiency can be rectified by more detailed definitions of the various categories and instructions as to scoring. An example of such explanations for rating ideas is shown in figure 9–2.

Although explicit definitions and instructions can reduce inconsistency, subjective elements cannot be kept out completely. For example, subtle ambiguities can creep into ratings when evaluators score criteria with varying intensities of conviction. One person judging an idea may be emphatic that it would be very good in meeting the standard of merchandisability. Another may rate the new product idea in the same manner yet have gnawing doubts about its ability to fulfill the high expectations of the evaluation. A refinement to obviate this difficulty calls for raters to express the degree of confidence they have in their scores. The addition of this nuance, modifying ratings by confidence level values, increases the complexity of the scoring system. But it is not at all certain that effectiveness or sensitivity would gain significantly. In that event, justification for such a trade-off remains problematical.[14]

---

[13] Paul E. Green and Donald S. Tull, *Research for Marketing Decisions* (3rd ed., Englewood Cliffs: Prentice-Hall, Inc., 1975), pp. 170–172, 184–191.

[14] Slocum, *op. cit.*, pp. 66–69.

Figure 9-2. Example of Definitions for Rating Criteria for Screening

	Very Good	Good	Average	Poor	Very Poor
4. MARKETABILITY					
A. *Relation to present distribution channels*	Can reach major markets by distributing through present channels.	Can reach major markets by distributing mostly through present channels, partly through new channels.	Will have to distribute equally between new and present channels, in order to reach major markets.	Will have to distribute mostly through new channels in order to reach major markets.	Will have to distribute entirely through new channels in order to reach major markets.
B. *Relation to present product lines*	Complements a present line which needs more products to fill it.	Complements a present line that does not need, but can handle, another product.	Can be fitted into a present line.	Can be fitted into a present line but does not fit entirely.	Does not fit in with any present product line.
C. *Quality/price relationship*	Priced below all competing products of similar quality.	Priced below most competing products of similar quality	Approximately the same price as competing products of similar quality.	Priced above many competing products of similar quality.	Priced above all competing products of similar quality.
D. *Number of sizes and grades*	Few staple sizes and grades.	Several sizes and grades, but customers will be satisfied with few staples.	Several sizes and grades, but can satisfy customer wants with small inventory of nonstaples.	Several sizes and grades, each of which will have to be stocked in equal amounts.	Many sizes and grades which will necessitate heavy inventories.
E. *Merchandising*	Has product characteristics over and above those of competing products that lend themselves to the kind of promotion, advertising, and display that the given company does best.	Has promotable characteristics that will compare favorably with the characteristics of competing products.	Has promotable characteristics that are equal to those of other products.	Has a few characteristics that are promotable, but generally does not measure up to characteristics of competing products.	Has no characteristics at all that are equal to competitors' or that lend themselves to imaginative promotion.
F. *Effects on sales of present products*	Should aid in sales of present products.	May help sales of present products; definitely will not be harmful to present sales.	Should have no effect on present sales.	May hinder present sales some; definitely will not aid present sales.	Will reduce sales of presently profitable products.

Lastly, the criteria themselves may not be quite independent of each other. For example, product characteristics are related to distribution channels. A low-priced, packaged food product will normally depend upon supermarkets as a major sales outlet. And both factors, product characteristics and distribution outlets, are associated with the type of promotional mix employed. This packaged food in self-service stores would undoubtedly be linked with marketing tactics that stress non-personal communication, such as advertising, sales promotion, and point-of-purchase displays. Consequently, screening forms might admit individual criteria that are closely correlated with each other. When screening criteria lack independent attributes, their ability to discriminate between success or failure of a project is accordingly diminished.

Freimer-Simon Model

One view that has received much attention, often referred to as the Freimer-Simon model after its authors, addresses some of the major problems inherent in screening, particularly those dealing with discriminating capabilities of criteria.[15] Freimer and Simon have argued that vaguely defined cutoff points combined with individual factors treated independently have rendered marketing decisions insensitive to changes in ratings. In their view, summated ratings are too crude to assess alternative courses of action, no matter how precise the assigned factor weights and score values. They advocate that such systems be used only after analyses can show that alterations in factor weights and score values can produce substantial changes in overall ratings and their standard deviations.[16]

Accordingly, the Freimer-Simon model postulates a multidimensional space, which encompasses the criteria by which an idea is judged. Two probability distributions are then located in this spacial configuration. One of these density functions represents successful products, the other unsuccessful ones. Such distributions may be constructed from past observations, subjective estimates, or both. Models based on objective information would require a company to have maintained historical data, with records lending themselves to such analysis.

Criteria weights and cutoff points in the Freimer-Simon model are developed by multiple discriminant analysis. This statistical technique can identify entities of mutually exclusive sets and thus is useful in isolating criteria that appear prominent in predicting market variation.

After realizing weights for screening criteria, the model proceeds by estimating the likelihood ratio of success or failure of a given idea.

---

[15] Freimer and Simon, "The Evaluation of New Product Alternatives."

[16] Marshall Freimer and Leonard S. Simon, "Screening New Product Ideas," *AMA Conference Proceedings* (Fall, 1968), pp. 99–104.

Bayesian analysis is then undertaken to evaluate the degree of risk inherent in a decision to accept or reject an idea.

The application of multivariate statistical techniques to screening lists suggests approaches for improving the choice of criteria and cutoff points.[17] Perhaps they can be made more meaningful and sensitive to marketing situations through sharper statistical analysis. Yet the Freimer-Simon model, for all its logically traversed reasoning, has not satisfactorily solved the most serious problems of screening.

Partly, the reason may lie in the analytical procedures used. Some experts, for example, have held that degrees of success or failure may be a better classification than the dichotomy that was actually employed.[18] But this modification would also increase the complexity and costs of screening, while potential benefits are yet to be demonstrated.

Another reason may be the type of data that the model requires. For instance, relatively few companies possess historically relevant data from which to build distributions of successful and unsuccessful products. When subjective data are used, the analysis falters before the assumption of unerring intelligence.

Perhaps the greatest value of the Freimer-Simon analysis has been the questions it raised. These are perennial ones and apply to practically all screening operations.

First, screening is subject to two types of errors: those of omission and those of commission. A potentially successful product can be rejected in screening. Contrarily, a potentially unsuccessful product can be accepted. But any analysis, including that of Freimer and Simon, can cover only the latter kind of error—ideas that were passed on for development on the basis of screening and failed later. It must remain silent about rejected ideas, some of which might have been successful had they been allowed to proceed to development and eventual commercialization.

A careful search will yield illustrations of successful rejects, to be sure. The classic example of a new product nobody wanted was the first copier machine, later named Xerox, which was turned down for development by more than twenty major corporations. The automatic model that followed was also adversely evaluated by several consulting firms hired by Xerox Corporation to study its marketing feasibility. Many independent electronic firms were started by frustrated scientists and engineers because their companies refused to exploit their new ideas.

But such examples are the exception, not the rule. The majority of

---

[17] See Allan D. Shocker, *et al.*, "Toward the Improvement of New Product Search and Screening," American Marketing Association, *1969 Fall Conference Proceedings*, pp. 168–175.

[18] David B. Montomery and Glen L. Urban, *Management Science in Marketing* (Englewood Cliffs: Prentice-Hall, Inc., 1969), p. 311.

rejected new product ideas are quietly laid to rest, and no one can tell what might have been. Nor would any company spend money experimenting along these lines—and there is no urgent reason why it should. How then can one establish a true cut off point whereby the two types of bad decisions are minimized?

The second major problem is that the effects of screening can seldom be completely separated from those of other operations that have no relation to screening. For example, R&D may conceptualize an idea in a unique way, so as to give the eventual product an enormous differential advantage. If this development was never contemplated in the screening process, was the score really a predictor of success? Or engineering may develop a new process or new materials hardly imagined by the evaluators after screening has been completed. Suppose further that these engineering innovations reduced costs so greatly as to give the new product a huge price advantage. In this instance, success would have little to do with screening because the really important ingredient was unknown at the time a preliminary evaluation was conducted.

Lastly, summated ratings have been known to display certain anomalies. For example, an idea may pass the screening test yet be deficient on an important criterion. This can be corrected easily, however, by specifying a minimum score not only for the overall value but for individual criteria that are deemed important.

All in all, an overview of preliminary evaluation intimates that the value of screening, perhaps arrived at intuitively, is primarily as a cost saver, not a revenue generator. It cuts expenses by sifting out the obviously bad choices. It does not enhance revenue by designating the obviously good choices, for these are not so obvious. The situation is somewhat analogous to the experience of broadcast executives having to select new programs by viewing pilot shows. They are able to spot a class D film with a fair degree of accuracy. But they cannot pick a winner, a show that will garner a high rating with any degree of consistency.

In like manner, summated ratings are indicative, not predictive, of an idea's potential. Small differences between ratings have no credence. In this sense, screening results serve as a guide to managerial decisions, never as a substitute for them.

Most firms that use screening arrive at cutoff points empirically. Those with large numbers of new products might attempt to associate different score levels with different probablilities of success. However derived, cutoff points are necessary, for they mark a critical point beyond which a company will not go to develop an idea. The focus thus remains on the positive, on the best-judged ideas, which are then analyzed in detail. The remaining ones are dropped, without regrets, qualms, or second guesses.

Early Stage Testing

Some companies, particularly those producing consumer goods, employ concept testing in their preliminary evaluations. General Foods and Green Giant, for example, conduct concept tests almost routinely as part of their screening process.[19]

Actually, concept testing may be done at various stages of new product evolvement, depending upon its purpose. Most testing probably takes place when the proposed offering is well along the road to commercialization, and planners are greatly concerned with advertising, product positioning, and customer usage patterns. This chapter directs its attention only to those tests that may be considered as part of preliminary evaluation, when the new product is still in a vague, undefined "idea" form.

At this early stage, concept testing attempts to assess new product ideas from a consumer's point of view. Specifically, its main purposes are as follows:

1. To see whether consumer views match those of company evaluators, and hence, whether marketing prospects are in conformity with corporate objectives.

2. To assist in choosing the best of several concept alternatives. There is a fine distinction between an idea and a concept; the former can be expressed by alternative versions or concept forms. For example, a powder mixed with water can be presented as a breakfast drink, a juice, a snack, etc. Or the idea may be formulated in several ways, with different physical appearances. Especially when new products tend to be line extensions, screening tends to concentrate on the selection of concept alternatives.

Early stage testing may also have secondary aims, though they are decidedly minor:

1. To indicate target markets or market segments for the ensuing business analysis.

2. To obtain clues as to possible promotional appeals.

3. To suggest modifications early, when costs are lowest. This is feasible when the new product is uncomplicated, technological factors are trivial, and specifications are of little concern to R&D.

Samples for testing consumer products run a wide gamut of possible designs. The most popular embrace focus groups, employees, central locations like shopping centers, consumer panels, and area samples of

---

[19] McGuire, *Evaluating New Product Proposals*, pp. 35, 40.

households. Omnibus surveys, of which there are several, afford a marketer the opportunity to add his own special questions in a national study. Michael Amoroso, Inc., recently announced a new syndicated survey called "Idea Screen," wherein companies can test an idea with 1,000 consumers in personal interviews for a fee of $900.[20] About twenty new product ideas are included in each study, and the client receives ratings, like those for TV shows, so that ideas can be gauged against concept norms.

Ideas are usually presented for early stage testing as short descriptions of one or two paragraphs. Because industrial products normally require visual aids, best results are attained at a later stage of development, when prototypes are available. Concepts may be tested singly, called monadic testing, or in clusters. Either way, measurements make widespread use of attitude scaling, which exists in numerous variations.

Although helpful in evaluating an idea, concept test results are often not clear-cut. The manner in which material is arranged and exposed to respondents can significantly alter research findings.[21] Intention-to-buy measurements, which are a prominent feature of most tests, can hardly be projected as an indicator of sales.[22] An immense chasm may exist between attitudes people express on a survey and their eventual behavior in the marketplace. Some companies use intention-to-buy responses as cutoff points. Bristol Myers, for example, requires 20 percent of product users as a minimum to state a definite intention to buy.[23] The limitations of concept testing do not seem to act as a deterrent to companies. But neither do they follow results blindly. Rather, planners must consider the shortcomings of such market research, handling results with caution and acting accordingly.

Computer Models

With the growing use of computers in corporate operations, mathematical models have made deep inroads in new product planning. A model is a representative of reality whether it is a system or a process. The representation can be complete or partial.

In this sense, models do not depend upon computers for their theoretical structures. A screening checklist, with criteria, weights, and score values, is in essence a model of the marketing process. It visualizes

---

[20] "Product Ideas Screened by New Service," *Advertising Age* (May 22, 1978), p. 22.

[21] See Edward M. Tauber, "What Is Measured by Concept Testing," *Journal of Advertising Research* (December, 1972), pp. 36–37; Russel I. Haley and Ronald Gatty, "The Trouble With Concept Testing," *Ibid.*, (June, 1968), pp. 23–35.

[22] Gareth W. Jones, "New Product Development," *The Conference Board Record* (September, 1976), p. 27.

[23] Interview with executives of Bristol Myers.

factors that determine success or failure, their relative importance, and their relationships to the eventual outcome and to each other. When relevant variables are left out, incorrect relationships among variables might be inferred from the model. Conversely, a screening model might contain superfluous elements, variables that are not related to an outcome. This is more easily corrected by analysis. In any event, highly refined models may still be insensitive to marketing outcomes.

There are basically two types of models, classified in accordance with their purpose. One kind may be called a descriptive model. Its purpose is to explain or predict a given result. The other type may be called a decision model, constructed to evaluate alternative courses of action. In both instances, the basic difference between computer-based and non-computer models is one of complexity rather than one of kind. The electronic devices permit infinitely more complicated relationships to be incorporated in computations and a volume of calculations that is inconceivable by sheer manpower alone.

In general, early stage screening has witnessed rather few attempts at computer-based methods. Most of them apply to operational control and business analysis, which follow the screening stage. But these sparse, somewhat irregular endeavors may yet be a harbinger of things to come.

Pessemeier Search Model

A somewhat unique approach is Pessemeier's model for new product search.[24] Its basic purpose is to select the best plan from among a number of alternative proposals that management considers suitable. But some definition of what constitutes "best" must be established before a choice can be made. In the Pessemeier model, the criteria for selection of a new product proposal are (1) an expected value, which represents an expected return on investment, and (2) a standard deviation, which can be interpreted as the degree of risk. On the basis of this trade-off between return on investment and assumed risk, management must determine which proposals fall within an acceptable range. From this standpoint, computer search also serves as a screening model. The rate of return, in effect, defines the cutoff point for discarding or proceeding further with an idea.

Although this model has been in existence for more than a decade, interest in it has been largely academic. The amount of information that must be supplied as input is rather substantial, with much of it comprising subjective judgment rather than hard data. At the same time, the computation burden may be heavy.[25]

---

[24] Pessemeier, *New Product Decisions*, pp. 39–71.

[25] Montgomery and Urban, *op. cit.*, p. 303.

The time and effort required to implement this decision model are far in excess of what corporations are currently expending for screening operations. Perhaps as computer utilization expands, efficiency gains are achieved, and data banks are developed, such computer models will enjoy wider usage. Meanwhile, this model appears to have limited potential, and cruder but cheaper screening methods prevail.

Oregon Innovation Center Model (IIES)

A somewhat different approach to model building was taken by Innovation Center at the University of Oregon. The center, with funding by the National Science Foundation, developed a computer screening procedure referred to as Invention and Innovation Evaluation System (IIES).[26]

Its main purpose is to evaluate, quickly and inexpensively, the offerings of independent inventors before any commitment is made for development or commercialization. A secondary aim is to provide inventors with feedback, so that they can better understand and appreciate entrepreneurial decisions relating to new products. In this manner, it is hoped, less time will be spent on fruitless ideas and creative effort will become more productive.

IIES is essentially a generalized rating system with certain niceties mixed in to meet its special goals. It contains thirty-three criteria pertaining mainly to the commercial feasibility of a proposal. The weights attached to each are described as derived from "inputs of experts in the field" and research as to discriminators of new product success and failure. But the description also notes that the weighting system is still under review and "might take a considerable amount of time and research before it can be formalized."

The salient features of IIES can best be understood by examining the rating format and its instructions. By way of illustration, a scoring sheet portion dealing with business risk factors is shown in figure 9-3.

As can readily be observed in figure 9-3, critical elements—those that preclude any further development of the project if scored negatively—are mingled with noncritical factors. For example, the first alternative under criterion 5 says the idea is not functionally feasible. It indicates the existence of a major flaw in logic or engineering design and practically renders the remaining evaluation irrelevant. The same might be said about the first choice of criterion 6, "impossible to produce now or in the foreseeable future." A product that cannot be made cannot be marketed. However, evaluators must complete the entire screening form, regardless of their scores on critical factors. Inventors will then

---

[26] G. G. Udell, *et al., Guide to Invention and Innovation Evaluation* (Eugene, OR: University of Oregon, 1977).

Figure 9-3. Sample Section of Scoring Sheet of IIES

BUSINESS RISK FACTORS:

5. FUNCTIONAL FEASIBILITY: In terms of intended functions, will it actually do what it is intended to do?

_____ The concept is not sound, cannot be made to work.
_____ It won't work now, but might if modified.   _____ DK
_____ It will work, but major changes may be needed.
_____ It will work, but minor changes might be needed.   _____ NA
_____ It will work—no changes necessary.

6. PRODUCTION FEASIBILITY: With regard to technical processes or equipment required for production, this invention will...

_____ Be impossible to produce now or in the foreseeable future.
_____ Be very difficult to produce.   _____ DK
_____ Have some problems which can be overcome.
_____ Have only minor problems.   _____ NA
_____ Have no problems.

7. STAGE OF DEVELOPMENT: Based on available information, there is...

_____ Only an idea with drawings and/or description; no prototype.
_____ A rough prototype which demonstrates the concept, but is not fully developed and tested.   _____ DK
_____ A rough prototype with performance and safety testing completed.
_____ A final prototype with testing completed; however,   _____ NA
minor changes might be needed.
_____ A market-ready prototype.

8. INVESTMENT COSTS: The amount of capital and other costs necessary for development to the market-ready stage would be:

_____ Greater than returns—should be dropped.
_____ Excessive—might not be recoverable.   _____ DK
_____ Heavy—probably recoverable.
_____ Moderate—recoverable within five years.   _____ NA
_____ Low—recoverable within two years.

Source: Udell, *op. cit.*, pp. 13-14.

receive a complete appraisal of their ideas. While not very promising, alternative approaches may still be possible.

The scoring sheet also has a place for "don't know" answers. Even though the evaluators are experts in their fields, their expertise does not extend to everything, to every criterion and every product. The "don't know" answer permits evaluators to gracefully disqualify themselves when unable to make an informed judgment. A relatively large number of "don't know" answers, however, generally implies a high level of uncertainty, and hence, risk.

The implications of IIES are much broader than those of its current operation. Although designed to appraise the output of inventors working on their own, the system can be altered easily to evaluate the creative efforts in a corporate environment.

Its diversion to such purposes would necessitate the inclusion of company-oriented criteria. As of now, IIES deals only with the question of commercial feasibility. Can the proposed new product be marketed profitably? When applied to a firm, the system must invariably incorporate criteria of that particular entity. Is that corporation desirous and capable of marketing the proposed new product?

Whether applied to individuals or corporations, IIES has much in common with other screening systems. Basically, it is an aid, not a replacement, for decision makers. At this stage, decisions must be made with imperfect and even inadequate knowledge. The output of any system is tied directly to the quality of its input. Thus, a screening system provides information, logically arranged and digested, for the decision-making process.

R E V I E W   Q U E S T I O N S

1. Discuss the purpose of the screening stage.

2. What would be the affect on the product development process if the screening stage were omitted?

3. Pragmatically, is the screening process a nebulous exercise, or is it a formal appraisal procedure with a specific beginning and a definite ending? Compare the pragmatic practice of screening to its academic formulation.

4. Since screening is itself part of a multistage approach to product development, what is the rationale for a multistage approach for the screening process?

5. Describe the screening procedures that would be appropriate for a small firm and for a large firm.

6. Companies A and B offer competitive products within the same industry and market segments and are of approximately equal size and financial strength. However, their product screening criteria differ significantly. Discuss the possible reasons for this difference.

7. Discuss the source of a firm's new product screening criteria. Prepare a list of screening criteria that might be employed by a grocery products manufacturer.

8. Formal screening devices, such as the weighted rating scale, are considered by many to be biased against revolutionary new products. Yet it is the revolutionary product (video disk playback system, for example) that frequently offers the best long-term profit potential. If this is true, should this method of screening be eliminated?

9. Compare a rating scale screening procedure for a simple yes-no question and answer technique.

10. Is a minimum acceptable return on investment a logical requirement for a new product idea entering the screening stage? Explain your answer.

11. Screening is not a foolproof process. It makes mistakes. What are the possible mistakes and why do they occur?

12. Mathematical models designed for product screening are scare. Why?

13. What is the meaning and significance of the new product concept statement?

10 / Business Analysis

Business analysis can be viewed as the dividing line between thinking and doing. An idea that meets management standards and is well liked is passed to development, where the new product concept is made into a concrete, tangible entity. Since development takes up the largest portion of new product expenses, the consequences of business analysis are of the highest order. A favorable decision often implies substantial commitments of corporate resources.

The decisions of business analysis hinge on three major considerations: demand, profitability, and return on investment. Will market demand be sufficient to meet the company's profit goals? And how much investment will be necessary? In recent years, all three considerations—demand, profit, and return on investment—have been incorporated into computer models. These afford management yet another means of thinking about new product possibilities and of deciding whether or not to act on such proposals.

Purposes of Business Analysis

Business analysis is merely a continuation of the evaluative process that began when the new product idea was first presented for consideration. It is a further assessment of those proposals that have evinced no "fatal flaws," serious violations of management-decreed constraints, and therefore survived the purges of screening.

The evaluation in this phase, however, is more detailed and exacting. It may cover the same basic points observed in screening. But the investigation now possesses broader scope and greater depth. Its orientation is also somewhat different, for it focuses on financial aspects and their implications. The major purposes of business analysis can be summarized as follows:

1. To serve as the basis for a decision as to whether to commit corporate resources towards the development of the new product idea.

2. To refine the product concept so that in the event it is approved an outline for a future program stands ready.

Yet this analysis, even with a decision to go ahead, can only be regarded as preliminary, as something not quite complete. Perhaps no plan is. But at this point a new product does not actually exist. Developmental work may lead to costs lower than initially estimated, prices less than first contemplated, and a promise of markets wider than originally visualized. Or the opposite may happen. The evaluation itself may be highly speculative, depending upon the proposal. At this point in time, the new product program can only provide a rough sketch for prospective action, and it usually must be modified in the light of future events.

Key questions of a business analysis deal with estimated costs and expected returns. What will be gained from the money expended to develop and market the new product? And are the gains worth it? When put in these terms, the problem is essentially one of cash inflows as compared with monetary outflows.

One way of reaching a solution is to evaluate demand and supply factors. The demand side concerns itself with revenue, the supply side with cost. Demand must be large enough to justify cash outlays for bringing forth and marketing the necessary supply. Accounting for both factors implies calculations of probable profits and return on investment.

Market Potential

A starting point for any analysis of demand is the concept of market potential. A potential is not a projection of actual sales. Rather, it is a theoretical construct that envisions the upper boundaries of industry demand under optimal conditions. The American Marketing Association has defined market potential as "maximum possible sales opportunities for all sellers of a good or service." As one author has expressed it, the potential for a market is "the limit approached by market demand as industry marketing effort goes to infinity . . ."[1] As such, a market potential represents the largest quantity an entire industry can hope to sell or the greatest dollar volume it can hope to realize if it expended its marketing effort to the utmost.

The logical potential for baby formulae, for example, might be conceived as total infants multiplied by some estimated number of feedings. The upper limit for regular gasoline might be viewed as the number of miles driven by older vehicles on the road divided by a measure of operating efficiency, such as miles per gallon.

Obviously the market potential for any product is dynamic, shifting and changing over time. Regular gasoline, for example, faces a contracting market as older model cars are constantly decreasing in number. On the other hand, the potential for unleaded gasoline grows steadily as more and more automobiles on the road have catalytic converters which are hypersensitive to lead. Even the birth rate, a bit more stable than the replacement of junked autos by new ones, is nevertheless a changing affair. A market potential must then be viewed as a series of estimates, broadening or narrowing with the passage of time.

---

[1] Kotler, *op. cit.*, p. 121.

Another characteristic of the theoretical maximum is its elastic nature. The market potential for most products does not emerge as an irrefutable, solitary figure that is routinely accepted by all members of an industry. Different companies might define their upper sales limits in different ways, even when the product is identical.

One firm, for example, might view the market for a fluoridated toothpaste as composed primarily of families with children and choose to ignore all others, the single, the childless, the retired. Another manufacturer with a similar product might include young adults as potential users and gear its commercial messages to a broader population grouping. Yet a third company might stretch its definition of possible customers to take in more mature citizens, seeing its potential market in the broadest terms. Or all three firms might settle on the same age groups but assign different degrees of importance to each.

Industrial marketers face the same situation as consumer goods manufacturers, but firms rather than people become the relevant units of estimation. In this respect, an extremely useful body of information is that of SIC industries, furnished by the Department of Commerce through its business census and other data collection activities.

The Standard Industrial Classification (SIC), initially developed in 1939, has become the basic taxonomical system for national accounts. It categorizes both industries and products.

All industries or economic activities are first divided into ten major groups, such as agriculture, mining, transportation, manufacturing, etc. Each of these groupings is then further subdivided into four-digit industries. For example, manufacturing in the 1972 census is broken down into 20 two-digit classes of industries (20–39). These 20 major groups are subdivided into 143 three–digit segments (201–399), which in turn are sorted into 451 smaller industrial groups (2011–3999). Each of these four-digit industries is actually defined in terms of related products, usually made of like materials and by similar processes. A seven-digit code describes each commodity in terms of the industry in which it is produced and of the "product class."

To illustrate how the system works, the seven–digit code 2023212 is the classification for canned, evaporated milk. The first four numbers, 2023, refer to the industry in which the product is manufactured, the condensed and evaporated milk industry. The first five digits, 20232, denote the product class, which in this instance is canned milk. The remaining two digits identify the individual commodity.

Information derived from the Census of Manufactures has provided the basis for the construction of input-output tables of the economy, which depict interrelationships among industries. They show the value of goods and services that industries buy from and sell to each other. This is illustrated by the following chart, which represents a slice of an input-output matrix (table 10-1).

Table 10-1

Interindustry Transactions (in Millions of Dollars at Producers' Prices)

For the distribution of output of an industry, read the row for that industry.

For the composition of inputs to an industry, read the column for that industry.

Columns (consuming industries):
1. Livestock and Livestock Products
2. Other Agricultural Products
3. Forestry and Fishery Products
4. Agricultural, Forestry and Fishery Services
5. Iron and Ferroalloy Ores Mining
6. Nonferrous Metal Ores Mining
7. Coal Mining
8. Crude Petroleum and Natural Gas
9. Stone and Clay Mining and Quarrying
10. Chemical and Fertilizer Mineral Mining
11. New Construction
12. Maintenance and Repair Construction

Industry No. / Industry	1	2	3	4	5	6	7	8	9	10	11	12
1 Livestock and livestock products	5,610	1,448	96	169								
2 Other agricultural products	8,379	905	105	507							80	3
3 Forestry and fishery products			34									
4 Agricultural, forestry and fishery services	603	1,335	45								161	19
5 Iron and ferroalloy ores mining					92	4						
6 Nonferrous metal ores mining	4	1			33	213	(*)			1		
7 Coal mining					(*)	1	400			3		
8 Crude petroleum and natural gas	2	119		(*)		5	1	(*)	5	(*)		
9 Stone and clay mining and quarrying						3	3		6	7	670	201
10 Chemical and fertilizer mineral mining		12						374		61	201	
11 New construction												
12 Maintenance and repair construction	233			44	30	16	23	476	63	8	26	4
13 Ordnance and accessories												
14 Food and kindred products	3,694	370	24						2			
15 Tobacco manufacturers												
16 Broad and narrow fabrics, yarn and thread mills		9			1	(*)	13		18		18	3
17 Miscellaneous textile goods and floor coverings	10	29	59	46	1		2	5	2		204	(*)
18 Apparel											49	4
19 Miscellaneous fabricated textile products	(*)	43	(*)	5			3				1	
20 Lumber and wood products, except containers	3	3		13	4	11	22		11	1	4,550	396
21 Wooden containers		105										
22 Household furniture											343	8
23 Other furniture and fixtures											222	9
24 Paper and allied products, except containers	15	1	(*)	(*)	(*)	(*)	(*)	1	21	4	247	45
25 Paperboard containers and boxes	2	3		123	(*)	(*)	(*)	(*)	(*)	1		
26 Printing and publishing	6	10	(*)	(*)	(*)	(*)	(*)	1	(*)	(*)	3	(*)
27 Chemicals and selected chemical products	75	2,297	3	21	28	50	50	164	48	27	136	18

Source: Dept. of Commerce, *Survey of Current Business* (February, 1974).

Figures in table 10–1 apply to broad, industrial classifications. Column data denote an industry's input, purchases from various sources. Row data reveal an industry's output and where sales are being made. Even a cursory examination of such a table indicates a wide diversity of supply sources and intermediate distribution patterns. For example, compare the row of figures for industry 27 with that for industry 22. Even on the basis of abbreviated data, the former can count every industry listed as a potential customer. The latter directs its output to only two industries, with a heavy concentration in new construction.

Since a new product may comprise only a small portion of an industrial market, the direct use of input-output tables may conceal the required answers in the all-inclusive aggregates. Additional information is often necessary. Nevertheless, a number of companies have been working at breaking down industrial classifications into smaller, more relevant units for purposes of estimating sales potentials.

The Census of Manufactures also reports on prime materials consumed by four-digit SIC industries, which is invaluable in forecasting demand for raw materials and semifinished goods. An illustration of such census reporting is that for cotton-weaving mills, portrayed in table 10-2.

Regardless of product type, consumer or industrial, estimates of market potential are easier when markets or industries are well defined. An industry with few users represents an analyst's dream. How wrong can one go in delineating the parameters of the auto industry, which is confined to a handful of manufacturers? But the expansion of users into many segments and submarkets may well turn that dream into a nightmare. Products flowing into numerous channels of distribution create similar difficulties, for each class of customers may have its own special characteristics and requirements.

Though the concept of market potential conveys an impression of grossness or inexactitude, it carries important ramifications. The process of denoting a theoretical maximum involves a description of marketing targets or segments against which sales and promotional efforts are directed. If the potential is defined too narrowly, sales opportunities will be passed over. If the definition is too broad, marketing effort will be wasted in pursuing impractical goals. Therefore, care must be exercised in combining those bits of information that make up the final definition.

Market Demand

Estimating actual demand of the market calls for a two-step procedure: projecting industry sales and projecting company sales. The ratio of company to industry sales designates a company's share of market.

If the new product is identical or similar to one already on the market, a typical situation, forecasts of industry sales offer few obsta-

Table 10-2
Materials Consumed by Cotton-Weaving Mills
Materials Consumed by Kind: 1972 and 1967

1972 Code	Material	Unit of Measure	1972 Quantity	1972 Delivered Cost (Million Dollars)	1967 Quantity	1967 Delivered Cost (Million Dollars)
	INDUSTRY 2211.—WEAVING MILLS, COTTON					
	Materials, containers, and supplies, etc., total[1]	......	(X)	1,268.0	(X)	1,600.0
013101	Raw cotton	1,000 bales	4,082.1	662.5	6,231.4	788.5
282305	Rayon and acetate staple and tow	Million lb.	76.7	25.5	66.1	18.8
282425	Polyester staple and tow	Million lb.	109.3	38.7	149.9	89.6
282421	All other manmade fiber staple and tow, except glass..	Million lb.	14.4	7.8	}	}
282301	Rayon and acetate filament yarn	Million lb.	16.2	14.9	23.2	27.0
282402	All other manmade filament yarn, except glass	Million lb.	11.7	8.6	48.0	8.0
010014	All other fiber (silk, jute, reused wool, waste, etc.)...	Million lb.	4.7	.9		
228101	Purchased spun yarn, all fibers including transfers from other plants of the same company	Million lb.	199.6	126.1	179.3	106.0
220211	Purchased broadwoven fabrics (piece goods) including transfers from other plants of the same company...	Mil. lin. yd.	363.1	162.2	623.6	215.1
286531	Dyes, lakes, and toners		(X)	29.0	(X)	42.1
970099	All other materials, containers, and supplies consumed		(X)	152.3	(X)	222.4
972000	Materials, containers, supplies		(X)	33.5	(X)	73.5

Source: 1972 Census of Manufacturers, Vol. II, p. 22A–28.

cles. Experience with the generic product class is a matter of record. Information sources are plentiful, the most common of which include private research companies, government, trade associations, and business publications. Each industry will favor some sources over others, depending upon prevailing conditions.

When the new offering departs markedly from existing products, forecasts become more subjective and uncertain. Practically all experts grossly underestimated demand for copying equipment in the formative period of Xerox. With only a paucity of factual data to go on, opinions form the hard core of sales projections. But this does not necessarily prevent their formulation in a logical, wholly consistent fashion.

A radical innovation, for example, might serve the same uses as conventional products on the market. In that event, the novitiate might elbow its way into the market as a substitute for what is currently available. Its demand would therefore be governed by the rate at which it replaced the old. The new product might also attract users who had previously shunned the contemporary, thereby expanding the market. This is referred to in economics as an "income effect." Thus, both income and substitution effects must be considered in market analysis.

In evaluating demand for a brand new product, the penetration patterns of an older product can sometimes be used if a parallel suggests itself. For example, consumer adoption rates of black and white TV in the late forties and early fifties served as a model for Corning Glass Works to estimate bulb and glass component sales to tube manufacturers of color TV when the industry was in its infancy.[2]

But at this point in time, both the rate of interproduct substitution and of new user accruals represent a large measure of guesswork, some educated and some nescient, some restrained and some wishful. The majority of all new products, however, do not contain highly novel features and do not necessitate such imaginative forecasts.

Share of market forecasts or share translated into dollar sales volume are similarly affected by the extent of product newness. But the newness refers to the company, not the industry.

Products that modify or revise or alter the company's existing brands offer the most predictable results. The old brand boasts a sales history, a customer base, a current demand. It represents an on-going business and provides a recorded body of information.

Products new to the company are less predictable. They are entities with no pasts and, in varying degrees, share greater uncertainties.

Their sales forecasts are further complicated by possible variations in marketing input. What a company gets, in part, depends on what it

---

[2] John C. Chambers, *et al.*, "How to Choose the Right Forecasting Technique," *Harvard Business Review* (July–August, 1971), pp. 54, 65–66.

does. But the productivity of marketing effort is unsettled and wavering, impelled and rebuffed by such factors as competitive activity, industry growth rates, and undisciplined preferences of consumers. A new brand may have to spend relatively large sums to gain customers when brand loyalty runs high or when the market is dominated by strong, established brands. On the other hand, dollar-per-new-customer expenditures may be relatively low in a market undergoing rapid growth.

The difference between market potential and industry demand is one indicator of overall sales expansion. The larger the difference, the greater the opportunity to gain customers by virtue of market growth, or of an "income effect." Conversely, a shorter distance between an industry's potential and its actual demand implies the new product must win converts mainly from other brands. This is the so-called "substitution effect." Both income and substitution effects may occur simultaneously.

A special case of substitution is when the new product gains converts from existing company brands. This form of substitution is known in the trade as "product cannibalism" and is common to multiple brand marketers. Manufacturers of automobiles, cigarettes, detergents, beverages, and breakfast cereals are but a few notable examples of companies flooding a market with a number of directly competitive items. Under such conditions, business analysis must take these substitution effects into account.

The usual situation, in which competitive brands are introduced to expand market share of a product category, can be viewed in much the way as intercompany accounts. They must be adjusted. Sales of a new product coming from other company brands represents no new business and no increment in revenue. Money has been taken out of one company pocket and put in another. Since this shift in sales means lower marginal contributions from the other company brands, the decrease can be regarded as an additional cost that should be borne by the new product. Incremental sales and resulting profits come only from "non-company" sources—from the substitution of competitive brands, customers new to the product category, or both.

If the new product is introduced for preemptive reasons—to prevent a competitor from making market inroads—then the analysis takes on a different complexion. For example, low tar cigarettes have grown at the expense of those with high nicotine contents. Consequently, a new entry with low tar can be expected to garner a portion of its sales from the company's regular brands. But some of that loss would have gone to competitors had the brand not been introduced. The net intercompany transfer is thus the difference between what would have occurred without the new product and what would occur with it. Estimation here becomes much more complicated, but the business analysis must address itself to such questions.

New brands are sometimes capable of touching off strong income effects in older, supposedly mature industries. This can occur when markets have been underpromoted and underdeveloped, and the new entrant comes in with a strong program. For example, the introduction of Scope, Colgate 100, and Reef in the mid-sixties with heavy advertising budgets was said to have about doubled the number of adults using mouthwash. The launch of Agree hair conditioner increased sales of the entire conditioner category by 30 percent within a year.[3] Life-Savers' introduction of Bubble Yum in 1975 enlarged the chewing gum market from $150 million to some $500 million.[4]

Regardless of circumstances, marketing policies have a significant impact on company sales. But at the business analysis stage, there is no actual plan in existence for a nonexistent product. In order to do a business analysis, assumptions about a possible marketing mix must be made. But the final plan at the time of commercialization can deviate sharply from that at the early phase.

Forecasting Techniques

Forecasting techniques are many and highly varied. Nevertheless, they can be grouped into three major categories: time series, causal designs, and qualitative methods.

Time series analysis relies primarily upon historical data, a set of observations ordered chronologically over time, such as monthly sales figures. Moving averages, exponential smoothing, and trend line extrapolations are the most common variations. Time series analysis has its greatest value when sufficient observations are available and trends are clear and stable. While this technique assumes that events of the past will continue into the future, it yields good short-term forecasts.

Causal designs range from simple correlation and regression to complicated computer-based models. But all such methods—absurdly simple or perturbingly complex—rest on presumed relationships between what is being forecast and other factors, called independent variables. Like time series, the establishment of causal relationships requires historical data. Here, the past also weighs heavily on the future, for estimates carry an implicit assumption that the relationships of yesterday will extend into all tomorrows. Causal designs are normally more expensive to employ, especially those constructed as complex computer programs.

Qualitative methods, too, are highly diverse. Their identifying feature is that they rest on opinions, from the informal ones of sales personnel and managers to the formal ones of panel experts and the famil-

---

[3] Nancy F. Millman, "Huge Campaign Will Back Launch of Agree Shampoo," *Advertising Age* (June 12, 1978), p. 103.

[4] Interview with Life-Savers executives.

Figure 10-1. Cost of Forecasting Versus Cost of Inaccuracy

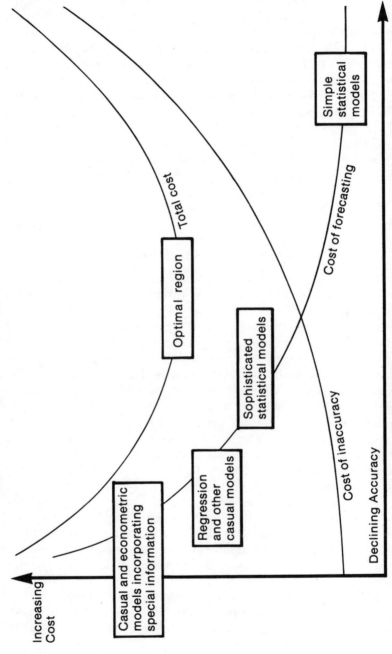

iar Delphi method.[5] Individual qualities of perceptiveness, discernment, and hard common sense are the overriding factors in the predictive qualities that ensue. These qualitative forecasts are used primarily when information is sparse or nonexistent.

The choice of method should fit the purpose of the forecast. In general, the greater the accuracy desired, the higher the costs. Such expenses cover activities of both estimation and search. But not all forecasts require the same degree of accuracy. An estimate of market potential, for example, usually calls for much less precision than one for setting budgets or evaluating alternative marketing strategies. Consequently, the increasing cost of greater accuracy must be traded off against its value, or the presumed cost of inaccuracy. A minimal sum of the two costs designates a theoretically optimal choice. Figure 10-1 illustrates this concept.

Profitability

The question of profitability in the business analysis stage is of momentous importance. Before funds are committed for development, all managements invariably ask: "How much will the new product return if it is launched?" The answer also becomes pivotal in subsequent appraisals of cash flows, payback, and return on investment.

On the most elementary level, profit can be viewed as a residual, the difference between money coming in and money going out. Revenue minus expenses equals profit. The first component in the equation was already provided by the sales forecast. It now remains to match these sales with costs and expenses to derive profit approximations.

The validity of cost estimates, like those of market forecasts, hinges in large measure on product newness. A slightly modified product should give cost accountants no difficulties. Current bills of materials can be used as prototypes. As the degree of product novelty becomes greater, problems multiply by leaps and bounds. These same estimators meet with wearisome obstacles when technical and engineering provisions are sketchy, as they often are before development. How does one estimate costs of manufacturing processes without detailed product specifications? For this reason, cost estimates in the business analysis stage are like sales estimates; they are preliminary and must be regarded as tentative.

The expense portion of the profit equation covers both production and nonproduction functions. Manufacturing costs are likely to include such diverse items as raw materials and supplies, warehousing, labor, machine time, utilities, maintenance, depreciation on machinery and

[5] See Steven C. Wheelwright and Spyros Makridakis, *Forecasting Methods for Management* (New York: Wiley-Interscience, 1973), pp. 191–193.

physical plant, service departments, etc. Nonproduction expenditures might include detailed breakdowns for selling and promotion, such as advertising, sales promotion, travel and entertainment, sales offices, customer service, and salaries and fringe benefits for sales personnel.

Actually, cost analysis began during the screening stage. If R&D thought the new product idea feasible, some rough cost estimates had to be assumed. Likewise, engineering could not have given the proposal clearance without some consideration of production costs. Screening also had to make some assessment of the proposal's compatibility with overall company resources. Business analysis simply continues this line of inquiry, but in more depth and with greater detail.

Sales and expense items are usually arranged in a particular accounting format employed by the company. An example of such a summary statement for product X, an industrial product, entirely fictional, is shown in table 10–3.

Table 10-3
Pro Forma P&L for Product X (in $000)

	Year				
	1	2	3	4	5
Revenue	4,800	6,750	8,250	9,260	9,750
Less cost of goods sold	2,880	3,350	3,650	3,700	3,800
Gross profit	1,920	3,300	4,600	5,560	5,950
Less selling and administrative	1,820	2,200	2,400	2,200	2,300
Profit before taxes	100	1,100	2,200	3,360	3,650
Taxes	48	530	1,060	1,620	1,750
Profit after taxes	52	570	1,140	1,740	1,900

A purist might object to imputed taxes on the grounds that corporations, not products, pay taxes. But neither can corporations avoid the government levies and keep for themselves the entire excess of revenues over expenses.

Many nonpurists might object to the figures in table 10–3 on other grounds, for as in the fanciful world of Lewis Carroll, things are not quite what they seem to be.

The bottom line, a seemingly hard and fast construct, is in reality an exceedingly elastic one. Bottom line figures may be raised or lowered by accounting practices. For example, a financial department may prefer accelerated over straight line methods of depreciation, taking higher write-offs in the early years of an asset. A new product can benefit from this procedure, for income taxes are deferred when sales are apt to be lowest. By the same token, anticipated profits are reduced and the new product proposal may take on a different complexion when related to the company's profitability standards. Similarly, the use of LIFO or FIFO for inventory evaluation affects the bottom line, heightening or depressing profits when prices are on the rise.

An interesting demonstration of how inventory evaluation affects profits is the case of Folger's coffee, a Procter and Gamble brand.[6] In the late sixties Folger's embarked on a program of national distribution, expanding eastward from its home base west of the Mississippi. In these eastern markets, Folger's could therefore be considered a new product, having to undergo an introductory period.

The steep rise in coffee prices in 1976 put a serious crimp into Folger's expansion program. By April 1977 the wholesale price of ground coffee peaked at $4.46 a pound, having swelled by some fivefold. The problem of falling demand was exaggerated by Folger's last-in, first-out (LIFO) system of accounting for inventory, which calculates the cost of coffee beans by the price of the last purchases made. Since the most recent purchases are more expensive than earlier buys, the period of rising prices found Folger's selling coffee at below the value its accounting system placed on its inventory. According to analysts, Folger's took a loss of about $55 million that year.

But by mid-1977 prices began to drop, and they declined steadily throughout 1978. Coffee margins improved, for the most recent purchases were now less expensive than the earlier ones and the differentials were reflected in earnings. Procter and Gamble's coffee-producing division was now making an important contribution to corporate net income and had to be given every encouragement in its quest for market share. The growing profits, helped in part by inventory valuation, enabled Folger's to resume its eastern expansion with greater vigor, pushing into Pennsylvania, New York, and New England, the last major areas for attaining national coverage.

The strongest objections to conventional profit reporting, however, revolves around the accounting practice called "absorption costing" or "full costing." Each product, the theory of absorption costing holds, must bear its full costs, those unique to itself and those fairly shared with other products from a common pool.

The unique or direct costs are generally accepted as legitimate charges. But sharing overhead is another matter. Critics of full costing argue that assigning overhead to new products is not relevant to a decision unless the allocation really represents an incremental cost. An example of such objectionable reporting would be administrative expenses for product X (table 10-3) if, in effect, no new expenses had

---

[6] Stan Luxemberg, "Folger's Scores in the Coffee Wars," *The N. Y. Times* (January 28, 1979), pp. D1, D5.

been added. If product X is thus burdened with phantom expenses, the argument goes, then other products should find their overhead charges reduced and profits enhanced. Should not this effect be taken into account, it is asked, when analyzing the profit contribution of a new product proposal?

A similar example is assigning factory overhead to the new product's costs of goods sold when plants are normally operating at less than full capacity. A cost already incurred, detractors of full costing point out, is a sunken cost and axiomatically cannot affect a future outcome.[7] An extreme position is perhaps that of Sam R. Goodman, vice-president of W. R. Grace and formerly chief financial officer of AMPEX and Nestle; Goodman accused traditional accounting philosophy with contributing "to the demise of more profitable products than many of the efforts directly related to the marketing of those products."[8]

An alternative to full costing is the application of "direct costing." As related to business analysis, this approach calls for a two-step procedure. First, it separates direct and indirect costs of the new product; then it breaks down the former into variable and nonvariable components. This application of direct costing is not sanctioned by the IRS, the SEC, or the Accounting Principles Board of the American Institute of Certified Public Accountants (AICPA). Consequently, financial reports to the public and government agencies abstain from direct costing. But the method can be used internally as an aid to business analysis.

Break-Even Analysis

A popular application of direct costing is that of break-even analysis. This form of analysis is an outgrowth of marginal concepts, which dominated microeconomics for more than half a century.

To illustrate how the analysis works, the first year's statistics of table 10-3 were rearranged in accordance with direct costing principles. All relevant or incremental costs for product X were classified into variable and nonvariable, or fixed, components. For the sake of simplicity, product X was assumed to have no inventory, being produced to order, and all fixed costs were considered incremental. Results of the *pro forma* statement, cast in a direct costing mode, are shown in table 10-4. The small contribution of $100,000 to the corporation's common cost and profit corresponds to the pretax profit in table 10-3.

The example in table 10-4 shows the unit price tag of product X at a round $2,000 figure. Because each unit has a variable cost of $1,375,

---

[7] Sam R. Goodman, *Financial Analysis for Marketing Decisions* (Homewood, IL: Dow Jones-Irwin, 1972), p. 140.

[8] *Ibid.*, p. 139.

Table 10-4
Pro Forma P&L Statement ($000)

	Year 1
Sales (2,400 units)	4,800
Less variable costs:	
Factory	1,880
Selling and administrative	1,420
Total variable costs.......................................	3,300
Marginal contribution	1,500
Less fixed costs:	
Factory	1,000
Selling and administrative	400
Total fixed costs	1,400
Profit	100

every sale can be said to make a marginal contribution of $625. This is the amount that goes towards meeting overhead, defined as all non-variable costs, plus profit goals.

The marginal contribution concept forms the basis of cost-profit-volume relationships. Since variable costs, by definition, are proportionate to revenue, every sale has the same variable unit cost and consequently the same marginal contribution. If the sale of one unit adds $625, two will add $1,250, three will account for $1,875, and so on. The break-even point is reached when the marginal contribution equals fixed costs. Here, profits are zero and revenue equals variable plus fixed costs.

The break-even point, in terms of dollar volume, can be derived from the formula $B/E = F/1 - (V/R)$, where:

B/E = Break-even point.

F = Fixed costs.

V = Variable costs.

R = Revenue.

Thus, $B/E = 1,400,000/1 - (3,300,000/4,800,000) = \$4,480,000$. At a price of $2,000 per unit, product X would have to sell 2,240 units in order to break even. The unit volume at which the marginal contribution would just cover fixed costs can also be calculated by the formula $B/E - F/MC$, where MC = marginal contribution per unit. By substituting for the terms of the equation, the break-even volume equals $1,400,000/$625, or total of 2,240 units.

Break-even analysis can be illustrated to executives in simple, easy-to-read charts. The cost-profit-volume relationships of this analysis are depicted graphically in figure 10-2.

Figure 10-2. Break-Even Analysis

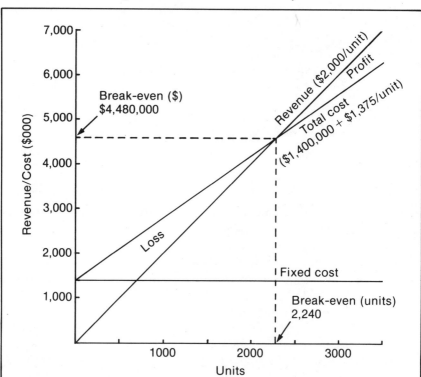

To calculate the break-even point as an end in itself is of little practical concern to a company. None will invest in a new product just to break even; it is not a corporate goal. Rather, the greatest value of break-even analysis in new product planning is its insinuation of risk.

On the negative side, the analysis is an indicator of danger. How low can sales ebb before the company loses money? Any other profit base can be stipulated. For example, suppose the company decides not to go ahead with a new product unless profit the first year reaches $250,000. In that event, sales of our conjectural product X would have to reach 2,640 units, or 400 units above break-even (400 × $625 = $250,000). This is indicated in figure 10-2 as the distance between revenue and total cost at the 2,640 unit volume. But the analysis also indicates the margin between the sales forecast and a catastrophic miscalculation, some lower than acceptable outcome that can run deep in the red.

On the positive side, the analysis indicates "leverage." The marginal contribution signifies the incremental profits associated with incremental sales once the break-even point is reached. Such estimates of profits for various sales levels are extremely helpful in developing a marketing plan for a new product.

Lastly, break-even analysis is a starting point for responding to the more sophisticated "what if" questions. These highly rated inferences can be forthcoming with only minor modifications in the basic technique.

Variants of Break-Even Analysis

A "what if" question is literally a subjunctive; it supposes something contrary to fact by introducing a future contingency. But this form of inquiry also becomes a quest for the possible, a search for outcomes that would result from changes in given relationships. Break-even analysis can be regarded in the same sense, for it is capable of examining effects that would ensue from alterations in the relevant variables of cost-profit-volume relationships.

To illustrate: the first year's projections for product X showed a profit of $100,000 (table 10-4). This profit rested on the premise that 2,400 units would be sold at $2,000 each.

But any number of contingencies can be introduced at this point of the business analysis. The problem might be restated thusly: "If the demand is 2,400 units, at what price must we offer the product in order to come out with a profit of $100,000?" Such questions are especially opportune when goods are produced to order, costs are fairly well known, and price results from negotiation, with normal industry profit serving as a guideline.

The answer to this question is easily arrived at by the equation

$$P = p/Q + F/Q + v,$$

where:

P = Price per unit.

p = Profit.

Q = Quantity.

F = Fixed costs.

v = Variable cost per unit.

Substituting the appropriate values and solving the equation for P, yield this result:

$$P = \$100,00/2400 + \$1,400,000/2400 + \$1,375$$

$$= \$41.67 + \$583.33 + \$1,375.00$$

$$= \$2,000$$

Or, the question can be so altered that price is given and quantity is regarded as the variable. For example: given a price of $2,000 per unit, how many units must be sold to make a profit of $100,000? The quantity needed to meet this profit goal can be estimated from the equation $Q = F + p/P - v$. Thus:

$$Q = \$1,400,000 + \$100,000/\$2,000 - \$1,375$$

$$= 1,500,000/625$$

$$= 2,400 \text{ units.}$$

In fact, there are many price-quantity combinations that would yield the same profit. A range of such alternatives is visualized by two iso-profit curves in figure 10–3.

Figure 10-3. Iso-Profit Curves

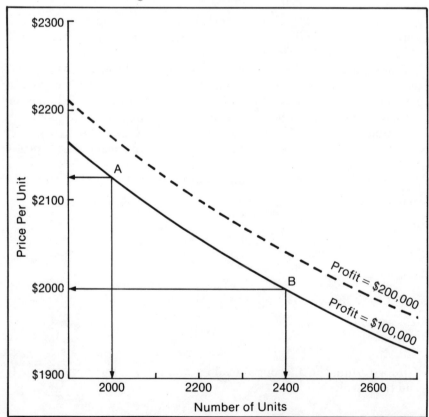

In the diagram (figure 10–3), all points on the solid line would yield the same profit of $100,000. To illustrate this proposition, consider points A and B. The respective combinations of price and quantity are marked off by the horizontal and vertical lines running from each point to the y and x axes. Thus, the A combination of a 2,000-unit sales volume and a $2,125 price would produce the identical $100,000 profit as the B combination, with sales of 2,400 units priced at $2,000 each.

Calculations can also be made for other profit levels. Accordingly, a $200,000 iso-profit curve based on the same cost-volume relationships is portrayed as a dotted line in figure 10–3. Plots of multiple profit levels depict changes that must be made in prices, sales volumes, or both in order to reach other strata.[9] Analyses of this sort permit considerations of various alternatives, for there is usually more than one way to get to a destination.

That the break-even concept adds perspicacity to business analysis is widely acknowledged. But like all techniques that appraise new product proposals, break-even, too, has its limitations. Variable costs are not always variable and fixed costs are not always fixed, particlularly over a wide range of output. Raw materials, for example, can often be purchased at a discount when ordered in larger lots. Fixed costs, at least in the long run, will rise with the creation of additional capacity. Both costs and prices are affected by volume, but break-even analysis treats these variables as though their values were completely known and entirely certain.

One way of introducing the assumptions of doubting, unsure, and fallible businessmen is the suggestion of a "probabilistic break-even," actually a form of risk analysis.[10] This variant, in common with other profitability evaluations, begins with a basic structure that supposedly represents all key revenue and cost relationships associated with the new product. But each variable is joined with a probability, which is solicited from the company's managers. In turn, these probabilities are transformed into a frequency distribution, or a density function.

It is often necessary to prepare estimates of the same variables but at different values. For example, raw materials may have different unit prices at different levels of economic order quantities. Consequently, the results may be many density functions to represent a probabilistic environment. The analysis might also, and usually does, outline several strategies for developing and marketing the new product. Again, each of these strategies and its numerous components will have sets of probability distributions associated with it.

[9] See Allan D. Shocker, "Iso-Profit Analysis," *Pittsburgh Business Review* (September–October, 1974), pp. 2–10.

[10] See Ted F. Anthony and Hugh J. Watson,"Probabilistic Breakeven Analysis," *Managerial Planning* (November–December, 1976), pp. 12–19.

Because of the large and complicated number of calculations, this method normally requires a computer. Electronic data processing can apply simulation, such as Monte Carlo, to estimate a probable break-even point by selecting values randomly from the inputted probability density functions.

This single iteration, however, is only one possibility drawn from a probabilistic universe of many break-even points. By the use of sampling techniques, the process is repeated until it ultimately yields a distribution of break-even points that is statistically reliable. Such a probability histogram for product X is illustrated below.

Figure 10-4. Probability Histogram of Break-Even Points

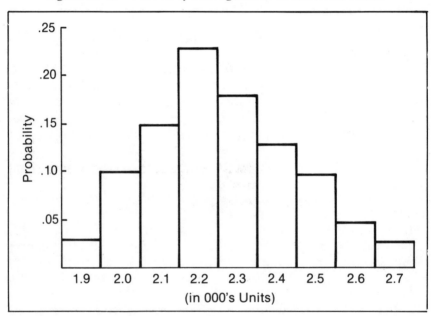

One claimed advantage of probabilistic break-even analysis is that costs and sales need no longer be viewed as being linearly related. Nor are relevant variables imbued with assumptions of unreserved certainty. Lastly, the probabilistic aspect introduces the element of risk. Managers can ask such questions as: "What are the odds of the break-even point for product X being equal to, or greater than, 2,100 units?" On the basis of figure 10-4, the apparent answer is .87, or nearly 9:1.

But for 2,200 unit level, the odds fall sharply to .72, or nearly 3:1. Risk considerations can also be extended to various alternative profit levels, prices, and quantities. In short, proponents of this probabilistic method maintain that it permits managerial uncertainty to be quantified.

Return on Investment

Regardless of its importance, profit is not the whole story of business analysis. Of equal significance is the expenditure that must be made for capital items that in the event of failure deteriorate into a sunken cost. Anticipated returns then must be judged in relation to the investment they necessitate. A new product proposal may promise large profits but may still be less desirable than many alternatives when compared with initial capital outlays.

Return-on-investment decisions involve four basic considerations of net returns: their amounts, duration, timing, and riskiness. For short-lived projects, timing is of small consequence. The amount of return, however, must be sufficiently large to justify the investment. For projects of longer duration, when returns are expected is as important as how much return is anticipated. That is, early cash inflows are preferable to later ones. As the old expression goes, time is money. The time value of money derives from the fact that money coming in early can be used to make more money.

The most common methods and variants thereof for assessing return on investment are payback, rate of return, and discount cash flow. A sample survey of 550 leading corporations indicated that a substantial majority (74 percent) used more than one method for capital budgeting. Some 71 percent of the companies studied reported accounting for risk in their calculations. The majority, however, did this not by formal probability techniques but by altering the targeted return.[11] For example, a high risk project would have to meet stiffer financial criteria in order to receive approval.

Payback

Though widely used, payback does not actually concern itself with return on investment. Rather, it is a liquidity concept, preoccupied with how long it takes a company to get back its initial investment. This line of reasoning adopts the common sense rule that all other things being equal, projects with shorter payback periods are more valuable than those with later net disbursements.

Apparent weaknesses of the payback method are many. First, net cash inflows occurring after the payback period are not considered in the analysis. Second, there is no explicit measure of profitability, and no importance is given to the time value of money. Third, critics claim that the method favors new product proposals with high short-term profits, while discouraging others whose impact may eventually be greater and more lasting.[12]

---

[11] Glen H. Petry, "Effective Use of Capital Budgeting Tools," *Business Horizons* (October, 1975), pp. 57–65.

[12] See Robert A. Grayson, "The Use of DFC Analysis," *Marketing Promotions/Marketing Dynamics* (January–February, 1972), p. 24.

Nevertheless, payback is popular with companies operating in an environment where projected cash inflows are highly uncertain. Many manufacturers of packaged goods, such as cosmetics and health care products, seemingly follow the principle that a quick investment recovery means lower risk. A payback period of one year or even shorter is not uncommon in these industries. The payback concept, with its stress on quick returns, can also be beneficial when new product proposals are numerous and sophisticated analyses are superfluous.[13]

Rate of return

The average annual rate of return relates net earnings to the cost of the investment. It can be calculated before or after taxes, but the latter is more common. The average rate of return can be stated as average net annual income/average net investment.

This method adheres closely to conventional accounting, and its format is familiar to practically all businessmen. To illustrate the calculation in the simplest terms, suppose an $8 million investment is projected to produce a net annual income of $400,000, on the average. The average investment is derived by simply dividing the initial outlay of $8 million by 2, which would roughly correspond to the midpoint of the life of the project. The average rate of return is therefore reckoned at 10 percent ($400,000/$4 million).

Rate-of-return computations take no notice of timing in monetary inflows and so fail to reflect the advantages of money coming in at an early date. A dollar expected ten years hence is accorded the same value as one projected for next year.

Discount cash flow

In the past decade, emphasis has shifted to cash flow rather than traditional methods of accounting for earnings. Although depreciation is taken as an expense for tax purposes, it also constitutes an important source of funds for many corporations. Similarly, net cash inflows from a project are available for all applications a corporation deems worthwhile—to reinvest in the business, to reduce debt, to pay dividends, etc.

The discount method for handling cash flow further accounts for the time value of money. Central here is the proposition that the future value of an investment is enhanced by the cash accumulating at compound interest. Future value can thus be calculated by the standard compound interest formula, $FV = I/(1 + i)^n$, where:

FV = Future value of an investment.

I = Initial sum invested.

[13] Homer A. Black, *et al.*, *Accounting in Business Decisions* (Englewood Cliffs: Prentice Hall, Inc., 1973), p. 668.

i = Interest rate for each period.

n = Number of periods in which interest is paid.

The more customary way of evaluating an investment proposal, however, is in terms of present value. This conversion from future to present value is accomplished by the formulation $PV = FV \, (I/1 + i)^n$, with PV denoting the present value of an investment. Using this formula, the expected cash flow from the new project is discounted to the present time at a coupound rate of interest and then compared with today's investment. Present worth tables are normally used to aid calculations.

To demonstrate how the method works, suppose our previous $8 million investment is expected to have a five-year life. Further assume that this expenditure will yield an after-tax profit of $400,000 per annum. If straight line depreciation is taken, then $1.6 million can be added back to produce an annual cash flow of $2 million.

The next step is to discount this $2 million annual cash flow by some designated rate of interest. The choice of interest rate is made in one of two ways. A firm can take the prevailing interest rate in the money market,which might then be regarded as its cost of capital. Or it can use the rate currently earned on its invested capital, which in this instance is an opportunity cost. Assuming a 10 percent rate after taxes, the problem can be worked out as follows:

Table 10-5
Example of Discount Cash Flow

Year	Cash Inflow	Discount Factor @ 10%	Present Value
1	$2,000,000	.909	$1,818,000
2	2,000,000	.826	1,652,000
3	2,000,000	.751	1,502,000
4	2,000,000	.683	1,366,000
5	2,000,000	.621	1,242,000
		Total	$7,580,000

In this calculation, the present value of earnings does not equal the present value of the investment. Stated another way, the present value (PV) ratio is less than 1.0 ($7,580,000/$8,000,000 = .95). Consequently, this project has not met the firm's capital cost requirement of 10 percent and should be rejected.

The greatest criticism of present value methods is the difficulty, if not the impossibility, of estimating net cash inflows over the entire life of a project. Further adjustments of present value may be necessitated by the recent waves of inflation. The use of a price deflator, however, renders these modifications even more tenuous. The manner of arriving at an expected interest rate and the level at which it is set may also affect acceptance or rejection of the new project.[14]

Computer Models

In recent years, both government and business have made increasing use of computer models both to forecast economic conditions and to plan future action. As late as 1969, the use of computers for such ends were far from common. A survey of 1,900 firms found only 63, or some 3 percent, working with computers for purposes of formulating strategies. By 1974, however, the situation seems to have changed drastically. A survey of 346 leading corporations by Social Systems, Inc., revealed that about 73 percent were using, developing, or experimenting with some form of corporate planning model.[15] This trend has undoubtedly spilled over into the areas of new product planning and evaluation.

New product models today are actually characterized by great variety, many of them competing commercially with each other. They also have different purposes, which range from simple forecasting to complex planning of new product development. For example, General Foods uses a number of submodels for different tasks. A program named TUPSIM, short for "trial-users package rate simulation," estimates sales potentials. Another computer program evaluates financial material, with a view towards forecasting statistics for profitability and return on investment. Not every model is necessarily employed for every new product proposal, for some are inappropriate and some are undesirable. General Foods can also obtain a rather comprehensive new product evaluation from PROBE, which combines a group of related submodels.[16]

The popularity of these so-called planning models is confined mainly to consumer goods, especially low-priced, frequently bought items. These new product models are composed of input and output linked to intervening factors. Input embodies advertising expenditures, sales promotions, product quality, and the like, but it also covers uncontrolled variables, such as competitive activity. The intervening factors refer to such agents as consumer attitudes, preferences, and shopping habits that in turn act upon the output. The latter comprises such elements as sales and profits, the end product of the analysis. All these

---

[14] See Harold Bierman, Jr., and Jerome E. Haas, "Are High Cut-off Rates a Fallacy?" *Financial Executive* (July, 1973), pp. 88–91; Edwin J. Elton and Martin J. Gruber, "Valuation and Asset Selection Under Alternative Investment Opportunities," *The Journal of Finance* (May, 1976), pp. 525–543.

[15] Thomas H. Naylor and Daniel R. Gattis, "Corporate Planning Models," *California Management Review* (Summer, 1976), p. 69.

[16] McGuire, *Evaluating New Product Proposals*, pp. 94–100.

factors work in the computerized universe with an inexorable logic, based upon postulated relationships.

DEMON[17]

DEMON, short for Decision Mapping Via Optimum Go-No Networks, is the oldest and perhaps the best known of a succession of models designed for new product planning. It visualizes new product decisions made not once but at various points as the proposal proceeds through a system or network. At any single point, there three choices, described as "go," "no," and "on." "Go" is a signal to get into full-scale production for national distribution. The reasons are so compelling that nothing could be gained by delay. "No" is equally definite, though negative; the proposal should be shelved because it will not meet management objectives. "On" connotes a maybe. The evaluation is inconclusive, but program development should continue. More work is needed in R&D, consumer research, or test marketing. The analysis then must be repeated subsequently until a definite go or no-go decision is reached. Figure 10–5 following depicts the network decision process.

Figure 10–5. The Network Decision Process

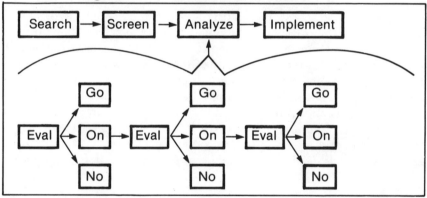

David B. Montgomery and Glen L. Urban, *Management Science in Marketing*, © 1969, pp. 295. Adapted by permission of Prentice-Hall, Inc., Englewood Cliffs, New Jersey.

Demand estimates are generated from assumed consumer response to marketing stimuli. For example, advertising and sales promotion is postulated as giving rise to awareness, depending upon the level of expenditures and the effectiveness of the programs. This awareness of the new product is supposed to lead consumers to purchase, and in accordance with their satisfactions, they may be converted to users or repeat buyers. Each stage in this hierarchy—from awareness to brand

---

[17] A. Charnes, *et al.*, "DEMON: Decision Mapping Via Optimum GO-NO Networks—A Model for Marketing New Products," *Management Science* (July, 1966), pp. 865–887.

loyalty—has a probability attached to it. Taking into account the probabilities of trial and usage at each stage will theoretically yield estimates of sales. Variation in probability values will produce measures of confidence levels. Costs can be estimated from various quantities of units sold. Consequently, the model provides profitability figures and the degree of confidence associated with these estimates.

At the business analysis stage, relationships between marketing input and sales are highly subjective, largely reflecting opinions of company managers. As more testing is done and information becomes available, empirically derived values are substituted for judgmental ones. At each stage of the network process, however, an exact plan and predetermined relationships are assumed to exist.

NEWS[18]

Another of the early computer models was the "New Early Warning System," called NEWS. Developed by BBDO, an advertising agency, the program was initially intended to forecast national sales from test market results. But it was later reported to have been used prior to test marketing, which makes it applicable to business analysis.

The heart of the model lies embedded in a pattern of consumer behavior that supposes individuals moving from a stage of initial awareness to that of routine buying. The rate at which they do so is seen as heavily dependent upon marketing effort. The exact number of consumers at each stage of this hierarchical structure is determined from a set of estimating equations functionally related to marketing parameters, such as frequency of purchase, levels of advertising retention, and conversion efficiency of advertising exposures to product awareness. Managers are often asked to assign values to these parameters in the early phases of new product development. Market share estimates are derived from the computed number of first time and repeat purchasers.

AYER[19]

Developed by N. W. Ayer, a Philadelphia advertising agency, this model was initially conceived of as an aid to planning introductions of packaged goods. Specifically, its intent was to predict purchase levels some three months after commencement of a test market or an introductory campaign. The rationale for this procedure, which produces only an estimate fixed at a single point in time, was that most introductions were planned in thirteen-week cycles and that this formative period, in large measure, foretold the fate of the new offering.

[18] David F. Midgley, *Innovation and New Product Marketing* (London: Croom Helm, Ltd., 1977), pp. 253–255.

[19] Henry J. Claycamp and Lucien E. Liddy, "Prediction of New Product Performance: An Analytical Approach," *Journal of Marketing Research* (November, 1969), pp. 414–420.

The model itself is composed of three interconnected submodels, which collectively postulate the familiar hierarchy of consumers being transformed from prospects to triers to regular customers. Estimating equations were derived from both empirical and subjective data. According to the authors of this program, the key link between trial purchase rates and advertising was a measure of "correct recall of advertising claims."

NEWPROD[20]

This model, developed by Gert Assmus, a Dartmouth professor, in cooperation with a large consumer goods company, is similar to those of its advertising agency predecessors. Its main purpose is to predict market share for the first year after a new product introduction. As such, it can be used as an evaluative and planning instrument.

Also like its forebearers, the predictions are made by visualizing a progression of awareness to product trial to repeat purchase. Regression equations describe relationships between consumer response and marketing input. A flow-chart of the NEWPROD model is depicted in figure 10-6.

In this particular model, both product awareness and initial purchase can come by way of advertising, free samples, and coupon redemptions. The model is flexible insofar as subjective judgments can be substituted for factual data in the business analysis stage.

SPRINTER[21]

These initials are an abbreviation for "specification of profits with interaction under trial-and-error response." Following in the footsteps of DEMON, this program features the well-known "go–no-go" decisions along a network route.

But the model is infinitely more complicated and detailed than any of its predecessors, containing some 500 equations to describe consumer response to marketing input such as advertising, pricing, sales promotion, distribution, and so on. Though the model represents consumer propensities for trial and repeat purchase as a set of highly complex relationships, its distinctive feature is its quest for optimization. Through a search routine using iterative procedures, the program selects the marketing strategy, or combination of input, that would presumably maximize expected profits. These returns are discounted at some designated rate of return and juxtaposed with their probability of occurrence.

---

[20] Gert Assmus, "NEWPROD: The Design and Implementation of a New Product Model," *Journal of Marketing Research* (January, 1975), pp. 16–23.

[21] Glen L. Urban, "SPRINTER: A Tool for New Product Decision Makers," *Industrial Management Review* (Spring, 1976), pp. 43–54, and "SPRINTER Mod III: A Model for the Analysis of New Frequently Purchased Consumer Products," *Operations Research* (September, 1970), pp. 805–854.

Figure 10-6. NEWPROD Flowchart

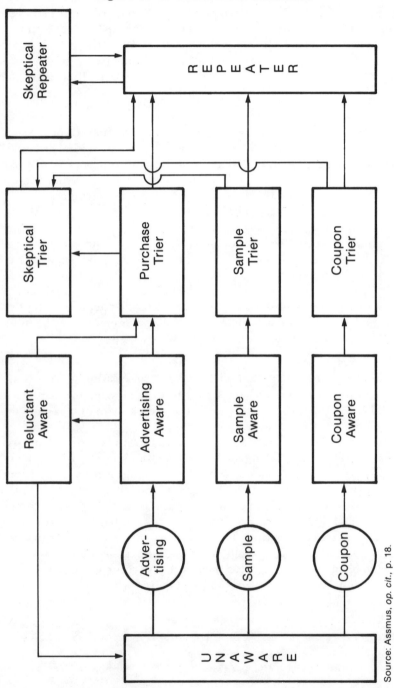

Source: Assmus, *op. cit.,* p. 18.

Evaluating a proposed nylon compound of a chemical company, SPRINTER systematically evaluated some 2 million alternative marketing programs to optimize the expected differential profit. The cost of computer running time was reported as a modest $650. But no figures were given for other expenses associated with the program, which can greatly exceed computer time costs. The basic concept of SPRINTER is illustrated graphically in figure 10-7.

Figure 10-7. Example of SPRINTER Decision Plot

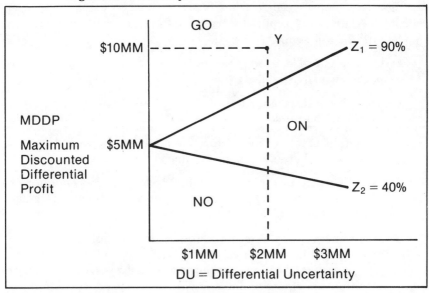

Glen L. Urban, "SPRINTER: A Tool for New Product Decision Makers," Spring 1967, Vol. 8, No. 2, p. 48. Reprinted by permission of *Sloan Management Review.*

The diagram (figure 10-7) shows maximum differential profits adjusted for the time value of money along the vertical axis. The amount of uncertainty, described as standard deviations in profits, is on the horizontal axis.

The line Z_1 indicates the company wants a 90 percent chance of being right concerning its investment of $5 million. At point Y, the expected differential profit is $10 million and the potential error, at the 90 percent confidence level, is $2 million. If these results were obtained for a new product proposal, the evaluation would be a clear sign to go full speed ahead.

The chart also shows a number of other relationships. For example, if profits happened to come in at $7 million, then the decision would fall into the ON area. More development work would have to be done and the evaluative process would have to be repeated. It is obvious here that the greater the expected uncertainty—or the more confidence management wants to have in being right—the higher the level of profits needed for a GO decision. The lower boundary that separates the ON an NO areas suggests that the company expects a 40 percent chance of reaching the target rate of return before an ON decision is made.

Advantages and Limitations of New Product Models

Today, the use of models is common in new business planning. The decision is often reduced to what type of model to use and for what purpose. Among the reputed advantages proffered by advocates of models are the following:

1. The procedure leads to greater consistency in assumptions, since input is usually supplied by several departments in a company.

2. Activities of different parts of the company in developing a new project are better coordinated.

3. Budgeting practices in product planning are improved because models make better estimates of time and resource requirements.

4. Assembling input for the computer model forces assumptions to become explicit. This highlights areas of management agreement and dissent.

5. Given the assumptions, numerous variations of a plan can be evaluated at the same time. What would happen if this were done instead of that? This form of sensitivity analysis provides insights as to the importance of decision variables in product planning.

Despite their claimed benefits, these models have so far opened no new vistas to brave new worlds. In fact, their very value to decision making has often been open to question.

A good model, it is held, should depict the world it represents with fidelity. But much of the market research data that goes into models are of low, unreliable quality. Consumer panels, important sources of information, commonly have less than 10 percent of the initial sample willing to cooperate and join in the test. Then how representative of the whole body of the nation's consumers are such survey results? Much of advertising recall and awareness measures come from small, single city tests in which response differences account for a substantial portion of the variation. Advertising exposure and audience measurements have been a continuous source of controversy even among advertising practitioners. The market research fraternity readily acknowledges that the major portion of survey error is of a nonsampling type, which is usually not measured in sample surveys. Yet all these anomalies, meticulously entered into a computer, are assumed to be projectable to the total population and predictive of its buying rates in response to marketing efforts.

Not even a complete lack of information is necessarily a deterrent to employment of computer models, for opinions of company managers can be used to feed the estimating equations. But do such procedures really convert uncertainty into risk? In classical statistics, a probability is a long-run frequency, derived from a large number of actual observations. It has an extremely high likelihood of occurrence, like the proportions of heads and tails apt to result from an almost infinite tossing of coins. From this standpoint, a manager's opinion of what he thinks might happen is hardly a true probability. The assertion that a number of marketing strategies can be assessed without risk of an actual new product introduction may be more illusory than real.[22]

If uncertainty is not, in fact, transformed into risk, it is surely concealed by hard numbers of the computer printout. This creates a false sense of security and an insularity from the realities of the marketplace. It also enhances the tolerance for unreliable data and the disregard for measurement problems. As one model builder confesses, "A model is a stone in the shoe for better data."[23] But the stone is not removed. Instead, it is rationalized that it is better to limp along with the stone rather than not walk at all.

In part, model creators themselves are to blame for the use of faulty data. They have separated form and content, evaluating the goodness of their designs solely by mathematical logic. But their articles in academic and professional journals are not those of disinterested observers, and their "proofs" are hardly beyond reproach. From a management point of view, the predictive value of a model is the difference between the error of using the model and that made without the model. Yet no author has ever sought to validate his creation in such terms.

It might be argued that models are much more than predictive tools. If employed in a decision-making role, they become feedback systems in the truest sense. They are a means of taking corrective action to reconcile disparities between goals and results. They seek ways to control, given a set of constraints, a company's operations and actions.

But the environment they seek to control is a contingent one, many elements of which are neither known nor knowable. A recent study of new products concludes that the failure rate is as high today as it was twenty-five years ago, computers and advanced mathematical tech-

---

[22] E. Eugene Carter, "What Are the Risks in Risk Analysis?" *Harvard Business Review* (July-August, 1972), pp. 77–79.

[23] John D. C. Little, "Models and Managers: The Concept of a Decision Calculus," *Management Science* (April, 1970), p. B–483.

niques notwithstanding.[24] A commission of the American Marketing Association appointed to study the effectiveness of research and development for marketing management arrived at similar conclusions. "A significant amount of marketing research effort, new knowledge development, model-building, and theorizing," the commission stated, "has had little impact on improving marketing" over the past quarter of a century. As one panel member noted, "The fact that the vast majority of new products put on the market turn out to be failures may be a manifestation of the phenomenon."[25]

The limitations of models are not sufficient reason to shun them, just as a diversion of actual results from intended action is not a good reason to do away with all planning. Rather, it is a matter of putting new product models into a proper perspective and setting realistic priorities. This has led some management experts to downgrade these academic means of dispelling uncertainty and to emphasize organizational aspects. Success, this group contends, depends not upon guessing right but upon doing right.[26] If uncertainty, and a modicum of adversity cannot be avoided, it is argued, a corporation with strong financial resources, a high-quality staff of managers and an *esprit* operating corps will better adapt to an ever-changing world. This kind of organization is bound to be successful because it has melded all the ingredients that make plans work. As one author so aptly phrased the proposition, "Fortune appears to smile more consistently on those who do the basics well."[27]

---

[24] G. Merle Crawford, "Marketing Research and the New Product Failure Rate," *Journal of Marketing* (April, 1977),p. 51.

[25] John G. Myers, *et al.*, "The Effectiveness of Marketing's R&D for Marketing Management: An Assessment," *Journal of Marketing* (January, 1979), p. 27.

[26] Bela Gold, "The Shaky Foundations of Capital Budgeting," *California Management Review* (Winter, 1976), pp. 51-60.

[27] Herman Bogaty, "Development of New Consumer Products—Ways to Improve Your Chances of Success," *Research Management* (July, 1974), p. 30.

REVIEW QUESTIONS

1. Business analysis is a continuation of screening. As practiced by some companies, it would be difficult to determine when one ends and the other starts. How then does analysis differ from screening? What does it seek to determine?

2. Compare the consumer goods manufacturer's approach to estimating market potentials with that of the industrial manufacturer.

3. Since market potential is a theoretical concept more than an actual forecast, how is it employed for business analysis?

4. Evaluate the difficulty of formulating an initial sales forecast for:
   a. a "me-too" product modification.
   b. a product that departs markedly from existing products.

5. Neither quantitative nor qualitative techniques of sales forecasting are without problems. Compare the drawbacks in the two approaches.

6. How can the known sales history of existing products guide the new products sales forecaster?

7. Profit can be viewed as a residual between money coming in and money going out. What are the problems of forecasting the amount of money that will go out—cost—for the first year's commercialization of a new product?

8. Profit estimates are subject to management treatment of various costs. The determination of anticipated product profits involves a degree of subjectivity and flexibility in the treatment of costs. Describe the problem. Discuss a number of profit concepts that are derived from alternate approaches to overhead expenses.

9. The treatment of new product development expenses will affect proposed prices for the product. Discuss two possible opposing approaches.

10. What purpose is served by performing a break-even analysis as part of business analysis?

11. Relate risk analysis to break-even analysis.

12. Is there a correlation between new product risk and profit? Discuss.

13. Criticize the concept of payback. Despite its shortcomings, it is a popular analytical tool and screening criterion. Why?

14. Discuss the application of computer models to the new product evaluation process.

15. If the business analysis stage ends with a "go" decision, a new product project proposal will be prepared via a report to top management. This report will provide guidance for the firm's future efforts. Prepare a proposed outline of such a report, indicating the type of information to be included.

16. Is it necessary to employ a scientific probability sample for concept testing?

17. Discuss the subjectivity and objectivity elements inherent in concept testing.

11 / Development

The early stages of development concentrate on technical and design problems, as the concept must be transformed into a physical product. As the process continues, emphasis shifts to production and marketing. Development necessitates the cooperation of various groups within an organization and creates a need for formal schedules.

An early form of scheduling was Gantt charting, which was first used in production. Though still used to represent major events and summary information, Gantt charts are inadequate for complex projects requiring many tasks. This void was filled by PERT, which is employed today in many different forms.

In addition to the traditional matter of product design, current engineering must be concerned with issues of product liability. Three basic principles have been used by the courts to determine whether a manufacturer has met all legal obligations—negligence, strict liability, and express warranty. Several governmental agencies, of which the Consumer Product Safety Commission is the most important, are empowered to order product recall of faulty goods.

Package design forms an integral part of total development and has two major aspects: physical distribution and merchandising objectives. Industrial products concentrate on the former. Certain consumer products, especially those selling in self-service outlets, are concerned with the latter. Packages designed to meet promotional objectives lengthen development and raise costs of the packaging system.

The adoption of a name for the new product depends upon the marketing strategy. Alternatives are the use of a distributor's name, a family name, or an individual one.

As the development stage nears an end, technology must be transferred from R&D to manufacturing. Five basic alternatives are available to effect this transition: product specifications and drawings, manufacturing participation in R&D, R&D participation in manufacturing, corporate coordinator, and transfer team. Lastly, the entire project must be transferred to marketing for commercialization.

The Development Stage

The development stage witnesses a transformation of the new product concept into a physical entity that is offered in the marketplace. This phase takes up more time and more expense than any other activity in preparing a product for the market. In general, the more radical the product, or its degree of newness, the higher the expenses. Since the development stage is the longest, its elapsed time becomes a major concern to new product management.[1] Long development times play havoc with planned costs in periods of inflation, as evidenced by cost overruns on lengthy government projects. Risks are also heightened, particularly when markets are susceptible to rapid change and high variability. There is no payoff in introducing a new product that is already obsolete or one that appears likely to be replaced shortly by another. But an accelerated development program usually demands larger current budgets and higher total costs. Decisions of this nature therefore involve trade-offs between the incremental costs of acceleration and the incremental benefits of earlier completion dates for the project.

The development stage manifests two main aspects: technical and marketing. But emphasis shifts from the former to the latter as development proceeds from concept formulation to product commercialization.

The early phases of development concentrate on design problems in the laboratory. Several departments, especially marketing, frequently contribute information used to draw up the product specifications. The collaboration of marketing and R&D is of utmost importance, for in the final analysis, the new product must meet the requirements of the market to have any chance of success. In fact, most new products are brought about by the pull of the market. There is also some evidence, though limited, that new products responding to market demand have a higher probability of success than those originating from engineering.[2] But essentially, the task of designing a new product is a technical one, employing the talents of engineering. As such, the approval of a new product idea commits the firm to an investment in R&D, at least in the initial stage of development. The largest investment takes place in the engineering end of the R&D spectrum, since the majority of new products call for applications of existing technology.

The design aspect, though begun early, is vital to the whole development process. It determines the product's features. It specifies the

---

[1] F. M. Scherer, *Industrial Market Structure and Economic Performance* (Chicago: Rand McNally and Company, 1973), p. 367.

[2] Arthur Gerstenfeld, *Innovation: A Study of Technological Policy* (Washington, D. C.: University Press of America, Inc., 1979), pp. 99–107.

materials and components that make up the product and designates the types of equipment that will be used in its fabrication. It thus locks manufacturing into definite processes and, in large measure, determines the cost of goods sold. The largest cost reductions are often achieved by designs that simplify manufacturing processes.[3] One widely used method of achieving cost reductions is value analysis, whereby engineers examine systematically all cost-function relationships to identify configurations that will yield comparable performance at lower costs. This may be achieved in a number of different ways, such as shifting to cheaper materials, reducing energy consumption in production, decreasing the proportions of rejections, cutting down on idle time in the manufacturing process, etc.

Towards the end of the development stage, emphasis shifts from engineering to marketing and production planning. The technology of the laboratory must be transferred to production operating under actual plant conditions. Marketing must at the same time produce a detailed plan for carrying out commercialization. This market plan, outlining how, when, and by whom various sales and promotion-related activities are to be performed, becomes the basis for the production schedule. The quantities and timing of the output must satisfy sales expectations and be produced in the most economical manner.

Between the two ends of the development stage—designing the new product and drawing up the marketing plan—lie a number of intermediate steps, such as building and testing prototype models, determining production rates and manufacturing standards, evaluating equipment and pilot plant runs, establishing quality controls for raw materials and components, and preparing documents for filing patents. Some steps leading to commercialization are sequential, while others are simultaneous. The process is highly complex as it involves the interactions of various groups whose activities must be coordinated. In turn, this gives rise to formal schedules, for each group must know what they are supposed to do and when. The what and when of each group must be related further to the activities of other groups.

Scheduling

A schedule is a plan of future action, the elements of which are arranged in time sequences. After objectives are formulated, the tasks necessary for achieving them are spelled out in detail. These tasks are then ordered in both time and sequence. A schedule thus describes what is to be done, at exactly what times, and by whom.

---

[3] Karger and Murdock, *op. cit.*, p. 108.

This work timetable is an integral part of planning. It permits a project to be planned in advance and its progress to be monitored. Formal schedules are intended to prevent haphazard and chaotic performance, especially for projects containing many parts and requiring a large variety of jobs. To be sure, a schedule by itself does not guarantee a smooth, efficient operation. But it does offer a means of preventing expensive delays and costly overruns, the symptoms of which can often be identified by progress reports. Timely monitoring permits corrective action to be taken before much damage is done. These reports, patterned on a management-by-objective philosophy, compare initial plans with actual performance. By analyzing the sources of variation between what was intended and what has taken place, useful insights emerge as to how to rearrange resources for improving performance.

Most large and medium-sized firms have a number of new product ideas in various stages of development. R&D may be conducting a feasibility study on one concept, working on the design of a second, testing manufacturing processes of a third, and so forth. In similar fashion, marketing may be conducting a product use test on one potential offering, drawing up promotional plans for another, and carrying out a sales area test with a third. To utilize given resources efficiently, these different activities must not only be coordinated but synchronized with each other. For example, engineering can specify certain materials on the basis of unit costs only if purchasing can line up enough suppliers and assure itself of adequate supplies when production begins in earnest.

One of the earliest forms of scheduling was introduced by Henry L. Gantt during World War I for production control. These Gantt-type charts are still used for overall planning—to delineate major events, broad goals, and summary information. An example of a simplified Gantt milestone chart is illustrated in figure 11-1.

The chart shown in figure 11-1, a somewhat refined version of Gantt charting, has time on the horizontal axis, individual tasks on the vertical, and milestones within each horizontal bar. These milestones are thus associated with particular tasks and related to time.

But the chart shows no relationship between tasks or between milestones. When projects are relatively simple with a low degree of coordination required among different tasks, the interdependence factor is not critical. Under such circumstances, Gantt charts can provide effective scheduling techniques.

When operations are complicated with many interrelated activities, Gantt charts have serious shortcomings. Unlike production, new product development is nonrepetitive; the product is developed only one time. Product development activities do, however, entail varying degrees of uncertainty and change. Their engineering aspects are charac-

Figure 11-1. Gantt Milestone Chart

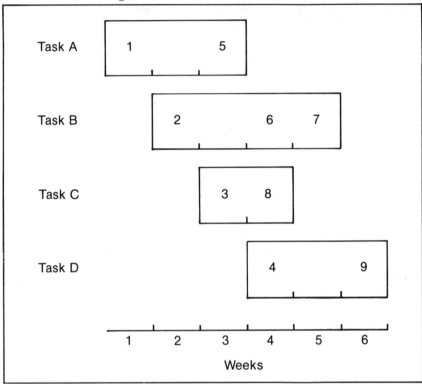

terized by low unit volume but often by large numbers of related tasks. When these conditions prevail, it is necessary to go beyond the typical Gantt chart for scheduling. This can be done by network analysis, which is a significant extension of Gantt charting. To convert the Gantt milestone chart of figure 11-1 into a network, it is necessary to show the sequence of relationships between milestones and possible constraints. This is illustrated in figure 11-2, wherein the original Gantt chart is converted into a network of events.

Although the milestone-derived network in figure 11-2 is an improvement over the Gantt milestone chart depicted in figure 11-1, even the improvement lacks the capacity for effective control of elaborate, large-scale operations. It lacks the capacity for the necessary analytic detail and predictive quality. These problems were addressed by the more sophisticated network analytic methods that emerged in the late fifties, such as PERT, and milestone networks remained confined, like their Gantt ancestors, to summary reports.

Figure 11-2. Gantt-Derived Milestone Network

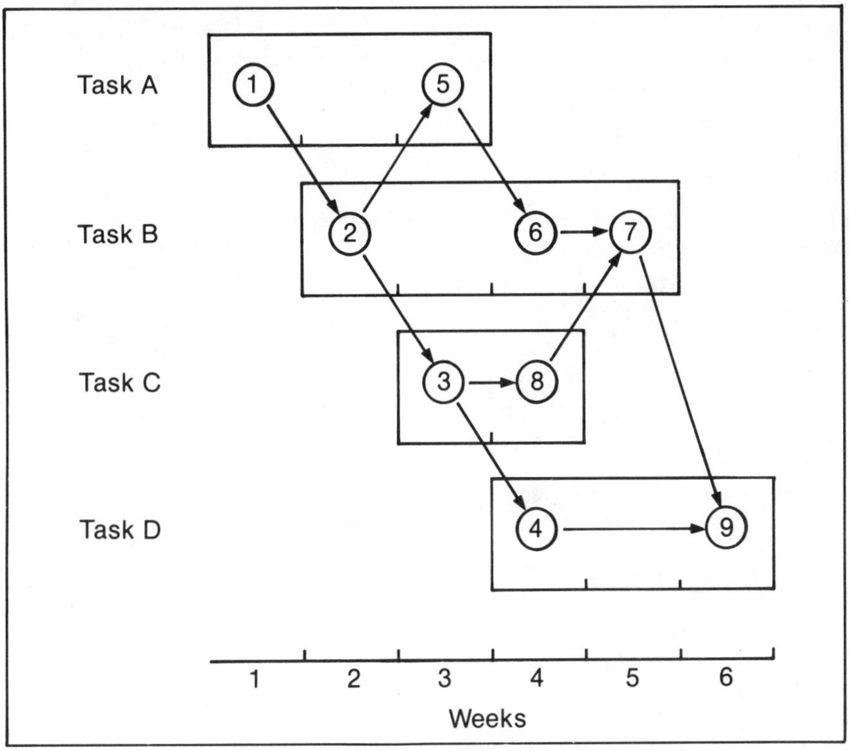

PERT

PERT, an acronym for Program Evaluation and Review Technique, was developed in 1958 by the Navy Special Projects Office in cooperation with Booz, Allen & Hamilton, a consulting firm. It was first applied to the Polaris missile program, which had to coordinate the efforts of some 250 prime contractors and more than 9,000 subcontractors. Its success with Polaris spurred its adaptation by industry. Over the years, many modifications and new features were added, and today the variations of PERT number well over a hundred.

A PERT network is comprised of two main elements, activities and events. Activities are jobs that take time and consume resources. These activities separate events, which are occurrences at specific points in time. As such, they demand neither time nor resources but signify the beginning and end of an activity. Stated another way, each event, except for the first and last, must have at least one preceding and one succeeding activity. Large, complicated arrangements of activities and events usually require that a network breakdown chart be constructed beforehand. This is an initial checklist of every function needed to bring the project to completion. A simplified version of a PERT network, showing the activities and events in the preparation of a sales promotion display and brochure, is presented in figure 11-3.

As shown in figure 11-3, events are numbered and set apart by circles. Ellipses or squares serve the same purpose. Arrows that join the circles represent the elapsed time for accomplishing a job, usually expressed in calendar weeks. Zero time activities are "dummies," as the activity between events number 6 and number 8. A dummy activity indicates a constraint that employs no resources but does not permit an event to begin until a prior task has been completed. For example, figure 11-3 declares that final brochure art can receive approval after final display art is authorized, and not before.

The time required for completion of any activity is postulated on an "expected value" derived from three sets of estimates—optimistic, pessimistic, and most likely. These terms are defined as follows:

1. Optimistic, designated by the symbol a. This indicates how long an activity would take if everything went exactly as planned. The chances of this ideal situation occurring are one in a hundred.

2. Pessimistic, described by the symbol b. This expresses the time a job would take if everything that could go wrong actually did. The probability of this gloomy outlook materializing is also .01.

3. Most likely, defined by the symbol m. This estimate represents the most frequently occurring length of time an activity would take if the job were done an infinite number of times under identical conditions in exactly the same way.

PERT assumes a beta distribution, which can be sloped positively or negatively. The calculated time for an activity, designated by the symbol t_e, is derived by converting the three different estimates into a single figure. This weighted average is calculated from the equation:

$$t_e = \frac{a + 4m + b}{6}$$

Figure 11-3 shows the three estimates—a, m, b—for each activity on top of the arrow and the t_e calculation beneath it. This represents the expected value of the beta distribution, expressed in weeks or fractions thereof.

Figure 11-3. Small Sample Network Preparing a New
Sales Promotion Display and Sales Brochure

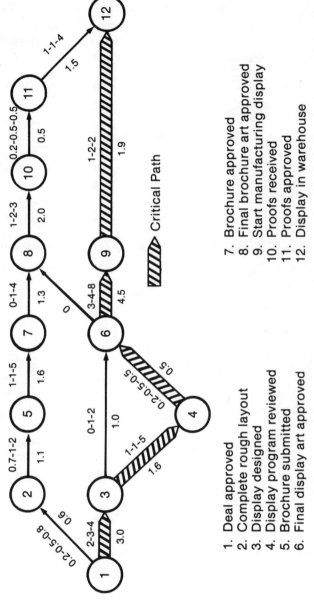

1. Deal approved
2. Complete rough layout
3. Display designed
4. Display program reviewed
5. Brochure submitted
6. Final display art approved
7. Brochure approved
8. Final brochure art approved
9. Start manufacturing display
10. Proofs received
11. Proofs approved
12. Display in warehouse

Reprinted from Uman, David B., *New Product Programs: Their Planning and Control* (New York: American Management Association, Inc., 1969), p. 86.

The earliest expected date for the completion of any event is the longest path leading to it from the beginning of a project. This sequence of events is called the "critical path," marked out in figure 11-3 as 1-3-4-6-9-12. This particular sequence indicates that the final sales brochure will be ready in $11\frac{1}{2}$ weeks, obtained by adding all t_e values along the critical path (T_e). Thus,

$$T_e = 3.0 + 1.6 + 0.5 + 4.5 + 1.9 = 11.5 \text{ weeks.}$$

The activities along the critical path govern the completion date of the entire project.

Events outside the critical path will usually have some slack. By calculating the latest allowable date, designated by the symbol T_1, planners can estimate how long it may take to do any job without causing delay in completing the project or the event at the end of the network. The amount of slack (S) is $T_1 - T_e$. Along the critical path, however, $T_1 = T_e$. Here, there is no room for error, no time to lose, no allowable slack or float. Here, completion dates must be observed exactly as scheduled, or the project will be late. Network analysis thus permits managers to determine which jobs must be done on time and which can be stretched out when advantages accrue from procrastination.

Perhaps the most valuable part of PERT is that of progress reporting, for it allows management to keep its finger on the pulse of projects. Information flows proceed both vertically and horizontally. The degree of detail should be related to the level of management for which reports are intended. In general, the higher the level, the less the detail.

The greatest value of monitoring, however, lies in the readjustment function. Plans seldom go exactly as initially anticipated, especially in new product development. There will be leads and lags in operations, as compared with original schedules. There may be frequent changes, necessitated by the arrival of newer, updated information. As development proceeds, networks usually must be reformulated to achieve better performance.

Readjustments can be accomplished in several ways. First, resources from one activity—those on paths with slack—can be shifted to other activities that are more critical. But these trade-offs can only be applied to resources that are substitutable. Second, technical specifications can be relaxed in order to save time. In many instances, this method is subject to severe limitations. Third, activities can be rearranged into different configurations. For example, activities that run concurrently will take less time than those that run sequentially. Converting activities, where feasible, from "series connected" to "series parallel" would therefore have the effect of shortening lead times. But this transformation to concurrent operations may also increase risks.[4] At any rate, periodic progress reports and simulations can produce alternatives for reallocating resources to improve the manner in which a project is carried out.

Design and Product Liability

The traditional issues of new product design revolve around such matters as standardization, consistency in production, quality control, reliability in use, durability, ease of maintenance, and levels of quality. In recent years, however, issues of product liability have loomed large in product design. Product liability is a legal term referring to damages sought because of defective products. Plaintiffs can be individuals or businesses seeking redress for losses or damages suffered.

The recent concern with product liability questions has arisen mainly from personal injury cases. Lawsuits have multiplied, partly because governments have made it easier for alleged injuries to get to court. Figures on the number of product liability suits filed with the courts are scarce, with cited figures ranging from close to a million, probably grossly overestimated, to a more conservative 85,000. But even the lower number represents a substantial increase over that of a decade earlier. Juries have also been prone to award larger sums, though many are reduced considerably on appeal. Nevertheless, the costs of insurance have soared, becoming a major problem to U.S. industry. The bill paid for product liability by manufacturing and retail firms in 1978 stood at an estimated $2.75 billion, as compared with $1.13 billion in 1975.[5]

In some industries the uncertainties associated with product liability have led to discontinuance of lines. Spaulding and MacGregor stopped making football helmets, claiming that "no helmet can prevent the type of injury associated with football." These firms were joined by Wilson Sporting Goods Co., whose spokesmen said the reason for withdrawing from the business was that court settlements were "bigger than the money the whole business generates."[6] But the risk of litigation is present in all industries, and the higher stakes prompted some authorities to recommend the participation of lawyers in product design. They argue that because the law deals with questions of harm, precautions, and warnings, procedures for designing products should examine the

---

[4] See Richard I. Levin and C. A. Kirkpatrick, *Planning and Control with PERT/CPM* (New York: McGraw-Hill Book Company, 1966), pp. 78–92, 114–118, and "How to Shrink Lead Time in New Product Production," *Business Management* (May, 1966), p. 81.

[5] "The Devils in the Product Liability Laws," *Business Week* (February 12, 1979), p. 72.

[6] Quoted in *Milwaukee Sentinel* (August 31, 1979), Pt. 2, p. 3.

same grounds as the courts.[7] In other words, the engineer should work closely with legal counsel when designing a new product.

The defect in a product may come from two sources: manufacturing processes or design. The manufacturer or seller is liable when he has failed to meet the legal obligations, which are determined by three basic principles—negligence, strict liability, and express warranty.

Negligence on the part of a producer involves unreasonable carelessness in making or designing a product. The norm by which the courts have judged a manufacturer's conduct is the "reasonable person" test. Has the firm acted "reasonably" in making safe products?

This rule has been extended, or made more stringent, by the "strict liability" doctrine. The focus here is the product itself. If a defect is established, irrespective of precautions taken, the manufacturer is liable.

But what constitutes a defect? The courts have held that manufacturers must strike a reasonable balance between risks and benefits. That is, they must design products not only for obvious uses but also for consumer misuses. They must anticipate the hazards and injuries that can result when consumers use products foolishly. For example, a teenager poured perfume made by Faberge over a lit candle to create a fragrant odor. The perfume ignited, burning a friend's neck. The injured party won a $27,000 award on grounds that Faberge did not warn users that its perfume was flammable. Faberge lost its appeal, despite its argument that there was no way to anticipate consumers pouring perfume over lighted candles.[8]

Product designers must be conversant with court decisions governing design and the weights assigned to various factors determining them. For example, a new ballpoint pen containing erasable ink raised banking concerns about potential forgeries and induced Gillette to carry a special warning on the package: "The American Bankers Association recommends that you should not use Eraser Mate to sign or endorse checks or other legal documents in order to guard against any possible alterations of these instruments." The refills for these pens were also designed so that they could not fit into any other pens, making it more difficult for forgers to take advantage of unsuspecting consumers.[9] Many manufacturers have seized upon labeling as a way to avoid product liability. But producers are not absolved from liability just because they properly warn against dangers inherent in a product.[10]

---

[7] Alvin S. Weinstein, et al., Product Liability and the Reasonably Safe Product (New York: John Wiley & Sons, 1978), p. 136.

[8] "The Devils in Product Liability Laws," pp. 72–73.

[9] Charles Perkins, "Manufacturer of New Erasable Pen Convinced by ABA to Include Warning," American Banker (March 6, 1979), p. ?

[10] Weinberg, et al., op. cit., p. 138.

The principle of express warranty engages the attention of marketing more than any other group involved in new product development. It relates to an affirmation of fact by a seller which is relevant when the buyer makes a purchase decision. Such representations can be made not merely for formal warranties but by advertising and even statements by sales people. For example, Toni "Very Gentle" home permanent in the late fifties advertised good results to users. An Ohio woman found her hair stiff and gummy after an application of the home permanent and claimed that her hair fell out after she removed the curlers. The Ohio supreme court upheld a judgment for the plaintiff on grounds that the advertising directed to the ultimate consumer created an express warranty. The user had every reason to believe, the court held, that no harm would befall her by washing her hair with "Very Gentle."[11]

Another peril that lurks in the way of new product design is the possibility of a government-mandated recall. There are a number of federal and state regulatory agencies that have the power to order the recall of defective or dangerous products. Most recalls, however, are made by companies voluntarily, without waiting for a legal writ. Their motives are various: to avoid later lawsuits, to prevent a tarnished corporate image, and to act in a manner consistent with socially responsible standards.[12]

Regardless of reason, product recall costs can prove exceedingly expensive. Recall of the Radial 500 was written off by Firestone Tire & Rubber Co. as a loss of $234 million.[13] Small companies with restricted financial resources may be unable to survive a major action. The King Candy Company of Fort Worth, Texas, closed its doors when the FDA labeled its chocolate candies as a health hazard and ordered a recall.[14]

Although any product can be subject to a recall order, the auto industry in particular has been plagued by mass-produced mistakes. The potential repair cost for correcting an exhaust defect in American Motors' 1976 models, estimated conservatively at $20 a car, would total approximately $6 million, more than double corporate earnings that year. In 1977, vehicle recalls of American manufacturers soared to a record 10.6 million, greater than the entire output of passenger vehicles in a normal year. The direct costs of product recall include communication to consumers, replacement of defective parts, and refunds. The indirect costs are more difficult to assess, involving adverse publicity and possible loss of customer goodwill.

[11] Anita S. Warren, "What to Do If Hair Falls Out; Or Are Companies Liable for Ad Claims?" *Advertising Age* (February 26, 1979), p. 54.

[12] Paul Busch, "Product Recall Grows as Peril for Marketers," *Marketing News* (June 1, 1979), p. 3.

[13] *Ibid.*

[14] John C. Boland, "Total Recall?" *Barron's* (August 7, 1978), pp. 22, 24.

Three major pieces of federal legislation deal with defective products. These are the Consumer Product Safety Act, the Occupational Safety and Health Act, and the Magnuson-Moss Warranty Act.

The Consumer Product Safety Act, enacted in 1972, created the Consumer Product Safety Commission, probably the most important agency today charged with protecting consumers against faulty goods. Headed by five presidential appointees for fixed terms, the commission operates with a staff of more than a thousand, including technicians, lawyers, and administrators. Its main responsibilities are to protect the public, assist it in evaluating product safety features, draw up uniform industry standards, and conduct research in product-related accidents and fatalities.[15] The commission can ban hazardous products if they pose unreasonable dangers to public health and safety when in use.

A consideration for firms manufacturing industrial products are the operations of the Occupational Safety Health Administration (OSHA), given legal status in 1970. This agency collects and analyzes occupational safety and health statistics, and the results of its research may be used by the Secretary of Labor to promulgate industry rules aimed at improving working conditions. The courts have upheld the doctrine that violations constitute negligence *per se*. Since OSHA rules are industry wide and in effect set minimum criteria for industrial product quality, manufacturers should design their output to conform with these standards.

The Magnuson-Moss Warranty Act, enacted in 1975, is of major concern to marketing. The main purpose of the act is the establishment of minimum disclosure standards for written warranties on consumer products. According to this law, terms and conditions are to be stated in easily understood language, without ambiguities or disclaimers. The Federal Trade Commission was empowered to draw up rules dealing with warranty content, and these should be strictly adhered to by marketing personnel when warranting or guaranteeing product performance.

Developing the Package

Except for commodities transported or distributed in bulk, products are enclosed in some sort of protective material. About 75 percent of all finished goods are so contained, and total U.S. expenditures on packaging in 1980 is projected at more than $43 billion.[16] There are two major

---

[15] See Paul Busch, "A Review and Critical Evaluation of the Consumer Product Safety Commission: Marketing Management Implications," *Journal of Marketing* (October, 1976), pp. 41-49.

[16] Alan Serchuk, "Packaging's Uncertain Road Ahead," *Modern Packaging* (January, 1978), p. 38.

aspects to package design: functions related to physical distribution and those associated with merchandising. The primary concern of raw materials and industrial products is the former. Many types of consumer goods, especially those sold in self-service outlets, must also concern themselves with package designs aimed at achieving merchandising or sales objectives.

Physical distribution aspects

The term *distribution packaging* refers to an integrated approach to package design.[17] The package engineer must first consider the essential properties of a package desired in a distribution network. This encompasses transportation, warehousing, materials handling—all activities necessary in a product's movement from factory to final destination. The idea is to select that particular design which minimizes not the cost of packaging only but overall distribution costs.

The reason for evaluating package design in terms of an entire physical distribution system is because the engineer's choice of package affects costs of movement and storage. For example, changing the shape, weight, or size of a package may make for easier handling and less warehouse effort. It may also lead to a reclassification of common carrier ratings and thus lower transport costs. Adding more protection to a package may accomplish the same objective by obviating the need for certain equipment and special handling. When lumber is wrapped in polyethylene film, it can be shipped in flat cars. This mode of transportation adds packaging costs but produces larger savings by eliminating the need for closed cars. The lowest cost package that fulfills a distribution objective is not necessarily the best selection. Rather, alternative designs must be evaluated on the basis of total physical distribution costs.

The focal point of package design for physical distribution is protection. A protective package must perform the following functions:

1. Enclose the material.

2. Protect the enclosed material against damage in the physical distribution process. The most common causes of damage are vibration and impact, which fracture, break, and distort products; punctures, which cause leakage and possible contamination; and compression, which leads to buckling and crushing.

3. Guard the material against environmental hazards, such as temperature, humidity, and foreign matter. These are normally beyond the control of logistical management. But package design can minimize or reduce risks from these sources of damage.

---

[17] See W. F. Friedman and J. J. Kipnees, "Distribution Packaging," *Distribution Worldwide* (August, 1977), pp. 32-37.

4. Maintain a uniform weight within the package. Most equipment in materials handling comes designed to handle packages that have a uniform distribution of weight.

5. Provide identification and shipping labels.

The type of protection depends on the nature of the product and its itinerary. Products that require refrigeration must have packages that facilitate air flow or heat transfer, so that spoilage is minimized when ideal conditions are not present. Food must be packaged for maintenance of palatability—taste retention, freshness, and preservation of color and consistency. Dry foods, such as breakfast cereals, cake mixes, and saltine crackers, call for packages with added moisture protection. Conversely, wet foods must be protected from drying out or absorbing moisture in storage, since they are moisture packed and permeated. Metal and other hard-surfaced products must be guarded against abrasion and corrosion.

The length of haul is also a factor in package design. The greater the distance a product must travel, the greater its exposure to the rigors of transportation and variations in climate. Exports normally require more protection than domestically delivered goods. Tropical destinations pose greater hazards, particularly if receiving and storage facilities are substandard.

Protection can be pretested by computer simulation and laboratory experiments. Some packaging materials manufacturers, seeking to sell entire packaging systems to shippers, do free testing for prospective customers. Various trade associations are engaged in the same types of research as a service to their membership. There are also in existence independent testing labs which specialize in package research.

A basic question is the degree of protection to incorporate in a package. There have been many attempts to establish standard cost ratios for different classes of products. But estimates vary widely, for package requirements are highly diverse. As a rule, the higher the value and fragility of the product, the greater the economic justification for more protection. For example, package costs for Xerox copiers comprise an insignificant portion of total costs, which run into $1,000 multiples per unit. These machines are shipped in specially made paperboard corrugated classified at the high end of the quality spectrum.[18] On the other hand, products that bear relatively low prices may not be able to afford such high levels of protection and must abide greater losses in shipment and storage. This practice is economical as long as the loss that can be eliminated does not exceed the additional physical distribution costs of an improved packaging system.

---

[18] Allen Pinto, "Packaging for the Long Haul," *Modern Packaging* (November, 1978), p. 25.

Some situations tend to favor a system of reusable packaging. Companies that do their own distributing may find their trucks running empty on return trips. Under these conditions, the cost of transporting reusable containers is virtually nil because time and distance of the return trip do not change. If common carriers are used, the container replacement cost must be greater than freight rates in order to justify material returns. This might apply to highly specialized containers, such as bins, assembly racks, pallet boxes, and hampers. In other situations, reusable containers may be mandated by government fiat. Many states and localities have passed laws to reduce environmental pollution from discarded cans and bottles and to encourage recycling of packaging materials.

Merchandising aspects

For many consumer products, especially those sold in self-service outlets, the package takes on functions other than those related solely to protection and handling in physical distribution. In the absence of sales personnel, the package must act as a merchandising vehicle at the point of purchase. It must attract the attention of would-be buyers in an atmosphere crowded with competitive offerings. It must communicate relevant information as to contents and product usage. It must intensify attitudes and impressions that marketers deem vital to building a "consumer franchise."

But the package does not serve as a merchandising aid to all products alike. It is extremely important to cosmetics and gift items, less so to frozen foods, and not at all to hardware.

Today's trends are away from flashy graphics and bombastic introductions and towards packages that are simple, contemporary, and functional.[19] But each designer may have a different interpretation of these attributes. For example, Miller Brewing Company packages are dominated by stylized lettering—"Lite"—which is described as masculine by Landor Associates, the package designer. The content information of the beer is stuck in an out-of-the-way place, where it does not distract from the logo. Color may also play a key role in package design. Pharmaceutical and personal care products often come in blue and white packages, which are thought to symbolize hygienic, antiseptic qualities. Cosmetic packages might be decorative, featuring pink and blue pastels, because they connote the softness that is usually desired in skin care. Poisonous products, such as insecticides, use strikingly harsh colors; black and yellow, for example, might give an impression of strong, toxic effects.

---

[19] "How the Top Designers Do It," *Modern Packaging* (February, 1978), pp. 34-37.

A package design may undergo a battery of tests for determining its effects at the point of purchase. One group of tests relates to perception, which can be measured by several available instruments. The tachistoscope is popular for conducting visibility tests because the length of exposure to images can be controlled in split seconds. The objective of such testing is to evaluate the legibility of lettering and art work and assess its causative factors. A "relative impact test" compares the proposed design with competitive packages by simulating a store shelf, or even an entire supermarket section. Consumers may also be shown slides of packages at different distances and at varying levels of illumination to measure the ease with which they can identify and locate particular brands.[20]

In addition to how it looks, a package can exert influence on consumer attitudes and behavior. Attitudinal measurements are obtained on consumer surveys through various types of rating scales, rankings, and preference questioning. Behavioral aspects may be inferred through numerous kinds of product usage tests and "buying games."[21]

The promotional elements of package design, however, cannot be viewed separately from those of physical distribution. Graphics and art work lengthen development time by as much as two to three times over that of designing a package for physical distribution only. Development of the packaging system is also costlier. Package development cost in the food industry, for example, runs to some 10 percent of total product development cost. Production and equipment also tend to be more expensive. Packaging can be conceived as a system of building blocks, with the smallest units at retail and the largest in transportation and storage. But the retail end can raise costs of distribution packaging by requiring added protection for the inner contents of the larger containers. Total packaging costs rise further above those of protection by the inclusion of more elements: more expensive printing, convenience features built into the packaging design, carrying cases and display racks for merchandising. In some instances, packaging costs comprise the largest component of total production costs. With the continued trend towards mass merchandising and high labor costs of sales personnel, package design with promotional functions should assume a greater significance.

Naming the Product

Another part of the development phase, and one that engages marketing, is the task of branding. This term refers to the practice of devis-

---

[20] David Schwartz, "Evaluating Packaging," *Journal of Advertising* (October, 1971), pp. 29-31.

[21] See *Ibid.*, pp. 31-32; William M. MacDonald, "Research is Vital Component of Package Design Process," *Marketing News* (May 18, 1979), p. 5; "Packaging Can Be Major or Minor Influence on Consumer Acceptance," *Marketing News* (March 24, 1978), p. 8.

ing names and trademarks which, when registered with the U.S. Patent Office, are given legal protection for exclusive use in conjunction with the new product. Not all products carry brand names, but the vast majority do.

The question of a brand name is closely linked with the marketing strategy adopted for the product and hence with the functions a brand name is expected to perform. Many products are marketed under a distributor name, in which case the manufacturer need not be concerned with a brand name. In fact, marketing functions in these instances are assumed almost entirely by the reseller, who also takes on the responsibility of branding. But when producers decide to market under their own labels, new products must be given names. This task includes name generation, checking against trademark references, screening lists of possibilities, marketing research with consumers, and legal work in brand registration. The amount of time and effort that goes into this job depends on product type as well as on the market strategy.

Most industrial products are given brand names perfunctorily, almost as an afterthought. A combination of numbers, letters, and company designation, such as IBM series 370, is considered sufficient. This is because the main purpose of the name in the industrial field is that of identification to facilitate ordering, shipping, and stocking. Buyers actively institute product search, and terms and conditions of sales are frequently negotiated. Product differentiation rests on product features, such as quality level and performance specification. The name by itself, commonplace or imaginary, hardly enters as a factor in the purchase decision. Then why make much ado about nothing?

Consumer products are often differentiated on the basis of advertising or promotion where consumer choice is influenced by psychological factors. Here, brand names do much more than just identify products. If adduced properly and creatively, names can contribute significantly towards the realization of overall marketing objectives. But they must be integrated with the promotional approach; they must blend with the advertising of which they are a part. For example, a name must be easy to read, remember, and pronounce if, as most marketers hope, it is to become a household word. It should be unique, easily set apart from other names. And probably the most desirable quality for an effective brand name is its ability to connote positive product images.

Several years ago, Thomas J. Lipton Co. introduced a meat extender called Pennsylvania Dutch Casserole. It tested well for taste, convenience, and price. It was packaged in an attractive carton and supported by an introductory advertising budget of $5.5 million. But sales lagged and the product failed. Later investigations led the company to single out the name as the cause of failure. "Pennsylvania Dutch," it was found, evoked no favorable image outside the Lancaster country area of the Keystone state, and the "casserole" descriptor brought up memories of making a meal out of leftovers. Two years later a similar product came to market called Hamburger Helper. Annual sales of some $50 million testify to its success.[22]

A name must also fit the product. It should communicate a message that conveys some central feature about the product, its performance, or its benefits. A case in point is that of Lowenbrau beer. Backed by heavy advertising support from Miller, the premium beer began its American debut with soaring sales. Then Anheuser-Busch filed a complaint with the Federal Trade Commission charging advertising deception because Miller implied that the product was identical to its German namesake. Sales plummeted as a consequence of the bad publicity caused by the lawsuit. According to Robert S. Weinstein, a well-known industry analyst, the now heralded "great American beer" made a fatal mistake in adopting the name of a venerable German brew and then producing a different commodity. "They (Miller) may have outfoxed themselves," says Weinstein, "by choosing a name that created a mental image they couldn't deliver. The product didn't fit the image."[23]

A manufacturing firm choosing to distribute under its own label has several choices of name strategy. First, the company can apply a blanket or family name such as practiced by Campbell, General Electric, Heinz, or Hunt. Second, it can use a separate, individualized name. Third, it can fall back on a combination of the two forms.

The family or blanket name possesses certain cost advantages, as budgets for name research are reduced or eliminated entirely. Promotional expenses may also be lowered, since the family name is already known. It thus renders superfluous advertising aimed at familiarizing consumers with a new name. The new product can also benefit from any prior associations that consumers have with the family name. This attitudinal transference may hasten the rate of consumer trial and consequently shorten the duration of the introductory phase. Greater ease in gaining distribution for a name brand already familiar to consumers reinforces early acceptance.

But a family name also has its drawbacks. This strategy is best suited to new products that are similar to others in the "family" in terms of product classification, distribution channels, and target markets. Otherwise, marketing synergism may be lacking. A multiproduct manufacturer like Procter and Gamble may purposely seek to avoid consumer associations of different brands or products. There may be a downright negative effect if consumers were to associate its Duncan Hines cake mixes with its detergents and cleansers.

---

[22] Willard H. Doyle, "Brand Still Crucial, But Now It's 'Manufactured,' Not Dreamed Up," *Marketing News* (February 10, 1978), p. 12.

[23] "Lowenbrau Big Factor in Reported Miller Slip," *Advertising Age* (August 27, 1979), p. 66.

When family names are used, the quality level of the new product should also be comparable to that of other items in the family line. A lower quality item may hurt sales of the better quality products. Similarly, promotion of a better quality product may result in credibility gaps among potential buyers. Previous experience is not easily forgotten or separated from new facts. Lastly, a new product failure may tarnish the reputation of older, successful brands.

New products with individual names must, of course, forgo the advantages of the group. Under no circumstances can they, to borrow a phrase from politics, ride on the coattails of the leader. Being individual entities, they must stand on their own feet. As a result, development costs and introductory expenses associated with the brand name are greater. But the firm is also afforded greater flexibility in its marketing program. Promotion can take more varied forms. Each brand may seek to create a different image, carve out for itself a different market position. Each brand may move in different directions, appealing to diverse market segments. Individual brand names thus offer a wider scope of marketing strategy and tactics.

The Transfer of Technology

If development is to prepare the new product for the marketplace, production must be able to fulfill demand requirements. Since most corporations encourage specialization—research by one group, design by another, production by a third—technology must be transferred from R&D to manufacturing. But the complexity of modern technology and the increasing numbers and varieties of new products have given rise to different methods of effecting the transition. There is no single method that suits all firms and all occasions. Rather, methods tend to vary in accordance with industrial organization and product characteristics. The subject of technological transfer has been given extensive treatment, among others, by Arthur Gerstenfeld, whose synthesis lists five basic alternatives which, in various combinations, cover the full spectrum of possibilities.[24] According to Gerstenfeld, these are as follows:

1. Product specifications and drawings.

2. Manufacturing participation in R&D.

3. R&D participation in manufacturing.

4. Corporate coordinator.

5. Transfer team.

---

[24] Gerstenfeld, *Effective Management of Research and Development,* pp. 43-53.

Product specifications and drawings

This technique requires R&D to prepare a set of specifications and drawings and forward it to manufacturing. Actually, specifications and drawings are made use of whenever technical information is conveyed from R&D to production. But here the documents themselves form the central feature. The blueprints and their interpretation by manufacturing become the focal point in the transition of responsibility.

The specifications and drawings method, relying primarily upon paperwork, keeps information to a minimum. It assumes that the recipients of the data can apply them with few explanations and clarifications. The method is, therefore, best suited for relatively simple products or for technologies with which production has an intimate familiarity. It also lends itself to situations in which transfer time is not a critical element. The reason is because the method entails sequential scheduling. First comes R&D, then documentation, followed finally by production planning. This one-step-after-another approach lengthens the time span of the operation. Finally, significant cost reductions are not to be expected from the specifications and drawings technique. The lack of manufacturing input in product design encourages R&D to overdesign the product. Higher tolerances than needed provide insurance against production slippage, it is reasoned. This tendency is reinforced by R&D's ignorance of plant capacity effects.

Manufacturing participation in R&D

This method calls for production engineers to be assigned to R&D. If done at an early date, manufacturing becomes involved with product design. The advantages of this participation are twofold. First, the integration of production know-how can lead to lower manufacturing costs by specifying cheaper raw materials, components, processes, equipment, or any combination of these cost reduction devices. Second, time is saved because of parallel operations. The production engineer can be laying out production procedures while the product is being designed and tested. However, development costs may run higher because effort is being duplicated. These extra costs should be weighed against the potential savings that can be achieved.

R&D participation in manufacturing

This is the converse of the previous method; R&D personnel are assigned to manufacturing. For all practical purposes, R&D engineers are given the responsibility for working out the manufacturing procedures. By having those who designed the product set up its production lines, time and effort are saved in technological transfer. This method is best employed in continuous flow production or in advanced technological industries. This method proves cumbersome, however, for companies with large numbers of new products.

Corporate coordinator

A single individual, regardless of title, is put in charge of the new product's developments. The technological transfer from R&D to manufacturing is the responsibility of that executive. Because the coordinator must follow through on the new product, it cannot be unduly complicated. The manager assigned to its development must be able to understand the critical features of the transfer process.

Appointment of a corporate coordinator can also facilitate transfer when the manufacturing plant and R&D laboratories are physically separated. Communication is hampered when people work apart, and cooperative effort is impaired. The corporate coordinator can bridge the distance gap by fostering commonality, a sense of common purpose and interest. To do this, he must promote a mutual interest among the participating groups in methodology, translate conceptual differences, and reconcile conflicting points of view. Others have also suggested that money can be used to negotiate equity positions in a project.[25] The interest and cooperation of development groups are "bought." This presumes that the coordinator has control over the project's budget.

Transfer team

The team approach combines specialists from R&D and manufacturing in a single, cohesive group. This team may be composed of groups permanently structured within the organization, such as new product committees, or they may be of a temporary nature, such as venture teams and task forces. Whether such teams are temporary or permanent depends in large part on the number of new products to be developed, as well as their characteristics. Proximity of R&D to manufacturing is also an important consideration, for team members must be in frequent contact with each other.

The transfer team can accomplish significant cost reduction because specialists from different disciplines contribute to each step in the development process. The interdisciplinary character of the group equips it to handle complicated products and complex technologies. The need for frequent meetings, however, may serve to lengthen development time.

The Marketing Plan

Before the development stage is over, a marketing plan should be in place. A great deal of preliminary work has already been done by business analysis, such as sales forecasting, estimation of unit costs at given production levels, and assumptions about the marketing mix that would be employed and its probable expenditures. In this respect, the marketing plan is an extension of business analysis; it adds all the necessary detail that makes planning operational.

---

[25] Steele, *Innovation in Big Business*, pp. 137–139.

A marketing plan has various purposes. Its main aims are:[26]

1. To weave all elements of marketing into a unified, cohesive entity.

2. To evaluate alternative methods of solving marketing problems and to reduce the likelihood of important ones being overlooked.

3. To draw up a budget for all marketing activities, with a timetable for expenditures and results.

4. To delegate authority for each task.

5. To submit a document that mangement can approve, reject, or modify.

There is no best way to prepare such a document, and companies call it by different names, such as business plans, operational plans, marketing plans. The exact name is of little importance, for it merely reflects a semantic preference. But the content of the document is of utmost significance, for it must include the key elements that are associated with sales generation. These can be condensed to three essential ingredients: situational analysis, marketing objectives, and strategy and programs.

The situational analysis reviews current market conditions and relates them to company strengths and weaknesses. Marketing objectives establish the outer parameters of the "product mission," as well as of specific marketing functions. Strategy and programs spell out in great detail what is to be done, when, and by whom in order to achieve the objectives set forth. Table 11-1 outlines the subject matter that might be included under each heading.

Since the situation for particular products will vary, marketing plans will address themselves to different questions and emphasize different aspects under each major heading. But the core of the marketing plan deals with elements that have commonly been referred to as the 4 P's: product, pricing, promotion, physical distribution. The plan for a new product contains little or nothing that is unique; it is essentially the same as that for an ongoing product. Because the 4 P's, or the marketing mix, form the backbone of many marketing books, the subject is considered as falling beyond the scope of this book. But pricing may deserve a brief discussion. Of all major decision variables of the marketing mix, pricing is the most complicated. It is also viewed as the most important single element of the marketing mix. It alone is directly embodied in revenue; all other variables are calculated as expenses. Despite the existence of extensive literature, business pricing practices veer sharply from price theory.

[26] Clarence E. Eldridge, *The Role and Importance of the Marketing Plan* (New York: Association of National Advertisers, 1966), pp. 2–6.

Table 11-1
The Marketing Plan

I. Situational Analysis

  A. Product category

    Sales trends (units, dollars) for the total product category and product types.

    Sales trends by region, customer characteristics, distribution channels.

  B. Competitive data

    Principal competitors and their marketing strategies, market shares, promotional effort, pricing, distribution patterns.

  C. Trade relations

    Markups, discounts, cooperative programs.

  D. Problems and opportunities

    These are inferences based on the above situational analysis.

II. Marketing Objectives

  A. Sales estimates over time, in both dollars and units, market share, contributions to profits and overhead.

  B. Subfunction objectives

    Subfunctions may include sales force, advertising, sales promotion, pricing, use of middlemen, physical distribution, inventory levels, technical service.

III. Strategy and Action Programs

  This section should include exact details by which the strategy is implemented and objectives are achieved. Contingency plans might also be included.

Pricing

Price is the exchange value of products in the marketplace. While companies use various methods of pricing, and often with little consistency, the subject of price can be approached from two directions, demand or costs. Firms adhering to either demand-oriented or cost-oriented pricing pay attention to both demand variables and cost factors. The distinguishing element is the emphasis given to one or the other.

Demand-oriented pricing

The method that stresses demand rests heavily upon marginal concepts of economic theory. The focal point is the demand curve which, in the usual sense, indicates price-output relationships for an industry's products. By delineating expected sales volume at various price levels, the demand curve also describes price elasticity, the ratio of the relative change in sales volume owing to a relative change in price. This statistic then measures the sensitivity of demand to changes in price.

In essence, the quantity demanded (Q) is viewed as a function of price (P). Thus, all given values of P or Q can be said to have different values of elasticity. This point value can be described as

$$\frac{dQ}{dP} \cdot \frac{P}{Q}.$$

It is more common, however, to use an "arc" or interval estimate. In this form, elasticity can be expressed as:

$$\frac{\Delta Q}{Q} \div \frac{\Delta P}{P} \text{ or in the alternate form } \frac{\Delta Q}{Q} \cdot \frac{P}{\Delta P}.$$

For example, let us suppose that a price increase from \$200 to \$220 per unit brings about a sales decrease from 550,000 to 500,000 units. Calculating price elasticity by the formula

$$\frac{\Delta Q}{Q} \cdot \frac{P}{\Delta P}:$$

$$\frac{550,000 - 500,000}{525,000} \cdot \frac{210}{200 - 220} = \frac{50,000}{525,000} \cdot \frac{210}{-20} = -1$$

The negative sign in the above example is dropped and the elasticity coefficient becomes 1, or unity. When the coefficient is unity, changes in price are proportional to changes in the quantity demanded. A sales volume change that is less than proportionate to a price shift means demand is inelastic. A converse result would imply a product with an elastic demand.

The above calculation employed values for P and Q that were averages of two periods, one before the price change (t_0) and one after (t_1). While other calculations are possible, the averaging method is recommended. The equation for price elasticity can thus be expressed as:

$$\frac{Q_1 - Q_0}{Q_0 + Q_1} \cdot \frac{P_0 + P_1}{P_1 - P_0}$$

As can readily be seen, the above equation will yield an identical answer to the example solved previously. Thus:

$$\frac{500,000 - 550,000}{550,000 + 500,000} \cdot \frac{200 + 220}{220 - 200} = \frac{-50,000}{1,050,000} \cdot \frac{420}{20} = -1.$$

In general, the larger the number of available substitutes, the higher the coefficient of elasticity. More durable consumer goods tend to be more elastic because their purchases can be postponed. Demand is also more elastic when price represents a larger proportion of buyers' incomes. This is often referred to as income elasticity.

The same principles apply to industrial products, though they are thought to be less elastic generally than their consumer counterparts. One reason is that many industrial products serve as input in manufacturing operations that in the short run follow the demand for finished goods. Procurement managers have freedom to shift the size and frequency of purchases, but they cannot alter greatly the basic demand from that derived by end-product fluctuations.

Nevertheless, there are differences among types of industrial input. When an input bears a low percentage to the total costs of producing an end product, demand is generally inelastic. Conversely, price has a potentially greater effect on sales volume when a component represents a high percentage of total costs. Lower prices for such products may sometimes induce more than proportionate decreases in prices of end products and thereby expand overall volume. This is often the case with new industries. Reduced prices of picture tubes are often credited with expanding the demand for TV receivers.[27] Lower input prices for hand calculators even brought component manufacturers into finished goods production as they integrated vertically towards rapidly growing markets.

The conventional wisdom of economics contemplates the firm as a profit-maximizing organization. If a total cost curve could be superimposed over a total revenue curve at various levels of demand, a firm would select the point at which the difference between cost and revenue is greatest. This concept is illustrated in figure 11-4.

In figure 11-4, total revenue for various levels of demand is shown as a second-degree curve. This accords with an assumption of quantity being inversely, but nonlinearly, related to price. Unit costs are regarded as U-shaped, declining as economies of greater volume take hold and then rising as operations approach the limits of their capacity. Until the firm reaches point B, which represents break-even, it operates at a loss. At point M, the difference between total cost and total revenue is greatest, and the firm will produce 0Q units. At the point of maximum profit, marginal revenue equals marginal cost per unit of output.

Whether it is practical for a firm to maximize profits through pricing is questionable. Businesses operating in competitive markets, such as commodities, can have no pricing policy. They must meet the going

---

[27] See R. Moyer and R. J. Boewadt, "The Pricing of Industrial Goods: A Departure from Conventional Wisdom," *Business Horizons* (June, 1971). p. 29.

Figure 11-4. Profit-Maximizing Concept of a Firm

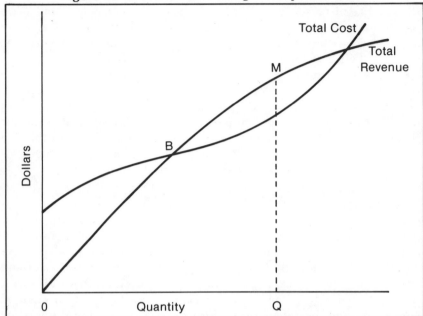

market price which, as in the day of Adam Smith, remains governed by "an invisible hand." The oligopolistic industries that prevail in the United States frequently display price leadership. One firm, usually the largest, assumes the role of price leader, and the industry, as though by consensus, tends to follow. But even leaders have trouble in ascertaining competitive reactions to price alterations. Mavericks are always ready to strike out in an independent course; opportunists are always watching to take advantage of a false move. Leaders must also be sensitive to noneconomic factors, such as customer relations, public opinion, and government scrutiny. But most important, companies cannot measure their demand curves. They cannot predict accurately what quantities will be demanded at different prices. Most companies, however, can estimate costs with a fair degree of precision. For this reason, the common method of pricing tends to be cost oriented.

Cost-oriented pricing

Because costs can be estimated for various quantities, companies can work backwards, fitting prices to costs. This entails adding a percentage or markup to the product cost in order to meet a given objective. The cost itself can be calculated on the basis of full costing, variable costs, or conversion costs. The latter is found by estimating direct labor and overhead required to convert raw material to finished goods, which in actuality amounts to value added.

The predominant strategy employed today appears to be a system called ROI pricing.[28] This stratagem implies an objective or some desired return on investment. The procedure calls for estimating costs for the most likely volume to be produced during the year. Unit prices are then set so that total revenue equals total costs plus targeted net income. In order for this procedure to work well, demand must be relatively inelastic.

Such cost-oriented pricing provides needed benchmarks. But marketing managers must make adjustments for a variety of factors: market conditions, possible competitive actions, industry operating levels. Pricing decisions must also be made in relation to other marketing mix variables. For example, pricing must be consistent with promotional and channel strategy.[29] It must also be blended with a product policy. A higher price may be commanded by a differentiated product, such as one of superior quality. Or it might contain some other characteristic to enhance its value in use. Many industrial products and expensive consumer durables have service features built into their prices. In any event, pricing is an art, not a science, proceeding empirically by trial and error and using no single method to the exclusion of all others.

Armed with a marketing plan, containing a pricing strategy and a marketing program, the firm is now ready to move out of development and take the next step towards getting the new product to market.

---

[28] Douglas G. Brooks, "Cost-Oriented Pricing: A Realistic Solution to a Complicated Problem," *Journal of Marketing* (April, 1975), pp. 72-74.

[29] See P. W. Ferris and D. J. Reibstein, "How Prices, Ad Expenditures and Profits are Linked," *Harvard Business Review* (November-December, 1979), pp. 173-184.

REVIEW QUESTIONS

1. Describe the characteristics of the overall new product development process relative to cost, risk, probability of success, and changing responsibilities.

2. An executive who was also an enthusiastic card player compared the new product development process to a poker game. The game starts with small risk and modest investment. As the game proceeds, both increase in magnitude. Continuing the gambling analogy, the player must continually evaluate risks, costs and possible rewards to determine if he should stay in the game or withdraw from the hand. What do you think of this analogy?

3. R&D people believe that the creative process cannot be scheduled. Therefore, a rigid time schedule cannot be established for the technical development of the new product. But the businessman knows better. Not only can R&D development activities be scheduled, but it is of the greatest importance that the agreed-upon schedule be met. Why is this true?

4. Should the R&D department be allowed free rein in the direction taken by their research and hunt for new products?

5. Smaller as well as larger firms will on occasion seek the services of an outside R&D organization. Why, particularly for the larger firm, should this be necessary?

6. PERT and CPM are frequently recommended scheduling tools for the management of new product development. Identify and explain the basic concepts and terms employed in PERT and CPM.

7. What information is required in order to fully describe each activity scheduled by PERT and CPM?

8. During the development stage, a proposed marketing plan covering the product's initial commercialization takes shape. This plan typically includes a number of sections. List and briefly describe each section.

9. A brand name for a new product may be the one used for a number of other related products (family brand), or the name may be made to order for the specific product (individual brand). Develop some principles that can guide the marketing person as to the appropriate path to follow.

10. Clothes make the man. The package for a typical consumer product does not "make" the product, but it is of considerable importance to the product's future. List the various considerations that may be referred to for a package design.

11. Assume that you have been appointed to be brand manager for a new product and have the responsibility of preparing the marketing plan. One component of this plan is the price at which the product will be introduced and probably sustained during the first year of commercialization. Develop a list of all possible factors that may affect your price recommendation.

12. Two possible objectives frequently cited for new product pricing are to:
    a. discourage competition.
    b. recover development costs within a given time period.
    Criticize these objectives.

13. Name two products of recent memory that you believe to have been priced in accordance with a skimming policy. Name two additional products priced in accordance with a penetration policy. Support your answer.

14. Discuss the different channels of distribution logical for a new product that:
    a. is similar to existing company products.
    b. does not involve the company's existing market.
    c. requires an aggressive introduction.
    d. is introduced by a small company lacking requisite resources.

15. Advertising expenditures for a new product may be very high initially, then gradually taper off to a lower level—or the reverse strategy may be followed. Explain the circumstances of the two opposing strategies.

16. Product liability poses a multifaceted hazard for the new product developer. Explain.

12/ Product Testing

A product testing program actually began in the development stage, which concerned itself primarily with technical testing. This stage tests products in the laboratory and with prospective customers.

Product testing programs with customers are highly diverse, but all can be broken down into three major types: concept tests, product use tests, and sales area tests.

The main purpose of the concept test is to guide R&D in transforming a vague concept into a tangible product. Most concept tests use sampling devices but do not select respondents with known probablities and hence cannot be generalized to population. There is also some question as to what a concept test really measures.

Product use tests are attempts to match the standards of earlier concepts with the actual, physical entity. Their main purpose is to assess customer reaction to product attributes of the new item and to compare them with those of competitive products in the market.

Most product use tests are "blind," with all identifications removed. A common method is that of paired comparisions, whereby prospective customers evaluate two products or pairs of products. Another popular technique is the monadic test, wherein respondents use the new item over a period of time and evaluate it in terms of their past experience.

Test marketing measures sales in one or more areas and aims to estimate the volume that would be obtained, as well as market share, if the product were distributed nationally with a given marketing plan. Decisions to test market a new product rest on the degree of perceived risk and estimates of comparative costs.

Nevertheless, test marketing is not problem free. It alerts competitors, involves high cost, and may not provide sufficient assurance about the outcome of a national introduction. Two basic approaches to overcome these difficulties are minimarkets and lab tests. Both of these marketing research methods are supplemental to test markets, not a substitute for them.

Testing Products with Customers

The development stage witnesses the beginning of a product testing program. Some of it is technical in nature, concerned with the composition and performance of the new product. Composition is determined through technical analysis, which breaks down the product into its component parts. That is, technical analysis studies the raw materials required in production and the processes by which the product is fabricated and assembled. Performance testing focuses on how the product actually works, and it attempts to simulate varying conditions of product usage. Procter and Gamble laboratories, for example, do laundry for some 500 employees each week in order to analyze the cleaning power of various chemical formulations.[1] Laboratory testing is a vital part of product development, for it helps in assessing the quality level in relation to competitive offerings. But most firms would feel more secure if the product would get an approving nod from actual users. In the last analysis, the marketplace, not the laboratory, determines the fate of the new product.

The exact purposes of testing products and their marketing programs with prospective customers are highly varied, but they can all be summed up as attempts to decrease the risk of failure. Firms seek to convert uncertainty into probability before committing substantial funds to bring a new product into the marketplace. If any negatives can be detected, if any defects can be eliminated, if any improvements can be made, the time to do so is before, not after, the new product comes to market.

Bernard Jaffee, president of a marketing research house, has characterized this inquiry into prospective new products as "replete with eccentricity" and as reflecting a "mosaic of methodologies."[2] And this description is not far off the mark in portraying the state of the art. Product tests display a bewildering array of survey designs and measurement devices. There are practically no generally accepted techniques, even among marketing research personnel within the same company. The choice of one variation over another is often made without any coherent reason. The different methods also yield different results, and researchers argue endlessly over their faults and virtues.

While diversity dominates marketing research in new products, some underlying common elements do suggest syntheses. The process of synthesis is necessary, imperfect though it is, to understand the testing phase. Synthesis must be undertaken to trace out basic patterns in the fabric of the methodological mosaic. When contemplated from this

[1] Peter Vanderwicken, "P&G's Secret Ingredient," *Fortune* (July, 1974), p. 77.

[2] "Eccentricity is Hallmark of Product Testing, Jaffe Asserts," *Marketing News* (March 24, 1978), p. 8.

perspective, new product testing can be broken down into three main parts: concept tests, product use tests, and sales area tests.

Concept tests usually come at the beginning of the testing series, since the concept must of necessity precede development. Sales tests are conducted towards the end of the research phase, just before actual commercialization. But in practice the three types of research do not occur in a strictly sequential order. There may be considerable overlap, and two or more different types of tests can be done at the same time as part of a single research project. Or evidence at a later phase may cause the new product to be returned for modification and testing begins again.

Concept Testing

A concept test done at this point is unlike any done earlier, the purpose of which was to search for ideas or collect data for preliminary screening. Now the product concept has been accepted; funds have been appropriated for its development. The main aim of concept testing now is to guide R&D in translating the concept into a tangible product, building a prototype, and incorporating necessary refinements or modifications. A secondary purpose is to guide marketing in positioning the new product and to building an advertising or selling program.

Concept tests are carried out with samples of would-be customers who are presented with a product concept and asked about their reactions. A wide variety of questions are possible, covering likes and dislikes, attitudes, preferences, intentions to buy. The interviewing forms are also highly diverse: questions may be unstructured or structured; open- or closed-ended; dichotomous or multiple choice. Many surveys employ ranking or scaling devices as interviewing techniques.

Some marketing research specialists have proposed elaborate procedures for testing concepts at this rather advanced stage of new product development. One such proposal visualizes concept tests, by studying consumer reactions to product attributes and promotional themes, as predicting the size of potential markets and segments thereof.[3]

A research service that comes close to subscribing to this philosophy is STEP, an acronym for Strategy Evaluation Program, conducted monthly by Eric Marder Associates, Inc. This syndicated study uses a sample of about 800 households, drawn by probability methods from telephone directories in 100 areas throughout the country. Each selected household is mailed a booklet that shows various products, all competitive, with their respective prices and brief descriptions. After answering a series of questions covering product usage and opinions about the illustrations and descriptions carried in the booklet, respon-

---

[3] Yorum Wind, "A New Procedure for Concept Evaluation," *Journal of Marketing* (October, 1973), pp. 2–11.

dents are requested to paste stickers, from a total of ten, underneath each product to indicate the likelihood of purchase in the future.

This concept test, according to its sponsor, "generates estimates of the potential share of market that would be obtained if the test strategy were implemented holding competitive marketing factors comparable and constant."[4] But even this statement on the meaning of survey findings, hedged with qualifications and reservations, makes no outright claim that "share of buying intention" will hold up in a real world situation or that it can be projected to total sales of the product category.

The majority of concept tests do not select respondents with known probabilities and hence cannot be projected to a given universe. But even probability designs do not obviate the criticism of external validity—the question of generalizing survey results to the population. Later concept tests, like earlier ones, are not immune from ambiguity. Are the measured reactions a reflection of the product concepts? Or do they represent a response to the creative quality of the presentations— descriptions, drawings, pictures, package or product mockups, promotional literature, finished advertisements? A wide gap may still exist between consumers' perceptions of vague concepts and those of an actual product they can see, feel, taste, smell, and understand. And there still remains a nagging inconsistency, a large and irreconcilable discrepancy, between what people say on surveys and what they do in real life situations. For these reasons, companies have, by and large, refrained from projecting concept test results to make market forecasts. Rather, firms have employed concept tests to derive rough, general magnitudes regarding reactions to product attributes and marketing approaches, so they can choose among feasible alternatives.

Product Use Tests

As compared with concept testing, product use tests can be looked upon as attempts to evaluate the product itself, often in relation to competitive ones. Abstractions give way to concreteness as research turns its spotlight on product prototypes. Can these samples, in the eyes of prospective customers, match the standards of the earlier concepts? Can these physical entities live up to the promises embodied in the earlier ideas? Do the items offer competitive advantages in terms of convenience, durability, and performance as evidenced by actual usage?

The product use test is still a step or so removed from matters of sales. It ignores questions of saleability. It turns a deaf ear to questions of whether new product features will account for greater sales and market share. Rather, its main purpose is to assess probable consumer

---

[4] Eric Marder Associates, Inc., *STEP* (New York: Eric Marder Associates Inc., 1966, revised 1973).

reaction to the characteristics or attributes of the proposed new product and to compare them with those of similar goods already on the market. Only if the intended novitiate indicates an equal or superior performance in use will the firm go ahead with a program leading to sales. If not, then shortcomings might still be corrected. Product use tests also provide insights into product applications, problem areas, and possible misuses by would-be customers.

Consumer goods that lend themselves best to product use tests are those with relatively high purchase frequencies, such as foods, cosmetics, and household supplies. Other products are not ruled out, but their testing is more difficult. Test data are collected in numerous ways: from consumer panels, attendance at public places, visitors to shopping malls and supermarkets, population samples, and focus group interviews. Few of these sample surveys select respondents in accordance with probability methods, and results are, therefore, not truly projectable to the population at large. But it is seldom necessary to estimate values of a given universe with great accuracy at this stage of development. More often than not, general magnitudes, rank orders, and broad comparisons will suffice.

Some companies conduct use tests among their own employees. These may be done on company premises, as in test kitchens, or by having employees take samples home with them. DuPont tests its hosiery by giving samples to female employees and having them fill out questionnaires pertaining to product usage and satisfaction. Auto manufacturers often have employees test out prototypes by using them in their normal driving. Such tests work best when a company has a large, homogeneous labor force whose tastes and buying patterns are similar to those of the general population. Results may be misleading, however, when employees perceive a vested interest in having the new product succeed.[5]

To keep interest focused on product characteristics without distractions from other influences, most product use tests are done blind. That is, all identifying labels are removed, so that products can be compared purely on their own merits, uncontaminated by such outside factors as price, brand name, or past associations.

A popular method of product evaluation is the paired comparison. It was carried over into marketing research from the psychophysics laboratory, to which it still bears a resemblence. Testing supposedly takes place under controlled circumstances within a common time frame. At the simplest level, this technique calls for a direct comparison of two products, the identities of which are masked. A single study may include several versions of the same product or a number of different products.

---

[5] McGuire, *Evaluating New Products*, pp. 40–41.

When more than two items are considered, each different unit must be compared with every other one.

Some studies have reported that the order in which items are tested may have a significant effect upon results. These systematic position biases seem more likely to occur when paired units have little perceptual difference.[6] The more two products are like each other, the greater the influence of seemingly minor variations in testing procedures. It has, therefore, become almost standard procedure to randomize the order of presenting items in paired comparison tests.

But randomizing techniques cannot do away with inconsistent answers on surveys. These faults are also associated with a lack of distinctiveness between items being compared. It is not completely unexpected for a person to prefer A over B, B over C, but C over A. Several methods have been devised to overcome the difficulty of handling answers that are internally inconsistent.[7]

One approach is the "repeat pair procedure." This technique asks respondents about their preferences for two items, A and B. The same routine is then repeated for another two items, which are actually identical to the first pair. This results in three categories of response:

1. People who preferred A on both occasions.

2. People who preferred B on both occasions.

3. People who were inconsistent, choosing A one time and B another.

The proportion of inconsistent answers can also be obtained from the "double pair procedure." This method exposes consumers to four products, only two of which are different. Or put in another way, the set of four items contains two A's and two B's. Respondents are then asked to designate which two out of four they prefer. Again, results yield a three-way breakdown: people who chose both A's; those who selected both B's; and those who made an inconsistent choice, preferring A and B at the same time. Because a certain proportion of people may be consistent by chance alone, the preferences for either item, A or B, are less than those showing up on the test.

Another way of determining whether the attributes of a new product can be distinguished from those of competitive products and whether they are preferred over them is the "triangular discrimination procedure." People selected for the survey are asked about their preferences for three products, two of which are identical. Respondents are then asked to pick out the unique product, the one least like the other

[6] Ralph L. Day, "Position Bias in Paired Comparison Tests," *Journal of Marketing Research* (February, 1969), pp. 98–100.

[7] David J. Luck, *et al.*, *Marketing Research* (4th ed., Englewood Cliffs: Prentice-Hall, Inc., 1974), pp. 386–387.

two. This method again provides a three-way grouping on discriminating ability: people who correctly designated the unique product; people who designated an identical item (A) as unique; and those who designated the other identical item (B) as unique. The last two possibilities are both wrong, and analysis may group them together.

Some market researchers may prefer staggered comparisons over the standard paired comparison tests. These are also referred to as "sequential monadic" tests. The difference between the two forms is mainly one of timing. Whereas the standard test compares two or more products at the same time, the staggered approach demands that individual items be used at different times. For example, one-half of the sample would be given item A and the other half item B. This type of split is made to avoid any position bias. Days or weeks later, the items would be reversed. The rationale for consumers trying one product at a time is that they normally do not use two similar products simultaneously.

Whether paired or staggered, all product comparisons have built-in flaws that detract from the confidence one can place in the results.[8] Inconsistent answers to questionnaires are always present in these marketing surveys. Products are used under contrived, artificially created conditions that may have no relevancy to those prevailing in the marketplace. If so, then how valid can such tests be? It is also held that consumers who participate in product use surveys are well aware they are being tested, and their behavior is consequently affected. They assume a role of judge and look for differences in product quality. But in playing out this role of expert, they are apt to magnify small differences far out of proportion to their actual importance. In short, respondents' behavior on surveys are quite contrary to the way they act in their usual, day-to-day routines.

There are other situations in which direct comparison would not be appropriate. In these instances, the new product can be tested by itself with a sample of prospective users. Such surveys are called monadic tests. They are thought to be closer to normal, real life conditions, in which consumers use and evaluate new products over a period of time in terms of their past experiences with similar items. In this context, adherents of monadic tests argue, consumer preferences and attitudes are more meaningful.

For industrial products, the product use test is often the most popular method of advanced testing because the products cannot be properly evaluated by any concept test. The main purpose of such tests is an evaluation of performance in actual use. Much of it is technical in na-

---

[8] See Harper W. Boyd, Jr., *et al.*, *Marketing Research* (4th ed., Homewood, IL: Richard D. Irwin, Inc., 1977), pp. 591–592.

ture, such as assessments under actual operating conditions of reliability, design features, operating costs, output estimates. In addition, these tests develop experience in plant operations and production. But marketing can also obtain relevant information about price alternatives, purchase influences within user firms, and market mix factors.

Firms agreeing to participate in product use tests are usually given trial supplies if the new product is of low unit value. Expensive, durable items, however, pose problems. Some manufacturers maintain pilot plants, where products can be evaluated in use under conditions that are similar to those of customers. If successful, these plants can be used for demonstration purposes, where prospects can witness the new product in operation. In instances where the new product is placed with outside firms, two policies are in existence. Some manufacturers turn over the prototype free of charge to the tester. Others contract to sell it at a reduced price on grounds that the user will have a vested interest in its success and will therefore exercise greater diligence in testing. Either way, it is often desirable to have a technician on the premises where testing takes place if the product is complicated and "bugs" are anticipated. The manufacturer should also be permitted to observe the tests, accumulate performance data, and make adjustments and modifications while the product is being tested in order to improve performance.[9] When prototypes are costly, as in capital equipment, placing a sufficient number of items in test plants presents a formidable obstacle, and decisions are often made on the basis of few tests.

Test Marketing

Test marketing is the final stage of new product development, coming just before commercialization. This is the last chance to evaluate the new product and its plan of introduction prior to its distribution in regular trade channels on a broad scale. In test marketing, the new product is distributed in one or more markets and sales measurements are taken. It is essentially a sales area test.

The purpose of the test market is twofold: (1) to estimate market share and sales volume were the product in national distribution; and (2) to correct any observable problem with the marketing strategy or with the product itself. The first objective is by far the more important. Test marketing is a costly undertaking, sometimes running into a million or more dollars. Before embarking on such expensive testing procedures, the firm should have ample evidence or solid assurance that both product and marketing plan are adequate. The test market is not the place to turn up major product flaws or look for hints of customer acceptance. Its role is in planning a national introduction and setting

---

[9] See McGuire, *Evaluating New Products*, pp. 73–75.

capital budgets.[10] Other objectives may be an investigation of buyer characteristics, trial and usage rates, purchase frequencies, product applications, results of altering marketing inputs and response from the trade. But these latter objectives are decidedly of secondary importance. Projections of national sales take primacy.

The popularity of test marketing stems from the fact that sales are measured where it counts—in the cash register. There are no conjectures, no interviews asking people what they would do in hypothetical situations and taking the replies to represent normal behavior. High costs and relatively long time requirements have led some market researchers to predict the imminent demise of test marketing.[11] So far, this prognostication has gone awry. Test marketing has not only persisted but flourished. The main reason is its presumed external validity, the belief that results are obtained under realistic conditions and can therefore be generalized. As one reporter put it, test marketing is the "only tool that comes close to predicting ROI."[12]

Not all products, however, are equally suitable as test market candidates. The decision to test market or not depends upon the degree of perceived risk and estimates of comparative costs. As a generalization, test marketing is desirable when risk is high and costs of a new product introduction are large. When opposite conditions prevail, there is less reason to test.[13]

Industries such as aircraft, autos, and steel, for example, have relatively high investment minimums. Outlays for fixed facilities are almost the same regardless of production volume. When the investment needed for large-scale output is not much different from that for producing small quantities, there is little to be gained from a test market. On the other hand, many industries are capable of adequately supplying test markets at a comparatively modest cost through pilot plants and temporary production lines. In these circumstances, test markets may prove advantageous because they may defer substantial investments until sales can be forecast with greater assurance.

The nature of products and markets is also a factor in testing decisions. Modifications and line extensions, requiring little or no investment in plant and machinery and offering low risk options, do not usually warrant test markets. Products with expected low sales volume

---

[10] David K. Hardin, "A New Approach to Test Marketing,"*Journal of Marketing* (October, 1966), p. 29.

[11] Saul Sands, "Can Business Afford the Luxury of Test Marketing," *University of Michigan Business Review* (March, 1978), p. 20.

[12] Sally Scanlon, "Calling the Shots More Closely," *Sales and Marketing Management* (May 10, 1976), p. 43.

[13] N. D. Cadbury, "When, Where and How to Test Market," *Harvard Business Review* (May-June, 1975), pp. 96–98.

fall into the same no-test category.

Budgets for new plants and equipment represent obvious investment decisions that test marketing may put on a sounder basis, but they are by no means the only ones. For many kinds of consumer products, especially packaged goods, expenditures for advertising and sales promotion run into the tens of millions of dollars. Inflationary trends have inexorably been pushing up these expenses. Though making a trial run in actual markets is costly, the outlays may well represent judicious spending. Why not use 2 percent of what would be expended on the new product introduction to get a firmer estimate of the probable return from the total outlay? This potential benefit casts test marketing as a protective device against commercial failure, but not as a profit-maximizing vehicle.

The first lots usually sold in a test market are said to be scooped up by competitors. Not only are they alerted to intended action, but they also have the opportunity to monitor the test market. They can test out counterstrategies, including those of developing product substitutes. When time is of the essence and the new product can be readily duplicated, risk reduction through test marketing may be zero or negative. On numerous occasions competitive items have appeared nationally while the new product was still being assessed by its originator in test markets. The decision variable in such instances hinges on the importance of time as a factor in the success or failure of the new product.

At times test markets have been willfully run long enough to allow competitors to react with product improvements, though admittedly such apparent magnanimity is rare. This seems to have been the case, however, when Procter and Gamble tested Rely tampons in Fort Wayne and Rochester, N. Y., for almost four years before its introduction to the trade in the summer of 1977. The advertising initially presented the brand as "the most absorbent tampon ever made . . . twice as absorbent as the leading tampon." Meanwhile, Kimberly-Clark, International Playtex, and Tampax all reformulated their products, and Johnson and Johnson showed up as a new entrant in the tampon market. By the time P&G went national, it could no longer make a superiority claim regarding absorbency. But it knew what competitors would do, having let them play out their hands, and was apparently ready with a refined program for national expansion.[14] A subsequent recall made the strategy academic. But that is another matter.

Many strange things have been known to occur in test markets, making a proper reading difficult. On occasion, competitors will step up their promotional expenditures in test markets to levels they could not possibly afford on a national scale. Desirous of succeeding, sales forces

---

[14] See Larry Edwards,"P&G Finally Expands Rely Test After Rivals Played Their Hands," *Advertising Age* (August 1, 1977), pp. 1, 69.

may also expend greater efforts in test markets and thereby achieve better product coverage in sales outlets. One company even reported that its test products were bootlegged—bought by the truckloads and shipped to other areas of the country where they sold for more than triple their suggested list price.[15]

Since the purpose of market testing is to derive a national sales estimate for the new product, selection of markets becomes a crucial matter. The process revolves around two basic questions: which markets and how many shall be tested?

The number of markets selected for a test is largely a function of reliability expectations. In general, the greater the number, the more reliable the results. A survey of major grocery and drug manufacturers found the average test market program contained three market areas.[16] Reliability can also be enhanced by expanding the testing area, such as going from Standard Metropolitan Statistical areas to TV coverage areas. The latter usually includes more than one of the former. Another way of widening a test market is by a "rollout," which adds successively larger portions of the population to the test area. Increasing the number of markets or expanding the size of the area decreases the chances of extreme deviations from the true norm. But it also brings with it higher research costs and, in the case of rollouts, possibly higher investment costs. An overly complicated research design with several variables to be tested might also necessitate an increase in the number of markets.

The choice of particular markets pertains to the issue of external validity. If results are to be projected nationally, tests markets must be representative of that universe envisioned in the marketing plan. The markets should therefore be typical of purchasing behavior with respect to the product class in which the new item falls or with which it will compete. Markets should also typify target groups, sales outlets, media patterns, and competitive marketing efforts. Lastly, markets should be self-contained. That is, all results must be capable of being ascribed only to the market tested and to no other. For example, the test market should possess no "waste" media circulation, promotion outside the confines of product distribution. Conversely, no strong outside influences should be able to affect sales within the test market.

Early sales may be poor indicators of eventual performance, particularly for products with high purchase frequencies. These products, with short buying cycles, often display "humped" sales curves. Their triers will build up rapidly at first and then decrease exponentially in succeed-

---

[15] Nancy Giges, "GF Keeps Carbonated Gum Test Hush Hush to Avoid Bootleggers," *Advertising Age* (July 31, 1978), pp. 1, 60.

[16] Quoted in A. J. Silk and G. L. Urban, "Pre-Test-Market Evaluation of New Packaged Goods: A Model and Measurement Methodology," *Journal of Marketing Research* (May, 1978), p. 171.

ing periods.[17] Such products must be tested long enough for the trial rate to level off and for repeat purchase patterns to take effect. The study of test market practices among grocery and drug companies cited earlier indicates a ten- to eleven-month duration for the average test market. The length of testing for big ticket items, the repurchase of which is infrequent or never, must take other considerations into account.

Yet the very strength of test marketing, its supposed external validity, has been surrounded by continuous debate and controversy. A Benton & Bowles' study of test marketing experience, spanning some ten years, compared brand shares in test markets with those in control markets. The advertising agency's analysis reported that 90 percent of the time the differences were no greater during the test period than at times when no testing took place.[18] Another study, done with seven Mennen products, simulated sales in different areas and concluded that no single market, or set of three markets, can predict with a high degree of accuracy how a new item will sell throughout the country.[19] The A. C. Nielsen Company compared the first-year results of fifty brands with market shares achieved in test markets using its research facilities. The products were in the health and beauty aids, household supplies, and grocery fields. The study estimated about half the time national market shares fell within 10 percent or less of test market results.[20] Forecasts of national sales from test markets can also be made by different methods, each of which has limitations and may yield estimates varying from each other.[21] Such anomalies have spurred attempts at improvements in two directions: to get better assurances from test markets and to develop more effective alternatives.

Test Marketing: Supplements and Alternatives

More than any other evaluative method, test marketing comes closest to measuring the end result of new product effort—sales in a realistic, market environment. Nevertheless, it has not been problem free.

---

[17] William F. Massey, "Stochastic Models for Monitoring New-Product Introductions," F. M. Bass *et al.*, eds., *Applications of the Sciences in Marketing Management* (New York: John Wiley & Sons, Inc., 1968), p. 85.

[18] Frank Stanton, "What Is Wrong With Test Marketing?" *Journal of Marketing* (April, 1967), pp. 43–47.

[19] Jack A. Gold, "Testing Test Market Predictions," *Journal of Marketing Research* (August, 1964), pp. 8–16.

[20] Nielsen Marketing Service, "To Test or Not to Test," *The Nielsen Researcher*, 30, No. 4 (1971), p. 4.

[21] See Gold, *op. cit.*, Edwin M. Berdy, "Testing Test Market Predictions: Comments," *Journal of Marketing Research* (May, 1965), pp. 196–198; Gold, "Reply," *Ibid.*, p. 199

Three difficulties in particular have confounded these sales area tests, posing strong challenges to the state of the art in marketing research.

First, a company deciding on a test market goes public with the new product before its time. The firm thus reveals its intended actions and gives competitors time to plan countermeasures.

Second, the test market is a costly way of assessing the probable outcome of putting a new product into commercial production. Consequently, many new items are deprived the benefits of test marketing, the expense of which cannot be justified. These high costs are further compounded when test-marketed products turn out to be failures. An A. C. Nielsen study, embracing 204 packaged goods in test markets, found that more than half the products were either aborted during the test or later withheld from commercialization.[22] It might be argued that spotting failures before commercialization is the primary role of test marketing and that this objective was therefore fulfilled. But this view can only be upheld if the test market can accurately project national performance.

This line of reasoning leads inevitably to the third and probably most important deficiency of test marketing. It may not give sufficient assurance of the eventual outcome of a national new product introduction, despite its high costs. And many products, of course, cannot be fitted into the test marketing mold at all.

Two basic approaches have been proposed to overcome these test marketing ills: minimarkets and a set of research methods referred to as lab tests. Both are capable of being combined into one, and sometimes they are. The lab tests are frequently used in conjunction with computer models.

Minimarkets

The minimarket can be regarded as a miniature version of a test market because testing is carried out in small-sized markets. The new product is distributed in sales outlets, promoted in actual media and trade channels, and monitored for market reaction.

But the small size of the minimarket offers a degree of control that cannot possibly be exercised in a typical test market. Limited in number, sales outlets can be visited frequently to make sure the item is in stock, point-of-purchase materials are in place, shelf facings are secured, and promotions are handled properly. Dealers can get their supplies directly, and discreetly, from the research company. Making deliveries outside of regular channels lowers the effectiveness of competitive intelligence.[23]

[22] Nielsen Marketing Service, "New Brand or Superbrand?" *The Nielsen Researcher*, 29, No. 5 (1971) pp. 4–10.

[23] See James H. Bowman, "Test Marketing Remains the Ol' Standby," *Advertising Age* (February 19, 1979), pp. S-1, S-24–S-25.

Who pays attention to what happens in Joplin? Or Spartansburg? Or Peoria?

These utopian conditions can actually be created at a much lower cost than that of traditional test markets. But they are also not apt to be repeated on a national scale. Futhermore, small town tastes, habits, and buying patterns cannot be regarded as typical of the nation as a whole. Therefore, minimarket results cannot be projected nationally.

The greatest advantage of a minimarket is its ability to test under controlled conditions alternative marketing variables, such as pricing, packaging, spending levels, sales promotions, and so forth. Pampers, one of the most successful products, failed the first time tested when selling for 10¢ each. The company subsequently simplified the package, reduced the cost of components, and reduced the price to 6¢ per item.[24] From this standpoint, the minimarket is a supplement, not a substitute, for the test market. It is a way of reaching the test market phase with the best possible plan or at least with the most effective alternatives from among those considered. Some critics of test marketing have implied that experimental testing in minimarkets is enough, that choosing most productive approaches makes the test market superfluous. But few firms will gamble on the correctness of this proposition when deciding whether to market test or not; the best efforts are not necessarily successful ones.

The experimental approach, often associated with minimarkets, is one that seeks evidence of causality in the new product's performance. One or more variables presumed to affect an outcome in an important way are manipulated under controlled conditions. Results are monitored and form the basis of the eventual analysis. By way of illustration, suppose a firm wants to test the effect of price. The new product can then be introduced into "matched" markets, one getting the lower price and the other the higher price. If all else is exactly the same and the two markets can be considered equivalent, difference in sales response can be attributed to differences in pricing. This form of experiment assumes, perhaps on faith alone, that all extraneous variables affect both markets equally.

An overriding consideration is to keep all factors equal except the variable tested. One method of doing so is to have both markets subjected to the same experimental treatment or to identical pricing. This can be accomplished by price switching. After a certain time, prices can be lowered in the high-priced market and raised in the low-priced market. Thus, the two price levels would be tested in both markets, and all extraneous variables would be averaged out. But results would be valid only if there were no interactions. The assumption of indepen-

---

[24] K. L. McGowan, *Marketing Research* (Cambridge, MA: Winthrop Publishers, Inc., 1979), p. 333.

dence in this pricing example is extremely dubious because of the pricing sequence. A sudden change after buyers have become accustomed to a given price level can produce a response that would not occur otherwise. Buyers may think an item is up for sale after seeing it selling at a higher price. Conversely, a higher price may bring forth a very negative reaction as buyers compare the new quotes with those of a prior period. If the marketing plan contemplates no such variations in pricing, an entirely new element would be added to the test—one that would not take place in the normal marketing operation.

Somewhat similar to this cross-over experiment is the Latin square, probably the most popular type of design applied to minimarkets. This form will accommodate a situation in which it is desirable to control two extraneous variables. To illustrate: a firm has developed three versions of a promotion to be used in conjunction with a new product introduction. Call these variations A, B, and C. Not to reveal the new item, the company has devised a plan to test these three versions with a similar product already on the market; they are assuming that any observable increment will apply to the new product introduction. But the time at which the promotion occurs is thought to be an important factor. Given three test markets, a 3 × 3 Latin square can be represented as shown in table 12-1.

Table 12-1
Latin Square Design for Three Promotions

	Market		
Time Period	1	2	3
1	A	B	C
2	B	C	A
3	C	A	B

In this design, one variable is evaluated, the promotion, although the factor takes on multiple values or different forms. Each version of the promotion is run in each market and in each time period. But the implicit assumption remains that interaction is completely absent. The Latin square also requires that each of the extraneous variables be broken down in categories equal to the number of factors tested. Thus, table 12-1 shows three markets and three time periods. But seldom do marketing situations contain such exacting equalities.

Two or more variables tested at the same time would necessitate a factorial design. Suppose the three promotion versions are to be run with TV commercials where there are two copy alternatives. If reactions to a promotion can be influenced by a TV commercial, and vice-versa, the two elements of the marketing mix cannot be regarded as independent of each other. To test promotions and commercials separately would tell nothing about how they would perform together. Such interrelationships are common features of marketing programs, the response to which may be of a greater magnitude than the sum of their parts. The relevant question here is not which promotion and which TV commercial is most effective; rather, the impact of two variables—promotions and TV commercials—is to be measured. There are three types of the first variable, called levels, and two of the second. This yields six possible combinations of variables and levels, which might be referred to as treatments. The relevant question thus becomes: which of the six possible combinations is most effective?

Analysis of variance can determine whether factors interact to produce a response and which factors are the most important. But a separate minimarket test must be run for each possible combination. This requirement has thrown up troublesome obstacles—coordination among markets, administrative control, high costs—which, for all practical purposes, have severely limited the use of factorial designs.

Lab tests

The lab test stands in sharp contrast to the test market in terms of the environment in which marketing research takes place. The test market may be viewed as a field experiment. Variables are manipulated but in a lifelike environment. Sales measurements come from actual sales outlets, and promotions are done in actual media and trade channels. A lab test also seeks to establish causation by controlling significant factors. But these experiments are carried out in a contrived setting, an artificially created situation that would possess conditions deemed desirable by the researcher.[25]

Research houses offering lab-testing facilities differ greatly in how they go about researching the new product. But they also display marked similarities in their attempts to reproduce real world results from simulated or feigned situations. Basically, each research agency enlists a sample of prospective buyers, exposes them to commercial messages—TV commercials, print ads, flyers, or direct mail—and then measures the group's subsequent purchase behavior. The environment is a synthetic one insofar as people are asked, and expected, to behave as they normally would, as though they were completely unaware that they are participating in a test.

For example, the model set up by Management Decisions Systems recruits consumers in shopping malls, where they are interviewed and shown advertising for the new product and existing substitutes. These respondents are then given an opportunity to shop in a simulated store.

---

25 Churchill, *op. cit.*, pp. 87–89.

Those who do not buy the new product are given free samples in an effort to simulate sampling. Sometime later, a telephone call obtains information about product satisfaction and repurchase.[26]

The Yankelovich Lab, another of several in existence, works in a similar fashion. Consumers are brought into its quarters, where they are shown advertising for the new product and for its competitors. Respondents are then given shopping money, about one-fourth of the purchase price of an item, and conducted on a trip to the company-operated store. They can browse, inspect merchandise, and make purchases. Immediately after the shopping jaunt, they are invited into group sessions, where discussions focus on why they bought the new product, why they did not, what they thought of the advertising, package, price, and so forth. These group interviews are meant to yield diagnostic material for purposes of planning advertising and promotions. Several weeks later consumers are called on the telephone, interviewed about their experiences with the new product, and asked about their intentions to buy it again. These follow-up calls supposedly measure the repeat buying rate.

Other research projects combine the lab experiment with the minimarket approach. One such system is that of ADTEL, which can control commercials reaching homes through dual-cable CATV. Sales and share of market estimates can be derived by store audits in minimarkets. But ADTEL also maintains a consumer panel that fills out purchase diaries. This source of information permits estimates of trials and repurchase rates and correlations of purchases with TV advertising weight.

Recently, the Universal Product Code (UPC) has emerged as a device for testing new products, combining features of both minimarkets and lab tests. Such a program is that of BehaviorScan, a product of Information Resources, Inc. Some 3,000 households in two small markets, one in the northeast and the other in the midwest, receive their television programs by cable relay. But instead of obtaining their purchase records from diaries, monitoring is done by automated scanning equipment in grocery stores. Panel members are given identification cards, which are scanned along with their purchased items. Because an individual can buy anywhere, Information Resources equipped all supermarkets in the test areas at its own expense with scan checkout systems.

To control as many marketing variables as possible, Information Resources coupled the scanner technology with a minicomputer-driven instrument that allows different TV messages to be sent to different

---

[26] Robert L. Klein, "Assessing the Difference: Simulation Can Mean the Edge," *Advertising Age* (February 19, 1979), p. S–12.

panel households at the same time on the same program. This makes it possible to link TV advertising with trial and repurchase rates.[27]

New products amenable to this type of experiment are low priced, frequently used, and distributed in self-service outlets. Their success depends upon a high unit volume of sales, indicators of which are trial and repurchase rates. These two activities, trial and repeat purchasing, can be conceived theoretically as moving towards a "steady state" as diffusion of the new product spreads among consumers. Thus, the interest in these measurements and in projecting them into the future is high.

Companies testing large numbers of new products have the opportunity to build up norms with which to gauge the prospects of success. Michael J. Barry of Kraft and William D. Hull of J. Walter Thompson told of their experiences with trier-repeat purchaser research in 1979 to a conference sponsored by AMA's Chicago chapter. According to Barry and Hull, better than 50 percent repeat purchase rates among buyers augurs well for a new product. Repeat buying in the 31 percent to 50 percent range presages success, but not a market leader. Figures below 31 percent indicate marginal products at best and failures at worst.[28] Different companies, varying in the way they obtain measurements and in the products they sell, are likely to have different norms as indicators of success and failure.[29] And all prognostications rest on certain assumptions about the future. Those of Kraft and J. Walter Thompson, for example, postulate no change in competitive pressures, promotional spending levels, product quality, price structure, distribution coverage, and even in patterns of product usage.

Some firms and lab testing services apply trial and repeat buying data to refined computer models. Management Decisions, for example, regards the self-administered questionnaires filled out by recruits upon their initial arrival at the lab facility as a "before" measurement. The probability of trial is derived from choices made on the simulated shopping trip, while repurchase data come from follow-up phone calls with the same respondents. Management Decisions' computer model, called ASSESSOR, generates two sets of predictions by two separate methods. The first relates product preferences to purchases. The second, which is more traditional, represents a fairly straightforward estimate of the steady state market share, which can be viewed as a long-run

---

[27] "New 'BehaviorScan' System Ties Grocery Sales to TV Ads," *Marketing News* (September 21, 1979), p. 7.

[28] "Not All Products Deserve Market Testing: Barry, Hull," *Marketing News*, (April, 1979), p. 8.

[29] See Jack J. Honomichl, "Repeat Purchases Hold a Key," *Advertising Age* (February 19, 1979), pp. S-20–S-21.

purchase level resulting from trial and repeat buying. Estimates are computed by a variant of the common representation, $M(t) = TS$,[30] where:

$M(t)$ = Market share for the new product.

T = Cumulative trial (the percentage of all potential buyers who ever try the new product).

S = Repeat purchase rate (the percentage of subsequent purchases in the product category by those who had tried the new product).

Do such computer-based predictions do away with the need to get into test markets? The overwhelming opinion of research users and suppliers alike shouts out in a resounding "No!" When substantial investments are at stake, few companies are willing to accept predictions resting on surveys with consumers, usually chosen by convenience sampling methods. Company managers feel more comfortable when measurements come directly from the cash register.

Nor were the lab experiments designed to replace test marketing as a way of assessing the sales power of new products. Robert Goldberg of Daniel Yankelovich sees the greatest advantage of lab testing as the reduction of test market failure.[31] Linda Cyrog, marketing research director at Foremost Foods Co., describes the Yankelovich LTM model as being used by her company as a "pretest market screening device." The lab test, according to Cyrog, offers "an opportunity to get an early prediction on how a product will probably perform in the test market."[32] The creators of ASSESSOR state their objective is "to aid management in evaluating new packaged goods before test marketing..."[33] Tracker, another computer model, was designed to predict year-end sales from early test results.[34] Clearly, the purpose here is to provide a means of making a quicker decision about a new product. Howard N. Gundee, vice-president of Elrick and Lavidge, in an article on the many virtues of the firm's sales prediction system (COMP), admits that the need for a test market is eliminated "not very often."[35]

[30] Silk and Urban, *op. cit.*, pp. 171–191.

[31] Robert Goldberg, "The Laboratory Test Market," *Marketing Review* (September, 1969), p. 10.

[32] "Market Simulation Cuts Risks of Product Failure: Cyrog," *Marketing News* (April 20, 1979), p. 8.

[33] Silk and Urban, *op. cit.*, p. 173.

[34] R. Blattberg and J. Golanty, "Tracker: An Early Test Market Forecasting and Diagnostic Model for New Product Planning," *Journal of Marketing Research* (May, 1978), pp. 192–202.

[35] Howard N. Gundee, "Prediction Systems Really Work; Outdo Market Testing," *Marketing News* (September 9, 1977), p. 5.

Lab tests and sales prediction systems seem to have added more research tools to an already full cabinet. But if they can reduce the time and money wasted on test market failures, a little crowding will not hurt.

REVIEW QUESTIONS

1. Briefly identify the various types of tests used in the testing stage.

2. Concept testing performed during and subsequent to development differs in scope and purpose from that performed prior to development. Explain the differences.

3. Differentiate between technical product testing and consumer use testing.

4. Convenience samples are used for concept tests and product use tests. Should this method of selecting respondents be improved upon? Would it improve accuracy?

5. Critics of traditional blind consumer use testing (product use) zero in on supposed shortcomings and ignore the true purpose of the procedure. What are the "shortcomings" and the "true purpose" of blind consumer use testing procedures?

6. A new product may be rated as very weak when tested against the leading brand in the industry. Nevertheless, the new product may be a perfect rendition of the planned concept. Explain.

7. Compare differences and similarities between industrial and consumer product use testing techniques.

8. Conduct your own blind comparison testing with two or three comparable brands of cola, beer, or perhaps liquor. What do the results suggest?

9. The decision whether or not to test market is an important one. Test marketing is time-consuming and expensive. What are the appropriate conditions for a "go" decision to test market?

10. Test marketing results are not uniformly definitive. The test does not precisely forecast sales and profits resulting from commercialization. Identify the more reliable and the less reliable information provided by test marketing. Why are there differences in quality of information and what can be done to improve reliability?

11. Test market sales results are typically projected to national totals using one or more different approaches. Design three simple projection formulas that expand test market sales results to a national level.

12. The new product manager in a large cosmetic firm recommended that the new product be test marketed before going national. The new product manager in charge of developing a new candy bar argued that the new product should not be test marketed, as "getting the jump" on competition was all important. What would be your argument in these two cases?

13. What is the role of minimarket tests and marketing experiments? Do these tests supplement or replace market testing?

14. Lab-type marketing tests are yet another means to reduce the risk of new product introduction. Specifically, what do these tests hope to accomplish? Are they successful?

13/ Diffusion of Innovation

The diffusion of an innovation is closely related to the product life cycle. The difference between the two is primarily one of emphasis. The product life cycle centers attention on sales, or the supply side, while diffusion focuses on usage, or the demand side.

The user may be an individual or an organization. Most consumer goods involve buying decisions that are individualistic. Industrial purchasing involves organizational behavior, and a separation often exists between users of an innovation and decision units responsible for its use.

The most common method of classifying adopters is on the basis of time—when they first start using an innovation. Adoption approximates a normal curve, and the cumulated number of adopters tends to take the form of a logistic curve.

The adoption of industrial innovation is influenced by two factors—the features of the innovation and the characteristics of firms. The proportion of initial triers at any given time is a function of the percentage having decided previously to use the new product or process. The rate of adoption is influenced primarily by two factors: profitability and size of the investment needed to install the innovation. Large firms are more likely to adopt faster than smaller firms.

For consumer goods, five characteristics are mentioned most often as affecting diffusion rates: relative advantage, compatibility, complexity, divisibility, and communicability. The characteristics of adopters seem to be situational, which covers a wide range of variables.

The adoption process, based on learning theory, visualizes a series of mental states that are referred to as a hierarchy of effects. These theories are the subject of much controversy, especially with respect to low-priced products introduced through mass media.

The Diffusion Process

The diffusion process describes how an innovation spreads among potential users. One way of measuring diffusion is to ascertain the rate at which an innovation is adopted. The term *adoption* refers to trial and continued use of a new product by individual consuming units. Whether diffusion proceeds quickly or slowly is governed by patterns of usage.

Studies dealing with the diffusion process assume importance insofar as they provide data for making inferences about possible success or failure of new products.

The diffusion of an innovation bears a strong affinity to the product life cycle. Both concepts rest on time series analysis. The product life cycle plots sales over time, while diffusion charts adoption by customers in a chronological order. The two curves must run a similar course, since the rate at which buyers try and repurchase a new item is related to its sales rate. To maintain this obvious parallelism, diffusion and adoption in this chapter will refer to generic groups of items that make up product categories. Another reason for this approach is that studies of diffusion, in the main, have dealt with product categories or industrial processes, and not with particular brands or individual company services.

While a product's sales rate and its diffusion level will display similarities, the product life cycle and diffusion concepts go off in different directions. Perhaps the main point of departure is one of perspective. The product life cycle views markets or segments thereof in the aggregate as indicated by the volume of sales. Interest, therefore, centers on a firm's strategies, on its input, on its resource allocations. How can it best respond to industry trends? How can it best influence its own sales charts, given sales configurations of a product category? In contrast, the diffusion concept turns its spotlight on potential buyers—even on individual consuming units—and consequently highlights the demand function. It seeks relationships among market factors that explain the rate of adoption. To be sure, demand cannot be divorced completely from seller activities. But diffusion shifts its emphasis to adopter units. What kind of buyers act first to embrace the new product? Are they different from later purchasers and, if so , in what respects? What factors are associated with the rate of adoption?

The user of an innovation may be an individual or an organization, such as a business firm, an association, or even a social or political entity. The variety of potential adopter units has given rise to diversity in the types of decision units. Studies of diffusion have uncovered at least three kinds of decisions with respect to the adoption of innovation—optional, collective, and authoritarian.[1]

The first type comes from an individual, irrespective of actions taken by other members of a society.That decision may be influenced by external forces in numerous ways, for no man is an island unto himself. But the choice to accept or reject a new product is subjective, residing in the mind of the individual. Buying decisions for most consumer goods involve decisions of this nature.

---

[1] See E. M. Rogers and F. F. Shoemaker, *Communication of Innovations: A Cross-Cultural Approach* (New York: The Free Press, 1971), pp. 269–297.

Collective decisions to adopt or forego an innovation implicate many people and require some form of consensus or approval by a majority. The affirmation may be nothing more than passive consent or acquiescence. The rate of adoption is thought to be positively correlated with the degree of power concentration. Nevertheless, collective decisions are made slowly because many individuals must be convinced that beneficial results will ensue from the proposed action. The fluoridation of a city's water supply is an example of such a process. But once the decision is made, everyone must conform.

Authority decisions are those in which adoption is forced upon an individual or group by someone in a position of power. The adoption of industrial products or processes is essentially mandated by a higher authority. Hence, the user unit and the decision unit, which may consist of one or more individuals, are usually not identical.

Interest in diffusion dates back to the turn of the century, when the sociologist Tarde stressed the role of "opinion leaders" in society's acceptance of new ideas. But the major impetus to research came in the forties and fifties from rural sociologists who investigated the spread of new agricultural techniques in farming communities. Studies in diffusion eventually spilled over into other fields: education, geography, communication, medicine, and economics, with each discipline proceeding separately in its own tradition.

The job of synthesis was undertaken by Everett Rogers, under whose direction some 2,400 publications on diffusion were collected by 1975 at the Diffusion Documents Center at Michigan State University.[2] The purpose of this project was to form an integrated body of knowledge from the vast storehouse of research. This is extremely important to marketing, which was a latecomer to diffusion research and remains dependent upon the accumulated findings of early researchers. However, data about diffusion as of now still relate to particular subjects: farmers in Iowa and Sweden, peasants in Colombia, doctors in some midwestern towns, etc. Disturbing questions therefore exist about the extent to which generalizations from other fields can be applied to marketing.

Classification of Adopters

Since the *rate* of adoption *influences the ways* in which diffusion unfolds, studies of the subject have sought to classify adopters. The most common method is that of Rogers, who uses a time dimension to define categories. That is, adoption units are grouped in accordance with the time they first began to use the innovation. From the standpoint of

[2] E. M. Rogers and J. D. Eveland, "Diffusion of Innovations Perspectives on National R&D Assessment: Communication and Innovation in Organizations," Kelly and Kranzberg, eds., *op. cit.*, II, 302.

marketing, time is vital in the introduction of a new product. Getting it accepted by the largest number of potential customers in the shortest possible time offers a distinct advantage to the innovating firm.

In examining past research, Rogers observed that adoption, when plotted over time, approximated a bell-shaped curve. This suggests that acceptance by consuming units is normally distributed in time. This pattern further implies that knowledge of two parameters, the mean and the standard deviation, permits computation of the entire distribution curve. The proportion of observations lying within any range can be determined easily from a "table of areas," which indicates the percentage of the area under the curve that is between two vertical lines erected from points on the X-axis. By transforming values to a mean of zero and a standard deviation of one, the percentages of the distribution contained between standard normal deviates are illustrated in figure 13-1.

Figure 13-1. Standard Normal Distribution

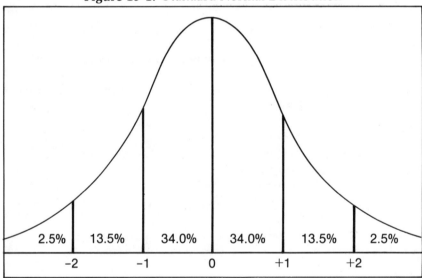

Emphasizing the need for standardization, Rogers has employed the concept of the normal standard distribution to categorize adopters, dividing them into five groups and taking standard normal deviates as breaking points.[3] The Rogers classification plan is described in table 13-1.

[3] Everett M. Rogers, *Diffusion of Innovation* (New York: The Free Press, 1962), pp. 159–164.

Table 13-1
The Rogers Classification Plan

Type of Adopter	Order of Adoption	Area Under the Curve
1. Innovators	First 2.5%	Left of –2
2. Early adopters	Next 13.5%	Between –2 and –1
3. Early majority................	Next 34.0%	Between 0 and –1
4. Late majority	Next 34.0%	Between 0 and +1
5. Laggards	Last 16.0%	Right of +1

Labeling the first 2.5 percent users of a new product as innovators is a somewhat unfortunate choice of description because the supplier of the item is also called an innovator. To avoid ambiguity and to differentiate demand from supply, the 2.5 percent who initially embrace a new product will be referred to as first adopters.

Rogers's five-part classification system has also posed operational difficulties for marketers of new consumer products. It may be desirable under certain circumstances to identify those consumers who would be the first to respond to a new product introduction. The traditional way of doing so is by sample surveys of the population. But a sample universe comprising only 2.5 percent of potential users renders surveys expensive and cumbersome devices for acquiring information. An extremely large number of interviews must be conducted in order to have a sufficient number of first adopters for statistically significant results.

To make sample surveys more practical, breaking points other than that of 2.5 percent have been advocated as a means of defining first adopters.[4] It seems that a 10 percent cutoff, equivalent to −1.65 standard normal deviates, has achieved the greatest popularity in marketing.[5] But the choice of this dividing line, in most instances, is made purely on the basis of expediency. Any other position on the normal curve might be equally valid or invalid, as the case may be. To avoid such arbitrary designations, the point of demarcation should be that which will produce observable distinctions between adopter categories.[6]

Regardless of how adopters are classified, the normal curve implies that the highest rate of adoption occurs at the time defined by the mean of the distribution. Further, the cumulated number of adopters derived from the normally distributed density function would tend to take a logistic form, as shown in figure 13-2.

---

[4] See David F. Midgley, *Innovation and New Product Marketing* (London: Croom Helm, 1977), pp. 54–55.

[5] Robertson, *op. cit.*, p. 85.

[6] See *Ibid.*, p. 87; R. A. Peterson, "A Note on Optimal Adopter Category Determination," *Journal of Marketing Research* (August, 1973), pp. 325–329.

Figure 13-2. Adopter Cumulation

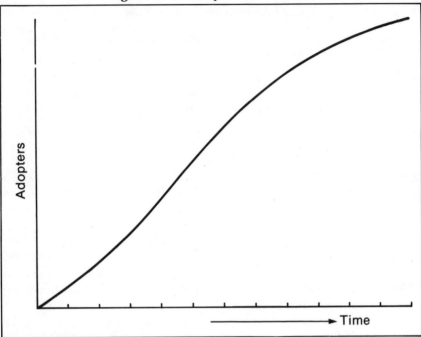

As indicated in figure 13-2, diffusion traces an S-shaped path, described by a Gompertz curve. This is similar to the classical configuration of the product life cycle, which postulates a logistic pattern. If diffusion and sales rates are related, then product modifications may exhibit diffusion that is described by an exponential curve rather than a logistic one. This seems reasonable insofar as there would be no introductory period characterized by low sales growth.

Diffusion of Industrial Innovation

Industrial innovation can be of two kinds: products and processes. The latter may include organizational as well as technical processes. In any event, diffusion of industrial innovation can be measured by several different methods. One way is to ascertain the proportion of an industry's firms or manufacturing plants that are using the innovation. This statistic indicates the extent of diffusion among firms. Another method is to estimate the percentage of an industry's output associated with a new product or process. This measurement is often employed to assess an innovation's impact on productivity. Other measures are productive capacity and employment of labor devoted to an innovation, expressed as a percentage of an industry's total capacity and labor force. There seems to be general agreement that, by virtually any measurement, industrial patterns of diffusion conform to the S-shaped logistic curve.

Sellers are concerned with diffusion for many reasons: forecasting sales for their new equipment; setting production schedules and inventory levels; planning investments in production and distribution facilities. But decisions to adopt an innovation also involve a reallocation of resources. Buyers must channel input from old processes into new processes. Skill requirements may change and workers may have to be retrained. Manpower levels may have to be recalculated and adjusted. New products and processes are highly sensitive to factors of price and quality, as well as potential returns. Thus, the rates of diffusion vary widely, depending upon the industry and particular innovation in question.

Diffusion in the industrial field is a relatively slow process. This generalization emerges unmistakably from Edwin Mansfield's extensive studies of the iron and steel, petroleum, coal, and railroad industries. The innovations studied were, for the most part, major ones. Their eventual prevalence could have been assumed with great confidence. It was only a matter of time until they were adopted, while outright rejection was almost unthinkable. Yet many of these innovations required twenty or more years before they were adopted by all major firms.[7] Old and new techniques, in varying degrees, tend to exist side by side for many years, with different uses having different cost efficiencies.

Two factors conspire to bring about variation in rates of adoption. One is the nature of the innovation itself, its perceived characteristics. The other is the characteristics of the adopter unit.

Innovation characteristics

Because the number of firms that make up an industry is limited, the proportion of initial triers becomes a function of the percentage having previously decided to use an innovation. The rapidity with which it is adopted, according to Mansfield, is determined by four characteristics: economic advantage, commitment, uncertainty, and risk reduction.[8] These can be explained as follows:

1. *Economic advantage.* Profitability is the yardstick that gauges the advantage a newcomer enjoys over older methods and processes. The greater this differential, the higher the probability of an innovation being adopted. Those that are perceived to be more profitable will therefore be used more rapidly than those with lower expected returns.

2. *Commitment.* Commitment is defined as the amount of investment needed to install an innovation. As the size of this commitment in-

---

[7] Edwin Mansfield, *Industrial Research and Technological Innovation* (New York: W. W. Norton & Co., 1968), pp. 133–136.

[8] *Ibid.*, pp. 136–152.

creases, calculating both direct and indirect outlays, the probability of adoption decreases. As more up-front money must be laid out, firms become more conservative. Financial arrangements also become more arduous to put in place. The rate of adoption is therefore inversely related to the size of investment required.

3. *Uncertainty.* This is the extent to which things can go wrong when a new technique is used. The amount of uncertainty associated with an innovation depends partly upon the degree of risk aversion held by a firm's management. But this factor is also related to the first two—economic advantage and commitment. Risk may seem diminutive when returns are expected to be large or when the necessary investment is relatively small.

4. *Risk reduction.* Risk reduction involves diminishing initial uncertainty with respect to an innovation's performance. Supposedly, the amount of uncertainty contracts with time as experience grows. Early deficiencies are eliminated, and accumulated learning begins to push operating costs downward. Performance comes to be taken for granted, while competitive pressures nudge holdouts towards adoption. But measurement of risk reduction is insubstantial and ethereal except in terms of profitability and investment size.

Mansfield's model, based upon regression analysis, indicates the existence of a linear relationship between an innovation's diffusion rate and its profitability and size of investment required. These two factors account for almost all observed variation in diffusion rates.[9] Studies of ten new industrial processes in Europe point to the same basic factors.[10] But this research undertaking also found that in certain instances capital tied up in existing technology tended to impede adoption of new techniques. The float glass process, for example, seems to have been adopted slowly by several large European companies reluctant to scrap equipment not fully depreciated or not deteriorated to a point where operations became costly.[11] Sometimes, the expectation of improvements in technology may influence a firm to wait rather than to adopt a technique that might be quickly outdated. Mansfield, too, alludes to the possible role of existing equipment, though his studies indicate no statistical significance of their effects upon the diffusion process.[12]

The rationale for the adoption of new agricultural techniques appears to parallel that of industry. The classic study by Zvi Griliches on regional development of hybrid corn pinpointed expected payoff as the

[9] *Ibid.,* pp. 140–152.

[10] L. Nabseth and G. F. Ray, eds., *The Diffusion of New Industrial Processes* (London: Cambridge University Press, 1974), p. 20.

[11] *Ibid.,* p. 210.

[12] Mansfield, *op. cit.,* pp. 146–147.

crucial factor. Some 60 percent of the variation in the rate of adoption was explained on the basis of profitability.[13] A study of agricultural practices in Sweden drew similar conclusions, citing economic advantage as the most important element in the farmers' use of new methods.[14] That profitability should emerge as prominent in diffusion of both agricultural and industrial innovations is not surprising. Farming is a business, the same as any other enterprise producing products for commercial purposes, and its practices cannot stray too far from profit objectives.

Characteristics of firms

Diffusion rates by themselves delineate overall trends in an industry. But an equally important question is one pertaining to adoption by individual firms. Do some companies respond faster than others and, if so, what characteristics differentiate them from late adopters?

Of all attributes by which a firm may be characterized, only size turns up as a statistically significant influence on adoption.[15] There are several reasons for this phenomenon. Large firms have more extensive facilities, and thus the probability that equipment will have to be replaced is higher. This, in effect, offers greater opportunities for a new capital good to be installed. The larger firm has a greater range or variety of operations, as compared with a small company. Since adoption is often determined by a particular situation, a greater scope of operations is more apt to give rise to situations in which an innovation can be tried. Trial also encounters relatively lower risk in a large firm, for more plants are available from which to choose should experimentation be deemed advisable. Lastly, the large corporation has greater command of financial resources. It usually has a higher ratio of cash flow to total investment, making an investment in a new process easier to justify. The amount of capital needed would also comprise a smaller part of the total investment in a large company than in a small one. The former also has better access to capital markets. Therefore, the amount of time a firm takes before applying a new technique is inversely related to its size.

Diffusion not only takes place among firms, but it also goes on within firms. A company using an innovation is, by definition, an adopter. But there are different gradations of usage. Companies can use innovations in varying degrees, as compared with their potentials. The series of steps a corporation takes, from first trial to complete adoption, can be regarded as another phase of the diffusion process. The intrafirm

---

[13] Zvi Griliches, "Hybrid Corn: An Exploration in the Economics of Technological Change," *Econometrica* (1957), pp. 501–522.

[14] Quoted in Rogers and Shoemaker, *op. cit.*, p. 154.

[15] *See Mansfield, op. cit.*, pp. 160–171.

adoption rates show how fast individual companies replace old methods with new ones after initial trial. These rates of adoption at the firm level add up to diffusion at the industry level.

Diffusion within firms, like those for an entire industry, displays a pattern that follows a logistic function. There is also a marked similarity between the intrafirm and interfirm level with respect to factors that influence the diffusion process. In both instances, speed of adoption depends upon profitabaility and the size of the monetary outlay an innovation requires. Put in another way, expected returns and size of investment significantly affect the rapidity with which a firm substitutes new techniques and equipment for older ones. Using these two factors, Mansfield was able to account for about 70 percent of intrafirm rates of diffusion.[16]

Management attitudes are often said to be important in how quickly a firm reacts to a new product or process.[17] But evidence on this score is only conspicuous by its absence. Perhaps this is because investigations on the subject, relying on regression analysis, have adopted a "black box" approach. Mathematical relationships are sought between input and output of the adoption process, but the inner workings of the organization are neglected. Hence, the internal mechanism accounting for the relationship remains a mystery. Or perhaps the economic factors—profitability and size of financial commitment—are so overpowering as to completely negate any differences in managerial outlook.

Diffusion of Consumer Innovations

Innovations in consumer products can be of two kinds: goods or services. Their adoption usually refers to trial and continued usage by individual consumers, though some studies have concerned themselves with trial only. In part, this anomaly may be the outcome of expediency. Most consumer surveys dealing with new products attempt to estimate purchases or purchasers at a point in time. Their design is cross-sectional; they present data about current users and triers of a brand. But the concept of continued usage requires a longitudinal study, whereby measurements are carried out over a given span of time. Goods with high purchase frequencies may also exhibit substantial amounts of brand switching, which leads to problems in how to define a continuing user. But this aspect is normally not the purpose of these surveys. Their main objectives, such as forecasting sales and designating marketing targets, can be accomplished without the niceties of adopter definitions or, for that matter, of the adopter concept itself.

Diffusion of consumer innovations, like those in the industrial sector, is the result of two factors. First, there are the features of the

---

[16] *Ibid.*, pp. 182–185.

[17] See Nabseth and Ray, *op. cit.*, pp. 20, 39, 50–51.

product itself, which can hasten or retard the rate of adoption. Second, there are the characteristics of the adopter units, which in this instance are comprised of individual consumers.

Innovation characteristics

Five characteristics are mentioned most often as influencing the diffusion rates of new consumer products. These five attributes have been enumerated by Rogers and can be described as follows:[18]

1. *Relative advantage.* This refers to the degree of superiority the innovation has over the products with which it competes. Diffusion is regarded as positively related with this factor; the greater the relative advantage, the more rapid the substitution of the new product for older ones.

2. *Compatibility.* Compatibility is defined as the extent to which the innovation is consistent with existing values and past practices. The old ideas, it is argued, are the measuring rods against which the new ideas are judged. When the two are close, the consumer is seen as having greater assurance that the innovation will perform properly and be worth the cost. From this standpoint, the implication is that greater compatibility lessens risk. There are also some who have argued that perceived risk should be regarded as an independent variable by itself.[19]

3. *Complexity.* Complexity involves the degree of difficulty a potential customer has in understanding and using the innovation. This factor is viewed as negatively related to the rate of adoption. It is an important reason, among others, for the slowness in diffusion of home computers. The spread of automatic tellers by banks was probably impeded by customers unable to understand completely how the machines work or what to do when something went wrong.

4. *Divisibility.* The divisibility attribute determines the degree to which an innovation may be tried on a limited basis. Its relationship to the adoption rate is positive. The factor also involves risk because the greater the possibility of experimenting with small quantities, the lower the risk. The opportunity of trying a new product at low cost is obviously more important at the early stages of its introduction when there may be few precedents to follow.

5. *Communicability.* Since buyers must be at least aware of the existence of an innovation in order to try it, communication is an important element in its diffusion. The ease with which an innovation can be described is thought to be positively related to its rate of diffusion. The extent to which a new product is visible to others can also be regarded as a form of communication. The features and results of the innovation are observed, and information to prospective buyers is thus imparted.

---

[18] Rogers, *op. cit.*, pp. 124–133.

[19] J. H. Donnelly, and M. J. Etzel, "Degrees of Product Newness and Early Trial," *Journal of Marketing Research* (August, 1973), pp. 295–300.

The above five characteristics were formulated from evidence collected largely from rural sociology.[20] Whether data pertaining to agriculture can be generalized to consumer products remains an open question.

As we have seen, relative advantage in agriculture as a determinant of adoption has been expressed in economic terms. This is possible, indeed desirable, because agriculture is run along business principles. Its structure may differ from that of other industries, but not its profit-oriented goals and economic orientation. But what does relative advantage signify to consumers? It can mean almost anything, depending upon their selective perception. Without resurrecting the older notion of an "economic man"—and there is no reason to do so—a relative advantage may comprehend a myriad of particulars, including the slightest whims and fancies of individuals.

This does not *per se* rule out the concept of relative advantage as a factor in diffusion of new products. Perhaps the vast multitude of mental images is what really exists, with variations arising from product to product. In that event, consumer perceptions of each innovation will have its unique set of central tendencies and dispersions. After all, a woman can see a new detergent as having completely different advantages from those of a new style in dress wear. The issue of meaning, however, does raise questions of measurements and generalizations.

Characteristics of adopters

The characteristics of different categories of adopters have aroused considerable interest in the marketing community. The center stage, however, is held by the first and early adopters, and for a variety of reasons.

First, if the initial wave of buyers is substantially different from later ones, then marketing influences change according to some form of progression. By the same token, marketing strategies must shift to accommodate these changes. For example, the pioneering consumers are the logical marketing targets at the beginning of new product introduction. As this early adopter segment approaches saturation, new users must come from other segments of the population. The timing of different strategies should therefore be geared to each oncoming wave of adopters, assuming it can be differentiated and accurately predicted.

Second, success or failure of a new product is largely determined by the early buyer segment. Its actions determine the sales penetration level during the product's formative period. If this level falls below expectations, pressures build for the company to abort the undertaking. If expected sales are surpassed, the company is impelled to go forward,

---

[20] E. M. Rogers and J. D. Stanfield, "Adoption and Diffusion of New Products: Emerging Generalizations and Hypotheses," Bass, *et al., op. cit.,* p. 243.

building production and distribution facilities for larger operations in the future.

Third, high buying rates encourage wider distribution when it counts. Dealers are more apt to stock products they think will be sold quickly.

Lastly, early users may influence the behavior of nonusers in many ways. They display the new product in use, not in a showroom but in the marketplace. They thus give the innovation visibility. Usage also imparts a certain element of legitimacy. Because early users are those with experience, they may be sought for advice and opinions by others. Such social interaction is referred to as opinion leadership. An interesting theory in this respect is that of David Midgley, who argues that the S-shaped diffusion curve comes about because of interpersonal communication. To Midgley, early adopters are individuals whose buying decisions need not be buttressed by opinions of others as they eschew social support. Midgley therefore advocates that products be designed to meet the expectations of early adopters because later buying is done on the "basis of their findings."[21]

The degree of opinion leadership inherent in the diffusion process, however, varies markedly from product to product. Higher priced items are generally believed to have greater social interaction than low-priced products. It seems to be pronounced for appliances but much less accentuated for convenience items.[22] Personal influence may also be prevalent for products subject to changes in style and fashion. One view is the "trickle down" theory, popularized by sociologist Georg Simmel. It visualizes the upper classes as setting standards for style and taste and the lower classes as emulating their betters. This point of view has been challenged by several authorities. For example, the transfer influence in fashion, by and large, seems to take place within the same social class rather than between different socioeconomic groups.[23]

Some time ago, there was much speculation about the existence of a generalized first adopter. It was hypothesized that some individuals are more prone to adopt an innovation at an early date, regardless of product. But the notion was soon dispelled as wishful thinking. One study, which investigated purchases of new items in appliances, clothing, and food, found little consistency in consumer behavior. Relationships were so low as to refute any idea that a group of individuals possesses a general trait of early adopter.[24] Another study attempted to measure adop-

---

[21] Midgley, *op. cit.*, pp. 34–36, 49–50, 70, 228–229.

[22] Robertson, *op. cit.*, pp. 100–110.

[23] Charles W. King, "Fashion Adoption: A Rebuttal to the 'Trickle Down' Theory," AMA *Proceedings* (1963).

[24] T. S. Robertson and J. H. Myers, "Personality Correlates of Opinion Leadership and Innovative Buying Behavior," *Journal of Marketing Research* (May, 1969), pp. 164–168.

tion of some 123 new products in six major fields: packaged foods, household cleansers and detergents, clothing, cosmetics, and small and large appliances. There was no discernable patterns of early buyers in one product field eagerly grasping at new products in dissimilar areas. In fact, the study concluded that early purchases were a function of situational variables unique to specific products and product categories.[25] The term *situational variables* can cover a multitude of possibilities an individual might encounter in the course of everyday affairs—a desire to taste some new food, a shortage of cash, a realization that an old item must be replaced, a chance glimpse of attractive new shoes, and so forth.[26] Such factors, particular to time and place, make it extremely difficult to predict how individuals will behave towards new products.

The Adoption Process

The traditional view of the way in which individuals come to use an innovation is referred to as the adoption process. It is steeped in learning theory, with later additions of decision-making concepts. The adoption process is conceived as being composed of a series of mental steps that an individual must take in order to reach continued usage of a new product. There are several different versions of these mental progressions, going from the lowly level of awareness to the top level of adoption. As such, they all belong to a single class of theories that can be described as a hierarchy of effects.

One of the first such models, called AIDA, was developed for marketing during the twenties.[27] AIDA viewed promotional efforts as adroitly bringing prospects from an initial state of awareness to one of interest and ultimately to that of desiring to buy the product. The model thus implied a multistage process by which potential customers were converted into actual buyers. First, they had to have their attention attracted to the product. The attention-getting phase was then superseded by an interest in the item which, if sufficient, aroused a desire to possess it. This favorable attitude, in turn, precipitated action whereby an exchange transaction could be consummated.

In 1955 a committee of rural sociologists postulated an adoption process consisting of five ascending steps: awareness, interest, evaluation, trial, and adoption.[28] This prototype was popularized by Rogers

---

[25] J. O. Summers, "Generalized Change Agents and Innovativeness," *Journal of Marketing Research* (May, 1970), pp. 178–185.

[26] R. W. Belk, "An Exploratory Assessment of Situational Effects in Buyer Behavior," *Journal of Marketing Research* (May, 1974), p. 157.

[27] D. A. Aaker and J. G. Myers, *Advertising Management* (Englewood Cliffs: Prentice-Hall, Inc., 1975), p. 103

[28] Rogers and Shoemaker, *op. cit.*, p. 100.

and became diffused in marketing as it was incorporated into models of consumer behavior.

Rogers subsequently revised his ideas and formulated a four-step hierarchy: knowledge, persuasion, decision, and confirmation.[29] The knowledge stage deals with receipt of information and is comparable to the awareness phase of the traditionalists. The persuasion stage is described as the formation of favorable or unfavorable attitudes. It, therefore, involves a cognitive process, which overlaps the interest and evaluative portions of the rural sociologists. It is concerned with the processing of information, or comprehension, and the eventual emergence of attitudes about a prospective product. The decision step is broad enough to comprehend all activities leading to the individual's choice, including trial. The last phase, called confirmation, is evidently an attempt to bring the hierarchy of effects into line with dissonance theories of psychology. These hold that people are ill at ease when cognitions are not quite consistent with their behavior, and therefore, they seek evidence to support what they are doing.

Regardless of particular version, the hierarchy-of-effects theory draws a picture of the consumer as a rational buyer. It presumes that purchase decisions are the outcome of deliberative acts. Many authors have gone so far as to compare product choice decisions with problem-solving methods. The hierarchy-of-effects theory further assumes that the mental processes that determine choice take place in a given order, right up to the final decision of acceptance or rejection.

There may be some value in such speculations. Almost every science has had them. But they have also engendered much debate in the industry.

One objection concerns the notion that learning must precede attitude formation. While evidence is hard to come by, what little exists indicates the contrary. Haskins's review of research studies dealing with the subject, most of them done with small samples under laboratory conditions, indicated a lack of relationship between changes in knowledge about a product and changes in attitude towards the item.[30]

A more serious challenge to the hierarchy-of-effects theory concerns the relationship between attitudes and behavior. Leon Festinger examined secondary sources for evidence that attitude changes bring about behaviorial shifts. His search turned up only three studies in the psychological literature, and surprisingly, they all indicated a negative relationship.[31]

---

[29] *Ibid.*, p. 25.

[30] J. B. Haskins, "Factual Recall as a Measure of Advertising Effectiveness," *Journal of Advertising Research* (March, 1964), pp. 2–8.

[31] Leon Festinger, "Behavioral Support for Opinion Change," L. Richardson, ed., *Dimensions of Communications* (New York: Appleton-Century-Crofts, 1969), pp. 105–116.

Herbert Krugman, delivering a presidential address before the American Association for Public Opinion Research in 1965, held that for many products learning might take place and buying might be affected by promotional communication, but attitudes could be unchanged or could be of such small magnitude as to be incapable of being measured.[32] There are basically two reasons for such results. First, many products evoke an extremely low consumer involvement. The promotional messages about these products represent trivia, and these trifles do not stir emotions strong enough to affect attitudes. How excited can one get about softness in a roll of toilet papers? Or in a new blue dot that adds cleaning power to a detergent? The only ones with strong attitudes towards such products are their managers, not consumers. The second reason is because the purchase is not the result of a rational, deliberative act. More recent research with brain wave frequencies suggests that reading and observing visual elements affect different parts of the brain. But the part affected by TV, which is the leading national medium for obtaining product information, stimulates mental processes that have little to do with reasoning or logical acts of deliberation.[33]

While their validity is open to question, the adoption models, for better or worse, have been instrumental in systematizing procedures and instituting discipline for promotional activity. Brain wave research may in time provide a better understanding of how the mind responds to commercially directed stimuli. This is still a long way from knowing the entire run of events by which individuals come to select specific products at particular times. But is it really necessary to detail the workings of these mental processes, though undoubtedly of importance to advertising and sales personnel, in order to comprehend diffusion? The act of diffusion is a behavioral, not a mental, phenomenon. Its patterns can be measured and employed operationally, even though the mental states of individual adopters remain very imperfectly understood.

---

[32] Herbert E. Krugman, "The Impact of Television Advertising: Learning Without Involvement," *Public Opinion Quarterly* (Fall, 1965), pp. 349–356; also see Krida S. Palda, "Hypothesis of Hierarchy of Effects," *Journal of Marketing Research* (February, 1966), pp. 13–24.

[33] "New Studies of Brain Functioning . . .," *Marketing News* (March 25, 1977), pp. 1, 7.

REVIEW QUESTIONS

1. The commercialization of a new product involves diffusion and adoption. Differentiate these concepts.

2. How has the concept of innovation diffusion affected the practice of marketing? What are the implications of this diffusion to marketing?

3. Sources of information may be characterized as impersonal, personal informal, personal formal, or personal impartial. Briefly describe each source.

4. Identify and describe the different categories of consumers purchasing a product for the first time. Identify the stage of the product life cycle when first purchased. Also identify the principal sources from which the necessary information and purchasing confidence was probably acquired.

5. Describe the effectiveness of mass media in achieving consumer adoption of a newly introduced product.

6. What factors influence the rate of consumer new product diffusion?

7. Diffusion in the industrial field is a relatively slow process. Why? What factors influence the rate of industrial new product diffusion?

8. The birth stage of a new product attracts the early buyers. This stage and these buyers contain the seeds that will determine the extent of future blossoming. What are these determinants of future blossoming?

9. Who are the opinion leaders? How effective are they?

10. Criticize the hierarchy-of-effect theories of the consumer adoption process.

11. Some writers have indicated that the small firm tends to be most progressive and the large firm is most conservative, tied in red tape. Yet studies of diffusion have shown the large firm more readily adopting and willing to purchase an industrial innovation than a small firm. Why is this so?

Five / The Environment for Product Development

14 / The Environment and Product Policy

The business firm operates in two broad environments, one physical and one social. These exogenous forces have assumed an ever greater importance, both to business units and society. The approach in this chapter will therefore depart somewhat from previous ones and relate environmental considerations to a macro point of view.

The exogenous system that makes up man's environment can be categorized as a combination of endowments, values, and institutions. The first is input for producing goods and services, measured aggregatively as gross national product (GNP). Society's values, operating largely through institutions, have a significance in how and to what purposes endowments are used.

A major problem in recent years, and one that will become even more persistent in the future, is that of diminishing supplies of raw materials. This trend has led some authors to conclude that a policy of exponential growth is incompatible with the limitations of a finite universe with nonrenewable resources. A more optimistic view, which accords with past experience, puts its faith in the problem-solving powers of technology to overcome resource scarcity.

The most obvious problem is that of energy, or rather, the heavy reliance upon petroleum for energy. Large quantities must be imported from parts of the world that have economic goals quite different from our own.

One possible solution is the substitution of other fuels for oil. Coal and nuclear power are the main alternatives. While these two sources of energy are expected to expand during the eighties, they also pose environmental problems. Another possible solution involves the substitution of capital for energy. But economists differ widely as to whether this is feasible.

Linked with resources is the question of ecology. When resource-using industries exude waste beyond the absorption capacity of nature, pollution is the result and the ecological balance is upset. To prevent environmental damage, a host of government agencies have sprung up. Business firms have also set up special departments to develop methods for environmental assessment. Nevertheless, a cleaner environment may not be conducive to national growth objectives.

Another major effect of environmental pressure has been greater public control over product policy. A good deal of consumerism is aimed at restoring to consumers what is regarded as their traditional rights. But other proposals collide with the conventional prerogatives of management over product policy.

The Environment

An environment can be conceived as exogenous, as a state of being that has developed on the outside. As related to products, the environment is commonly viewed as being outside the business firm, which produces most of our society's goods and services. Because environmental forces are settings for economic activity and not directly involved in strategic decisions, they are often regarded as a constant. It is conventional for discussions of product management to treat the environment as something that is given. But these external realities make themselves felt in product decisions, and their influence looms greater and greater with the passage of time.

In the normal course of operations, the firm must at the minimum be engaged in two environments, one physical and one social. The physical universe embraces the warm sun and chilling winds, the green-covered forests and mineral-laden soils—all natural phenomena that mankind has exploited for its use. The social environment includes not merely the man-made organizations to harness nature but also all relationships of human beings to each other. The exogenous system that forms the environment may be approached from many different directions. From a functional standpoint, however, it can be viewed as an arrangement consisting of three main entities: endowments, values, and institutions.[1]

Endowments are defined as classes of input for the production of goods and services. These encompass what economists refer to as factors of production, such as capital, labor, and raw materials. The issue of nonrenewable resources presage an ever-increasing importance for product policy in the years ahead. Related to resource use is the ecological issue, which is also bound to grow in importance.

Values can be described as deeply held beliefs by which individuals or groups judge modes of conduct and goals of society. The pervasive web of human values entangles the means and ends of product policy, for these values affect how endowments are used and for what purpose. What is acceptable in styles of dress, preparations of food, forms of housing, designs of furniture, and manners of recreation depends in large measure upon the preferences and tastes of individuals. American values, which put great store in materialism, are also exported along

---

[1] Kelly and Kranzberg, *op. cit.*, pp. 47–119.

with the products and technologies of the industrial world Americans have created.

Institutions are closely linked with values, for societal preferences become institutionalized. They give legitimacy to organized actions. They also vary from country to country, maintaining a unique flavor in each particular culture. In socialist countries, for instance, the means of production are owned collectively. In other systems, notably that of the United States, most of society's assets are owned by individuals or private institutions. However, asset managers do not necessarily act in strict accord with the desires and interests of owners. In any event, values serve as constraints to what will be done and in what manner, regardless of economic systems and national boundaries. For example, Japan's powerful International Trade and Industry in 1974 was reported to be carrying out a feasibility study for a completely automated factory. But the agency's officials were quick to point out that the personless plant would eliminate only routine, monotonous tasks, and not the guaranteed lifetime jobs that have been traditional in Japan.[2]

American corporations likewise cannot step too far beyond the bounds of institutionalized values. They yield to the force of public opinion like palm trees bending in a strong wind. They advertise themselves as equal opportunity employers, fashionable today but emphatically unorthodox some two decades earlier. Perhaps the greatest strength of American business is its resiliency, its ability to adjust to changes in preferences and attitudes of society at large. Though variable, values are nevertheless socially binding ingredients. They bind man's memories to his past and man's hopes to his future. They bind society's endowments to its institutions. As an ideal, Americans still cherish free enterprise. But freedom for business enterprise to use endowments as it wishes is becoming weaker and weaker, while the voice of the public over control of productive input is growing louder and louder.

The high level of America's gross national product and its continued growth rest on two basic supports. One is social in nature. It includes such diverse elements as the state of technology, efficiency of economic organizations, stability of political institutions, education of the labor force, and national goals to which the country's leaders pledge commitment. For the most part, these are positive. While shortcomings evidently exist, both in private enterprise and public institutions, they have thus far exerted no serious threat to economic performance. A veritable pillar of strength is the generally held opinion that sees well-being as measured by the amount of products society consumes. Corporate officials and government bureaucrats may often differ among themselves

---

[2] *The N. Y. Times* (November 2, 1974), p. F15.

over ways and means. But they remain united as to purpose, the desirability of achieving exponential growth.

Though a favorable social climate is necessary for economic progress, that alone is not sufficient. It must be joined with an adequate stock of physical resources, the other main support for economic advance. But the likelihood that ever-growing quantities of physical resources can keep pace with economic growth is not encouraging. While attention stays riveted on petroleum, other natural resources have evinced faltering activity. Supplies of platinum, gold, zinc, and lead have been so depleted that they are no longer able to fill all demands for their use. Silver, tin, and uranium are expected to become scarce by the end of the century if present usage rates continue.

Physical Resources

The achievement of exponential growth in a world with nonrenewable resources presents society with a serious problem, the answers to which are mainly in the realm of opinion. One view, which settles on the pessimistic side, came from the prestigious Club of Rome. In April 1968, thirty people from ten countries came together to discuss the dilemma of national expansion programs and apparent shortages of resources. This meeting resulted in a computer model by Jay Forrester of MIT. This model was later used as the basis of a more detailed study under the direction of Dennis Meadows.[3] Both studies, with the help of computer science, revived the century-old view of economics as the dismal science.

According to these global models, exponential growth leads to faster depletion of finite and irreplaceable resources. Meanwhile, economic expansion requires larger supplies of material resources to feed the industrial machines. More capital is also required to extract from the physical universe the same amount of dwindling resources. As man approaches these natural limits, the efficiency of capital must fall, less investments can be put aside to increase plant and equipment, and finally, depreciation will exceed new investment. At that point, the industrial base will collapse and catastrophe will overtake the world. Even if technology should push back the limits imposed by given resources, the industrial process will overload the waste absorption powers of nature. Or food production will not be enough to sustain the earth's growing population. These ominous events will come to pass in the next century, the models predict, for man cannot hope to foster without end a self-renewing growth in a finite world.

---

[3] See Donella H. Meadows, *et al., The Limits to Growth* (New York: New American Library, 1972).

This neo-Malthusian view has brought many cries for restraint to industrial expansion. Some have advocated a return to the small-scale production of yesteryear.[4] Some have heaped scathing criticism on the materialistic ethic, urging rejection of mindless consumption in favor of psychic and spiritual values.[5] Others, such as Meadows and his associates, have proposed the search for a system that is "sustainable" or stable and in line with the capabilities of man's external environment.[6] But all of these varying opinions, some more so than others, imply that future business strategies must concern themselves with managing products in a stagnant, or even in a negative-growth, economy.

But zero or negative growth conditions have never been accepted as a legitimate goal by contemporary society. The "grow or perish" dictim reigns as an article of faith among corporate management. No federal legislator or administrative head has ever proposed a program for winding down long-term economic growth. The popular demand is for more, not less: more jobs, more housing facilities, more food on the table, more discretionary income, more worldly goods. Such is the stuff that makes up the American dream!

This optimistic view of progress, ever onward and upward, is deeply rooted in experience. Indeed, all Western nations have witnessed the miracles of technology causing the heavens to open and shower upon mankind the treasures of more. And so the West, year after year, for a period spanning several centuries, has followed the biblical injunction "replenish the earth and subdue it."

The economic expansion of Western society, not always proceeding in a straight line, can be traced back to the so-called commercial revolution of the fifteenth century. What made it all possible, however, were the advances of science and technology. These developments gave man the capability of substituting one material for another, or one endowment for another, when the one in use became depleted or too costly to obtain. This was accomplished in a variety of ways. First, man developed wholly new materials. Plastics and polymers, for example, took the place of natural materials such as cotton and rubber. Such innovations decreased man's dependence upon certain items, though not upon resources in general. Second, science and technology raised the productivity of each given resource unit, as by permitting the use of lower grade materials, more abundant ones, or scrap and waste. In each instance, the substitution bore a lower cost relative to output. Third, relative costs of exploration and recovery were lowered, making the extrac-

[4] E. F. Schumacher, *Small is Beautiful* (New York: Harper & Row, 1973).

[5] Carter Henderson, "The Economics of Less," *Business Horizons* (April, 1979), pp. 25–28.

[6] Meadows, *et al.*, *op. cit.*, pp. 163–188; Kafalas, *op. cit.*

tive process itself more productive. Materials could be coaxed from the earth at lower and lower unit costs.

Then how can any computer model project a scenario of gloom and doom unless past experience was injudiciously disregarded? On what grounds can it be assumed that human ingenuity will become enfeebled as we approach the twenty-first century? Or that man will fail dismally in his mastery of nature? Or that *homo erectus* will revert to his ancestral form and once again walk the earth with an ape-like gait?

Like most models, conclusions depend heavily upon the assumptions made. Thus, Robert Boyd, using the same Forrester model, inserted a set of technologically optimistic values and derived a printout of no foreseeable limitations for per capita output of goods and services. Substitution, Boyd concluded, will continue to eliminate any particular scarcity, while technology will continue to increase productivity and the standard of living.[7]

But this optimistic view, uplifting to the spirit, is no more assuring than the assumption that give it nourishment. It supposes an almost endless range of possibilities for substitution. But probabilities may be another matter, and their values are unknown. They appeared extremely high in a past age because relatively small numbers were involved in the onrush of industrialization. Today, more people all over the world are participating in the industrial process and clamoring for an equitable share of material goods. If the American economy alone were to continue its historic growth, averaging some 3.0 percent per annum, real GNP in twenty-five years would double from its present $2 trillion base.

There has also been a marked shift in the control of physical resources. In a past age, a few dominant nations exercised control over the earth's raw materials and made decisions to conform with their national goals. Today, control is more diffused, and the utilization of natural resources is subject to the conflicting aims of many nations.

The optimistic view was flawlessly expressed by Backman and Cezepiel, who wrote: "Society has always found ways to economize on the use of scarce resources and will do so again."[8] But this is a hope, not a promise. Yesterdays cannot be re-created in a concatenation of tomorrows. To assume as the optimistic view does that sometime, somewhere, someone will achieve a technological breakthough is an act of faith. And that faith may well rest not upon a rock but on a thin reed.

---

[7] Robert Boyd, "World Dynamics: A Note," *Science* (August 11, 1972), pp. 516–519.

[8] Jules Backman and John Cezepiel, "Marketing Strategy: Some Basic Considerations," Backman and Cezepiel, eds., *Changing Marketing Strategies in a New Economy* (Indianapolis: Bobbs-Merrill Educational Publishing, 1977) p. 9.

Energy

Of all physical resources, the most important are those used for energy. These will offer corporate management its greatest challenges, as well as opportunities, in the decade of the eighties.

The prime reason is that America depends to a large degree on oil and natural gas to fuel its plants and power its machines. But these supplies are running out. U.S. proved reserves of petroleum have been falling at the rate of a billion barrels a year since 1970. For every ten barrels produced, only six barrels of proved reserves have been added—and there is a strong likelihood of ever smaller replacements. Yet demand keeps expanding. The Energy Department predicted that energy consumption will rise from about 80 quads in 1979 to 101.5 quads by 1990.[9] A quad is the amount of energy derived from a half-million barrels of oil a day for a year or from one trillion cubic feet of natural gas.

Since demand has far outstripped the availability of domestic supplies, the shortfall must be made up by imports. By the late seventies, the level of foreign petroleum products had grown close to 50 percent of total U.S. requirements. But the increasing amounts of imported petroleum have exacerbated, not ameliorated, the energy problem. Exporting nations have orchestrated policies to further their own social and political ambitions, not those of their customers. Production quotas may be out of tune with the articulated goals of American economic growth, for they are directed in accordance with the aims of crude oil producers. Output is set at a rate geared to development plans for their economies and to resource depletion for their objectives. And it is not realistic to expect otherwise.

Energy prices have soared, pushed up by a growing demand, higher marginal costs for new supplies, and the commands of OPEC. A cartel-mandated price hike is equivalent to an excise tax levied on U.S. consumers and has had similar effects. An increase in the price of energy, all other things being equal, leaves consumers with less money to spend on other things. Higher costs of home heating means cutting back on alternative uses of money, less saving or less spending on other goods and services. Higher prices of energy have also spread to other products, the costs of which rise in accordance with their relative energy content. Such inflationary pressures have brought changes in consumer behavior and shifts in demand towards goods and services that use less energy. The American public has curtailed its love affair with big, gas-guzzling automobiles, for example, and has exhibited stronger preferences for small, more efficient cars. The way energy-induced changes in

---

[9] *Wall Street Journal* (December 19, 1979), p. 1.

costs affect the demand of any particular product depends upon its price elasticity. In general, the pattern of industrial output has moved in the same direction as demand—away from energy-intensive products and processes—as business firms have altered their input in response to changing conditions. This trend, in the absence of government-directed edicts, is swayed by the elasticity of substitution between current methods of energy utilization and other primary input. It implies a proposition that changes will be made when the value of energy saved exceeds the costs of inaugurating the change.

One form of substitution has been to develop alternative fuels for different uses. The main ones in the eighties are apt to be coal and nuclear power.

United States coal reserves are plentiful, estimated at about 200 billion tons. A ton of coal contains roughly the same amount of energy as three to four barrels of crude oil. At the current rate of consumption, coal supplies in the ground are enough to last some 200 years.

The largest portion of coal output at present, about 75 percent, is consumed by electric utilities. During the eighties coal production is expected to increase about 5 percent per annum—not much faster than the projected 4.5 percent rate in the peak load demand for electricity.[10] Although greater use of coal will help offset the dwindling oil supplies, it will also pose environmental problems. More than half the U.S. coal is surface mined, which is more economical than underground mining. But the less expensive method scars the tired earth, and restoration of the land reduces the cost advantage. Some coals produce sulfur emissions which, objectionable to environmentalists, can be removed by "scrubbers," but these are expensive and create waste disposal problems. Lastly, science is not quite sure how increases in carbon dioxide and heat in the atmosphere will affect man's environment.

Nuclear energy, entirely confined to electric utilities, is potentially the fastest growing fuel, replacing oil and gas. Its early enthusiasts envisioned the major part of the nation's electricity generated by nuclear power as early as the turn of the century. As late as 1976, Exxon was forecasting a more than fivefold output of nuclear energy, with a 16 percent share of the U.S. total by 1990.[11] Today, any prediction seems tenuous as the nuclear issue becomes mired in politics. The storm of protest after the Three Mile Island accident caused the Nuclear Regulatory Commission to declare a moratorium on new construction and issuance of operating licenses. Though the ban was temporary, nuclear power suffered a severe setback, and future increases in the numbers of nuclear power plants are bound to proceed at a slower pace than the

---

[10] *Ibid.*, p. 32.

[11] "Looking Ahead to 1990," *Exxon USA* (First Quarter, 1976), pp. 28–29.

Exxon projections, which but a few years ago would not have been described as unduly optimistic.

Quite apart from the safety issue, nuclear energy faces a host of problems. Operating costs have skyrocketed, partly because of more stringent safety regulations. These higher costs have narrowed the differential advantage over coal-burning facilities, the main competitors of nuclear plants. Storage of nuclear wastes, which creates hazards lasting for centuries, remains an unresolved issue. And domestic reserves of uranium, estimated at about a billion pounds, must contend with impending shortages by the middle of the eighties. Meanwhile, newer technologies are enveloped in controversy. Development of the more efficient breeder reactors has been held back because mankind has not been able to resolve its differences without the possibility of mass homicide. Breeders have thus been held back by fear that the technology will encourage a proliferation of nuclear weapons. Research in fusion, which would permit reactors to be fueled by vast amounts of hydrogen from the oceans, has enjoyed generous government backing. But even the most ardent supporters of these projects do not expect significant commercialization before the next century.

Unconventional fuels have not been assigned a major role for the eighties, either by government or energy company officials. The much heralded research program in synthetic fuels, such as coal liquids and gas, shale oil and liquid biomass materials, is a long-term affair. Though hopes run high, the emergence of a synthetic fuel industry supplying a significant portion of America's energy needs is hardly contemplated before the twenty-first century. About the same time span is visualized for solar energy, currently suffering from a limited technology.

The substitution of one fuel for another, especially for the shrinking supplies of oil and gas, is obviously an increasing necessity. Such changes tend to alter the mix of both company output and consumer purchases. But it is problematical whether they act as a stimulant to the gross output of goods and services, as indicated by real GNP. The upward trend in energy costs is not dampened significantly. In fact, substitution of new fuels may eventually turn out to be more expensive than the traditional ones. Gasohol, pushed by the Carter administration, is costlier to produce than no-lead gasoline. The government strategy for building a synthetic fuel industry would have to contend with bringing water to semiarid regions and creating new cities in unpopulated areas of Colorado and Wyoming. All this is in addition to developing plants and distribution facilities.

If energy costs become a higher proportion of total costs, the productivity of capital is diminished. Changes in fuel usage may be a necessity; it may be better to settle for lower productivity than to produce nothing at all. But when a change in fuel is the dominant factor in the switch, capital outlays involved in the process may yield a lower relative output.

As related to GNP, the role of technology and capital formation to support it forms the core of the elasticity of substitution issue. Unfortunately, economic opinion is widely split, and econometric models have yielded highly conflicting results. One school argues that energy and capital complement each other, in which case a reduction in the use of one brings a similar effect in the other.[12] Under such conditions, the government's conservation policies bow to necessity but are at odds with growth objectives. If capital is an effective substitute for energy, as held by economists with a more optimistic bent, energy restrictions need not depress economic growth.[13] A high coefficient of substitution elasticity can result in economic growth and less energy at the same time. According to some authorities, the elasticity of substitution between energy and an aggregate of all other economic factors must be about 0.5 for this to happen.[14]

Historically, the relationship between capital and energy supports the complementary thesis. Technology in the past tended to reduce labor per unit of output, while energy and capital maintained a fairly constant ratio between them. R&D thus served the function of replacing labor by machines run by more gas and electricity.

But the thrust of R&D as a labor-saving mechanism took place when energy was a relatively small part of total cost and its price was falling. In recent years the price of energy has undergone a sharp reversal, and industrial designers pay much more attention to possibilities of lowering energy intensities. With relatively small incremental costs, new facilities can be designed to produce raw materials using 20 percent to 60 percent less energy than existing facilities. Commercial buildings can be renovated to achieve 25 percent savings in heating and cooling, while new structures can cut fuel bills more dramatically.[15] The transportation industry, which in the absence of a scientific breakthrough depends heavily upon petroleum products, has witnessed substantial gains in energy reduction of vehicles. In 1980 alone, General Motors budgeted close to $7 billion in capital spending for improving fuel economy, as

---

[12] See E. A. Hudson and D. W. Jorgenson, "Energy Policy and U.S. Economic Growth," *American Economic Review* (May, 1978), pp. 118–123; E. R. Berndt and D. O. Wood, "Technology, Prices and the Derived Demand for Energy," *Review of Economic Statistics* (August, 1975), pp. 259–268.

[13] S. Ozatalay, *et al.*, "Energy Substitution and National Energy Policy," *American Economic Review* (May, 1979), pp. 369–371; J. M. Griffin and P. R. Gregory, "An Intercountry Translog Model of Energy Substitution Responses," *Ibid.* (December, 1976), pp. 845–847.

[14] Ozatalay, *et al.*, p. 369.

[15] Lee Schipper, "Another Look at Energy Conservation," *American Economic Review* (May, 1979), pp. 363–365.

well as safety and emission control. The comparable figure in 1979 stood at about $5.3 billion.[16] Until 1970, there was a one-for-one relationship between changes in energy and changes in GNP. Today, the ratio between the two is roughly 0.6; a 1 percent change in GNP requires a 0.6 percent change in energy.

But the change in energy usage by substitution of capital is a slow process accomplished mainly at the margin. Major reductions occur only when large proportions of existing capital are replaced. This replacement rate rests on demand and the ratio of marginal costs from old facilities to capital and operating costs of new ones. Whether technology is equal to the task remains a question that only the future will answer.

Ecology

The issue of natural resources has direct links to that of ecology, a term derived from the Greek word *ikos,* meaning "place to live." Human ecology thus refers to the study of man's relationship with his habitat, part of which includes the physical universe.

The use of natural resources is a two-way process. Man not merely extracts substances from nature but also returns resources to nature. Industrial production exudes wastes, which are raw materials or their derivations that do not go into the product. These raw materials have transformed atoms and in this new shape find their way into the air and soil and water. Man also discards products in the form of garbage and sewage. All these effluents go back to nature and are reprocessed into substances that become part of the physical environment. Resources thus move back and forth between man and nature. When the quantities of effluents exceed natural, waste absorption capacities, pollution has tipped the ecological system out of balance.

Pollution is a product of modern society. Economic growth, accompanied by advances in technology, has been a qualified accomplishment. It has greatly expanded the quantity and variety of material goods and raised the standard of living. It has brought comforts to the remotest parts of the earth, eradicated plagues and pestilence, and prolonged human life. But it has also damaged the physical environment and sometimes threatened the very life it was meant to succor. Geographic shifts in economic activity, promising greater efficiency and lower prices to consumers, have left large urban areas with decaying buildings, like the now abandoned mining towns of the old west. A pall of sickening haze overhangs many of our largest cities. New detergents, which reduce the tiresome household chores, are impervious to antibac-

---

[16] *Wall Street Journal* (December 24, 1979), p. 2.

terial action, poison the soil, and threaten the water supply. Powerful chemicals to destroy harmful insects kill beneficial ones as well. Rachel Carson's *Silent Spring*, written in 1962, still stands as an eloquent testimonial to the damage pesticides can bring about when used without thought of consequences.

To counter the ill effects of environmental damage, society has responded with a host of governmental agencies on the state and federal levels. The most important is the Federal Environmental Protection Agency, established in 1969. Though its prime task is to set standards for environmental quality, it also monitors and enforces its regulations.

Today, extensive environmental studies must be filed with regulatory agencies before any work can begin on new structures that might affect the environment. Industrial plants and utilities have to be built with pollution control devices, for atmospheric emissions and waste water discharges must meet government-mandated standards. Older plants, if not retrofitted to reduce pollution within allowable limits, are usually made to burn low sulfur oil or coal. Automobile manufacturers must equip their new cars with antipollution devices and fuel systems that take no-lead gasoline.

Business firms have also responded to the call for a clean environment, which is patently in their interests. They have incorporated ecological criteria into product design, especially for capital goods. They have set up departments of environmental affairs, charged with the responsibility for developing methods of evaluating the environmental effects of their operations. Many companies have gone far beyond governmental standards for protecting, and even enhancing, the environment in which their plants and offices are located. For example, plans to build a chemical plant for Union Carbide sixteen miles upstream from the Gulf coast on the Colorado River included extensive biological studies of the region. The proposed layout for the site envisioned the preservation of swamp lands and open water, deep forests and wildlife havens. Administrative offices were set apart among groves of wild pecan trees, so as not to harm the 200-year-old stands. According to the company, a facility "planned in this way can be a model of harmony with the environment..."[17]

Few would question the need to protect the environment and enhance the quality of life. But it is impractical, if not impossible, to build production facilities, roads, houses, and shopping centers and keep the environment unchanged. It is impractical, if not impossible, to continue expanding production and increasing population and at the same time to add absolutely no waste to the environment. Ecological issues

---

[17] *Union Carbide Profile* (New York: Union Carbide Corporation, 1974), p. 4.

are thus concerned primarily with degrees of control and their trade-offs. How far should society go in its effort to eliminate pollution? By 1981 American business is expected to spend more than $11 billion for pollution control. What is the reasonable thing to do, considering costs and benefits?

Adherence to environmental standards usually involves substantial expenditures, which add little or nothing to a product's end use. An electric utility that installs scrubbers to its generating plant does not change the form or capability of its product, electric power. But it will add substantially to the cost of its output. This is not to say that the incremental cost is unjustified or wasteful. But all products are not affected alike. Environmental costs vary widely from item to item. Services, for example, normally require less pollution control expenditures than goods, for they use less energy and raw materials per unit of output. There is also considerable variation in the pollution potential of goods, both in their production use and disposal. Environmental considerations have therefore come to influence product policy decisions.

A clean environment also involves trade-offs in the utilization of capital. Spending more on pollution control leaves less funds to expand production and distribution. The same money doesn't stretch as far; it builds smaller or fewer facilities. Output as a proportion of investment grows smaller, thereby decreasing the productivity of capital. There is thus a trade-off between environmental protection and real GNP. It might be argued that a healthier environment is conducive to greater output, thus offsetting the higher capital costs, but there is little or no evidence on this score.

In the long run, the physical environment may be a contrary force and impose constraints, or even absolute limits, on our present policy of economic growth. One aspect of more goods and services is an increase in energy utilization, the bulk of which comes from fossil fuels. No matter how the resource question is resolved, higher production levels and more people implies a greater output of energy. When fossil fuels are burned, carbon dioxide is released into the atmosphere. Part of the emission is absorbed by the oceans, but part remains in the air. Nuclear power does not give off CO_2, but it introduces an even greater hazard that remains radioactive for centuries. And both kinds of fuel, fossil and nuclear, radiate heat that warms the atmosphere. A continuing increase in thermal pollution could theoretically reach a point at which disastrous climate effects would ensue. Warmer winters might prove a pleasant change in colder climates. But if the earth's temperatures were raised high enough to melt the polar ice caps, the oceans would rise and roll over vast land masses.

Of course, the world is probably a long way from such a calamity. But the limits of thermal pollution and CO_2 additions are not known. For this reason, many have cautioned that a policy of growth must be commensurate with the external environment's absorption capacity.[18]

Perhaps advances in technology will in the future permit economic expansion with no thermal pollution. Discarded materials might be recycled, and waste heat might be fed back into the productive process rather than ejected to pollute the air. A larger proportion of energy might come from the sun, which would not raise atmospheric temperatures over what they would be normally.

But these "mights" represent man's hopes and perhaps an undue faith in the power of technology to solve his problems. Moreover, these problems are not wholly technological ones. Many involve social values, and sole reliance on engineering solutions often results in what has been called a "technological fix." Its action resembles that of a vicious cycle. The solution gives rise to other problems, which in turn look again toward technology for solving what it has created. For example, industrial activity gives off waste. We have employed technology to reduce pollution levels. But it has also raised energy requirements and put additional strains on tight resources. Technology is then once again called upon to reduce energy usage. In another example, traffic congestion induces air pollution. Construction of more and wider highways can lessen congestion, but now more cars are on the road. If environmental hazards are to be overcome, technology must be blended with human values.

Public Control and Product Policy

Product policy is formulated within an economic system commonly described by such words as competitive and free enterprise. To most Americans these words also carry value-laden connotation: goodness, wholesomeness, even sanctity. But they are also at variance with realities, and the distance between theory and practice is widening. As such, the twin concepts of competition and free enterprise increasingly are becoming catchwords, keeping their form but losing their meaning.

The basic character of economic institutions invariably changes, regardless of the terms used to describe them, with every encroachment of the public in business decisions, either through private organizations or government agencies. One such intrusion onto the business scene came from consumerism, a force that has been gathering momentum over the last two decades. This movement essentially aims at increasing the rights of the public in commercial transactions.

---

[18] Meadows, *et al., op. cit.,* pp. 78–93.

Some of these rights are traditional ones which, in an atmosphere of benign neglect, were disregarded by sellers. These transgressions include such practices as vending defective products, making sales claims that add up to puffery, failing to divulge relevant information, advertising with hard-to-notice qualifiers, and dealing with the public in a manner considered unethical. Consumerist attempts to rectify such practices can be viewed as adherence to conventional, generally accepted values.

Another set of proposals is meant to protect the public from harm and to enhance the quality of life. These regulations, too, represent no sharp break with traditional values. Keeping watch over the public health and safety has always been regarded as a legitimate function of government and can be supported with ample precedents. Under this commonly accepted power, government monitors food ingredients for health hazards, prevents dangerous toys, sets rules for drug products, and requires safety caps on containers holding potentially harmful products. But these regulations, by marking out which products and product prototypes can and cannot be produced, collide with traditional management prerogatives over product policy. Options available in the past are no longer so, partly because society has expanded the interpretation of what constitutes health and safety, partly because government bureaucracies continuously seek new service areas in their attempt to perpetuate themselves.

Government regulatory agencies have mushroomed, with federal funding for regulation growing nearly sixfold during the decade of the seventies to some $4.8 billion.[19] Regulation has extended into so many aspects of business that there is hardly a firm whose product decisions are exempt from government surveillance. Until 1970, regulation was primarily industry specific. During the seventies it began cutting across all industries. As put by Julian Scheer, senior vice-president of LTV Corporation, "The chief executive has seen increasingly that more and more of the day-to-day decisions are made, not in his boardroom, but in Washington."[20]

Unable to stem the tide of regulation, business had no choice but to go with it. In the fifties and sixties, firms sought to keep out of government's way if they were able to do so. By the seventies, recalcitrant avoidance gave way to solicitous association. Corporations expanded and upgraded government-related activities and placed them under the direction of a top-ranking officer. While lobbying remains important, it has lost its primacy. The main objective of the new relationship is to

---

[19] Vasil Pappas, "More Firms Upgraded Government-Relations Jobs Because of Sharp Growth in Federal Regulations," *Wall Street Journal* (January 11, 1980), p. 42.

[20] *Ibid.*

gain an understanding of political cross-currents that affect govern-ment policies so as to be prepared for them and, if possible, lend a hand in shaping them. Bureaucrats have welcomed the *rapproachement*, for they regard accommodation as preferable to confrontation. They have opened their doors to business representatives and bid them enter. As public servants, they cannot deny accessibility to their constituents, especially those with political clout. They also buttress their legitimacy by bringing into their conclaves groups that would upset their stability. But by doing so, they become more responsive to the sectors they are supposed to regulate. It is for this reason that regulatory agencies are sometimes accused of being controlled by the regulated.

While government and business draw together more closely and the product policy of the firm becomes more dependent upon Washington, the notion of free enterprise waxes stronger. Bureaucrats must act within the law, not arbitrarily. They are sworn to uphold legal institu-tions and protect society's values, not destroy them. It then follows that all regulations are designed to strengthen, not weaken, an economic system that the public almost equates with individual freedom.

Business, too, finds it in its interest to perpetuate tradition but for exactly the opposite reasons. Regulations not to its liking can be painted as sinister attempts to undermine the free enterprise system, while those which they favor, obviously, have a contrary effect. Thus, steel companies can brand government's high-handed attempts to dampen price increases as interference with free market forces but praise trigger prices on foreign steel as a vindication of the competitive system. Simi-larly, the same auto executives who denounced burdensome regulations as sapping the strength of free enterprise—which they probably do—see nothing wrong with their system when bailed out of bankruptcy by government guarantees. In a pluralistic society such as America, how-ever, differences of opinion exist in the business community. Thus, the Business Roundtable, made up of leaders from the largest corporations, disapproved of federal loans to Chrysler. Nevertheless, theory and practice tend to drift apart.

Similar inconsistencies prevail with respect to supply-demand rela-tionships. For more than a quarter of a century, executives responsible for product policy, by and large, have accepted without qualification a corporate philosophy known as the marketing concept. Briefly stated, the theory assumes that demand, wholly independent of supply, stems from consumers acting to satisfy their needs. In this form, the market-ing concept is derived from the traditional theories of classical eco-nomics, particularly those of utility and consumer sovereignty.[21] If

---

[21] W. S. Sachs and G. Benson, "Is It Time to Discard the Marketing Concept?" *Business Horizons* (August, 1978), pp. 69–70.

demand is a function of independent-minded consumers maximizing their satisfaction, should not products march to the beat of want-satisfying drums? Business is thus enjoined to make products to fulfill consumer needs and is promised rewards in accordance with its ability to do so.

But even the warmest advocates of the marketing concept readily acknowledge, that it is not generally practiced.[22] The fault lies not with bad or wicked men in the seats of power but with the theory. It is impractical. The very best of men, all good and true, could not practice what is preached unless they made products for unreal people in an unreal world.

A firm is anything but a passive instrument in getting products to market. Advertising and sales promotion expenditures for consumer products run into many millions of dollars. Advertising agencies boast of the persuasive power of their messages in the trade press, client meetings, and new business solicitations. Much of these claims can be discounted, to be sure. But the promotion techniques also work, and therefore they are widely used. If market demands can then be influenced, it is a contradiction to implore firms to satisfy market demands.

That does not say that Madison Avenue can produce sales upon demand. Quite the contrary. Demand is generated by a host of factors, many of which run counter to the objectives of any paritcular firm. An advertising campaign therefore involves great uncertainty, as evidenced by the high failure rate of new consumer products. But uncertainty does not negate the influence that is brought to bear upon consumer choice. The relevant question for product managers pertains not to what consumers need but to what they will accept—not to what they want, but to what they will buy.

Precepts diverge from reality because business is part of the American establishment. Like politicians, corporate officers are dedicated to the preservation of traditional values though not to the maintenance of the *status quo*. But change must come, if it does, within the framework of a value system that is time-honored and cherished. The ideals of the individualistic ethic run deep, and the mere hint of big business trying to manipulate the public brings antagonism and conflict. Then why conjure up demons when business can enjoy the image of a public servant satisfying freely determined, self-directed needs and wants?

Other reasons why companies cannot practice the so-called marketing concept are business rivalry and industrial structure.[23] Imitative

---

[22] E. g., see Peter F. Drucker, *Management: Tasks, Responsibilities, Practices* (New York: Harper & Row, 1974), pp. 64–65; Herbert Zeltner, "Beware of Reefs: Where Our Modern Marketing Process is Running Aground," *Advertising Age* (September, 1976), pp. 71–72.

[23] See Sachs and Benson, *op. cit.*, pp. 72–73; Ronald W. Stampfl, "Structural Constraints, Consumerism, and the Marketing Concept," *MSU Business Topics* (Spring, 1978), pp. 5–16.

products and imitative strategies are dictated by competitive pressures. No firm can abstain from making "me-too" or parity products and hope to prosper, or even survive. When combined with technological restraints, differences among company offerings tend to become minimal.

Technology has other effects as well. Capital-intensive firms relying upon mass production techniques must adjust their outputs to their resources. To be manufactured efficiently, such goods must fit into a flow production mold. The items are all the more preferable if they have an existing demand because that makes for low risk. In such firms, operating under what Galbraith has called the "technological imperative," the mode of production is the prime consideration in product development.[24] Competitive advantage and industrial leadership derive from efficiency and lower production costs. Product options here do not hinge on what consumers want but on what they can get. The technological organization provides output parameters. Given a set of alternative products, marketing determines how much of each consumers can be induced to take.

Organizational and technological constraints in product development also make themselves felt in service industries though not to the same extent as in manufacturing. New services must accommodate themselves to computerized management information systems, vital to the exercise of proper control over operations. Changes or alterations in these systems are costly and time-consuming. Service firms, like manufacturers, are dependent upon the cooperation of specialists, each having an expertise in a narrow area. Services falling outside a firm's area of dominant competence, even in related fields, can only be developed at substantial cost and effort. A life insurance company is not necessarily in the "protection business." Depending upon its staff's ability, the firm may have as much trouble writing casualty or home insurance as railroad executives would have in trying to run an airline. A savings and loan association may find itself in a strange, new world were it to fan out into portfolio management.

In recent years, another philosophy has arisen in the most respectable circles to challenge the traditional role of the corporation and its products. The proponents of this view point out that consumer preferences, as for large cars and overheated rooms, are often incompatible with the interests of the nation as a whole. In contrast to the atomistic view of society, this philosophy embraces a welfare concept. Corporate objectives, it holds, should be directed towards social ends and the "wider goals of society."

---

[24] See John K. Galbraith, *The New Industrial State* (Boston: Houghton Mifflin Company, 1967), pp. 11–21; Joan Woodward, *Industrial Organization: Theory and Practice* (London: Oxford University Press, 1965).

If this philosophy were to prevail, the corporation would be transformed from an economic to a social or political entity. Product development would become less concerned with monetary returns and more concerned with such issues as creating jobs, renewing urban blight, training disadvantaged youth, subsidizing artistic and cultural endeavors.

Many of these undertakings are surely worthwhile, and corporations do many of these tasks now. But they are unimportant in their scheme of things, peripheral to their main aims, which are primarily economic. Product policy remains governed by sales, costs, profits. Any change in these corporate functions would introduce more profound questions which the present cannot answer. If economic forces and prospects of pecuniary gain will not determine what should be produced, and how the output should be allocated, what and who will?

REVIEW QUESTIONS

1. Discuss the business implications of the neo-Malthusian view of the future state of man's physical resources.

2. Discuss the implications of a national energy shortage on the rate and direction of future product development.

3. Many people believe that a solution to the energy crisis will parallel the solution to other problems of past centuries based on the principle of a lower cost substitution of one resource for another. Discuss the applicability of substitution as a possible solution to declining energy resources.

4. Ecological concerns increase in importance as the world becomes more crowded. How will this affect a firm's future operations?

5. Public control impinges on business product policy. Discuss the nature and results of this impingement.

6. Does the marketing concept determine a firm's product mix? Explain your answer.

APPENDIX

Major U.S. Legislation Affecting Products

Federal Food and Drug Act (1906)

The law prohibits the manufacture, delivery, or receipt of any food, drug, device, or cosmetic that is adulterated or misbranded. Violators can be imprisoned for not more than one year, fined not more than $1,000, or both. Violators with previous convictions under the law, or whose violations were committed with intent to defraud or mislead, can be imprisoned for not more than three years, fined not more than $10,000, or both.

The Food and Drug Act was expanded by the Food, Drug and Cosmetic Act in 1938 and amended by the Food Additives Amendment in 1958. It was further modified by the Kefauver-Harris Amendment of 1962, which dealt with pretesting drugs for safety and effectiveness and labeling drugs by generic names.

Federal Meat Inspection Act (1907)

For purposes of preventing adulterated meat products, the Secretary of Agriculture, or his delegate, is responsible for inspecting all animals before they are slaughtered and all meat before it is packaged.

The act prohibits sales, transportation, and manufacture of adulterated or misbranded meat products. Violations are punishable by imprisonment of not more than one year, a fine no more than $1,000, or both. But if the violation involves intent to defraud or an attempt to distribute an adulterated product, punishment upon conviction can be a jail term of up to three years, a fine of up to $10,000, or both.

Flammable Fabrics Act (1951)

The law prohibits the manufacture or distribution of any product or fabric that fails to conform with flammability standards. Any violation shall be deemed unlawful as an unfair method of competition or as an unfair, deceptive practice in commerce under the Federal Trade Commission Act. Violators shall be guilty of a misdemeanor, subject to imprisonment of not more than a year, a fine of not more than $5,000, or both.

Refrigerator Safety Act (1956)

The law requires that manufacturers must equip all refrigerators with a device that enables the door to be opened from the inside. Violators shall be guilty of a misdemeanor and, upon conviction, shall be subject to imprisonment of up to one year, a fine of up to $1,000, or both.

Federal Hazardous Substances Act (1960)

The act prohibits the following practices:
1. The sale of any misbranded or banned hazardous substance.
2. The adulteration, destruction, or removal of the whole or any part of a label of a hazardous substance in interstate commerce.
3. A false guarantee.

Violations can result in fines of $500 maximum, up to ninety days in jail, or both. Offenses committed with intent to defraud or mislead are subject to penalties of not greater than a year in jail, a fine of $3,000, or both.

Federal Cigarette Labeling and Advertising Act (1965)

The law makes illegal the manufacture, import, or distribution of cigarettes with packages that fail to bear the following statement: "Warning: The Surgeon General Has Determined That Cigarette Smoking Is Dangerous to Your Health." Subject to the jurisdiction of the Federal Communications Commission, advertising of cigarettes and little cigars in electronic media is prohibited.

Fair Packaging and Labeling Act (1966)

All packaged consumer goods must be properly labeled, identifying the commodity and bearing the name and place of business of the manufacturer, packer, or distributor. The net contents or quantity shall be separately and accurately presented in a uniform location on the principal display panel of the label. The authority to promulgate regulations concerning food, drugs, or cosmetics is vested in the Secretary of Health, Education, and Welfare. Regulations on all other commodities is given to the Federal Trade Commission.

Child Protection Act (1966)

The law bans the sale of any toy or article intended for use by children that is a hazardous substance. The Child Protection Act was amended in 1969 by the Child Protection and Toy Safety Act. The latter law extends the prohibition to electrical, mechanical, or thermal devices that pose hazards to children.

National Traffic and Safety Act (1966)

The law empowers the Secretary of Transportation to establish appropriate motor vehicle safety standards. Each standard must be stated in objective terms, be practicable, and meet a public need for motor vehicle safety. The law prohibits the manufacture or import of motor vehicles that fail to meet such standards. A maximum fine of $1,000 was set for each violation, with a penalty not to exceed $400,000 for any related series of violations.

Truth in Lending Act (1968)

The law requires lenders to state accurately the cost of money to consumers. The annual percentage rate to any extension of consumer credit is to be determined in accordance with regulations of the Board of Governors of the Federal Reserve System. This body was also empowered to set regulations for all classes of transactions under the act.

National Environmental Protection Act (1969)

The federal government declared its responsibility for enhancing the quality of air, water, and land resources by setting environmental standards in cooperation with state and local governments. Heads of federal agencies must ensure that all facilities under their jurisdiction conform to the following requirements:

1. Air and water standards.
2. Regulations for dumping material into ocean water.
3. Guidelines for solid waste recovery, collection, storage, separation and disposal systems.
4. Federal noise emission standards.
5. Guidelines on radiation.
6. Application and manufacture of pesticides.

The Environmental Protection Agency was established in 1970 under the provisions of this act. It was also given power to pursue environmental research and development in addition to setting and maintaining environmental standards.

Occupational Safety and Health Act (1970)

The Secretary of Labor was given responsibility to promulgate regulations for occupational safety and health. In the event there are conflicts among federal standards, the Secretary of Labor shall determine that standard which assures the greatest protection of safety and health to employees.

A National Advisory Committee on Occupational Safety and Health was established to make recommendations to the Secretary of Health,

Education, and Welfare relating to the administration of health and safety standards.

Poison Prevention Packaging Act (1970)

The law permits the Secretary of Health, Education, and Welfare to set standards for special packaging for products dangerous to children. The purpose is to protect children from personal injury or serious illness. The standards must be feasible, practical, and appropriate for rectifying the problem.

The law also permits marketing of noncomplying packages for the elderly or handicapped in the event such persons are unable to use regularly packaged products. UNder certain conditions, a manufacturer can package any household item in a single size if he also supplies that item in a special package that conforms with the law. However, the package that does not conform with the law must bear a label which states conspicuously: "This package for households without young children."

Consumer Product Safety Act (1972)

The act created a Consumer Product Safety Commission to gather and maintain information on the causes and prevention of death, injury, and illness associated with consumer products. The commission is also authorized to set safety standards consisting of the following:

1. Requirements as to performance, composition, contents, design, construction, finish, or packaging of a consumer product.
2. Requirements that a consumer product be marked by clear and adequate warnings or instructions, where necessary.

Manufacture and sale of products that do not comply with product safety standards or that have been banned as hazardous are prohibited.

Magnuson–Moss Warranty/FTC Improvement Act (1975)

Any warranty of a consumer product shall conform to the rules set by the Federal Trade Commission and disclose fully and conspicuously in simple and readily understandable language the terms and conditions of the warranty.

In order to meet FTC minimum standards for warranty, the warrantor must remedy the defect within a reasonable time and free of charge. The FTC shall prescribe rules for minimum requirements for any informal dispute settlement procedure that is incorporated in a warranty. The rules should provide for participation of independent or government entities.

Case Studies

J. B. Manufacturing Company

J. B. Mfg. Co. is a diversified manufacturer of electro-mechanical products, most of which are sold as components to other manufacturers who incorporate them into more complex 'systems.' For example, one of their divisions makes electric motors, varying in size from $\frac{1}{16}$ to 1 horsepower. These motors are sold to manufacturers of forced air furnaces, vacuum cleaners, major appliances, etc.

J. B.'s electric motor division is a dominant influence in fractional horsepower motors, and has the largest market share, 55 percent. The business is dependent on the general state of the economy in terms of consumer purchases of major appliances, and the management of this segment of the business has a strong desire to diversify in an attempt to level out their business cycle by adding new products that are counter-cyclical to present ones.

The present organization is structured for maximum efficiency to achieve low costs and retain J. B.'s dominant market position. Technical production and marketing functions are kept at very low levels, and there is practically no cushion of effort to apply to product development.

Management of this division is hesitant to add personnel, thereby increasing operating expense. Management incentives and bonuses are based on profits, and every additional item of cost can have a direct negative effect on individual bonuses.

J. B. corporate management has told the management of this division that it wants to see some diversification but at the same time, does not want to see operating profits fall.

There appear to be four potential solutions:

1. Form a group at the corporate level to search out and develop new products for the electric motor division. Costs of this effort would be borne by corporate staff, so that the division would not be penalized in its current earnings. As soon as the new product was ready for manufacture and sale, it would be turned over to the electric motor division for exploitation.

2. Provide an accounting mechanism to report costs of new product development separately and not include them in the calculation of managers' bonuses. All work to be performed directly by the electric motor division.

3. Corporate management could demand that the division undertake to diversify with its own funds and people. While this would probably reduce bonuses temporarily, the addition of new rev-

enue and new profits from the new product would eventually compensate division management adequately. Because the division has no excess personnel to assign to the new task, it would have to add to its staff, and probably set up its own new product development task force.

4. Acquire a going business which has the right business cycle characteristics, and will fit the capabilities of the electric motor division. The corporation has done this in the past, and been quite successful at it. Corporate management has the feeling that, while this has been a successful route in the past, the ability to do this is becoming more limited due to governmental restrictions, and ability to digest multiple acquisitions. If this choice is selected every time, the ability to develop products within the organization wastes away, and the company's ability to expand relies on what is available for sale, rather than the kind of product the company should really have.

1. As the president of J. B. Corporation, which alternative(s) would you select and why?

2. As the general manager of the electric motor division, which alternative(s) would you select and why?

Gruff Whiskey

"We have come to a decision. Even though each of you has good reason for your point of view, it is obvious that we can move in only one direction."

These were the words of the executive vice-president of a leading distilling company as he faced his colleagues of the management team. It was considering the future of what was once a leading whiskey brand which, for purposes of maintaining confidentiality, we shall call Gruff Whiskey. There were three choices considered: 1) do nothing—continue as is; 2) milk the brand and eventually discontinue it; 3) try to resuscitate the brand by changing the market strategy, the product attributes, or both.

Gruff Whiskey still accounted for almost $10 million in annual sales. But the profits were marginal, and sales had undergone a long-term decline. Within the past decade alone, sales had fallen off from 900,000 cases to 300,000 cases. Declining sales was a fact for the entire domestic whiskey category. While total distilled spirits increased, the relative share of domestic whiskey was growing continually smaller. The domestic products were losing ground to two groups: 1) non-whiskey categories, such as vodka, gin, cordials, rum and brandy; 2) imported whiskeys.

A survey of consumers of drinking age done by the marketing research department indicated the following:

1. Gruff Whiskey was recognized by a large proportion of drinkers.

2. Consumers believed that Gruff was a good whiskey.

3. Gruff had the smallest percentage of any major brand in the fifth size, which is the most popular take-home package in most areas.

4. Gruff was absolutely dead in suburban areas. Its major market was among low income groups.

5. Gruff users had an older age profile, as indicated in the following table:

	Percent of Customers	
Age of User	Gruff	Major Competitors
Under 30 years..............................	11%	25%
30–45 years	42%	46%
46 years + ...	47%	29%
Total	100%	100%

Selling liquor is different from any other type of marketing. A basic plan requires many variations, because regulation of the liquor business has grown out of local traditions. Laws vary widely from state to state. In Massachusetts, for example, privately-operated bars and stores buy from privately-owned wholesalers. In other places, the state itself is both the wholesaler and retailer. Some of these states also sell to privately-owned bars. Others have no bars. One state operates as the sole wholesaler, vending liquor to privately-owned stores and bars. Several states have county or municipal systems which own and operate liquor establishments. Regulations governing advertising and sales promotion within states are equally varied.

Gruff Whiskey is sold directly to the state or county distribution systems in 17 states, plus Montgomery County, Maryland. In the remaining parts of the country Gruff Whiskey is sold through a dual distribution system. The brand is handled by some 80 wholesalers, the sales force of which call on bars and stores. These agencies handle a broad variety of lines, including brands which are directly competitive with Gruff Whiskey. Since the brand is not a leading one, it is doubtful whether it is of great importance to any distributor. The company salesmen carrying Gruff Whiskey also carry other brands. About 60 percent of all Gruff's sales are written by the company sales force.

A summary of Gruff's financial position was as follows:

Sales	$9,870,000
Less: Cost of Sales	
Materials	3,750,000
Direct labor	1,380,000
Factory overhead	700,000
Gross profit	4,040,000
Less: Selling and Administrative	
Sales salaries	1,000,000
Sales commissions	350,000
Advertising, promotion	1,200,000
Other out-of-pocket	700,000
Sales office expenses	400,000
General and administrative	500,000
Marginal contribution	(110,000)

Gruff Whiskey was being produced at facilities which were being utilized at some 82 percent capacity. It accounted for about 8 percent of utilization. Items such as sales salaries, sales office expenses and general and administrative were allocated to the brand. Since sales people carried other brands, their portion of salaries assigned to Gruff was done on proportionality to sales. Sales office expenses were also assigned on the same basis. Even part of the "out-of-pocket" expenses were not truly variable, since they included such items as "travel and entertainment." Because sales personnel would do the same traveling whether or not they carried Gruff Whiskey, that portion allocated to Gruff can actually be considered a non-variable cost. In all, about 50 percent of the "other out-of-pocket" was really variable. The remainder was not.

After considering marketing and financial data, the management group came to the conclusion that Gruff Whiskey should be milked and eventually discontinued.

Questions

1. Do you agree with the decision? Why or why not?

2. How would the financial picture alter under a milking or harvesting strategy, assuming that sales drop by 10 percent?

3. At what point would you recommend that Gruff Whiskey be discontinued?

Superior Foods Company

A large manufacturer of packaged foods is organized in the marketing area along lines of a product manager system. Each brand is the responsibility of a particular group, headed by a manager. This individual reports to a product group head, who, in turn, reports to the V.P. of marketing.

The recently established product development department for this company is headed by a director, who reports to the Vice President in charge of marketing. The director of product development is responsible for planning, development and execution of complete marketing programs, plans and budgets for all new products to expand brand and product lines. The product development department undertakes the search for appropriate product concepts, directs product-packaging development work, and can employ outside organizations and agencies to forward the new product activity.

The duties of the Director of Product Development are outlined by the following job description:

1. Directs the planning and development of marketing plans for all new products from concept stage to national launch. Guides product-conception activities and supervises the necessary testing stages for determining the profitability of the national introduction of new products.

2. Directs the pace of the company's new product activity and determines what resources can and should be put behind the total program and its individual components.

3. Ensures company and agency cooperation through the research, development, testing, and introductory market-launch phases of the product(s).

4. Reviews analyses of evaluations of consumer wants and needs with respect to product performance and recommends corrective and progressive action.

5. Receives and evaluates new product ideas from internal and external company sources and determines what part they should play in our new products program.

6. Directs development of all product packaging for both new and established products taking into consideration aspects such as function, cost, practicality, materials, graphic design and esthetic appeal of all packaging items.

7. Coordinates the activities of own and other organizations in planning and executing a new product's market release.

8. Directs the development of national marketing plans and test market translations, including the complete marketing mix: marketing strategy and objectives, advertising (copy and media), sales promotion (trade and consumer), and publicity.

9. Approves and presents for further approval total marketing plans and budgets for all new products.

10. Coordinates the efforts of own and market research personnel in developing research programs for evaluating new product progress in test marketing stages.

11. Coordinates the work of agency, design and internal advertising/sales promotion personnel on development and optimal execution of marketing, media, creative, packaging, and promotional objectives and strategies. Exercises approval or disapproval authority subject to agreement at higher level.

12. Maintains productive contacts with appropriate marketing, trade, and industry groups to keep current on new developments and trends.

13. Cooperates with key members of the marketing division and other divisions to ensure the successful implementation and execution of approved marketing, advertising, and sales promotion plans.

14. Provides continuing reports on work in progress and results of current efforts.

15. Develops specific marketing policies for recommendation to the marketing vice-president.

16. Administers the company's trademark program in conjunction with trademark attorneys.

Questions

1. Considering the responsibilities of product development, what kinds of personnel should the director look for in staffing the department?

2. What type of personnel problems might the director expect to encounter?

3. What kind of intercompany conflicts might the director anticipate which would involve his department?

Great Eastern Manufacturing Co.

Great Eastern is a diversified specialty chemical manufacturing company. Annual sales are $500,000,000, about half of which comes from sales to high volume industrial accounts and the other half to the retail market through supermarkets and drug chains. Essentially, the materials they manufacture are formulated products, such as cleaners, deodorants, polishes and waxes.

About 30 percent of the items they sell are based on proprietary chemicals which Great Eastern manufactures in house, and include special detergents, emulsifiers, brighteners, and the like.

Great Eastern has a chemical research and development laboratory manned by 30 professional scientists and 50 technicians, supervised by a vice-president of research and development.

The marketing function is split into independent groups, industrial and commercial, and retail, each headed by a vice-president.

All manufacturing functions report to a vice-president of manufacturing.

Great Eastern also has a vice-president of engineering who is responsible for all plant equipment, buildings, process engineering and safety.

All corporate staff departments, such as purchasing, personnel, legal, and financial report to a vice-president of administration.

All of the vice-presidents report directly to the president.

Great Eastern's business is highly competitive, and leadership in share of market can only be maintained by a constant stream of new products and updating of existing products.

There has never been a dearth of new product ideas. Being a leader in its field, Great Eastern receives hundreds of ideas from all types of sources: independent inventors, research institutes, universities, etc. It also maintains contacts with a select network of venture capitalists, business brokers, and investment bankers, who keep them aware of new start-up companies and companies available for acquisition.

Over the past several years, the number of new products actually reaching the market has started to dwindle and the president set out to find the reason.

All ideas submitted to Great Eastern pass through a patent lawyer who determines if the submitter of the idea and Great Eastern are adequately protected legally. He passes on those which qualify legally to a new product review committee, consisting of representatives of all the functional vice-presidents. Each idea is read and given a cursory evaluation for general company interest and 'comfort factor.' Probably three-fourths of the ideas do not get by this review. As exaggerated examples, an idea for a new type of seat belt for automobiles, or a new urban transportation system would, of course, be rejected as outside of Great Eastern's field of capability.

The remaining ideas are classified in two categories: those in which technical feasibility is the key point, and those in which marketing considerations are dominant. Those that need confirmation of technical feasibility are passed on to research and development, those whose marketability needs confirmation to the two marketing vice-presidents.

Any ideas that are thought to be feasible by these groups come back to the new product committee for final judgment and selection.

Very, very few ideas find their way back to the committee from either the marketing departments or the laboratory, and the president decides that these are the bottlenecks that must be widened first.

He talked with the vice-president of research first, and asked him to pick, at random, a few of the ideas that had not passed muster technically. It was apparent in every case that the technical examiner had taken a completely negative approach and had sincerely believed his mission was to 'find out what's wrong with the idea.' Since all the ideas being examined were not worked out in great detail, it was relatively easy to find flaws or potential flaws which could be legitimate logical reasons for rejection.

The president subsequently talked with the two vice-presidents of marketing. His conclusions were exactly the same, i.e., the approach was predominantly to look for faults, not advantages.

The president also got the impression that the research and development and the marketing departments had an inherent jealousy of others' ideas, particularly if they were from outside the company, and this intensified the unconscious desire to find fault.

The evaluation and concomitant recognition of 'good' ideas is well accepted as being one of, if not the most important ingredient in successful new product development.

What can the president do to improve the odds of Great Eastern's evaluation process?

Bradford Company

The Bradford Company was built on the base of a single product line, for which it purchased patent rights 20 years ago. The patents were held valid by the courts in several infringement lawsuits, so that Bradford had the market to itself during the effective life of the original patents. These original patents matured three years ago, so they no longer provide protection.

Bradford was fortunate in having a management that continued research and development over the past years, and has built a patent estate consisting of improvements, modifications, and new features, all

of which will protect their technological leadership in the market segments in which they operate. However, after Bradford had built its
original business to total sales of $200 million, demonstrating the exist-
ence of a sizable market, ambitious competitors appeared immediately
upon expiration of the original patents.

In spite of the dominant technical position, and the high quality of
its products, Bradford was adversely affected to the extent that profit
margins eroded nearly 25 percent before management took the new
competition seriously.

Cost reduction programs were started in all functional areas of
the business in an attempt to restore previous margins. Prices were
reduced, new marketing programs initiated, production procedures
revised, engineering costs reduced, and administrative expenses cut to
the bone.

At the same time, it was suggested that perhaps the old levels of
profitability would not be regained and that the ultimate solution was to
find other new product lines in which Bradford could obtain the same
sort of protection (and profit margin) it enjoyed in its original line. To
do this would obviously cost money, making further drains on profit
margins, hopefully temporary.

Bradford Company's original product was an office copy machine,
employing mainly electrical and mechanical technology, but sprinkled
with other disciplines, such as optics, thermodynamics, inorganic, or-
ganic, and physical chemistry. In fact a broad spectrum of sciences so
that there are few limitations on the technical skill base.

Sophisticated industrial marketing skills are also available. While
most office copy machines are sold direct to commercial and industrial
users by a company sales force, their line is also handled by independent
dealers in smaller communities, giving them experience in this mode of
distribution.

Bradford has no experience in the retail over the counter market,
and, in fact, is not comfortable even thinking about mass merchandising, and the risks associated with it.

Bradford's financial position is basically strong. Their high profit
margins in the past generated sufficient money to provide working
capital as well as capital for physical expansion, so consequently is debt-
free. The state of the present business is such that there are no major
new capital expenses required, so that profits can be topped for some
modest new product development costs. Because Bradford has followed
a very conservative dividend payout policy, it is unlikely that these will
have to be reduced, at least for the next two to three years. There is no
question, however, that net earnings will be directly affected by whatever amount is spent on research and development aimed at entirely
new products. Management feels that this reduction of earnings will

not be interpreted by the financial community as weakness, and if re-sults can be produced in a reasonable length of time, the price of the company's shares should not fall substantially.

Bradford's board of directors has met and approved, in principle, the idea of continuing to exert every possible effort to improve profits on the copy machine business, and, in addition, to establish new product lines via internal development, acquisition or other means, with the stipulation that such lines have higher return on sales and return on investment than copy machines.

Company management was instructed to present to the board, within 30 days, a detailed plan, including strategy, organization, and tactics for searching, evaluation, and development of new products/ businesses.

1. In view of the present situation at Bradford, what form of organization would be most desirable?
   a. Product group reporting to a line operating executive.
   b. New product group at corporate level reporting to top staff executive.
   c. Outside organization specializing in new product develop-ment.
2. Bradford Company has obviously been a 'product-oriented' com-pany in the past. Should this orientation be changed and how?

Sunshine Manufacturing Company

A large well-known manufacturer of national advertised toiletry products was experiencing unanticipated new product failures and below average success in new product sales. As part of a contemplated general reorganization, the Sunshine Manufacturing Company was also casting a suspicious eye on its new product organization.

Mr. John Markham, vice-president of marketing, was very troubled by the apparent lack-luster effectiveness of his new product organiza-tion, and was considering use of an outside management consultant to review the organization and operation of his new product area. The new products organization had been established only three years past. Previously, the individual product managers and research and develop-ment had the new product responsibility.

Hoping to avoid the necessity for an outside consultant, which Mr. Markham considered would be a blow to his prestige, he appointed a committee to conduct an internal audit of the company's recent new product history. This committee consisted of Mr. Andrew Adwar, the advertising manager, Mr. Edward Rosche, Jr., the marketing research manager, Mr. Ken Prodis, the new product group manager. The committee was to be chaired by Mr. Markham and was to receive assistance, when needed, from the research and development and production department.

Following two months of investigation, the committee came up with the following facts and opinions:

1. *Recent new product experiences:*
   a. a new deodorant product and a reformulated bath powder were abandoned after each struggled through two years of test marketing.
   b. a new toothpaste achieved a fair degree of market success, but it required five years rather than the initially budgeted three years.
   c. a smaller competitor beat Sunshine to the market with a new type hair curler. A similar device had been in a Sunshine test market for one year.

2. *The control and coordination of commercial new product development involved a number of individuals, as outlined in Chart I and detailed below:*
   a. Product managers were responsible for minor package and product modification relating to the brands under their control. The Sunshine Company was a strong believer in the power of mass advertising, devoting an average 25 percent of sales to this marketing tool. As a consequence of this faith, the product managers of commercialized products (as contrasted to new products managers) reported to the advertising manager.
   b. The new product group had resulted from the prior reorganization. Mr. Prodis had been appointed the first manager and currently held the same position. He reported to the marketing vice-president. Reporting to him were four new product managers and the marketing research people. This group was responsible for the creating and assembling of new product ideas relating to the assigned product lines and the subsequent initial screening, evaluation, concept testing and detailed business analysis of these ideas. New product ideas came to the new product group manager from various sources within and without the company, including creative input from his individual managers. The new product group manager's responsibility included a recommendation as to possible future development of the idea, based on information inputs to date. Marketing research provided much of the information input from external sources. When new product ideas were cleared for technical development, the new product project was turned over to the development manager.

The new product manager that had been assigned to screen and direct the business analysis procedure was also given the responsibility to prepare the initial marketing plan and guide the product through test marketing. In view of this person's specialized knowledge about the product, it was common practice at the Sunshine Manufacturing Company to promote the assigned new product manager to product manager of the commercialized new product. If not commercialized, he remained in his current position.

c. A new product development manager was responsible for guiding the project through development and testing. This manager reported to the vice-president for research and development, serving his boss as interface with the marketing department's new product organization. The development manager's initial procedure is to prepare a detailed schedule and budget for the balance of the development project. Information is provided by his research and development department, the new product group, and the marketing vice-president. It then became his responsibility to monitor development and subsequent testing progress and to prepare a recommendation as to whether or not test marketing was advisable. The project's responsibility was then handed over to the appropriate new product manager.

d. A new product committee consisted of the aforementioned new product group manager, new product development manager, Mr. Adwar, the advertising manager, Mr. Rosche, Jr., the marketing research manager, and a representative from the legal department. The committee was chaired by Mr. Markham, but was also frequently attended by the executive vice-president, Mr. Herbert Press. The responsibility of this committee was to oversee new product planning, establish policy, and make the final go/no go decision relative to development, testing and commercialization.

An analysis of this committee's actions during the prior two years indicated that they were largely involved in monitoring new product progress and budgets, and relying almost completely on the recommendation of the new product members and marketing research people as to the crucial new product decisions.

3. *Opinions:*

a. Mr. Prodis, the new product group manager, was a firm believer in research—extensive marketing research, consumer product testing, testing of each major element in the marketing plan (4 P's) and test marketing. This belief was founded in his fear of failure and possible effect on the reputation of the Sunshine Manufacturing Company. Such extensive research had obvious effects on product development time, but the results of the research were considered to be worth the time and money expended.

b. Mr. John McIntyre, a product manager responsible for Natural Soap, was of the opinion that the new product people were empire builders and had frequently encroached on the product managers' territory. He cited the example of Anti-Itis Soap, a product developed a number of years ago by research and development, designed to deep cleanse and lessen the irritating symptom resulting from sunburn, allergies, rashes, and similar causes. Mr. McIntyre was of the opinion that this product was an extension of his soap line and, therefore, development and marketing responsibility should have been so assigned. However, the new product development manager viewed this product as reaching a different market and reserved the development/commercialization responsibility for the new product people. Mr. McIntyre believed that the product was mishandled and had not reached its proper sales level because it was divorced from the regular soap line.

c. Mr. Markham had become increasingly concerned as to the validity of complete old/new product separation. Both old and new products required the preparation of marketing plans, and who was better qualified than the product managers of existing products? He was increasingly of the opinion that product managers of existing products should have a larger role in new products.

d. Both the production and research and development departments expressed dissatisfaction with communication between their respective departments and the new product people. Changes in the specifications were subject to extended discussion and delays, the production people were frequently suspicious of requests from research and development, and there was a general lack of cooperation.

Reading the committee's findings, Mr. Markham experienced a growing feeling of depression. Should he bring in an outside consultant or should he attempt to correct the problem from within? In fact, he was not certain there was a problem that could not be corrected by a few simple changes.

Does the reader have any suggestions? Does the new product organization require any changes, or perhaps additions? Are the recent new product experiences symptomatic of any problems?

Excelsior Publishing Company

The Excelsior Publishing Company is planning to introduce a new consumer magazine. This publication is to appeal to a dual audience, men and women. To be successful, and make a significant contribution to company profits, a subscription circulation is projected at about 3 million paid copies. This level is expected to be reached in about three years.

The editorial content is planned to deal with subject matter of general interest, such as people and events of wide significance, travel, places of interest, business, literature, entertainment, art. However, the editors have various options, both as to focus and editorial mix. They also have alternatives as to the magazine's format, such as size, graphics, paper and reproduction quality, advertising-editorial layout. These decisions are product-related, and are thought to have an important effect on the sources of revenue, subscriptions and advertising. The publisher is also of the opinion that, from the standpoint of audience, male readers compose the crucial variable. That is, success or failure rests on the reactions of male readers.

The publishing company thus undertook a research project to explore how men perceive different magazines, especially those appealing to mass audiences containing material related to editorial decisions. The research department recommended a research approach called multi-dimensional scaling.

By its very definition, the act of perception is a subjective one, pertaining to this and that individual. The images which are evoked, in a literal sense, are in the eyes of the beholder.

Measurements of perceptions can therefore be regarded as psychological ones. Most of them rest on the premise that the way people see things is related to the attributes of the objects preceived. Accordingly, the survey involved two things: 1) magazine characteristics (attributes) and 2) media vehicles (objects).

The attributes studied were of two kinds, editorial and advertising. The former were derived from editors' opinions on which attributes they deemed relevant to their decisions. These characteristics were as follows:

Editorial
Aesthetic, artistic qualities
Prestigious, good reputation
Thought provoking, absorbing
Imaginative, innovative
Broad range of topics, content
Intellectually stimulating
Interesting

For the sophisticated
Informative
Entertaining
Enjoyable

The editors deem all of the above attributes as desirable. The more positively readers would respond to these characteristics, in the opinion of editorial people, the better the magazine. They realized, however, that any single magazine cannot have all these attributes perceived as positive, and that people may regard some as more vital than others.

The advertising attributes were made up from input by both editorial and sales personnel. Advertising attributes are only partially under the control of media. For example, a magazine has the option of not accepting ads for certain products. It has the option of deciding where, within the front and back cover, ads are to appear. But a publication has little control over the content of an advertising message, once an advertising category is accepted. The attributes studied were as follows:

Advertising

Advertising carried is in good taste
High quality of products advertised
Believability of advertising claims
Reliability of products advertised
Confidence in products advertised
Carries advertising by outstanding companies
Advertising does not interrupt reading

The study focused on how men perceive publications in terms of these attributes, editorial and advertising. The objects to which these attributes applied included a set of six magazines which, in varying degrees, were selected because they were thought to represent various prototypes of mass circulation books appealing to dual audiences. These were as follows, together with estimates of their paid circulations:

Magazine	Circulation (000)
National Geographic	8,400
Newsweek	2,950
Reader's Digest	17,750
Sports Illustrated	2,250
Time	4,250
TV Guide	18,300

National Geographic and Sports Illustrated were selected to personify special appeals publications, travel and exotic in the first instance and sports in the second. Perhaps the Reader's Digest might also be classified in the same category because of its unique editorial contents, which summarizes or reproduces articles initially printed elsewhere.

The selection of National Geographic, however, came primarily for reasons other than special appeal. Its graphics and reproduction quality, in the opinion of the editors, were outstanding. It also had a more restrictive advertising policy than all other magazines studied. Liquor and cigarette advertisements are not accepted. The publication also does not comingle ads and editorial. All other magazines included in the study do, in the belief that ads get greater exposure when mixed with editorial matter. The choice of Time and Newsweek were because they contained many articles which would form the subject matter of the new publication, though there would be no focus on a news orientation. TV Guide was thought to satisfy a utilitarian or "service" book concept.

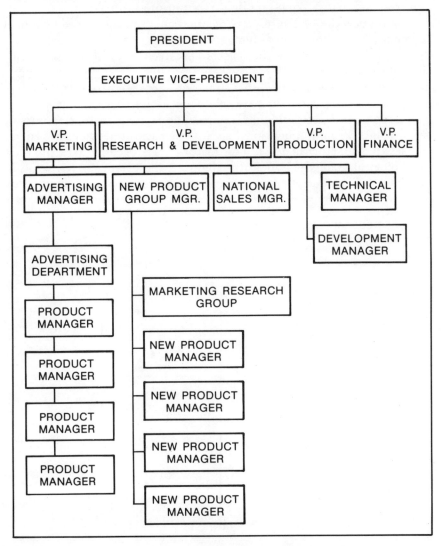

The study was based on a sample of upper income neighborhoods of seven metropolitan areas in and about New York. These Standard Metropolitan Statistical Areas (SMSA's) consisted of New York, Nassau-Suffolk, Newark, Bridgeport, Danbury, Norwalk, Stamford. Upper income areas of these SMSA's were highly relevant to the publishing firm, since syndicated audience studies indicated that magazine readership was economically upscale.

Each respondent was asked to rank each media vehicle in the set of six on each attribute. The order of particular magazines was rotated (from one attribute to another), so as to avoid any position bias which may arise. Respondents were also told there were no right or wrong answers, and that rankings are only a matter of personal judgment.

Based upon the responses, a perceptual map was developed by multidimensional scaling. This assumes that while people perceive things in terms of the attributes of the objects perceived, they do not see each characteristic by itself. Rather, objects are perceived as configurations of attributes, linked to each other in various arrangements. In multidimensional scaling, attributes are related to each other and considered simultaneously. Specifically, media perceptions are transformed into a set of points in multidimensional space. The basic dimensions are then extracted by factor analysis. The factors then become axes on the psychological map which indicate salient attributes and "psychological proximity." The perceptual map from the computer was as follows:

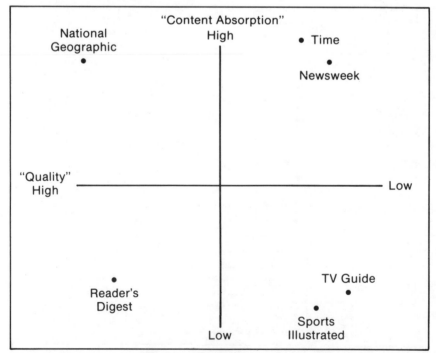

The dimensions labeled "content absorption" and "quality" are in reality composites of various attributes. The "attribute mix" of these dimensions comprises the following groupings:

Dimension 1 "Content Absorption"	Dimension 2 "Quality"
Interest	Aesthetic
Informative	Entertaining
Broad range of topics	Enjoyable
Advertising believable	Advertising does not interrupt reading

1. Analyze and interpret the research findings.
2. If you were the editor of this intended magazine, what editorial features (format and content) would you recommend?

Acme Engineering

Acme Engineering was founded in 1951 to produce mechanical and hydraulic power transmissions. This is still an important product line, though the company has grown remarkably since its establishment. By 1979 Acme Engineering could boast of $120 million in net revenue, some $13 million in net income after taxes, and about 8,000 employees.

But over the years the company added substantially to its product mix, mainly in related lines. It greatly expanded its compressed air products, which include machine tools, blowers, reciprocating and rotary compressors. Some of these products, along with mechanical transmissions and other drive components are custom designed to fit individual needs. Because customers' machinery undergoes a high rate of change, product development serves an important function at Acme.

In fact, Charles Morton, the chief operating officer, is strongly of the opinion that the company's future growth must come from new products. He stated at a board of director's meeting that in the next ten years some 60 percent of sales have to come from products that the company does not have now, if growth targets are to be met. Research and development expenditures for the past several years have been about 10 percent of sales, on the average.

Although Mr. Morton's statement about the role of product development in meeting future goals was a strong one, it was hardly exaggerated. New machines powered by compressed air had contributed significantly to earnings growth. One reason was because advances in air technology reduced noise levels in outdoor work and in plant. This advantage permitted the firm to make significant sales inroads in hospitals, medical centers and food processing plants.

New compressor technology also has wide application in modern manufacturing operations. For example, compressors are widely used by the transportation industry in the production of automobiles, aircraft, marine engines and trucks. Printing plants and metal fabricating units represent other operations which make extensive use of compressed air. Because compressors serve such a wide variety of industrial processes, the potential markets for Acme's products offer bright opportunities for expansion. But the strong trend towards automated equipment virtually makes it mandatory for the company to emphasize product development, if it hopes to compete successfully in these markets.

In recent years, Acme products have found a strong demand in the electronics and communications industries. This was particularly so for the tools and automatic machines to make solderless electronic connectors. These devices are presently coming into use with respect to miniature transmission cables, the conductors for which are as fine as a human hair, separated by as little as .025 of an inch. These connectors go into cable assemblies which supply communication links between minicomputers and word processing equipment.

The trends in the machinery industry has propelled Acme more and more into solid-state electronics and modularity. Currently under development, among other projects, are new machines for splicing and applying connectors to cables. These machines include programming units which supply them with instructions on the appropriate sequence for inserting wire.

Despite its impressive growth, Acme Engineering is still a relatively small company by industry standards. For many years, product development was the responsibility of a new products committee, composed of ten members and including the chief executive officer. This group was responsible for all new product ideas that come before it. Most of the new concepts came from the research and development department and from technical personnel involved in support and servicing. But in recent times the number of new product ideas seemed to have increased beyond the capacity of the committee, the members of which were engaged in full-time activities other than product development. Criticism was also voiced by several department heads that the organizational structure failed to exploit profitable sources for ideas.

To rectify the situation, Mr. Morton established a small group to do exploratory research. But this move presaged a number of ideas to be evaluated, and an even heavier burden for the overworked committee to carry. Hence Mr. Morton sought to lift this weight from the committee's shoulders completely.

According to Mr. Morton's plan, a group of lower echelon executives would be given the job of screening ideas coming from the exploratory group. The ideas that passed the first test would then be passed on for more detailed analysis. Only those that qualified would go to the committee for a decision as to whether money should be appropriated for development. In this way, the new products committee, free of routine, administrative tasks, could concentrate on the functions of senior management. It would provide directions for search, set stanards for evaluation, and make the final decisions on development and commercialization.

But before this plan could be put into operation, the company needed a formal, evaluative system. Mr. Bailey, of the market research department, was appointed to develop such a system for screening ideas.

Mr. Bailey examined company records to see what criteria the new products committee had used previously, since there were no written criteria. Mr. Bailey also investigated what other companies in similar fields were doing. After several months, he submitted a screening procedure.

The screening form had four main categories: environment, financial, marketing, technical/production. Twenty criteria were spread among these four categories. Ideas were to be rated on each criterion, using a five point scale. Since each criterion was accorded an equal weight, the division of criteria into the four basic groups was really irrelevant. Each product was rated on each criterion, which made the maximum number of points that an idea could score equal to 100. To qualify for business analysis, an idea had to score a minimum of 70.

The values of scaling itself—1 to 5—were made dependent upon a subjective probability. If the scorer thought an idea had a high likelihood of meeting a given criterion, the concept would get a 5. If the probability was deemed to be low, the point count would drop to 1 on that criterion. A copy of the questionnaire is appended to this report.

Before presenting the screening procedure to the committee for approval, it was decided to subject the system to a trial run. In this way, the committee could judge the procedure not merely on the basis of form but by how the system works. Accordingly, five new product concepts were chosen and given for evaluation to the committee members, who were to serve as the guinea pigs.

When responses to the questionnaire were tabulated, and analyzed, they were sent to Mr. Morton, who promptly passed them on to the members of the new products committee. But he did so with little enthusiasm and a great deal of misgivings. Of the five new product ideas screened, two scored above the qualification point of 70. But in each instance, four out of the ten evaluators rated the idea below par. Even more disturbing, the four scorers who turned thumbs down on one idea were not the same who were negative on the other. In other words, there was a large amount of variation among the executives evaluating the same ideas—too much variation for comfort. The same thing held true, the analysis showed, on an item-by-item basis. The degree of uniformity for ratings on some criteria, especially those pertaining to marketing, was not much higher than that which would obtain by chance. Then if ratings of senior-level executives lacked consistency, how could another group of managers hope to produce results which reflected the preferences of the new products committee? And in turn, how would this committee go about deciding, logically and objectively, the fate of new product ideas?

Mr. Gay, head of research and development and a member of the new products committee, raised another serious objection. He charged that the entire rating scheme was biased, ostensibly because of Mr. Bailey's marketing background. In the high-technology markets served by Acme Engineering, Mr. Gay argued, technical or performance features were the most important factors in product acceptance. Yet the screening questionnaire contained only five criteria dealing with technological aspects but nine pertaining to marketing factors. Therefore, Mr. Gay pointed out, marketing factors were given a weight of .45 in the total score (9/20), while technological factors received a weight of .25 as a contribution to the total (5/20). This order of importance, Mr. Gay asserted, was far out of line with the realities of business.

Mr. Stern, chief financial officer and also a member of the new products committee, objected to yet another aspect of the screening program. Mr. Stern, observed that the expected return-on-investment criterion had a possible maximum value of 5 points out of the 100-point total (1/20 × 100). This was illogical, Mr. Stern insisted, for a new product idea might be rated poorly on profitability but come up with a total score of better than 70. The more expensive business analysis would then prove a waste of time and effort, because no responsible executive body would approve an investment that posited meager financial returns.

Lastly, Mr. Morton himself had concerns about the cutoff point. "How can we be sure that 70, like the ideal room temperature, is the right figure?" he mused.

If a score of 70 should turn out to be too low, Acme Engineering might be investing in products that would fail. Conversely, a too-high cutoff point might cause the firm to forgo opportunities.

But one thing was certain: product development could not be permitted to drift much longer. Decisions about screening had to be made. His mind filled with doubts, reservations, and misgivings, Mr. Morton nevertheless called a meeting of the new products committee to decide how to proceed with screening new product ideas.

   a. If you were Mr. Morton, what would recommend?

b. How might the screening procedure be improved?

c. Are there other methods by which the product development objectives of Acme Engineering might be achieved?

Screening Form

Below is a list of 20 criteria. You are to rate each new product idea on each criteria. The rating will be a number from 1 to 5.

Scoring will be done as follows:

You are to score an idea...	If you think the idea has a probability of meeting the criterion which is...
5	more than 80%
4	61% to 80%
3	41% to 60%
2	21% to 40%
1	20% or less

The scores and probabilities are illustrated graphically below.

Rating:	1		2		3		4		5	
	0%	20%	40%	60%	80%	100%				

Probability of Meeting Criterion

Now enter the product idea identification number, and rate the idea on each criterion.

Idea ID No._____

Criterion   **Rating**

Environmental Factors

1. Product liability standards and all government regulations can be met with little effort .... _____

2. Product will pose no potential hazard or side effects under all conditions, including misuse .... _____

3. Manufacturing and use will result in no environmental pollution .... _____

Financial Factors

4. The payback period will be five years or sooner .... _____

5. Investment costs can be funded from current earnings without causing financial burdens to ongoing operations and present product lines .... _____

6. Profitability will be enough to yield a 20% return on investment, before taxes .... _____

Marketing Factors

7. The potential market for the product is at least $30 million per year in terms of total sales .... _____

8. Potential company sales will, after three years, reach a minimum of $3 million per annum .... _____

9. The product life cycle is likely to be at least 7 years........ _____

10. The demand for products of this type is growing at a rate of better than 4% per annum .... _____

11. Relative to competitive products, the new product can be sold profitably at a lower price .... _____

12. The product can be distributed through channels presently used by the company.......................... _____

13. The product can be serviced, and given technical support, by the staff already available .... _____

14. The product can attain a market share of 20% within a period of three years .... _____

15. The costs of promoting the product benefits, including expenses of the sales personnel, will not exceed 10% of revenue .... _____

Technical/Production

16. The product will perform more efficiently and effectively than other products designed for similar functions .... _____

17. The product is more durable than substitutable products.. _____

18. The product can be patented, without any need of secrecy .... _____

19. Production processes will be relatively problem-free....... _____

20. Research and development to reach production on a commercial scale will be relatively simple to accomplish .... _____

National Analytical Services

National Analytic Services is a small public relations and promotion firm, with gross sales of about $10 million. Its president, who is responsible for all new business, was recently made an offer by a major airline to license certain computer programs which could be used by commuter airlines. In turn, National Analytic Services would market these programs to the commuter airlines, and pay a royalty of 10 percent of gross sales to the licensor.

The programs were of four kinds: financial reporting, maintenance and engineering, operational reporting, material inventory. these programs could be sold individually, in accordance with the requirements of the user. They were designed for the IBM 360 and 370 series. Nevertheless, National Analytical Services would have to modify them somewhat in order to have commuter airlines employ them efficiently. National Analytic Services would also have to undertake program development to keep the programs up-to-date and to fulfill the changing needs of the commuter airline firms.

National Analytic Services investigated the field, and found the commuter airline market a favorable one. The industry was experiencing a current growth rate of close to 20 percent per annum, and government deregulation was expected to give further impetus to growth. Increasing volume applied to both passenger and cargo traffic. In fact, even the recession of 1974–1975 did not seem to seriously affect the industry's annual growth rate, which did level off, but then resumed its upward course.

The problems of the commuter airline industry were seen as those associated with rapid growth. To meet the enhanced demand, most airlines must expand their fleet of planes, and frequently with aircraft of larger size than those in current use. However, the industry is hampered in this endeavor as ceilings on promised Federal equipment loan guarantees are the subject of endless debate by Congress. Nevertheless, expanded traffic implies more clerical personnel. Insofar as the computer programs are substitutes for labor, they should appeal to commuter airline managements. Prospects for marketing these programs are especially favorable since only about half the commuter lines currently use computers at all, and there is no strong competitor offering alternative systems. The largest negative to marketing the programs is that the entire market is limited to about 242 firms, which are widely dispersed geographically.

National Analytic Services decided to analyze the proposal to market the computer programs. If the decision would be favorable, management contemplated setting up a separate division of the company. The

Table 1

Pro Forma P&L for 12 Months after Start of Project

	Month											
Revenue	1	2	3	4	5	6	7	8	9	10	11	12
Leasing	—	—	3,330	6,670	10,000	13,360	18,340	23,340	28,340	33,340	36,670	40,010
Installation	—	—	3,000	3,000	3,000	3,000	4,500	4,500	4,500	4,500	3,000	3,000
Total revenue...	—	—	6,330	9,670	13,000	16,340	22,840	27,840	32,340	37,840	39,670	43,010
Programs & Sys.												
Salaries & fringe benefits	5,400	5,400	5,400	5,400	5,400	5,400	5,400	5,400	5,400	5,400	5,400	5,400
Space/utilities	300	300	300	300	300	300	300	300	300	300	300	300
Telephone	100	100	100	100	100	100	100	100	100	100	100	100
Supplies, misc....	200	200	200	200	200	200	200	200	200	200	200	200
Computer time.....	2,000	2,000	1,000	300	300	300	300	1,000	1,000	1,000	1,000	2,000
Travel	100	100	100	100	100	100	100	100	100	100	100	100
Installation	—	—	3,000	3,000	3,000	3,000	4,500	4,500	4,500	4,500	3,000	3,000
Total	8,100	8,100	10,100	9,400	9,400	9,400	10,900	11,600	11,600	11,600	10,100	11,100

Table 1 *(continued)*
Pro Forma P&L for 12 Months after Start of Project

							Month					
	1	2	3	4	5	6	7	8	9	10	11	12
Revenue	24,500	28,500	27,000	26,800	27,300	30,800	30,050	31,490	32,250	33,000	32,000	33,500
Sales Expenses												
Salaries & fringe benefits......	8,700	8,700	8,700	8,700	8,700	8,700	8,700	8,700	8,700	8,700	8,700	8,700
Space/utilities......	400	400	400	400	400	400	400	400	400	400	400	400
Telephone......	400	400	400	400	400	400	400	400	400	400	400	400
Travel/enter......	3,000	3,000	3,000	3,000	3,000	3,000	3,000	3,000	3,000	3,000	3,000	3,000
Promotion......	—	4,000	—	—	—	3,000	—	—	—	—	—	—
Servicing @ 5% of lease revenue..	—	—	170	330	500	670	920	1,160	1,420	1,670	1,830	2,000
Royalties......	—	—	330	670	1,000	1,330	1,830	2,330	2,830	3,330	3,670	4,000
Total	12,400	16,400	12,900	13,400	13,900	17,400	5,150	15,890	16,650	17,400	17,900	18,400
Genl & admin.	4,000	4,000	4,000	4,000	4,000	4,000	4,000	4,000	4,000	4,000	4,000	4,000
Total costs & expenses	24,500	28,500	27,000	26,800	27,300	30,800	30,050	31,490	32,250	33,000	32,000	33,500
P&L......	(24,500)	(28,500)	(20,670)	(17,130)	(14,300)	(14,460)	(7,210)	(3,650)	90	4,840	7,670	9,510

effort, it was reasoned, did indeed constitute a new business, completely different from that of business consulting. To implement the decision, a business analysis was undertaken and a business plan of operations was drawn up. This can be outlined as follows:

The market development program must emphasize personal selling and follow-up service. The latter is particularly important, as customers will be small companies with little experience in computer utilization. The sales force should therefore be made up of personnel with technical or engineering backgrounds.

The buying process may well involve several persons, each considering the proposition from the vantage point of his own functional area. Because of multiple purchase influence, salesmen must assess each situation as it occurs. Because purchase decisions may take several weeks, or even months, the salesman will have to make a number of contacts before a decision is made. Coupled with wide geographic dispersion of commuter lines, sales coverage has limitations. Therefore, it is contemplated to cover only half the potential of 242 the first year, concentrating on those closest to the home office. The remaining half will be solicited the second year.

Based on this sales strategy, it is proposed to hire three salesmen, who can also do service follow-ups. As more sales are made, and the market potential covered, sales effort will gradually shift to servicing rather than getting new customers. Though individual companies may lease different programs, it is contemplated that the average sale will be for a lease arrangement of $20,000 per annum, plus $1,500 for installation and training when the system is initially installed. The $1,500 covers the estimated out-of-pocket cost only. Payments on the lease are to be made monthly.

Considering price and alternatives available to commuter airlines, National Analytic Services can expect to achieve a 20 percent market penetration. If sales effort is directed at half the market the first year, estimated sales are then 20 percent of 121 or 24. The same amount of new sales are expected to be attained during the second year, yielding 48 lessees. To proceed at a faster pace, though desirable, is deemed beyond the resources of the company.

The company also intends to hire two computer system analysts to modify the programs, which should require about two months. Afterwards, these personnel can install the systems when sales are made. Actually, the work involves instruction and training in application, and takes about two weeks at each installation. This should allow the systems people to spend about half their available time on program development work and the other half on instruction and training for each installation. As presently contemplated, the programs will run on a batch processing system, either on the premises of the client, or a service bureau. It would be possible to alter the programs specifically for a customer in some other arrangement. But this would require an additional cost, which can be tacked on to the price as a one-time charge. A real time system is feasible in the future, but should not be considered until National Analytic Services has had experience with the present mode. The life of these programs, without substantial alterations, is expected to be four years.

Estimating both revenue and cost, a *pro forma* P&L statement for the first 12 months of operations is shown as table 1.

After analyzing projected revenue and expenses for the first year of operations, management of National Analytic Services decided to go ahead with the project. However, there was considerable disagreement about the plan of operations. It was agreed that the new venture could be financed out of current earnings, which was the prudent thing to do. But cash flow would be very tight, and some outlays for the main business would have to be deferred. Some of the managers even feared that if the plans did not materialize as projected, the company would suffer an important setback. These individuals therefore suggested substantial modifications in the operating plan. The proposal was therefore tabled for further study, and a meeting set at which alternatives were to be discussed and a decision made on how to go about marketing the program.

Questions:

1. On the basis of breakeven analysis, what can be said about the degree of risk for this company? About the potential profit leverage?
2. In what ways would you suggest to reduce company risk in this venture?

AgriMedi Products, Inc.

AgriMedi Products is an old company, founded at the turn of the century. It started as a family business, selling farm supplies to rural communities in the midwest.

In the 1940's, with government emphasis on producing more food for the armed forces of the nation and its allies, the firm moved into animal health products.

The company experienced its greatest growth in the years following 1950, notably the 1960's. Sales increased better than 10 percent per annum, on the average, and net profits traced a comparable course. During that time the company was transformed from a family-owned concern to a public company. Today, the company boasts of slightly

more than 3.5 million stockholders. Its sales volume in 1979 amounted
to $134 million, with $2.80 earnings per share of common stock. Some
20 percent of net earnings are currently being paid out in dividends on
this common stock, amounting to about $3.6 million. Despite this com-
paratively low payout, the stock had been selling at a premium because
the firm was labeled a "growth company" by financial analysts, at least
until recently. A ten year financial summary is attached to the end of
the report.

The major portion of corporate growth had come about because of
biochemical products in the human health field. These prescription
drugs are marketed to drug wholesalers and retailers, hospitals, clinics
and other institutions. Research support to customers is also a requirement in this industry. Yet AgriMedi Products is a small company, as
compared with the giants in the field, and does not have sufficient
resources to meet the large firms head on. The company has therefore
adhered to a policy of emphasizing certain segments which have been
neglected by the large firms. When its research and development laboratories developed biochemical products with wide application,
though patented, the company has been content to license its patents
and to receive royalties on sales. In this manner, it has been able to
substantially reduce risks and still maintain an active program of product development, which seems an absolute necessity to future growth
and well-being.

But within the last four years, the rate of growth seemed to decline.
A number of reasons conspired to produce this ominous result. First, a
number of patents had run out. Two, others were made obsolete by new
developments in the field, and the company was finding much sharper
competition than hitherto. Three, FDA rules for testing drug products
had become more stringent, with development time more than doubling
and costs skyrocketing. This meant that for the same dollars, the
amount of new products coming from research and development were
sharply reduced. This trend was exacerbated by inflation, which ran
into two-digit figures. Since the largest portion of research and development expenses are in the form of salaries, higher than normal re-
muneration had to be granted to scientific and technical personnel to
prevent a high turnover in a field where demand for such skills is high
and supply tight. Four, the research and development budget had always been set as a percent of sales. As sales growth slowed, so did the
flow of funds available for research and development. Thus, while the
sales department was demanding more new products, research and
development output was declining.

The issue came to a head at the annual budget meetings to set
appropriations for 1980. Since research and development was regarded
as a crucial area, the method of budgeting for product development

focused on that area. The discussion of the finance committee revealed two different schools of thought. One opinion was that of the controller, which defended the practice of budgeting for research and development as a percent of sales. The other agreed with the controller that research and development should be accounted for as a period expense in reporting financial results. But from a management point of view, this group argued that research and development projects should be treated as investments, and budgeting should be revised accordingly. A summary of the arguments presented by both groups is as follows:

Arguments of the group to change the percent of sales method.

1. The percent of sales method has no relation to the needs of the company. The determinant of spending for product development is sales, rather than sales being a determinant of development.

The method worked well in the past because sales were expanding rapidly, and research and development had adequate funds to meet management objectives. The fact that sales growth has decreased does not *per se* mean a change in objectives. It merely means that more money is needed to accomplish them. If management still maintains its goals of a 10 percent per annum increase in sales and profits, then it must be flexible enough to allocate more than it had for a critical area. The budget should therefore be governed by the tasks required of research and development, and not by a current sales projection. To do so is to allow the tail to wag the dog.

2. An investment criterion is already being used when proposed projects are being sent along for development. Business analysis, for example, evaluates these projects on their expected return on investment. Then should not budget procedures be made consistent with selection procedures for the same projects? This would imply that funds be allocated on a project-by-project basis, especially since all company-sponsored research and development are targeted.

3. Research and development costs need not, and should not, be deferred and amortized in the future. But neither should custodial accounting determine how funds be allocated to specific tasks. These are two separate questions. There is nothing to prevent the company from charging research and development costs as it does now to the period in which they are incurred and budgeting projects on the basis of expected returns.

4. The average period from beginning of development through testing takes about six to seven years. Then in effect, the company is spending now for revenue to be generated in future periods. This is investment by any definition. Then budgeting on the basis of investment criteria would permit better evaluation and control over operations, and lead to better decisions.

5. Given current objectives of corporate growth, new products are essential. In view of increased costs of product development, spending for research and development is badly out of line with company goals. It is better to forgo current earnings, so as to build for the future. A larger investment in research and development projects now would mean greater profits later.

6. If investment criteria are used, we would be matching current costs with future revenue, discounted by the value of money. This seems to be far more sensible than the present rule-of-thumb methods for allocating, what are in reality, investment funds.

Arguments of the group defending the percent of sales method.

1. The method is not a fixed, inexorable percentage, to be applied regardless of circumstances. It can be altered or adjusted. It has been kept because, in our judgment, there was no compelling reason to increase it. This is a judgment decision. But so are most others related to budgets when results cannot be traced directly to an acitvity.

2. For this reason, research and development is not an investment in the same sense of plant and equipment. There is no way to predict revenue over the effective life of a project. In fact, we cannot readily predict how long a product concept will be in development, let alone its cash flow for a number of years thereafter. Under such circumstances, revenue expectations from research activity is highly speculative, and to make budget allocations on such flimsy data would be most unsound.

3. Even if we guessed correctly about a project's returns, we cannot tell what contribution was made by research and development. We cannot tell what proportion can be attributed to research and development and what proportion can be credited to other causes, such as production efficiency, marketing acumen, promotional effort. Hence, there is no practical way of matching current effort of research and development with discounted future revenue resulting from such efforts. If that is so, the idea of using investment criteria for budgeting is an illusion.

4. Because of the impossibility of handling research and development as an investment, it is prudent to treat it as an on-going activity, both in reporting and in managing its operations. This would imply it be expensed, the same as sales, promotion, administration. By setting the budget for these activities as a percent of sales, the charges become variable and cash flow can be managed more effectively.

5. Since research and development costs are treated as variable, they have a tendency to rise with higher prices owing to inflation. On the whole, unit costs and unit prices owing to inflation have been pretty much in line. Government regulations are another matter, and one over which we have little control. But neither do our competitors.

6. Even with substantial increases in the costs of research and development, partly mandated by government, the budget is not inconse-

quential. In fact, it is almost as large as net profits, $12 million vs $18 million. The R&D to profit ratio is higher now than it was in 1970. If this is insufficient to close the gap between corporate objectives and projected sales, then this raises a number of questions other than those relating to how to budget for research and development.

For example, if we increase the research and development budget, which we can do, are we more assured that the desired growth in sales will ensue? And if we do not borrow, the increase in the research and development budget would have to come at the expense of other activities, such as funds from other departments, proposed investments, profits, other balance sheet items. In short, the requests of research and development, no matter what budget procedures are used, must be balanced with those of other parts of the company, including those of stockholders for higher profits, increased dividends, and good stock prices in the market.

7. If we grant that the decline in sales growth came about because of a fall in R&D output, which is hypothetical, it still does not follow that budget procedures ought to be changed. Can we say that the budget procedures caused the drop in output?

Nor should we simply increase the allocation for research and development. That is not to say an increase would not do the job. But that approach would only be trying to correct a deficiency by considering only one possible solution—that of research and development. There are many other alternatives for meeting corporate growth objectives, and management should carefully consider them. And these go far beyond the question of how to budget for research and development.

Though the president attended the meeting of the finance committee, he read and reread the summary of the minutes, and pondered over the question raised. What should he do?

Ten Year Financial Summary
(Dollar Amounts in Millions Except Per-share Figures)

	1979	1978	1977	1976	1975	1974	1973	1972	1971	1970
Sales	134	123	115	102	90	77	67	57	51	44
Cost of sales	51	48	45	39	33	26	24	19	17	14
Gross profit	83	75	70	63	57	51	43	38	34	30
Marketing/admin.	40	36	34	29	24	22	19	16	14	12
Research & develop.	12	11	11	10	9	7	6	5	5	4
Interest	2	2	2	2	2	1	1	1	1	1
Income before taxes	29	26	23	22	22	21	17	16	14	13
Taxes	11	10	9	8	8	8	7	7	6	6
Net income	18	16	14	14	14	13	10	9	8	7
Earnings per share	2.80	2.50	2.20	2.18	2.19	2.03	1.60	1.41	1.22	1.02

Duralake Plastics, Inc.*

Duralake Plastics, Inc., is a large producer of plastics which are sold to industrial concerns for use in making their consumer products. Duralake's productive output is measured in millions of pounds per year and its customers are located throughout the world.

In the late 1960's a polymer was discovered by the Technical Center that had some promising properties. With a proper mix of chemical compounds and a suitable catalyst a highly reactive, low weight polymer could be prepared. The chemical properties of this new polymer were judged by the Technical Center research staff to be of potential value as an intermediate product to other products not currently manufactured by Duralake. Therefore, although the polymer was not typical of Duralake's other products, it was decided to pursue the development of the product. The compound was named Malake and it was patented by Duralake. Developmental research was done in cooperation with firms that did produce those products.

By the early 1970's two firms cooperating with Duralake proceeded to develop proprietary applications of Malake in their production processes. A large chemical firm found that, even with the relatively high price, Malake had significant advantages in a particular type of cleaning compound. In the other case a major glass manufacturer developed a patented manufacturing process based upon Malake. Both of these companies encouraged Duralake to finalize the chemical-property design of Malake and place it in commercial production since such action would be of great benefit to these two firms in their respective market places.

There was no doubt that the sales volume forecasted for the foreseeable future would not justify Duralake's investment in the specialized production equipment. However, the pricing of Malake did promise a profitable product. More importantly, the two firms which would purchase Malake were important customers for other Duralake products, and Duralake felt some pressure and obligation to meet all of the product demands of these customers. The product commercialization plan that was developed included two elements not typical of the firm's normal operations. First, the product would be manufactured by an outside firm under a custom manufacturing arrangement. A custom manufacturer, called a toller, is a production firm that manufactures a product to the client's specifications. Second, the market development of the product was assigned to a single individual within the marketing department.

---

*Summarized from the case prepared by Professor Jay H. Coats of West Virginia University and Thomas Coyner, an MBA candidate at West Virginia University.

The custom manufacturing arrangement is usually an extremely profitable and flexible relationship for both firms involved. It also involves some potential dangers for both firms. The client firm retains liability for the product produced by the toller and is also ethically, if not legally, responsible for the safety and good manufacturing practice of the toller. The toller does have certain responsibilities. It is required by the client firm to produce the correct quality product in the proper volume within a given time. The toller is also normally held responsible to provide the product based upon a specified manufacturing process provided by the client. Legal agreements prevent the toller's selling the product to other than the client firm.

Contact is maintained by the client firm via a liaison group. This group is charged with (1) providing the toller with the necessary technical and informational support, (2) minimizing Duralake's liability in connection with the product and the toller, (3) protecting the security of trade secrets which may be transferred to the toller. Duralake proceeded to establish a liaison group and a workable relationship was established with a custom manufacturer. Malake was commercialized with initial sales to two cooperating firms in the chemical and glass industries.

Duralake felt that there was a large range of possible applications for this product. To uncover such applications, space advertisements were placed in chemical trade magazines giving technical information about Malake but without specifying applications. The response was very encouraging and literature was followed-up with samples of the product as requested.

Late in 1974 a laboratory technician noticed an unexpected crystalized material under the lid of the drums containing the Malake received from the toller's plant. Chemical analysis determined that it was a by-product of the catalyst used in the manufacturing process and that it was a highly dangerous compound. Low levels of the by-product were present in all of the product. Upon receiving this information Duralake immediately took four actions. First, the two existing customers purchasing Malake were notified of the presence and characteristics of the toxic material. They were also provided with recommendations as to how the product could be handled safely. Second, the custom manufacturer was provided with the same information. Third, the Technical Center began a project to find a suitable substitute to replace the offending catalyst. Fourth, an outside consulting firm was contracted to do a toxicological analysis of the product to determine its possible hazard to ultimate consumers.

As a consequence of the toxicity problem, the chemical firm determined that they could no longer use Malake in their cleaning compound. They reformulated their product to exclude Malake, and those sales were lost to Duralake. The glass manufacturer performed an industrial hygiene survey of their facilities using Malake and concluded that the toxic by-product did not present a problem for them and they continued to purchase the product. Duralake's effort to replace the catalyst was not successful. The consulting firm reported that Malake was considerably less toxic than the crystalized substance and that Malake was not toxic by the standards of the Occupational Safety and Health Administration (OSHA). Production of Malake was continued throughout 1975 and 1976 in order to meet the needs of the purchasing customer. Even with the low volume and tolling arrangement, Malake remained a very profitable product.

In January of 1977, as a result of internal organizational changes, a new manager was assigned responsibility for the marketing of Malake. During the transfer of responsibility, the new manager developed several concerns about the handling of the toxicity problem with Malake. The glass manufacturer had been notified of the toxicity problem (in 1974) only by a telephone call. Without any written record of Duralake's having informed the glass company, Duralake's liability concerning any legal action caused by the toxicity could not be defined. It was further discovered that Duralake's internal product control procedures had been unintentionally by-passed by the custom manufacturing operation. In early 1977 it was determined that many of the internal control procedures for Malake were either never implemented or else review forms were signed in a perfunctory manner after a brief or nonexistent review. No information on the safety or toxicity of the product had been given to any of the hundreds of firms which had been sent samples of the material.

The status of Duralake's relationship with the toller was also questionable. No contractual agreement had ever been made between the two firms. The product was ordered and produced on the basis of a simple purchase order system. The lack of a contractual agreement raised the question of legal liability concerning the toller's treatment of toxic by-products removed from Malake as it was being manufactured. Additionally, the toller did not, nor was he required to, test the products for the level of toxic contaminant. The new manager of the Malake product developed a program to minimize the liability of the firm while providing for the adequate protection of both customers and the custom manufacturer. The basic premise was that any product could be sold as long as it was properly represented to the customers, the manufacturer and the firm. Not only minimal, but complete safety and health information was provided to all who were involved with the project. Clearly, the concern was for principle not profit.

On the recommendation of Duralake's legal department (1) all customers and potential customers who had received quantities of the product were notified about the problem, (2) the toller was notified of the potential disposal problem associated with the toxic by-product.

The firm's legal department made three recommendations. First, it decided that it was in the best interest of the firm to continue to manufacture outside without a contract. Their opinion was that common business law was sufficient to protect both parties regardless of the toxicity and waste disposal problems. They also decided that Duralake was only required to inform the manufacturer that his waste disposal system was probably insufficient and that Duralake was not required to provide an adequate disposal method. Third, the legal risk of using the toxic material could be controlled by proper documentation.

Questions:

    A. Discuss Duralake's management of Malake's (1) development (b) commercial exploitation (c) subsequent toxic problems.

    B. What is Duralake's moral obligation with respect to the future of the new product, with respect to control over the toller?

Medical Electronic Instruments, Inc.

In April 1976, Fred Young, product manager for Non-Destructive Testing Products was considering the problem of releasing a new piece of non-destructive test equipment to the field sales and service organization of Medtronics.

Medtronics is a manufacturer of a wide variety of medical electronic equipment used in industry, hospitals and large clinics. Sales for 1975 exceeded $10 million, and at least a 20 percent increase was expected for 1976. The corporate headquarters and major manufacturing facility was located in Minneapolis.

Fred had recently received his M.B.A. degree in marketing from the University of Minnesota. He felt that he could apply the techniques of operations research to his problem, particularly network planning.

The product to be released was a highly technical product which would be different in many ways from those the sales force currently handled. In order to make a major impact on the industry, Fred had decided to introduce the product at a major trade show, the National Convention of the American Society of Non-Destructive Testing, held Aug. 1–5 at San Diego. The product would be released to the national sales force immediately following the show.

This case was prepared by Professor Robert H. Collins, Ph.D., of Oregon State University. and Mr. Jim Browning, MBA Candidate, Oregon State University. Copyright © 1977 by Robert H. Collins, Ph.D.

There were many things to get done before this trade show. Fred was able to group these activities into nine major categories.

A. *Provide product training to the field sales force.* This activity included both lectures and hands-on equipment training in the use of the product. It would take approximately five days to train the sales force.

B. *Provide product training to the service force.* While it was essential for the sales force to possess product knowledge, a completely different training program had to be developed to teach the service force how to maintain the product. This training would also take about five days.

C. *Preparation of service kits.* Each serviceman must have a tool kit to service the new product, and be trained in its use. It would take about a day and a half to prepare these kits.

D. *Preparation of sales aids.* Each salesman would receive a sales manual, plus assorted flip-charts, literature, product mock-ups, and visual aids to assist him in communicating with the customer. Sales aids must be prepared prior to the sales training program, and preparation would take about seven and a half days.

E. *Preparation of warranty and service contracts.* As more industrial customers show reluctance to provide their own service, warranty and service contracts have become more important as competitive product features. Hence the sales force and the servicemen must be aware of them. It will take about five days to draw up these contracts.

F. *Designate factory support teams.* Factory support teams act as a backup to the field sales and service force. It will take about one-half a day to select these personnel.

G. *Preparation of instruction manuals.* Proper operation and maintenance by the customer is a major factor in ensuring product satisfaction, reducing warranty costs, and creating an overall favorable image for the manufacturer. Preparation will take about 25 days.

H. *Pre-release promotion.* Prior to the actual release of the product, promotion must be directed at potential customers. A combination of direct mail and trade advertising is used to create interest in the product, and announce Medical Electronics Instruments' attendance at the ASNDT trade show. It will take approximately five days to prepare this promotion.

I. *Preparation for the trade show.* It will take about six days to construct an effective exhibit.

Fred felt that a PERT chart would be of assistance in scheduling the many activities required to release his new product to the sales force. Therefore he summarized these activities, and completion times in the following chart.

Table 1

Activity	Predecessors	Time Requirements Number of Days a	m	b
Train Sales Force (A)	D, E, G	4.5	5	6
Train Service Force (B)	C, E, G	4.5	5	6.75
Prepare Service Kits (C)	None	1	1.5	2
Prepare Sales Aids (D)..............	F	5	7.5	10
Prepare Warranty/Service Contracts (E)	None	4.5	5	6.25
Designate Factory Support (F)	None	.25	.5	1
Instruction Manuals (G)	None	20	25	35
Pre-Release Promotion (H)	D	4.5	5	6
Prepare for Trade Show (I)	E, G, H	5	6	9
Attend Trade Show (J)	A, I	5	5	5

a — Most Optimistic Completion Time
m — Most Likely Completion Time
b — Most Pessimistic Completion Time

Questions:

1. Draw a project network (PERT chart) which depicts the logical sequence of events required to introduce Jim's new product.
2. What is the critical path, and how many days will he need to complete the project?
3. What is the near critical path? What is the probability that the near critical path will become critical? What are the consequences of a shift from the critical path to the near critical path?

Subject Index

Name Index

A

Aaker, D. A., 346
Abbott, Lawrence, 6
Abell, Derek F., 104, 111
Abrams, George J., 18
Adler, Lee, 136
ADTEL, 328
Agree, 57, 73, 203, 257
Alford, Charles L., 196
All dishwasher detergent, 118
American Association for Public
    Opinion Research, 348
American Bankers Association, 292
American Can Company, 82
American Home Products, 73
American Institute of Certified Public
    Accountants, 262
American Management Association,
    156
American Marketing Association,
    150, 250, 280, 329
American Motors Corp., 293
AMF, 10, 89-90
AMPEX, 262
Anchor Hocking, 131
Angelus, Theodore L., 16, 18
Anheuser-Busch, 58, 300
Ansoff, Igor H., 65, 91, 98-99
Anthony, Ted F., 267
Aram, John D., 151
Armstrong Cork, 65
Arrid, 72
Assmus, Gert, 275-276
Association of National Advertisers,
    154
AT&T, 124
Ayer, N. W., 274

B

Backman, Jules, 356
Bailey, E. L., 16, 18
Bales, Carter F., 86
Barnett, Norman L., 49

Barry, Michael J., 329
Bass, F. M., 323, 344
Battelle Memorial Institute, 12-13,
    22, 121-122, 214, 229-230
BBD&O, 202, 274
BehaviorScan, 328
Belk, R. W., 346
Bell Telephone, 144
Benson, George, 166, 168, 170,
    172-173, 175-177, 206, 366
Benton & Bowles, 323
Berdy, Edwin M., 323
Berndt, E. R., 360
Best Foods' Knorrs, 18
Bic, 7
Bierman, Jr., Harold, 272
Black & Decker, 99
Black, Homer A., 270
Blattberg, R. C., 50, 330
Boeing, 215
Boewadt, R. J., 307
Bogaty, Herman, 280
Bohmback, D., 96
Boland, John C., 293
Booz, Allen & Hamilton, 16-17,
    132-133, 174, 222, 224, 287
Boston Consulting Group, 66, 69,
    72-73, 99-102
Bowman, Edward H., 103
Bowman, James H., 324
Bouchard, T. J., 189
Boyd, Robert, 356
Boyd, Jr., Harper W., 200, 318
Brand, Milton I., 26
Bristol Myers, Inc., 73, 243
Brooks, Douglas G., 309
Bubble Yum, 257
Buell, Victor P., 154-155
Bumphy, Paul J., 131
Burger King, 115
Burgi, Walter, 49
Busch, Paul, 293-294
Business Roundtable, 366
Buzzell, Robert D., 16, 108
Byrne, Harlan J., 41

421